BEAUTIFUL, ALSO, ARE THE SOULS OF MY BLACK SISTERS

BEAUTIFUL, ALSO, ARE THE SOULS OF MY BLACK SISTERS

A History of the Black Woman in America

JEANNE NOBLE

PRENTICE-HALL, Inc.,
Englewood Cliffs, N.J.

To my nephews
John, William, Keith, and Michael—
may they grow strong, wise, and giving; become men like
Albert, Alex, Alvin, Ben, Bill, Edward, Ivory, Lamar,
Lonnie, Norman, Roscoe and Vernon;
and love strong, sharing, and sensitive women like
Aurelia, Barbara, Betty, Dorothy, Ellen,
Enid, Jerry, Josephine, Judy, Jean,
Lena, Leontyne, Lillian, Patricia, Ruth, and Thelma.

Printed in the United States of America

Prentice-Hall International, Inc., London
Prentice-Hall, of Australia, Pty. Ltd., Sydney
Prentice-Hall of Canada, Ltd., Toronto
Prentice-Hall of India Private Ltd., New Delhi
Prentice-Hall of Japan, Inc., Tokyo
Prentice-Hall of Southeast Asia Pte. Ltd., Singapore
Whitehall Books Limited, Wellington, New Zealand

10 9 8 7 6 5 4 3 2

Library of Congress Cataloging in Publication Data

Noble, Jeanne L
Beautiful, also, are the souls of my Black sisters.

Bibliography: p.
Includes index.
1. Afro-American women. I. Title.
E185.86.N6 301.41'2'0973 77-27408
ISBN 0-13-066555-X

CONTENTS

MY PEOPLE

The night is beautiful,
So the faces of my people.

The stars are beautiful,
So the eyes of my people.

Beautiful, also, is the sun.
Beautiful, also, are the souls of my people.

—*Langston Hughes*

PART I

THE PAST

What is Africa to me:
Copper sun and scarlet sea,
Jungle star of jungle track,
Strong bronzed men, or regal black
Women from whose loins I sprang
When the birds of Eden sang?

COUNTEE CULLEN[1]

1

What Is Africa to Me?

For centuries under this copper sun, while diamonds were silently lying deep within the earth and rich veins of gold lay waiting in darkness, the greatest treasures of Africa were its people. Highly developed communities, with richly endowed traditions, responsible life styles, and humane social structures, were always there for explorers to discover, had they truly set out to gain knowledge and exchange ideas and goods. But such was not the white man's mission in Africa.

While Imperial Rome, Greece, and later England, Portugal, and America among others, plundered the outer edges of Africa in a greedy grab for its natural resources, its interior remained largely a land of mystery. Little wonder that this continent captured the imagination of explorers: it was a fascinating yet frightening challenge, offering great wealth matched by awesome danger to match.

The white world has always viewed Africa with mixed feelings and drives, including greed and guilt. To reconcile such ambivalence, a special vocabulary and intelligence emerged that defined Africa as a Dark Continent occupied by inferior humans—all in need of the white man's religion to save souls, white culture to bring about civilization, and white technology to develop the land's resources. Furthermore, those self-imposed undertakings were piously assumed as "the white man's burden." Now the heirs of these colonizers are confronted with the historic burden of blame placed on them by the African descendants. Demand for accountability and even restitution for historic wrongs has become today's "white man's burden." Slowly at first and then militantly in the Black Revolution days of the Sixties, blacks from the halls of the

United Nations to the dusty roads of Selma, Alabama, began to unleash pent-up feelings about how it was then and now to be historic victims of colonization, slavery, and segregation.

There flows also from this history a "black problem" that we American descendants of those captive Africans bear. We internalized too long the lies and myths which taught and preached that our African ancestry was inferior, shameful, and best forgotten. We have been faced with exorcising from our psyches the trauma of self-hatred which resulted from such historic "putdowns." Ours became the obligation to build among ourselves an increasing confidence in unique capabilities and in black abilities equal to those of all people, including the descendants of former colonizers and slavers who still possess superior economic and political world power. This was and is the onerous "black burden" for us. It is certain that those who would be free must first see themselves as adequate, able, good, and beautiful!

It is not enough to intone: "I'm black and I'm proud." Deep in the marrow of our bones we must know this is truth, not sloganeering. And this foundation of knowing, built on the accumulated knowledge that scholars and black leaders have gained little by little over the years, perhaps most intensely and systematically during the Sixties, must be continuously strengthened. Never again in history should black adequacy and equality be questioned and doubted. The civil rights struggles of the Sixties have resulted in some social advances for blacks, as well as many disappointments. Yet to slide backward into that old cesspool of collective self-loathing borne of a distorted and denied history, to surrender the positive gains in self-consciousness which came of those struggles, helped by an emerging black history, would be the worst outcome of all.

"History," writes Lerone Bennett, "is knowledge, identity, and power."

> By telling us where we have been, history tells us where we can go. . . . By providing historical roles and models, we can attempt new and difficult conquests . . . history is the scaffold upon which personal and group identities are constructed . . . a people without a historical sensibility cannot respect themselves, nor can they free themselves of the tyranny of the here and now.[2]

Self-respect and the tyranny of the here and now—it will take the first to overcome the second. We know the strength of "The Self-Fulfilling Prophecy":[3] by communicating our expectations to an individual or group, we affect the predicted changes in their resulting behavior or performance. This can be a positive force of enormous value, but when its negative power is turned against a people, the effect can be poisonous. The prophecy for blacks has historically been that we are inferior and doomed to be losers. Consider that blacks entered American society as slaves, as property, investments from which an owner was determined to get a financial profit. How, then, could we be expected to recognize or project ourselves to our children as strong, positive images? Little wonder we wandered through the years trying to escape a negative reflection, trying to gain acceptance into the very society which denied our history and ignored our humanity. That such individuals as Harriet Tubman and Sojourner Truth emerged from slavery as giants of energy with wills strengthened in the fires of pain, is witness to the triumph of the human spirit over the tyranny of negative conditions.

Only such strong resolve, based on the self-confidence of many, many individuals, collectively organized for change, can favorably alter the black condition. The first step begins with respecting who I am, who you are. Personal identity has a dimension of collective awareness, based on membership in a reference group one is proud to call "mine." Furthermore, black consciousness and self-respect depend on valid and reliable written history, constantly confirmed and expressed—not only in scholarly treatises, but also in prose, poetry, song, dance, and art.

As the Black Revolution of the Sixties gathered strength, black scholars were stimulated to research African history for an understanding of a past which had for so long been distorted into making us despise ourselves. What they, and others, brought to light were records of ancient Africa with established themes concerning a quality of civilization which forms the basis of a proud legacy.

> . . . Black people have survived on this earth at least two million years—for at least as long as man has been known to exist. We are an old people with wisdom to share.
>
> . . . Black people have built complex, humanistic social systems which served our ancestors well in their time and from which much good can be learned today, as we cope with poverty and with rearing children in an increasingly dehumanizing and mechanized society.
>
> . . . Black people have continually fought for freedom from tyranny and oppression, sometimes winning and sometimes losing, all the while learning the art of survival.
>
> . . . In interpreting the acts of birthing, loving, living, and

> dying, in the form of dance, music, art, and literature, black people have immortalized expressions of life that transcend racial distinctions and speak eloquently of the universality of the human condition. This is SOUL. And it's hard to identify with our history and *not* have it.

As important as this understanding is to all blacks, it is most vital for black women. In the quest for historical truth, we are raising searching questions about ourselves as blacks *and* females. "What can we learn," we ask, "from both the black and female experience? What themes evolve from African history that might provide insight into our struggle against racism and sexism? And what African models can be used as we raise the timeless question: 'Who and what and why am I?' "

There is much to give us answers!

WHEN THE BIRDS OF EDEN SANG . . .

The earliest traces of life have been preserved for us in those rocks that are the very foundation of Africa. Dr. Kohl-Lewer discovered the remains of one unnamed predecessor there, and from the soil of Africa, Professor Raymond Dart brought "Rhodesian Man" to light. Ironically, both scientists underestimated their finds, believing them to be more apelike than manlike. Both stirred controversy and doubt throughout the world: first, few scientists were prepared to accept Africa rather than Asia as the womb of mankind; also, perhaps, the long-established stereotypes of black people being apelike stood in the way of scientific objectivity.

The noted husband-wife archaeological team of L. S. B. and Mary Leakey were convinced, however, that a previous fossil discovery made in 1931 was an earlier ancestor of "*Homo sapiens.*"[4] They made the claim that subsequent fossils found in Africa represented the form of creature which most resembled our human ancestors.

Then in 1962, from the diggings of Olduvai Gorge, Tanzania, the Leakeys unearthed the fossil that helped forge the links of probability into near certainty that humans, as we know them today, did begin life in Africa.

What further made the Leakeys' discovery of interest was that it established this fossil as a concrete record of a female who had lived approximately 800,000 years ago. The Leakeys nicknamed their fossil "Cinderella," a very "ofay" name for a black woman of any era, but she had a scientific name too—"Homo habilis woman," meaning "woman with ability," and that is a distinction of note. We are able to learn a great deal about the conditions of life in prehistoric times from "Cinderella"—including her ability to speak, walk, and eat meat. It is also believed that she worked with tools, perhaps even fashioned them.[5]

It is appropriate that "Cinderella" entered the human record with the designation "woman with ability." For ability has consistently characterized black women—the ability to work with tools in antiquity, and other implements in later times; the ability to toil relentlessly so that her family might survive and her people advance; the ability to laugh and sing and create, in good times and bad—all abilities which mark the history of the black woman. Homo Habilis Woman: A Worthy Ancestor.

THE LEGENDARY IN AFRICAN HISTORY

We did not learn about ourselves from archaeology, other sciences, or the written records alone. Legends enter the human consciousness and form impressions, attitudes, feelings.

Legends and facts, the latter subject to the biased interpretations of historians, combine to give a people a sense of their worth. The people of Africa are no exception. Important in the legends of Africa are the stories of women. It has been suggested that an actual historic woman of exceptional attainment might have been regarded as a freak, a human sport, whereas to invent or embellish the story of a female and build a legend around her showed a readiness to believe in the accomplishment and authority of the female.[6]

Legends of African women give us a sense of the esteem felt toward women, and even the fear. They describe the qualities highly valued in women. Many of these legends were handed down through oral tradition—a communication technique widely used in Africa—later, others were passed along in pamphlets, poorly printed or simply mimeographed; the assertions in such stories were often unable to meet the tests of modern scholarship.

Two legends come along in such ways.

The Legend of Queen Moo[7]

Leakey speaks of the gaps in the story of human evolution and specifies the Americas as a fertile land for future exploration. Perhaps in years to come the story of Queen Moo, allegedly a black woman who engineered the building of the sphinx along the banks of the Nile in Egypt, will be lifted from legendary speculation to truth. Certainly, the Negroid features of the sphinx have long been a matter of puzzlement to spectators and scholars.

It is claimed by one scholar, Le Plongeon, that when the Egyptians in the valley of the Nile were beginning a civilization, there existed on the Western continent a nation called Maya. The exact boundaries of Maya are unknown, but it included the Yucatan, where important archaeological discoveries have been made.[8] Maya had a high degree of culture in arts and sciences. Its people were exceptional navigators and explorers whose seagoing feats are illustrated in the epic "Ramayana."[9]

Their predecessors were called by modern historians the aborigines of India. As the people of Maya journeyed across the Syrian desert, they finally settled in the valley of the Nile, and named the district of Nubia, Maiu, after the mother country. These travelers became the nucleus of people who welcomed Queen Moo when she was forced to flee from Maya and take exile on the banks of the Nile. It is said that there she commanded the building of the sphinx to honor her brother-husband, Prince Coh.

How Moo got there is a mystery. That she actually existed and built a temple and mausoleum in Maya to house her husband's remains is fairly well established.

In many ancient kingdoms brothers and sisters married each other in order to preserve the royal lineage. Moo and Coh, brother and sister, were a happy couple and benign rulers. Prince Aac, their brother, jealous of both their reign and marriage, assassinated his brother and attempted to force Moo to marry him.

Moo, as the story goes, was heartbroken by the death of her husband. She rejected Aac and devoted herself to her dead husband's memory. In a grand gesture of love and respect for Coh, she ordered the building of a memorial hall and mausoleum in Maya.

The cruel Aac resented Moo's rejection and her efforts to keep her husband's memory alive. He finally plunged the country into civil war and threatened her life. Moo fled Maya and sought refuge among her fellow countrymen in the land now called Egypt. Here she was worshipped as a goddess, and she designed and ordered the building of the mysterious sphinx, whose features were exactly like those of Coh.

LePlon claims that in his excavations in the Yucatan he found the charred heart of Coh. He makes comparative notes on the similarity of the inscriptions found both in the Maya temple and at the base of the Egyptian sphinx. Particularly convincing is his comparison of the two languages and the portrait in the monument of the leopard with human head, so alike in both countries. It is thought that Moo associated this leopard with the strength of her husband.

The solution of the sphinx mystery may very well be found in the ancient Maya archives, where it is waiting to be mined by future scholars and archaeologists. And among the hypotheses to be tested is the idea that a black woman may indeed have designed the sphinx!

The Legend of Nitocris[10]

Perhaps the story of Nitocris, which Herodotus, the father of history, recorded, reached the ears as a legend; perhaps it was factual. It is well known that historians consider Herodotus a useful guide to antiquity but consider his explanations speculative and mythological.

He speaks of Nitocris as an Ethiopian queen who was placed on the Egyptian throne after the Egyptians killed her brother. She demonstrated remarkable engineering insight during her reign. She routed the Euphrates so that it would pass a certain city. She built a large basin so that the river could form a reservoir. She lined the embankment with stones, according to Herodotus, displaying an unusual interest in conservation. She built a stone bridge across the largest span of the river to unite two halves of her city and had it constructed so that the bridge planks could be taken up at night, thereby discouraging nocturnal crimes.

Nitocris was also quite revengeful. In order to retaliate for her brother's death, she constructed a chamber and invited his enemies to a banquet. By means of a secret duct, the water from the river flowed in and drowned them. Afterward she threw herself in a room of ashes in order to escape her enemies. But alas, she choked to death!

There are many legends of women who sacrificed all for love. What is remarkable about Moo and Nitocris is their alleged roles as builders, architects, innovators, and artists. Love might have motivated Moo, but Nitocris was less a femme fatale than an outstanding engineer, conservationist, and city planner—really the first in human recording to combine all these talents into a blueprint for city living!

"THOSE REGAL BLACK WOMEN FROM WHOSE LOINS I SPRANG. . . ."

Female slaves were often described as "regal" or majestic. Today many older black women are respectfully addressed as "queen mothers." Down through the ages, the image of majesty has come to the black girl in the admonition: "Walk proud! You are the descendant of queens!"

Legends now yield to facts. Only those "ebon black" Nubian and Egyptian queens, seldom mentioned in literature, and Ethiopians are discussed here, though acknowledgment of the popularly accorded Cleopatra and Nefertiti is duly noted. Considering these two popular queens and the others, less well known, Africa has indeed produced an unusual number of black queens remembered not because they were consorts of kings but because they were rulers in their own right.

QUEENS OF ETHIOPIA

Queen Sheba: Black and Comely[11]

Though some historians have sought to make Sheba's historical feats more legendary than real, the *Kebra Nagast*—the Book of the Glory of the King, the holy book of the Ethiopians—gives an account of Makeda the Queen, whom we know as Sheba.

Intelligent, curious, and enterprising, beautiful Sheba presided at court on many occasions when merchants traveling between her realm and the courts and marketplaces of the world gathered to tell of affairs beyond her realm. Over the years their tales of King Solomon's handsomeness, and particularly his great wisdom, aroused her curiosity, and she decided to travel to his court and learn from him. Traders commuting between both courts had also spoken often to Solomon about Sheba, whetting his curiosity about her reputed talents.

Solomon and Sheba may have been curious for different reasons. She was hungering for knowledge and a view of the world beyond her castle. Solomon, who already had 700 wives and 300 concubines, may have been attracted by the beauty of Sheba; but also, the richness of her treasury, some of which she took to him in gifts, was a factor in her favor.

Sheba, by all accounts, makes her mark in history as an eager student anxious to learn everything possible from Solomon. Law, justice, and social order were her preoccupations, and she eagerly besieged Solomon with questions and debates. Happy to oblige such an eager student, Solomon became an agreeable teacher, but inevitably sought a more romantic relationship. Being also a perfectionist, he was determined to discover if the rumors of Sheba's birthmarked foot (either a "foot of a goat" or a "hairy foot") were true. He had the courtyard flooded so that Sheba had to raise her skirts and thus reveal her deformity or cosmetic imperfection.

Solomon then worked out a cure. It might simply have been the discovery of depilatory!

Sheba the scholar and Sheba the woman were difficult to unite. Perhaps Sheba resented Solomon's harem. Maybe her chastity vows as queen blocked her feelings. In any event, Solomon finally tricked her into bed by daring her to agree that if ever she took something from him she would accede to his wishes. Being quite independent, this seemed like a wager Sheba could easily win. Solomon then staged a banquet with a menu of highly spiced foods. He forbade the serving of water and wine and their presence in the bedrooms. That night, half crazed with thirst, Sheba stole into Solomon's bedroom looking for water. As she reached for the pitcher beside Solomon's bed, he said, "Alas, you have taken something of mine." "But it is only water," replied Sheba. "Yes, but what is more important to take than water from a friend?" And so a love relationship began.

Menylek, a son, was born. Sheba was called home to Ethiopia. Her people accepted the boy child as their future king. Solomon's parting gift to Sheba was a royal ring and his promise that if Menylek presented the ring in the future, Solomon would acknowledge him as son. Menylek grew strong and brilliant under his mother's tutelage, and was brought up to observe Solomon's religion and philosophy. With Sheba's blessing, he later took the royal ring to his father and studied with him.

Before leaving Jerusalem to fulfill his duty to Ethiopia as ruler, Menylek became so obsessed with the Ark of the Lord from the Holy of Holies in Jerusalem that he stole it and carried it back to Ethiopia. The Ethiopians believe that this act moved the sect of Jehovah from Jerusalem to Ethiopia.

"Thus we know," says the *Kebra Nagast,* "that of a surety the King of Ethiopia is King of Zion and the first-born seed of Sheba, and that God loveth exceedingly the people of Ethiopia, and hath made for the Kings of Ethiopia more glory and grace and majesty than for all the other kings on earth."

Mistresses and Candaces

Between 748 and 664 B.C.—a period of more than eighty years—Ethiopia ruled Egypt. During that time a series of eight Ethiopian queens called "Mistresses of Kush" reigned.

One of these, Queen Amenertas, bore the full insignia of authority, the uraeus crown and double cartouches. Both her mother and father were of royal lineage. Her Ethiopian father,

Kashta, is often depicted with his daughter on his right hand.

Amenertas was a priestess-sovereign devoted to the service of Amon. She is noted for her beautification of Thebes and the restoration of the works of her predecessors that had been destroyed in war. She also built chapels in her own name and left many examples of her beautification program in other cities including Aswan and Memphis. Queen Amenertas, "a vigorous ruler, administered her kingdom in peace and prosperity, both as its political and spiritual leader."[12]

Though Amenertas shared the crown with her two brothers, whom she married in succession, it is her name that illustrates the progress of that time. The Temple of Osiris, which she either built or restored, is undoubtedly one of the most important monuments of antiquity. This temple was adorned with statues of her, including a life-sized figure of the queen which bore the following inscription: ". . . I was the wife of the divine one, a benefactress to her city (Thebes), a bounteous giver for her land. I gave food to the hungry, drink to the thirsty, clothes to the naked."[13]

A black granite statue of Amenertas, found in mutilated condition, still remains.

Her daughter, Shepenapt, was the last of the Ethiopian queens to rule Egypt.

A long line of near goddesses and great women have played significant roles in Ethiopian life. The Ethiopian women of antiquity may have set the style for modern ideas of male-female equality. Indeed, a close study of Ethiopian women helps black women understand something of the resoluteness and independence that has come to characterize us as a group.

Throughout the ancient world, Ethiopia was a country highly respected and even immortalized. Herodotus wrote eloquently about the natural beauty and bravery of the Ethiopians. The Greeks considered Ethiopia the home of the gods and goddesses; little wonder there was also a "special kind" of female image associated with this section of Africa.

Ethiopian and Egyptian art is not merely ornamental but a faithful accounting of historical deeds and life. Heeren speaks of the portrayal of kings and queens particularly in the monument of Naga. Viewing this Ethiopian monument, one sees queens alongside kings, not just presenting gifts or sitting in respectful attendance, but appearing as conquerors and warriors who bear arms and destroy captives.

The reliefs of Naga show five male and five female deities. There is one god represented with a double head and four arms.

The king comes from one side and the queen from the other. Power there was considered to be a shared process.[14]

The Ethiopians have drawn great strength from their historic greatness—a greatness that included being "the most just, the most powerful, and the most beautiful of the human race."[15] And regardless of Ethiopian attitudes toward women today, it is certain that "regality" came from the women of Ethiopia, before the white man came and possibly, just possibly, brought male chauvinism along!

"Candace" was a royal title used exclusively in Nubia. Ethiopian queens are sometimes confused in the literature with Nubian Candaces. One Candace of Nubia whom Shinnie refers to as Amaninenas[16] drove down the Nile just after Rome had vanquished Cleopatra and become mistress of Egypt. Her soldiers captured Syene (Aswan), enslaved its inhabitants, and in contempt threw down the statue of Augustus. Rome retaliated by razing Napata, Candace's royal city and one-time Nubian capital. Considering the fact that this brought a period of Nubian and Ethiopian rule to Egypt, it is unfortunate that so little is written about this Candace[17] and others who reigned in what is now the Sudan.

QUEENS OF EGYPT

Egypt has produced great and illustrious queens, excitingly glamorous queens! Black women have long romanticized and idolized them, particularly Cleopatra and Nefertiti. Probably every black actress at one time or another has wanted to play Cleopatra. Walk into any African boutique and you will see trinkets and other adornments for women bearing the label "Nefertiti!" But this fascination certainly is nothing new. Many of the Pharaohs took their wives from Ethiopia. It was said that an Egyptian ruler who married an Ethiopian wife might one day produce a crown prince who would restore the lost Paradise and bring about universal brotherhood.[18]

For all this continuous interest, surprisingly little attention has been paid to two of the greatest Egyptian queens of earlier times, Nefertari and her great-granddaughter, Hatshepsut, both more easily identified as black and closer to the Nubian blood line than either Cleopatra or Nefertiti.

Dynasty XVIII, in which both of these earlier queens lived, is generally considered to be the greatest age of Egyptian history. Arts, crafts, and literature flourished. The quality of life, especially the people's dedication to justice and compassion, marked this age as one of the most humane in history. The treatment of women as equals, the respect for their minds and talents, created an atmosphere that allowed their self-confidence to develop.

The concept of matriarchy might have started here. At least one scholar deemed Egyptian women to be first-class citizens who could own, inherit, build, buy, and sell property. Enjoying great independence, they participated in government of the family, religious ceremonies, and business affairs conducted outside the home.[19]

It is not surprising then that Nefertari and Hatshepsut grew in stature to astonishing heights of power and eminence scarcely matched in the Western world.

Nefertari

The founder of Dynasty XVIII, King Amose I, husband of Nefertari, would certainly be considered a liberated man today. Not only did he write of his deep love for the women of his family, "he gave them authoritative powers that equaled his own."[20]

His deepest love and respect, however, was reserved for his wife, Nefertari. "The complexion of the Ethiopian Queen was Ebon Blackness."[21] This likeness is illustrated in a statue of Nefertari which can be seen today in the Berlin Museum. Nefertari and Amose were purported to be brother and sister; this fact may have been what prompted Evelyn Wells, the distinguished Egyptologist, to ask after viewing Amose's remains: "Is there in that sleeping face a trace of Nubia?"[22] Once again the question of who is black in Egypt is raised. One disquieting fact that persists, even for those who deny the blackness of Egyptians, is the riddle of Nefertari's color and that of Amose!

Nefertari shared the throne of Egypt with her husband for twenty-five years, establishing a peaceful and humane reign, and even after his death she refused to resign her authority. She was the first queen who scorned the inactivity of the harem and actively fulfilled the duties of a sovereign.[23] Even when her son Amonhotep came to power she continued to wield influence and continued guiding building projects, including the shrines and temples in Upper Egypt.

Nefertari was one of the most venerated queens in history. A kind of religious mystique surrounded her. Amose I, her husband, bestowed on her the title "God's wife" as well as "Great Royal Wife."

She not only ruled her people in life but dominated their

minds as a goddess after she died. A popular cult devoted to her memory lingered for many years after her death.

Hatshepsut

Nefertari must have been a role model for her great-granddaughter, Hatshepsut. She never met the venerated queen, but Hatshepsut's grandfather, Amonhotep I, must have imbued her with his admiration for his mother's wise and humanitarian works. As a royal princess whose duties included acts of worshipping royalty, especially of her own lineage, Hatshepsut probably made oblations in Nefertari's memory. She seems to have embodied Nefertari's strength and wisdom, for she was, in the opinion of modern historians, "the world's first great queen," "the first great woman in history."[24]

Many of her interests, though much broader in scope, paralleled those of Nefertari. She, too, was a beautifier and builder, her greatest monument being the beautiful terraced temple of Deir el-Bahri west of Thebes.[25]

Hatshepsut was groomed to reign like no other queen of Egypt. She was her father's favorite, and despite other royal children, there appeared to be no question that her intelligence and manner made her the ideal choice to assume the throne. Wearing a boy's kilt, Hatshepsut learned to hunt and participate in sports. She was tutored by priests and scholars in all the lessons needed to rule Egypt. Her father gave her the title crown prince. However advanced this society, it would seem there was still a greater premium put upon being a "prince" than on being a "princess"!

Departing from custom, her father decided to make Hatshepsut co-regent of Egypt before his death. In an elaborate coronation that took the royal party to two cities, Thebes and Heliopolis, she was crowned "king of Upper and Lower Egypt, Living Forever," when she was barely twenty.[26]

By the time she came to full power, Egypt was used to a strong male presence, and even for Hatshepsut, her sex became a liability.[27] She was the only remaining fully royal Thothmesid, a line of royal descent, and the first sole woman regent. For a time, she ruled alone, but in accordance with royal obligations and social pressure, she finally chose a half-brother to rule with her as a husband. He took the name of Thothmes II, though his mother was not of royal birth. He was not aggressive—perhaps Hatshepsut liked it that way—but he gave her two daughters to assume the continuation and fulfillment of royal expectations.

Thothmes II died young and once again Hatshepsut ruled

alone; but this time, to put down a palace coup, she had herself crowned king. Using all of her dead father's royal titles, she assumed a stronger reign and was able to go on to build some of Egypt's greatest monuments, including her Deir el-Bahari temple. Everywhere, splendid new temples and buildings were rising. Egypt was prosperous, art flourished. There was good government and lively commerce. Being an astute politician, Hatshepsut recognized the claim to the throne of her husband's son by Isis, his concubine. Thus, Thothmes III was married to her daughter, making him co-regent; but he waited impatiently in the wings, for Hatshepsut ruled in total power.

Hatshepsut, a pacifist, had no taste for war. She sought to keep Egypt self-contained, beautiful, and at peace. In the end, her son-in-law won a political advantage by becoming a great soldier, showing his fitness to wage war.

Thothmes III started a propaganda campaign to get rid of this peace-loving woman. "He wears what she cannot—the codpiece of a soldier," was whispered everywhere.[28] In a desperate move, Hatshepsut sent an expedition to Punt, hoping to offset Thothmes' claim to the throne as a soldier-conqueror. Though she did not know the exact location in Africa, she thought the Punt expedition would achieve peacefully what war would do violently—gain treasure and wealth, including myrrh and jewels. She sought to trade for these acquisitions, not wage war. The expedition succeeded, but this was not enough. The Egyptians, goaded by Thothmes' friends, soon grew tired of prosperity and peace and overthrew the queen; her violent, ruthless son-in-law then plunged Egypt into an era of war and aggression.

Not content with replacing Hatshepsut, so great was Thothmes' hatred that he erased her name and face from most of her lovely monuments. Until fairly recent times, even historians scarcely realized that Hatshepsut was, indeed, a woman.

QUEEN WARRIORS

Africa, south of the Sahara, produced queens of great intelligence and varied talents; but almost all of them were forced to prove their abilities on numerous battlefields.

Judith the Fire

After Sheba established the Solomonic line of kings in Ethiopia, another woman, Judith, fought and vanquished the Christians in tenth century Ethiopia. Judith succeeded in dethroning Delna'ad and placed on the throne of Ethiopia the first of eleven Zague kings who dispossessed the Solomonic kings for 354 years. Delna'ad's son was smuggled out and it was his descendant who finally reclaimed and took up the Solomonic line of rule.

As usual, very little can be found about Judith in literature. She, like other female warrior-rulers, is called several names. The one that persists is "The Fire."

She deserved both the name of Judith and The Fire. Like the heroine of the Book of Judith in the *Apocrypha,* Judith the Fire was an ardent fighter for the cause she believed in.

In addition to driving out the long established Christian monarchy, she burned all the churches and the capital of Axum. She was a wild fighter according to the scant legend about her, and was motivated by the desire to establish Judaism as a religion, which indeed she did for over three hundred years.[29]

Zinga

Among all the historical figures of Africa, few equal the Queen-Warrior Zinga, or Ginga, as she is sometimes called. Born in 1582 in Angola, she is noted for her bravery, intelligence, and resolute efforts to keep the Portuguese at bay in the early stages of colonialism. Lydia Child's account in 1836, interestingly, is the fullest account of Zinga.[30] Others seem to note her name only in passing.

Zinga was sent by her brother, the king, as an ambassador to negotiate peace with the Portuguese. She was shown all the pomp and circumstance due a royal visitor. She became incensed, however, over the difference in seating accommodations prepared for the Viceroy and herself. His chair of state was more magnificent than hers; it rested on a richly embroidered rug with cushions of finest tapestry and jewels all around it. Zinga, not to be outdone, ordered one of the women in her entourage to kneel in front of all this splendid regality. She seated herself upon the woman's back and gravely awaited the entrance of the Viceroy. The Portuguese were duly impressed with this "regality," showing her to be no stranger to protocol (a feat the Chinese duplicated in the Sixties by causing a furor over the shape of the conference table in Paris).

The Portuguese attempted to negotiate an alliance that would have required the Angolese to pay tribute once a year to the King of Portugal. Zinga denounced this stipulation, saying, "Such proposals are for a people subdued by force of arms; they are unworthy of a mighty monarch who voluntarily seeks the friendship of the Portuguese and who scorns to be their vassal."

She finally concluded a treaty upon the single condition that all Portuguese prisoners held by her people would be returned.

Zinga tarried perhaps too long in Portugal, very much impressed with the lavishness of the entertainment. While there, she either was converted into Christianity out of belief, or chose to be baptized for political reasons. She was forty years old at the time of her baptism.

After she returned to Angola her brother broke the treaty and made war against the Portuguese invaders. He was defeated and later died of poisoning; some say Zinga poisoned him because he did not follow her advice. After she ascended the throne, she strangled her nephew in revenge for her own child's life that had been taken by her brother earlier.

The Portuguese grew fat and wealthy in Zinga's land. Her people became restless and resented their "occupying" presence. Zinga finally contrived an alliance with the Dutch and several neighboring chiefs and went to war with the Portuguese again. She obtained several victories, but lacking the firepower of the Portuguese, was finally driven from her kingdom.

The Portuguese placed a black puppet king on the throne. This so exasperated Zinga that she renounced Christianity and swore everlasting war on the Portuguese. Leading one of the most gallant and merciless bands of soldiers, Zinga made constant forays into Portuguese territory and harassed them continually for over eighteen years.

The Portuguese attempted to negotiate several treaties with this fierce warrior, but she demanded an absolute return of all her land. She outsmarted them when almost at the end of her resources. Asking if she could retire and reflect on the terms of surrender, she took her soldiers across the river by night and raided Portuguese territory in another region.

Total defeat and the death of her sister weakened her resolve and softened her vengeance. The priests who were among her captives kept reminding her of her Christian vows, and she finally declared that she had returned to the church and signed a treaty of peace. She dedicated the capital city to the Virgin Mary and erected a large church.

When the Portuguese forbade polygamy and polyandry, Zinga, at the age of seventy-five, entered a monogamous marriage. She spent her last years doing good works, founding new cities and building churches. She was never too old to punish neighboring chiefs who broke the treaties she had signed. Yet she never submitted to the humiliation of becoming a vassal of the Portuguese king.

She sent a personal representative to the Pope requesting more missionaries for her people. The Pope granted her request. At a festival in her honor, celebrating the Pontiff's affirmative reply, she and the ladies of her court performed a mimic battle in the dress and armour of the Amazons! Though she was eighty years old, she danced with the skill and agility of a twenty-five-year old woman.

On her death at the age of eighty-two, she was buried in a Catholic habit, with a crucifix and rosary. But before this burial she lay in state in the clothes of Angolese royalty, with a bow and arrow in her hands. This more than her conversion to Catholicism symbolized the life she led: Queen-Warrior.

Chaka: The Zulu Queen

Chaka was a great African Zulu chieftain. Through her extraordinary military strategies and brilliance she united many tribes in Central and South Africa into what became known as the Bantu nation. At one time this nation occupied two-thirds of black Africa.

These people, who varied in color from the black of the Amaswazi to the yellowish-brown of some of the Bechuana,[31] are collectively called Zulus. The name was given them by Chaka, whose original tribe membership was Zulu, but who conquered most of the other territory and formed the nation that played such an important part of the political history of South Africa during the nineteenth century.

Chaka united the entire Zulu nation against the Dutch and English "with a military genius unique in history."[32]

Queen Mothers

A role of great prestige in the history of Africa, unparalleled anywhere else in the world, is held by Queen Mothers. A story which illustrates the role of the Queen Mother in the psychology of Africa describes the surrender of the Ashanti people to the British.

The reigning king, Asantahene, had successfully held Ashanti country against the British. But after five successive wars, the British, with superior firearms, overwhelmed him. They promised him peace and honor but they went beyond any code of military honor and demanded that he submit himself to some public act of submission in order to prove that he accepted the British as ruler of his country.

This, according to Claridge,[33] was a great blow to this great Ashanti king's pride. To present himself before the British in a demeaning act symbolizing powerlessness and defeat was devastating to him. Once before in history a ruler had sent a deputy to an enemy to stand in proxy for him at a moment of surrender—but never had a king personally stood before his people in such a humiliating posture.

The story relates that he stood momentarily fingering the ornaments of his garment, looking as if he might alternately cry and scream. Then, he "slipped off his sandals, and laying aside the golden circlet he wore on his head, stood up with his mother, and hand in hand—mother and son—they walked across the court to where the British governor sat. Then, halting before him, they gave each other a long agonized look, prostrated themselves and embraced the feet of the governor, then Sir Francis Scott.

"Thousands of their Ashanti brothers and sisters sat mute as they watched the mother and king walk these humiliating steps to deliver their people to these foreign invaders. The Ashantis sat as if turned to stone, and mother and son, whose word was a matter of life and death and whose slightest move constituted a command, were forced to humble themselves in the sight of the assembled thousands."[34]

Joint Rulers

There were joint rulers of men and women. One writer says: "Among the Mandingoes of Sierra Leone a beautiful custom prevailed among these people to pronounce the names of the king and queen conjointly in the pulpit; the Queen called Kaza, being in the government also regarded as the consort of the ruler."[35]

There are names of black women that illuminate the earliest beginnings of African tribal history. The history of the Sala of Northwestern Rhodesia started in 1820 when a female chieftain named Namumbe appeared from a district to the northwest of Lusaka and "founded a village." When Namumbe died in 1835, her sister Maninga inherited the chieftaincy. The names of African female tribal chiefs are too numerous even to mention.[36]

AFRICAN WOMEN WARRIORS

That ancient women were capable of warring should not be surprising. In modern times, when hearth and home are under siege, and one's man is elsewhere, it is considered appropriate, even heroic, for a woman to grab a gun and defend self and property. American history is full of white heroines who won high esteem through acts of defense. Rarely, however, are women lauded for offensive aggression in any cause. Not only is the deliberate and purposeful act of taking up arms to defend a country or fight for a way of life prohibited by law, but negative attitudes against "fighting women" are ingrained in the public mind.

The women warriors in Africa's history are unique because they plotted military strategies and successfully waged aggressive battles. They fought not to protect themselves or their homes, but aggressively to preserve their own country and way of life. Many female names are associated with attempts to stave off the white expansionists who plunged Africa into the deplorable period of colonialism.

There were several female generals, though most fought battles because of their primary roles as chieftains and queens.

The most amazing story of historical note is that of the Corps of Dahomey, or the heroic Amazons.

The Amazons of Dahomey

Strange that the word Amazon, when associated with black women (or any other woman, for that matter), carries negative connotations. It is associated with the attitude that it is unfeminine for women to fight, which is quite different from the attitude that neither men nor women should fight or wage wars. Eldridge Cleaver's fellow prisoner whom he quotes in *Soul on Ice* is only one of many who associates the word Amazon with negative meaning. "The white man . . . turned the black woman into a strong self-reliant Amazon." To him an Amazon black woman was "that steel . . . I hate."[37]

The white man did not turn black women into Amazons. The Amazons existed long before white men beat their way into the back lands of Africa. King Gezo, or Guozo, is responsible for reorganizing the Amazons from the original group of unfaithful wives and criminals who guarded the king, to an elite group of unmarried girls, numbering over four thousand. Young girls considered it important to serve in this army and by all accounts they were as handsome as they were fierce.

Without the Amazons' assistance, King Gezo could not have held his powerful position among African kingdoms. Time after time the rest of the army of King Gezo scattered when faced with attack, but the Amazons stood their ground, and once "were hacked to death rather than yield one inch of ground." Their strenuous training was observed by eyewitnesses who claim that they charged through obstacles formed of cactus, thorny bushes, and spikes!

Some writers refer to the Amazons as the "wives of the King of Dahomey," because their sexual lives were regulated by him. Their duties included guarding King Gezo, and their equipment included bows, arrows, and drums. Some Amazons cut off their right breast in order to better hold the butt of the gun![38]

Gezo was one of the greediest slave traders among African chiefs. When his greed matched that of the white slavers, all kinds of vile deals were made. One white slaver became so obsessed with the Amazons that he desperately set out to trade new types of guns for six Amazons.

John Charity Spring and Harry Flashman, two white slavers, recorded fascinating accounts of their interest in the Amazons.

> . . . and such women! They must have been close on a man's height, fine strapping creatures, black as night and smart as guardsmen . . . [they were led by] a great ebony Juno naked to the little blue kilt at her waist, with a long stabbing spear in one hand a huge cleaver in her belt . . . a broad collar of beadwork tight round her throat, and a white turban over her hair . . . at her girdle there hung two skulls and a collection of what looked like lion's claws . . . each one carried a spear, some had bows and quivers of arrows, and one or two even had muskets. . . . I never saw anything on Horse Guards that looked as well-drilled and handsome—or as frighteningly dangerous.

> . . . These are the cream of the Dahomeyan army—the picked bodyguard of the king. Every voyage I've made, I vowed I'd bring back half a dozen of them, but I've never been able to make this black Satan part with even one. He'll part this time, though. . . .

> We'll keep one, perhaps two. The others will fetch a handy price in Havana . . . what? Think of the money they'll pay for black fighting women in New Orleans! I could get two—no, three thousand dollars a head for creatures like those![39]

Gezo's greed for new "fire power" finally overcame his better judgment and he reluctantly consented to sell Spring six of his cherished Amazons. But even as the men sealed the contract and marched off with the Amazons, Spring and Flashman begun to fear the Amazons' sullenness despite their discipline. Clearly they obeyed the king—but with great resentment;

> . . . By Jove, it was a long minute's walk to the gate of the stockade, through the double file of those black Amazon furies, their faces sullen with anger and grief at the sale of their fellows, while the great crowd of townsfolk roared in protest behind them. But the

> discipline of those women warriors was like iron; the king had said, and that was that. . . .[40]

But tragedy met the white slavers. On the return to the Balloit College (already stacked full of slaves and ready to sail), they were attacked by the Amazons, who captured their six sisters and killed five of the men for good measure. Spring's disappointment was singular:

> . . . I lost that black slut. All those years, and I lost the sow! Even that single one . . . she would have done! My G–d, I could have used that worm![41]

AFRICAN WOMEN IN MARRIAGE AND FAMILY LIFE

It is tempting to weigh history in biographical terms—the sum total of great personages becoming the proof of this or that idea. Certainly the queens and warriors of Africa give testimony to the fact that strong, brave women have helped shape African history. But the unique and the striking tell us little of the everyday themes of human struggle. We have to examine the external aspects of a civilization—visible expressions of attitudes and habits as seen in institutions, agencies, and life styles. The personal qualities of a people—probably the most important aspect of all—define those intellectual and moral values which make, preserve, and advance a civilization. The moral and intellectual qualities of humanity—especially those to which so-called civilized societies pay lip service: respect for the individual; the collective responsibility and care for the young, the old, and the sick; and the pursuit of the aesthetic—determine, in the last analysis, the character of a great civilization.

Such a view of history takes us from an emphasis on the "great women theory" to that of African women as a collective force in molding African civilization, particularly the institutional life of marriage and family.

The position of African women in marriage, family life, and society has been historically interesting to scholars, explorers, and colonizers. Tales of "women possessed of charms such as the white world never knew" were accompanied by descriptions of them as independent, strong, and courageous. Many learned travelers, including Ibn Battuta and Mungo Park, combined curiosity with some disapproval of the independence they observed in African women.

White men at that time idolized their women with words like

dependent, weak, emotional, and retiring. Any demonstrated female vigor beyond zestful coquetry (which allowably added spice to the romance between the sexes) was thought unfeminine, in both Arab and European worlds. It is not surprising, then, that the colonizers resented the African women's independence and aggressiveness in home and community affairs.

Aggressive decision-making usually suggests a matriarchy, which was first associated with Egypt and was considered commonplace until the Greek rulers sought to introduce foreign concepts. Egyptologists generally referred to the fact that the Egyptians allowed their women a remarkable degree of freedom, yet somehow the corrupting matriarchal theory seemed to creep into their descriptions of women's aggressive roles.

The prominent position of the women in the family led generally to a prominent position of women in Egypt. No people, ancient or modern, has given women so high a legal status as did Egypt.[42]

Elsewhere in Africa, women occupied equalitarian positions. Even when explorers and colonizers sought to impose their male chauvinistic views on African social systems, they met resistance. When, for example, Mohhamed Askia the Great attempted to reform Timbuktu, he ordered the women draped from head to toe. But when he died the country returned to the accustomed freedom between men and women.[43] Neither paternalism nor monogamy fitted easily into the traditions of Africa.

Sexual relations between unmarried boys and girls was seldom a tribal taboo; it was even encouraged, with little importance given to prenuptial chastity.[44] The art of love was as much a value as was warring. One account glorifies cheerful love-play, stating that "the hero must show a soft hand when courting."[45]

The matrilineal system of kinship, in which inheritance succession and political allegiance are determined by the female line of descent, was widespread in Africa, a situation often associated with a matriarchy. One all too often concludes that in such a system the woman exercises domination over men similar to that exercised by men over women in modern patriarchal society. Such domination was alien to the matriarchal elements in African society. Both men and women were producers. Both had power positions in the accumulation and disposition of property and wealth.

Furthermore, the African social system was more family oriented than marriage minded. Decisions were made for the good of the entire family, marriage between a man and a woman being a "coming together" of two families.[46] Since only a woman can truthfully certify the paternity of children, authority over kinship lines rested with her in a matrilineal system.

Many systems favored a congenital brother-sister bond. The Akan people of the Gold Coast had a matrilineal system which dictated special terms for mothers' brothers, and the difference between direct and collateral descent was ignored. "A woman may not know who fathered her child, but she does know who will always be its uncle."[47]

All persons bearing a common clan name were related by blood and descended from a common ancestress. Although the descent was matrilineal, the lineage head was a male in whom was vested political and legal authority. The female head held high moral authority. As wives did not always live with their husbands, it seemed that they preferred to continue living with their own kin. Clinging to their mothers, they returned to their mothers' homes during the day.[48]

Matrilocal marriage and matriarchal societies existed in one form or another among tribes in every part of Africa. Among the Bechuane tribes there was a proverb: "Happy is she who has borne a daughter; a boy is the son of his mother-in-law." Among the Zulus and tribes of Southern Nyasaland, grooms lived in the house of their wives, and remained there five years before building their own home. Among the Pygmies of the Congo forests the daughters continued to live with their parents even after they were married, and the husbands placed themselves under the orders of their fathers-in-law. The countries now known as Nigeria and French Sudan have been characteristically matriarchal, descent being traced through the woman and property being transmitted by a man to the children of his sister.[49] Parenthood, in most cases, was more highly valued than marriage.

Polygamy served to support the system of values, not to deprecate women, though conquerors and missionaries denounced no feature of African life as much as polygamy. It has been viewed as heathen, sinful, the core cause of all perceived backwardness of Africa, and insensitive to the feelings of women.

It is difficult to speak well of polygamy when the widespread acceptance of monogamy is sanctioned as morally right, socially approved, and worthy of God's highest blessings. Chastity, continence, and monogamy formed the basis of Western morality.

And yet, as one writer tells it:

> If we could put aside prejudice we would have to admit that no section of humanity has so far devised a comfortable, successful,

> smooth running system for mating, breeding and satisfaction of sex desires of men and women. Our way is disfigured by woe and wrangling. And since legends began all the world has tangled with the management of its sex life. We must accept that any attempt to contrast various systems—pagan Africa's, our own, and all the others—is but a comparison of inefficiencies.[50]

Polygamy appears to have functioned adequately in precolonial Africa. We know this from the accounts of African women who were the chief supporters of the system. The fact that they may not have known of any other system does not weaken the case, nor does the fact that modern, educated African women reject polygamy as undesirable today demean its past significance.

Actually, many African women resisted monogamy. European missionaries were often shocked to hear them defend polygamy in words that conveyed two essential points: "We never marry anyone we do not want to, and we like our husbands to have as many wives as possible."[51]

In most cases the sole wife of a man became an object of other women's sympathy. The concept of exclusive attachment between a man and woman was neither understood nor preferred. Tribal wives actually coaxed their husbands to take other wives, even helped them to find compatible companions. Numerous wives were conceived as prestigious for the entire family unit, facilitating the work of all and increasing family wealth.[52]

African history describes a general social system which valued children and ascribed to them positions of respect and affection. Compared to societies where children are romanticized and overprotected, in Africa's past the children appear to have been "taken in stride." Disciplined in the ways of the tribe, African children were taught special respect for old people and lived for the greater good of the tribe and the collective well-being of the total group. African society was "group-oriented" instead of "child-oriented."

African motherhood was not based on exclusive attachment to one's biological children. Among some tribes the first child was taken from the mother at birth and suckled by another woman. Widespread was the custom of distributing children among aunts, uncles, and other relatives. The "foster family" system produced close relationships between the children and adults. In fact, rather than asking, "What is your father's name?" or "What is your mother's name?" missionaries had to word the questions: "Who is the father who begat you?" "Who is the mother that bore you?" If they had simply asked their names, they would have been answered with the names of four or five fathers and as many mothers without the biological parents even being included.

The social system from which our African slave ancestors were captured and brought into slavery produced a woman whose self-concept, values, loyalties, and lifestyles foretold an impossibly difficult adjustment to America. The individualistic, competitive social system of America was strikingly different from the sharing, collective group life these women had lived in their tribes. Though some had long been accustomed to African slavery, it was certainly never as inhumane, never as life-binding as American slavery. Our African foreparents headed into the most brutalizing and humiliating institution in the history of mankind—American slavery—and their survival and that of their children is the greatest monument to humanity ever yet recorded.

Consider the odds against the African woman's survival in slavery—and even later:

. . . From a society that valued the naturalness of her sexuality, she faced a repressive Victorian code of morality which enshrined virginity as the highest form of respectability and morality.

. . . From a family life which treasured children as honored members of the collective group, she faced childbirth as a lonely vigil—knowing that the child she birthed belonged not to "her" people but to a plantation system; often not knowing the paternity of her child because she was mated by the will of her master. She also reared it in a society that looked on premarital and extramarital relations as immoral. When later forced to leave her children with others in the black community because she had to work, America soon considered her action as "child abandonment" and she was forced to feel ashamed.

. . . From a family-oriented society, she came to a marriage-oriented one where "one man for one woman and that for all times" pulled against the traditional socialization of African women against exclusive attachments to one man. And as her values changed over time, where were the men numerically available to marry her?

. . . From tribes that produced strong, brave, regal, self-reliant women, accustomed to hard work, she came to a slave system, then to a tenant system, then to the slums and ghettos—to work that would test that strength for generations to come. And in doing so she and her daughters would live until this day in the shadow of negative comparisons with white women whose images as ideal feminine women are entrenched in the folklore and myths of America.

"WHAT IS AFRICA TO ME?"

The overriding summation of the African woman's past is simply the fact that she has always demonstrated strength and self-reliance—necessary qualities for survival. There was among black men a definite respect for the mental as well as physical acumen of women. Female equality is enough of a historical thread in the history of Africa for women *never* to have developed a concept of themselves as worthless or dependent. The men and women of Africa had developed more egalitarian relationships in ordering the affairs of the tribes than any other civilization. Though the records are scant on this score, one is bound to correlate: The white man in his garb as missionary and his cloak of conquerer instilled in African men the concept of "male chauvinism." That, and the image of white women as beautiful, came with colonization, exploitation, and plunder and, like any other negative foreign concepts, soon became entrenched in the fiber of African life. But not before the vestiges of egalitarianism carried in the minds of those Africans sailing as slaves bound to America.

Alex Haley describes the ancient African attitude of men and women toward a woman's value.

> Nightly now, it was on the eve of the annual harvest, circa 1760, every female in the village over twelve rains old, was boiling and then cooling a freshly-pounded saydame leaves solution, in which they soak their feet to a deep, inky blackness up to the ankles; as well as the palms of their hands, as all men felt that the more blackness a woman had, the more beautiful she was—and especially if she was obviously physically strong. So the mothers of unmarried daughters were quick to tell them, "you are beautiful, but you learn to work, for you cannot eat your beauty."[53]

As the daughters were captured, bound, and dragged to the shores of the West Indies, South America, and the United States, the historical virtues and traits which had made them strong and brave and hardworking, a kind of strength-constancy, were those that enabled them to survive. Frail "clinging vines," overly dependent, become extinct, like *Homo erectus.* The strong and self-reliant survive—as did Cinderella—*Homo habilis.*

And survived we have! And multiplied, endured, built, resisted, and persisted. And at last

> *Now* do our hearts and minds
> at last realize
> They and I are civilized.

CHAPTER 1
NOTES

[1]Countee Cullen, "Heritage" in *On These I Stand*, p. 121. Copyright 1925 by Harper & Row, Publishers, Inc.; renewed 1953 by Ida M. Cullen. By permission of the publishers.

[2]Lerone Bennett, Jr., *The Challenge of Blackness* (Chicago: Johnson Publishing Company, Inc., 1972), pp. 194–198.

[3]Robert Merton, "The Self-Fulfilling Prophecy," *Antioch Review*, VIII (1958), 195. For fuller discussion, also see Jeanne Noble, "Guidance and Counseling Minority Youth," in *Guidance Personnel Work, Future Tense*, ed. Margaret Ruth Smith (New York: Teachers College, Columbia University Press, 1966), pp. 105–122.

[4]L. S. B. Leakey and Vanne Morris Goodall, *Unveiling Man's Origins* (Cambridge: Schenkman Publishing Company, Inc., 1969). Also see Melvin M. Payne and Joseph J. Schenschal, "Preserving the Treasures of Olduvai Gorge," *National Geographic*, 130, No. 5 (November 1966), 701–706. In the latter reference the author Melvin Payne and photographer Joseph Schenschal describe in photographs the skeleton of the woman, *Homo habilis*, "Cinderella," and her man and child found in Bed I in Olduvai Gorge. *Homo habilis* is thought, by Leakey, to be ancestral to *Homo erectus*, a skeleton-like Java and China primitive finds. Leakey believes that "*Homo habilis* is leading toward modern man, while *Zinjanthropus* and *Homo erectus* mark dead-end branches in revolution's tangled growth."

[5]*Ibid.*

[6]Galbraith Welch, *Africa Before They Came* (New York: William Morrow and Company, 1965), p. 308.

[7]Augustus Le Plongeon, *Queen Moo and the Egyptian Sphinx*, 2nd ed. Published by author, 1900 (Library of Congress). In this publication, the author was not able to establish a scientific claim of Queen Moo's blackness, or her direction in building the sphinx. His major evidence is the striking similarity between inscriptions and symbols found on the sphinx and that of Prince Coh's tomb in the Yucatan. Yet the discussion is convincing enough for future scholars to research in more depth.

[8]*Ibid.*, p. 1.

[9]*Ibid.*, p. 2.

[10]Herodotus mentions Nitocris in Book I (Chapters 185–187) and Book II (Chapter 100). See *The History of Herodotus*, trans. George Raweinson (New York: E. P. Dutton & Company, 1910). For commentaries see H. C. Tolman and J. H. Stevenson, *Herodotus and The Empire of the East* (New York: American Book Company).

[11]See Wallis Budge, *The Queen of Sheba and Her Only Son Menylek* (translated) (London, Liverpool and Boston: British Museum, Medici Society, Limited, 1922); Norman Hill, *Queen of Sheba* (London: Albert Maritt Company, 1930), a fictionalized version of Sheba; A. H. L. Heeren, *Historical Research into the Politics, Intercourse and Trade of the Carthaginians, Ethiopians and Egyptians* (London: Oxford University Press, 1938); Edward Villendorf, *Ethiopia and the Bible* (London: Oxford University Press, 1968).

[12]Evelyn Wells, *The Queens of Egypt* (New York: Doubleday and Company, Inc., 1969), p. 207.

[13]*Ibid.*, p. 209.

[14]Heeren, *Historical Research*, p. 393 (see footnote 11 above).

[15]Bennett, *Challenge of Blackness* p. 5.

[16]Margaret Shinnie, *Ancient African Kingdoms* (London: E. Arnold, 1965), p. 29.

[17]Welch, *Africa,* p. 14.

[18]Sterling Mean, *Ethiopia and the Missing Link in African History* (Harrisburg, Pa.: The Atlantis Publishing Company, 1945), p. 35.

[19]Wells, *Queens of Egypt,* p. 31.

[20]Evelyn Wells, *Hatshepsut* (New York: Doubleday and Company, Inc., 1969), p. 35.

[21]Heeren, *Historical Research,* p. 39.

[22]Evelyn Wells, *Queens of Egypt,* p. 31.

[23]Janet Buttles, *The Queens of Egypt* (London: Archibald Constable & Company, Ltd., 1908), p. 6.

[24]See Christiane Desroches-Noblecourt, *Tutankhamen* (New York Graphic Society, 1963); and James Henry Breasted, *A History of Egypt* (New York: Charles Scribner's Sons, reprint 1959).

[25]*Encyclopaedia Britannica,* Vol. II (Chicago: William Benton Company, 1968).

[26]Wells, *Hatshepsut,* p. 113.

[27]*Ibid.,* p. 150.

[28]*Ibid.,* p. 232.

[29]Welch, *Africa,* pp. 28–29.

[30]Lydia Marie Child, *A Brief History of the Conditions of Women in Various Ages and Nations,* 5th ed. (New York: C. S. Francis & Co., 1845).

[31]W. E. B. DuBois, *The World of Africa* (New York: The Viking Press, 1947).

[32]*Ibid.*

[33]Walton W. Claridge, *A History of the Gold Coast and Ashanti,* Vol. I (London: John Murray, 1951), p. ix.

[34]*Ibid.*

[35]N. Cameron, *The Evolution of the Negro* (Schomburg Collection, 1939), p. 19.

[36]Basil Davidson, *The Lost Cities of Africa* (Boston/Toronto: Little Brown & Company, 1959), p. 18.

[37]Eldridge Cleaver, *Soul on Ice* (New York: McGraw Hill Book Company, 1968), p. 162.

[38]Robert Briffault, *The Mothers,* Vol. I (New York: Macmillan & Company, 1927), p. 453; Childs, *Brief History,* p. 253; and Welch, *Africa,* p. 309.

[39]George MacDonald Fraser, *Flash for Freedom* (New York: Alfred A. Knopf, 1972), pp. 67–69.

[40]*Ibid.,* p. 72.

[41]*Ibid.,* p. 77

[42]Briffault, *The Mothers,* p. 387.

[43]Felix DuBois, *Timbuctoo* (New York: Longmans, Green & Co., 1896), p. 176.

[44]Briffault, *The Mothers,* p. 69.

[45]Oscar Koenig, *The Masai Story* (London: Michael Joseph Co., 1961), p. 93.

[46]Jomo Kenyatta, *Facing Mt. Kenya* (New York: Vintage Books, 1962)

[47]M. S. Field, *Serial Insecurity* (London: Faber & Faber, 1960).

[48]*Ibid.,* p. 26.

[49]Briffault, *The Mothers,* pp. 274–284.

[50] Welch, *Africa,* p. 317.

[51]See G. T. Basden, *Among the Ibos of Nigeria* (New York: Barnes & Noble, 1966),p. 97; M. M. Grun, *Ibo Village Affairs* (London: Sedgwick & Jackson, Ltd., 1974), p. 76; and Briffault, *The Mothers,* pp. 605–606.

[52]*Ibid.*

[53]Personal letter from Alex Haley to the author dated February 18, 1970.

To be a slave.
To be owned by another person, as a car,
house, or table is owned.
To live as a piece of property that could be
sold—
A child sold from its mother, a wife
from her husband.
To be considered not human,
but a "thing" that plowed the fields . . .
To be a slave.
To know, despite the suffering, deprivation,
that you were human, more human than he
who said you were not human.

JULIUS LESTER[1]

To Be a Slave

They were never just things and property; for the basic human qualities of caring and nurturing, as well as strong survival skills, remained inviolable. Black women just went on mothering, for generations of black and white children began their infancy on their laps, growing into adulthood relating to them often as the primary mother figure. Slavery was just another brutal test of black femininity which they in time would overcome.

But how did they come to be slaves? These men and women were not the prizes in a tribal war; they did not come to serve a rival chief whose power could be respected. They were trapped and taken from their natural habitat like animals that have suddenly taken on great commercial value, only these creatures presented some unique problems.

At first, capturing them was not too difficult. Because their society and civilization did not match Western standards, it was easily ignored. Some of the traders, for example, recognized the seeming innocence that caused some women to be attracted to scraps of red flannel that they would pick up, planted there by the slave traders to form a flaming trail through the cool green of Africa right onto the gangplank of their slave ships. The women laughed as they joined in this strange new game until the trap was sprung and suddenly they found themselves chained on board, unable to buy their freedom by returning the bits of cloth they'd thought so valuable. For many, it would be the last reason they would have for laughing.

It was easy, at first, to capture many young boys as they played in the forest, away from their villages. The slave traders had only to take them by surprise, scoop them up, and get them quickly on board the waiting ships. By the time their families discovered that they had not been taken by rival tribes for possible ransom, their children were well on their way to a new life of pain and suffering, never to be seen again.

Naive as the Africans were, they were not stupid. After a few human losses, they formed vigilante corps to protect themselves and avoided those outlying paths between villages and rivers which were so indefensible. As tribes became aware of the danger, slave traders were forced to devise more cunning ways of capture.

Although the slavers could not see their African prey as human in the same way they knew themselves to be, they soon realized that some were subject to the familiar emotion that was most suitable to their purpose: greed. To the African chiefs, slaves were wealth; so were guns, but guns brought a different kind of power. It made sense to trade some of their slaves taken in tribal wars for guns and ammunition; besides, they were only moving their captives from one form of slavery to another. There was no way for them to know that the system as practiced in the Americas was unlike any other mode of enslavement ever known in the world. None of their people ever returned to tell of the cruelty and degradation suffered from their white owners. So, some African chiefs played into the hands of the slavers. This evil collaboration helped to corrupt the spirit and independence of Africa.

History notes at least one chief who entered into the slave system hoping not for guns and whiskey but for teachers, doctors, and carpenters. His original name was Mari-Congo; he was later to adopt the new one of Don Alfonso when he adopted Christianity. Even Don Alfonso was to be cheated. He received the usual luxuries and guns, only to lose his land and the precious lives of his people.[2]

Surely this was the most dreadful page in black history. Slave or be enslaved. If a chief did not gain the advantage in weapon power to protect his village from other chiefs, he ran the risk of being enslaved; but the only means of gaining the necessary fire power was by bargaining for them with human coin. To save his people from slavery, he was therefore forced to commit his neighbors to it. What madness lay in that riddle!

There was still another avenue open to those early, enterprising hunters. African priests, they discovered, were as susceptible as chiefs to the idea of trading off people for power. The Aros, for example, were a fierce people, considered to be holy oracles of the god Umu-Chukwu. It was to Aros priests that the Ibo clansmen paid tribute for the safety of their crops and cattle. When the Aros demanded a "fine," it was in the form of an errant child, or one whom the priest called errant. Under pain of dire consequences, the one deemed unworthy was surrendered to the holy men to be "eaten" by the mighty Chukwu. Indeed, the families thought that was the fate of their unfortunate ones, since those "fines" disappeared from the face of the earth. For the victims to find themselves sold by the holy men to traders and later to white owners from the auction block might indeed have been as ominous an alternative as being eaten by the vengeful gods.[3]

As cruel as their betrayal was, it would be impossible to accuse those African priests of inhumanity without also acknowledging that for the most part the Christian church sanctioned slavery, though it might have been presumed that those who claimed to represent a holy and beneficent God would have cried out against it. Had the Christian church regarded Africans not as mere pagans, but as human beings worthy of its protection, would slavery as we know it in this country have been allowed to grow and flourish? As academic as this question is, it should be considered before casting stones at the African priests; they had no knowledge of the One who is followed by those in the West as the Son of God, and who said: "Inasmuch as you have done it to the least of my brethren, you have done it likewise to me." Slave dealers in black flesh found it easy to look upon their primitive captives as less than human, so they treated them like animals. They were branded and herded, often three hundred at a time, into the holds of slave ships, stacked and packed by engineering logic to make each crossing well worth the trouble. But, there was plenty of trouble with these Africans. Unlike animals, they mourned the loss of their families and their freedom. They did not take well to chains or to the confinement which allowed only six feet by fifteen inches per person, space enough for most of the captives to lie only on their sides. In many cases, weak babies were tossed overboard to save maximum room for the fittest, often the women from whom they were torn fought with all the power left them. Chained as they were, some leaped in the water after their children, dragging others with them; others struggled until arms or legs were broken against the metal that held them, and unable to die with their young, died on board some days later from their wounds and refusal to eat. The responsibility of such potentially valuable cargo weighed heavy on those captains, their charge being to deliver as many alive as possible, at the lowest possible cost. Since these slaves were thought to be lacking in the refinements of civilized folks, however, it was deemed enough to throw yams down the hole for their feed. There were concessions to health made on some ships, which allowed exercise once a day, and twice each day hoses were turned on to wash away the excrement. After all, each captain knew of some others less wise in their treatment of similar human freight who had lost entire shiploads to epidemics. Such a waste to go to all the trouble of loading and chaining and feeding, then to end the journey with nothing for their trouble!

Closely confined as they were, some captives managed to commit suicide rather than face an unknown future as a slave in some strange land, but others, especially those black women who nursed the sick and comforted frightened children, began a journey of survival which is still going on today. They drew on many ancient African customs and a rich heritage of music and dance, though brutalized and humiliated on that long trek across the sea. Out of their tears, sorrow, and the personal redemptiveness of joy and laughter, many of their creative capacities gained artistic expression. Like their Ashanti, Mandingo, and Dahomean mothers before them, black female slaves came through the Middle Passage as sensitive, strong, and self-reliant women.

THE NEW WORLD

> "Going high, going mighty slow, a little while to go.
> Bid 'em in, bid 'em in.
> The sun am high, the sun am hot, us got to git ham tonight."[4]

So chanted the auctioneer in Charleston, South Carolina, as the crowd milled around, each man hoping to get the best buys in good working or breeding stock. Did he want well-muscled men to go to the fields, or had his wife sent him for a couple of reasonably bright-looking girls to be trained for service in the main house? Did he perhaps judge potential house slaves with a sharper eye toward more personal service he would exact from them? Whatever he needed he would find it on the auction block at Charleston; the only trick was to look beyond obvious weaknesses brought on by the harsh, cramped journey the Africans had just completed. A wise buyer had to know which wounds would heal with the least damage, which limps would be permanent. He had to try to guess which frightened, sullen looks, which flashes of outright hate and hostility could be tempered into productive submission by his particular means of discipline, whether it be by the lash or through a kind of humane paternalism. It was, after all, an investment.

They came from the ship as naked as they had traveled; no need for niceties with savages; besides, the buyers wanted to see exactly what they were bidding on. For these African brothers and sisters there was no shame in their bodies, but they were to learn much from reflected attitudes and open jibes of the white man who carefully inspected the young black women for sale, since ". . . a large portion of white men . . . had one or more sexual contacts with slave women."[5] The young white men of the Big House, and often the masters, were almost expected to sow their wild oats on the pallets of young house slaves, for whom, when they bore mulatto babies, there was neither censure nor shame, just eventual replacement by a younger female slave. As for those babies, half black, half white, they formed a new class; they were seldom reared with slave children but played with whites and other mulattos, often taught by their very isolation that they were somehow better than their pure black brothers and sisters. Sometimes they were the means of freedom for their mothers and themselves. For although perpetuating the system, at least some slaveholders rebelled against having their own flesh and blood live out their days as chattel.

And so, the breeding capacity of slaves or their potential for the owners' personal sexual enjoyment were all figured in with both the auctioneer's expectations and the bidders' eagerness to vie with one another for the strongest and what whites deemed to be the most attractive black women. The women bore their anguish alone, for black men were powerless to offer protection or solace—they too were slaves!

There was also a certain value even to older female flesh, although not as great as for young breeders; someone had to take care of the babies while their slave-mothers were busy with more profitable work. It was soon learned that many of the older women were also skilled in healing, and that they made good nurses for the master's own children; so, a relatively sound old body might easily bring $100, though such a sale created little excitement or competition.

Some new owners did not want the bother of taking nursing babies; it was at best a distraction to the young slave who needed to learn new rules and a new way of life. These surplus children were simply taken away from their mothers and either were given to an old black Granny already on the plantation, or were left screaming at the auction site while the mother was driven away with that dreadful sound filling her soul.

Caring for the young was handled in different ways on different plantations. One description that has come down to us is of a great, long, old cradle for the babies which an overseer built to cut down on the time wasted by black women stopping their field work to nurse them. The communal cradle was under a big cottonwood tree and served well until one day a sudden thunderstorm came up; when the mothers raced to protect their young ones, they found the trough filled with water and every baby in it floating dead. So violent was the reaction, that in order to stem a possible rebellion the plantation owner was virtually forced to set up a kind of day care center where older slaves kept an eye on the babies left there.[6]

DIVISION OF LABOR

In general, there were three classifications of slaves, each separate and distinct in their work and in their social standing among their peers. Lowest in the structure were the field hands. These were often the strongest slaves, best able to stand the heat and able to bear the heaviest burdens. They were sent to plow and plant, to hoe and pick cotton, that "white gold" their lives depended so upon. Some of the women were given simple shifts to wear, but more than half of the work group was entirely naked. Slave owners could see the value of food, but seldom saw the relationship between clothing and work productivity.[7] The whip could be used liberally on them, as they were thought to be all brawn and no brains. They planted, they harvested. But they also plotted! That they were capable of plans for insurrection was mercifully not obvious to even such a sensitive woman as Fannie Kemble, a noted actress of the time, whose husband owned many slaves, and who wrote that the field hands were "the more stupid and brutish of the tribe."[8]

According to one scholar, "These laborers lived, some dozen men, women and children, in meager log huts. There was no furniture of any description, beds were made of straw and old rags, thrown down in a corner and boxed in with boards, each had a single blanket. The wind whistled and the rain and snow blew in through the cracks, and the damp earth soaked in the moisture till the floor was miry as a pigsty."[9]

A possible and probable scenario might well go like this: Just before sunrise the conch shell would summon them all from their fitful sleep. In ordinary times they labored in the fields starting at sunlight, and it was not until noon that breakfast of cold bacon and water came; supper came when the remainder of the workday was over. Only during harvest season were there three meals. Rations of corn and bacon were given to the women each week, and these meager staples they pooled. There most likely was only a small hand mill to grind the corn, and usually there were no pots or cooking pans provided; the slaves had to improvise as best they could. Their bacon was just thrown on the coals to broil and the corn meal was mixed with a little water and put on rocks in the ashes to bake. When it was "done brown," ashes were scraped off these corn pones and everybody sat around on the ground and ate.

By the time these workers ate their night meal, it was usually close to midnight. In spite of the day's burden and their miserable conditions sometimes one peson would manage to strike up a tune on a homemade instrument or start the others singing. That they could sing under such inhuman circumstances was proof to their owners and the rest of the white world that they obviously had no feelings, no sense of the fitness of things. What these critics failed to see was that only through their music and the recreation it brought them were those weary slaves able to retain their sanity and to keep alive some shreds of hope . . . which in turn kept them alive.

If, after the fires had died down, a black man slipped under the blanket of one of the women who slept near him, the sexual ease they both found in such brief encounters and even the children which might be born of them were still other means of survival.

The second category of slaves was the "yard slaves" who comprised the middle social strata. These slaves possessed skills in carpentry, furniture making, blacksmithing, sewing, and nursing. They lived apart from the field hands in somewhat better conditions, and their rations might include such luxuries as rice or grits. They were respected by both whites and field hands and were fiercely proud of their handiwork and fully conscious of their contribution to the well-being of the plantation system. Many Southern diaries pointed out the beautiful workmanship demonstrated by this group, and it was through them that some few advantages were won from their white masters. Because they worked in closer contact with their owners, this middle group was able to know and incorporate some of the customs and habits of the Big House in their lifestyles while at the same time keeping alive many African traditions, especially nursing and medical skills.

With all their privileges, even these skilled artisans were not always treated fairly. Fannie Kemble recorded her outrage when her husband kept some $60 earned by the sale of a boat built by two of his skilled slaves, but why not, the men in question *were* his property!

Because of their skills and prized abilities, yard slaves were also the ones to be "hired out"; they found their way into cities to make money for their owners, and sometimes in their spare time they earned money to be saved for their eventual freedom. Later, of course, due to their marketable talents, it was this group which fared best during Reconstruction.

The third classification took in all those who worked in the Big House, cared for the yards and gardens, drove carriages, and performed the duties of personal servants. These "house slaves" were seen as favored to some degree, although they were often laughed at by the other slaves who thought them snobbish. Household staffs appear to have been equally divided between men and women. There were laundry women, seamstresses, housemaids, dairy-women, and often several cooks in each category among the female workers. Sometimes the head of this domestic group was a woman, usually the old cook, but in most cases the black male butler supervised the domestics on orders from the mistress of the plantation.

Psychologically these house slaves were forced to curry favor through the use of their personalities. Since they had no highly marketable crafts to fall back on like those of the yard slaves, they lived in dread of being sent out to work with "those dirty, smelly niggers" in the fields—a fear seldom shared by the skilled slaves. Some of the young house slaves were treated like pet sheep who sleep like puppy-dogs in bed chambers."[10] Many grew up as confidants of whites. From this group came imitators of white behavior patterns, but unlike the middle groups of skilled laborers, house slaves tended to let go of their African traditions, and they thought themselves superior to all the other blacks. They probably knew better than others the complex inner feelings of a slavemaster or mistress in relationship to their slaves and also knew well their deepest personal fears and drives. But so enmeshed were they in their own love-hate, loyalty-disloyalty patterns with whites, so fearful of field work, and so proud to be in the "privileged" class, that they seldom used their knowledge to help break the back of slavery that Stampp was to immortalize as "that peculiar institution." Many of the insurrections were sold out by house slaves, and most of the strife that threatened to disunite freedmen after emancipation is traceable to the antipathy between house and field blacks.

Of course, on those farms where only a few slaves lived and worked, there was no such division of labor.[11] Each slave did a little of everything, indoors as well as out. The only division was between the whites who owned the land the blacks who tilled it. There was usually neither paternalism nor cruelty in their common exchanges, neither love nor hate, trust nor distrust—just two groups, black and white, caught up in the circumstances of the time, each keeping to themselves. In later chapters there will be illustrations of some prime examples of "house" or domestic slaves and the generation that followed them, as seen through the eye of fiction, but that was to come after the fact of slavery itself. Here we are concerned with what we know from various records made at the time by those who lived through it.

FAMILY LIFE

It is difficult to speak of the American nuclear institution of "family life" as such under American slavery; there was so little of it. Establishing ties only caused trouble when one of a pair was to be sold or traded. Although some owners did permit marriages by a preacher, such ceremonies were rare. For most of those who wanted to live together there was merely a sham ritual called "jump over the broom," but when that was all they were permitted, that had to suffice. As with everything else governing slaves' lives, this depended on the mood of their master. From a tribal system based on laws that enabled each man and woman to know how family life was to be regulated, Africans were thrown into a system where the rules changed according to the master of the moment. If a slave found herself owned by a cruel man, there might be the hope at least to escape into a more benign form of slavery through resale. The reverse, of course, was also true; while in the best of circumstances, there was always the dread of being sold or willed to a less humane master.

What did family life mean to an African slave in an alien society, cut off from her history and heritage?

Contrary to some opinions which express a belief that there is a disintegrated black family life stemming from slavery, scholars from Stampp to Robert William Fogel and Stanley L. Engerman reinforce slave accounts which prove that slaves cherished and developed stable family lives. The greatest punishment a master could mete out was not the sting of the whip, but the threat of family separation. The most common objective of a runaway slave was "to get back home"—to parent, to spouse, to children. These slaves did not need legal ceremonies or papers to bind them psychologically to each other in common kinship bonds that characterize all cultures. Husbands and wives made vows to each other, and clung together in caring and protective ways without legal contracts imposing obligations or penalties for marital and family violations. Whites were protected by laws which governed their sexual, marital and family acts, even including such nebulous grievances as alienation of affection and misrepresentation of one's intention to marry. Not one law prevailed among slaves to encourage monogamy, fidelity, or child care. Lacking the support of any legal foundation, the fact that many strong black family structures evolved is remarkably commendable. Within "the peculiar institution" of slavery it was not plantation codes, as some claim, which set up norms and standards recognizing aggregates of individuals living together as families, but the slaves own internalized values passed down through the generations which taught well the meaning of sharing, caring, and protecting each other in group units. During slavery, white families were strongly patriarchal, so it is understandable that some would see black husbands and fathers as submissive to black women, and it was at this historic junction, no doubt, that the onerous word matriarchy reared its hideous head. While Stampp argues that black women were in control of family life and Fogel and Engerman take the opposite view claiming that black men were clearly heads of their families, the truth is surely somewhere between these two polarities. Observers might well conclude that the slave father was powerless, lacking the economic and legal foundation to fight off arbitrary interference of whites with a slave's wife and children. Unaccustomed to women sharing in the provider-decision-making role, the observer could further suggest dominance on the part of the slave woman. But, it is more reasonable to conclude that both slave man and woman pooled all the meager resources they had, intellectually, spiritually, and materially, and together developed an equalitarian family structure. After all, there had been family sharing by their African forebears and this was acceptable before the white man imposed his values on Africa. Now the circumstances of slavery welded men and women into another sharing structure. This too was acceptable, until whites defined it otherwise.

To be sure, most plantation owners recognized slave families by giving them housing accommodations. For many owners it made sense to encourage family life as a constructive institution which made for peace and harmony. And peaceful slaves were good business. But after all, slaves were securities for loans, divided among heirs upon death, and expensive to keep if crops failed. No matter how compassionate some owners might have felt, as property human chattels were expendable, and family unity at the expense of financial loss or gain meant the destruction of the black family.

So, in the final accounting, black family life was shaped by slaves who were determined to live together "for better or for worse." And along the way some endured the negative circumstances they faced; others didn't, for good reasons. But for most slaves, family life was a necessity most fought to keep intact.

RELIGION

Christianity was readily accepted by slaves. They responded eagerly to its message of hope, its promise of better times to come, and they began singing their praise of God in their own way. Out of the singing that so delights audiences all over the world today came gospel songs and spirituals. Actually, gospel songs come from the texts of the Old Testament, echoes of an earlier time when Israelites were slaves and the words they sang were of walls tumbling down, of the Hebrew children saved from the fiery furnace, and "Go down Moses . . . let my people go!" The gospel black slaves proclaimed was the gospel of Freedom! Some heard the music and were moved to seek that Freedom by their own wits, and some, not waiting for that "great gettin' up mornin' " in the "sweet by and by," got up and ran away.

RUNAWAYS AND RESISTANCE

> "Runaway, a Negro woman and two children; a few days before she went off, I burnt her with a hot iron, on the left side of her face. I tried to make the letter M."
>
> "Runaway, Mary, a black woman, has a scar on her back and right arm near the shoulder, caused by a rifle ball."
>
> "Runaway, the Negress Martha—she has lost her right eye."[12]

Many, many slaves attempted escape. The penalties were severe, and yet history records that countless numbers attempted it over and over again.

One female slave "about eighteen or twenty, whose independent spirit could not brook the degradation of slavery, was in the habit of running away; for this offense she had been repeatedly sent by her master and mistress to be whipped by the keeper of the Charleston workhouse. This had been done with such inhuman severity as to lacerate her back . . . a finger could not be laid between the cuts. But the love of liberty was too strong to be annihilated by torture. As a last resort . . . a heavy iron collar with three long prongs projecting from it, was placed around her neck, and a strong and sound front tooth was extracted, to serve as a mark to describe her in case of escape. Her sufferings at this time were agonizing . . . this slave, the seamstress of the family, was continually in her [the mistress's] presence, sitting in her chamber to sew . . . with her lacerated or bleeding back, her mutilated mouth and heavy iron collar. . . ."[13]

Black women were involved in virtually every organized resistance to slavery. In several instances, Negro women killed their masters, not infrequently, by poisoning them.

We have a record of one couple's imaginative and highly successful bid for freedom. William and Ellen Craft married and were determined to live together as man and wife. William Craft was an accomplished apprentice cabinetmaker who saved enough money working overtime to carry out a bold plan he and his wife formulated.

In December 1848, Ellen, a mulatto, cut off her hair and donned the garments of a "fine young Southern gentleman." She bandaged her face as if suffering from a toothache and added a pair of dark glasses to finish the disguise which was to open the doors to freedom for herself and her husband. William's part of the charade was somewhat easier to carry off, for he was to be traveling as a "faithful and trusted slave," certainly an appropriate choice to accompany the fictitious Mr. Johnson on so long a journey.

Their first test came when tickets were purchased for Mr. William Johnson and slave. The station porter who had once wanted to marry Ellen called her "young massa," and respectfully obeyed her orders.

There were other close calls, but William made a great fuss over "his young massa's delicate health," which kept many people from talking to Ellen. Some ladies even got romantic notions about "him"!

Mr. Johnson was so unusually cordial toward William, thanking him for his care and smiling at him, that several passengers thought it necessary to give lectures on slave-master etiquette: "Don't say thank you to niggers . . . it swells their heads." Several people offered to buy William. Others warned Johnson not to risk taking him North, where his slave was bound to run away.

Getting tickets for the pair to Philadelphia proved an unexpected problem. By this time there were so many fugitive slaves escaping to the North that critical checkpoints had been established. Papers had to be shown in order to continue journeying through to the North. Fortunately, some of the other passengers took a fatherly interest in Mr. Johnson, supporting his claim that William was really his slave. Finally the captain sold him the ticket, saying,

"Sorry, Sir, but so many abolitionists come this way stealing slaves that we have to be careful."

At the same time, many sympathetic Northerners on the train tried to persuade William to escape. They gave him names of abolitionists, who eventually helped the couple to reach Boston, where William secured work as a cabinetmaker and Ellen as a seamstress.

For two years they lived a fairly prosperous and happy life. This one "intact" monogamous family just might have made it in America, except for the 1850 Fugitive Slave Bill, which forced people all over the country to send back all escaped or captured slaves or face severe punishment. Thousands of black families who were beginning to put down family roots and take up self-supporting occupations constantly had to pull up stakes and seek hiding wherever they could, most often in Canada. There were agents everywhere, and the harassment was so unbearable that in order not to be forcefully returned to the South, some simply gave themselves up.

Unable to capture the Crafts through trickery, the slave owners applied to the United States Court in Boston and obtained a warrant to arrest them as fugitive slaves.

The Craft case became a cause célèbre. Mass meetings were held by sympathizers and freedmen in the city, while Ellen and William hid out with Quakers and abolitionists. Finally, not wanting their white friends to be punished for sheltering them, they secured passage to England.

In England they became respected citizens and reared a family of four children. Later, William Craft became a leading merchant, trading with Africa for exchange of goods, firmly committed to the idea that Africa should not have to sell humans to gain the goods she desired. Ellen's artistry and skill with a needle enabled her to become one of England's leading modistes. Both the Crafts remained ardent abolitionists to the end of their days.

From the planning of their bold escape to its happy conclusion, Ellen and William Craft proved that they would go to any length to maintain themselves as a family unit. And America once again proved it did not care one whit for black family life.[14]

But there were those who did care and who helped slaves escape, chief among them, Harriet Tubman.

HARRIET TUBMAN[15]

Harriet Tubman was not content with her own escape, but devoted her life to leading untold others to freedom. She called herself a "conductor" on the underground railroad: history calls her "The Moses of her people."

"In all my years as a railroad conductor," she allegedly said, "I never run the train off the track, and I never lost a customer."

Harriet Tubman ran away from her Maryland slave home while still in her early teens. Either intentionally or unintentionally, she blocked the doorway when an overseer was chasing another slave. He hurled a two-pound piece of steel at her head and seriously injured and deformed her. Harriet never recovered from this injury and often sank into "speechless spells" for long periods of time, or fell asleep in the most unlikely times and places. Her enemies called her "the woman with the sleeping sickness."

But while her slavemaster and others discussed her half-wittedness, Harriet made plans to escape.

One night she and two of her brothers started out, but the boys became frightened and returned home. Alone she hid and ran, taking nourishment from the woods, until she was "free at last."

Harriet might have been content with her personal triumph over slavery, but she was determined to bring out as many slaves as possible. Over the next twelve years she returned nineteen times, bringing out over five hundred slaves, sometimes whole families. She used paregoric to drug the babies to sleep, and when someone became afraid she did not hesitate to pull out a pistol and say: "Keep going. A dead nigger tell no tales, either you go on or die." On and on, she conducted her passengers "cross Jordan," she said, "to the real promised land."

She was the most sought-after fugitive in the country. The price on her head rose from $3,000 to $4,000—at a time when the going rate was $100 a captive!

Some say she was a voodoo woman, possessed of extraordinary powers; others said she was demented and therefore unaware of her danger. But her cunning and wisdom in contriving escape plans and timing her trips did not support such a description of Harriet. She had the resoluteness of Ginga and the warrior sense of the Dahomean Amazons. She was no legend. She was real.

In between trips she made speeches raising the necessary money for her expeditions. In Syracuse she fought in a race riot.

When the Civil War came she signed up as a nurse. Before the end of the war she planned and executed the Combahee River Campaign, acting as a scout, spy, and raider as well as nurse. She received a letter of commendation from President Lincoln for her service to the government, but drew only twenty days' rations from the government for four years' dangerous work. She drew no salary for her military work, but sustained herself and other soldiers by her own resources.

Like most black heroines, however, she died almost penniless and quite pathetically. She had made many friends among the abolitionists, but there was little remunerative work for her. She was honored by Queen Victoria who invited her to attend Court, and sent her a Diamond Jubilee medal. Thirty-five years after the Civil War she was awarded a pension of eight dollars a month, and in 1899 the amount was increased to twenty dollars. This was not compensation for her own service in the war but a widow's pension!

THE EMERGING BLACK WOMAN

No single prototype of black femininity emerged from slavery. No single word like "matriarchy" summarizes the life styles of the black women in slave systems that differed greatly, depending on whether one was a house, yard, or field slave and lived in a large, small, urban, or rural slave institution. No one family pattern can be said to have embraced all black women, whether they were sold as a family unit or separated. And no concept of mothering can be associated with them, whether they were fortunate enough to rear their own biological children or not. And certainly no one female slave's reaction to her own personal slave status can be said to apply to all slaves.

The white Southern belle image was generally accepted as the measuring rod for determining the appropriate behavior, dress, manners, and all around "goodness" and "badness" of women. The age of chivalry flourished again on large plantations, and even wives of poor white men who had to work hard to help sustain their families paled into insignificance when compared to the "Southern belle." The phrase "poor white trash" was coined for them. And black women were considered even lower.

The black woman entered Reconstruction with few role models indigenous to her environment that could fairly measure her worth. On the other hand, she faced the ludicrous spectacle of being constantly evaluated against the white female Southern belle image. Even if this model had been desirable, it was and is a role model that centuries of African and slave history and experience worked against.

What could be said of black women at the close of slavery?

First and foremost, black women were brought to this country to be laborers. Their mothers had proved themselves to be hard workers in Africa and the enslaved daughters proved their industriousness so well on this continent that hardly any division of labor developed between male and female slaves. Black women worked in the fields along with black men. They worked the same hours. And they received the same pay—nothing! The only difference was that in their spare time they birthed and cared for children.

The black woman as worker is the single consistent thread in black femininity. Freed black women looked around them and found only role models of working women whose initiative was needed for survival.

Institutions like marriage and family life which dared to compete for black women's time and attention were doomed to be crushed. It made sense to the white slaveholder (who rationalized it with lies) to institutionalize work and forbid a strong marriage and family pattern of living. It became predictable even in slavery, that as long as black women's labor was needed in the American economic system—as it is today in the service occupations—the black woman's role as a laborer would be a realistic part of her selfhood, and as important as visions of her as homemaker. (A current example of America's preoccupation with the black woman's working role versus her family role is a proposed welfare reform stipulation which would demand that welfare mothers—many of whom are black—work when there are "available jobs" and leave children in day care centers. If Americans valued marriage and family life for blacks, they would reorganize their "reform measures" to support their ideals. The fact is, only lip service is paid to the ideals.)

It is a certainty that few, if any, black women had become solely "housewives"—not even the freed women in cities could be so classified. Ladies who spent their time adorning their homes for husband and family were foreign to their experience. Really caring for a home and comforting a weary husband require freedom from an unfulfilling job requiring long hours, with only short pay. This freedom black women have never known. Often required is a reciprocity of role functions, with the husband playing the protector and provider roles, and the woman the comforting and nurturing ones. Since slavery had completely eliminated these roles from black male-female relationships, black women had had little experience to assure them that they could let go of their working role and be supported.

Those slaves who had worked in the Big House, or the slaves from small plantations where the division of labor was not narrowly drawn, did observe the relationships between white husbands and wives. They were able to pick up imitative patterns, but little of the substance of housewifery was internalized enough for them to forsake their role as breadwinners. Most of them tried to imitate white women and be themselves, as they do today. But, the art of "being taken care of," the security of "knowing the man will eventually come through," which might have caused them to relax in the marriage role, simply was beyond the reach of all but a very few. Those who did try to be imitative took on to themselves most of the burdens of both roles, and when they failed to orchestrate them successfully, a very critical society denounced them for not doing them equally well.

It has already been pointed out that the African woman who came to this country was not accustomed to a romantic-monogamous marriage pattern. Had the early slaves been left alone they probably would have followed the customs of their homelands, distributing themselves into "collectives," working out ways to care for the children and the elderly. Had there been an imbalance of the sexes, they probably would have become polygamous. This was natural for them. Gradually as the generations came, a stability indigenous to their environment would have developed and the pathology which followed the abolition of slavery might have been avoided.

But marriage, either on small or large plantations, was, too, generally discouraged and broken up at the master's will. Collectives could not develop because of the mobility of slaves. Yet, romantic ties must have taken place since many of the runaways were spouses trying to reach their families! In time, slaves might have adopted the monogamous marriage patterns of whites, but they were even denied a good try!

That the words "licentiousness" and "immorality" would be applied to black women because they participated in sex outside the marriage pattern simply reinforces the stupidity of slaveholder mentality. But this too was a psychological "putdown," an attempt to corrode the black woman's self-concept, an effort to shame her. Black leaders soon picked up this cry for respectability and demanded that chastity and sexual continence be enshrined in the black community. But how do you break a sexual pattern overnight? What was the payoff for large numbers of black women? A man? An intact family? Is it reasonable to suggest that they forfeit sex altogether? For what purpose, what promise? Perhaps the most impossible and undesirable dream of our leaders has been that black people could ever imitate the white nuclear family. Looking back, one wonders what difference it might have made if polygamy had been allowed to continue, even as long as it did with the Mormons?

Thus the newly freed woman slave emerged after slavery with a will to work and the skills of a domestic or farm laborer. She was expected to develop a monogamous relationship with one man and build a nuclear intact family! Yet men were jobless or exploited and could not provide the necessary economic base. Furthermore, nothing in her experience, and none of her African heritage, prepared her for such a life pattern. That many of them did it quite well is a credit to their adaptability.

The family centeredness of Africa was reinforced during slavery. Many female slaves had their children torn from them, but most tried every possible way to keep them. When other stray children came upon black women they were welcomed; there were plenty of "substitute" mothers to rear them. Many slaves reached out to "the white family" with open arms—for the mothering instinct was perhaps the most highly developed trait among black women and most were strong enough to express this in many ways. This kind of nurturing drive made many black women "joiners" right from the start. Female slaves were ardent churchgoers and camp meeting members. This movement toward "collectives" made them participants in insurrections, for they were as eager to gain freedom as every other human being.

CHAPTER 2 NOTES

[1]Julius Lester, *To Be a Slave* (New York: The Dial Press, 1968), p. 28. © 1968 by Julius Lester. Reprinted by permission of The Dial Press.

[2]See Basil Davidson, *The African Slave Trade* (Boston/Toronto: Little Brown & Company, 1961), pp. 115–153.

[3]*Ibid.*, pp. 210–213.

[4]B. A. Botkin, ed., *Lay My Burden Down: A Folk History of Slavery* (Chicago: The University of Chicago Press, 1945), p. 154.

[5]Kenneth M. Stampp, *The Peculiar Institution* (New York: Random House, Vintage Books, 1956).

[6]Botkin, *Lay My Burden Down*, p. 119.

[7]Lester, *To Be a Slave*, p. 70.

[8]Frances Anne Kemble, *Journal of a Residence on a Georgia Plantation* (New York: Harper Brothers, 1863), p. 25.

[9]Lester, *To Be a Slave*, p. 173.

[10]Kemble, *Journal*, p. 23.

[11]Stampp, *op. cit.*, p. 31. According to Stampp, in 1860 only one fourth of the slaves lived on farms with fewer than ten slaves. One half lived on farms with more than twenty slaves and another fourth on units with more than fifty.

[12]See Theodore Weld, ed., *American Slavery As It Is: Testimony of a Thousand Witnesses* (New York: American Anti-Slavery Society, 1839).

[13]*Ibid.*, p. 22.

[14]Lydia Marie Child, *Freedman's Book* (New York: Arno Press, 1968).

[15]See Sarah Bradford, *Harriet Tubman: The Moses of Her People* (New York: Corinth Books, 1961); Earl Conrad, *Harriet Tubman: Negro Soldier and Abolitionist* (New York: International Publisher, 1942); and Benjamin Quarles, *Black Abolitionists* (New York: Oxford University Press, 1969). See also Marcy Heidish, *A Woman Called Moses* (Boston: Houghton Mifflin Company, 1976), Historical afterword.

Free at last
Free at last
Thank God Almighty
I'm free at last . . .

NEGRO SPIRITUAL

Free at Last

And how they thanked God! They sang his praises profusely and joyously! "A great human sob shrieked in the wind, and tossed its tears upon the sea—free, free, free."[1]

With equal fervor they thanked Abraham Lincoln, their Great Emancipator! They idolized him, worshipped him. It would take generations before their descendants would really believe that Abraham Lincoln meant what he said to Sojourner Truth—he didn't free the slaves out of humane concern for their lot—he did so in order to preserve the Union. But to the slaves Freedom was a personal gift from Mr. Lincoln to them—a direct response to their misery.

A FEW ALREADY HAD FREEDOM . . . OF A SORT

At the time of emancipation a little less than 500,000 of the black population were already free. Some freed themselves by running away. Others gleaned scraps of freedom as Union armies swept across the South. Sherman had taken some of the Sea Islands in Georgia and South Carolina and divided 485,000 acres among 40,000 Negroes. There, they worked the rice fields, little realizing that the land would be reclaimed from them after only a few years and all their efforts would be worthless. Others were freed by manumission, rewarded to them as trusted servants, usually through a legal provision in some master's will. Much of the free population consisted of mulattos, 37 percent in fact, persons born of a white and a black parent. In a few instances, white women produced offspring by black men, but by far the larger percent of the mulatto population, both slave and free, were children born of black female slaves and a white male. Most of these offspring enjoyed few special advantages, but a few "white fathers" provided some of them with land and money. As these mulattos intermarried, they in turn produced further generations of free blacks.[2]

Before the Civil War, free blacks congregated mostly in the large cities of the East, with Charleston, South Carolina, and New Orleans, Louisiana, being exceptional gathering places for mulattos. In urban cities most of the free population had learned to read and write, and in most cases as newly freed slaves entered the cities, they found schools already established by blacks. They were enterprising and well motivated. In fact, "the number of adults who could *not* read and write was negligible,"[3] a fact suggesting the seriousness of their efforts to fend for themselves and to be good citizens. The church became the focal point for worship and recreation. "There was a growing recognition of a class of thrifty, ambitious Negroes,"[4] with both husband and wife working side by side. Black men were distributed in several trades, but Negro women were mostly domestics.[5]

Among the occupations held by black women, the modiste or seamstress became the most prestigious job. This was a good profession by any standard, but interestingly enough, it was valued by the black community because a modiste was often in close contact with white aristocrats. Although blacks have always had to endure the pretenses of kinfolk domestics who have been quick to compare everything black with "how it's done in the white folks' house," the domestics' view was always "from the back of the house." The modiste, however, sewed in the parlour or somewhere that was a gathering place for the master's family. She worked on garments that were treasured by white women and thus earned their respect. So these seamstresses were early established as the final authority on white folks' doings.

One such modiste, Elizabeth Keckley, gathered intimate information concerning Mary Todd Lincoln into a book, but unlike subsequent members of personal Presidential staffs who publish the "inside intimate stories" of their employers, Elizabeth made little money on the book and died penniless.[6]

THE WITNESS OF ELIZABETH KECKLEY AND THE LINCOLNS

Elizabeth was a slave until she was over thirty. She was a house slave. As a child of four, her assignment was to take care of the master's newborn baby, rock it, keep the flies out of its face, and not let it cry. She liked the job because it gave her a sleeping place in the master's house, away from the crude slave cabin. "True I was but a child myself . . . but then, I had been raised in a hardy school . . . had been taught to rely upon myself and to prepare myself to render assistance to others . . . I can bless slavery for . . . the important lesson of self-reliance."[7]

Self-reliance was to serve her until she died. She began her career by rocking the baby so hard that she threw it on the ground and she was severely beaten. Because Elizabeth was so reserved in manner, she was often beaten for impudence. She was also attractive, and as was all too often the case with others, she was made pregnant by "a white man—I spare the world his name." A son was born of this union. He died fighting in the Union Army, never reaching full manhood.

The family Elizabeth served grew very poor and in order to keep them from hiring her old mother out in service, she offered to "take in sewing." For two years and five months she was the sole provider for seventeen persons and she developed a reputation as a skilled seamstress. Her master agreed to a fee of $1,200 for her freedom and that of her boy. She had married a man named Keckley who had told Elizabeth he was a freedman; they parted, however, when she discovered he was still a slave who was only expecting she would purchase his freedom. Then, as a tribute to her work, some of her customers raised the necessary money for her freedom and that of her child.

She moved to Washington and her business grew steadily, attracting many famous women including the wife of Jefferson Davis. Elizabeth claimed that the dress the Confederate President used to camouflage his unsuccessful escape was a chintz wrap she made for Mrs. Davis.[8]

She later became Mary Todd Lincoln's modiste and confidante, spending considerable time at the White House, often in the presence of Mr. Lincoln. The right-hand glove the President used on the day of his second inauguration was given to her as a memento. It was she to whom Mrs. Lincoln turned for solace at the President's deathbed, "being Mrs. Lincoln's only companion, except her children."[9]

Elizabeth, in the ways of many "houseslaves," overidentified with Mrs. Lincoln, helping her pack the family's things in preparation for turning the living quarters over to President Johnson, and greatly neglecting her own business. The former First Lady became more and more dependent on their friendship. Elizabeth shared both Mrs. Lincoln's grief and anger. Elizabeth was enraged that President Johnson "... never called on the widow, or even so much as wrote a line expressing sympathy for her grief and the loss of her husband,"[10] and Elizabeth refused to sew for the "Johnson ladies," an act that surely did not help her business.

Mrs. Lincoln gave Elizabeth "the cloak, stained with the President's blood," as well as "the bonnet worn by Mrs. Lincoln on the night of his assassination."[11] Later Elizabeth donated these mementos to Wilberforce University, but they were lost in a fire.

It was Elizabeth who accompanied Mrs. Lincoln to Chicago, further neglecting her trade. When she returned to Washington to reopen her business, she was surprised that so few of Mrs. Lincoln's friends knew of the widow's poor financial state. And since fewer still moved to help, Elizabeth's "loyalty" caused her to close out what had once been a thriving business and move once more to Mrs. Lincoln's side.

The two women went to New York to dispose of some of the assassinated President's clothes in order to pay bills. Masquerading as Mrs. Clarke and maid, they hunted second-hand clothes' dealers in a futile effort to dispose of the things anonymously. Mrs. Lincoln thought it could all be done quietly, but there was no market for such old clothes, elegant and historical though they were. The brokers thought that bold, hard-sell salesmanship could turn the items into profit, but both Mrs. Lincoln and Elizabeth vetoed those tactics. Finally, one of the brokers did leak the story of the "forlorn broke widow" to the press and Mrs. Lincoln fled to Chicago, leaving Elizabeth to transact the details.

It is now history that Mrs. Lincoln was severely maligned for her actions, destitute though she was. Little noticed, however, was her friend and modiste Elizabeth, who wrote letters to countless editors rebuking them for their criticism of Mrs. Lincoln. Elizabeth explained that the Empress of Russia disposed of such items in like manner and was not thought disgraceful, so, why not Mrs. Lincoln?

Elizabeth stayed on alone in New York to sell Mrs. Lincoln's effects, but since there was no money to pay her, she was forced to set up a modiste business there. By then her name was linked with the sale of the clothes and she too was rejected by old friends, many of them black. She wrote her memoirs while shipping most of Mrs. Lincoln's things back to her in Chicago.

The book of Elizabeth's reminiscences, meant to raise funds to help the widow, was denounced as "scandal and trash" by Robert Lincoln, who had all available copies bought from the market, suppressing the book.

Elizabeth's loyalty to Mrs. Lincoln was evidence of a special quality house slaves brought into relationships with whites for whom they worked. They were misunderstood by those who on one hand extolled the loyalty of house slaves, but on the other, doubted that loyalty when money became the issue. Elizabeth clearly saw herself as sturdier than Mrs. Lincoln and obviously enjoyed the role of "strong, loyal confidante." She had often said that slavery taught her to rely on herself. In the end she used some of this strength and self-reliance to aid a friend. In doing so, she too became a pauper.

Though certainly laudable, Elizabeth Keckley's devotion to one individual is overshadowed by another black woman's dedication to more people than her arms could encircle. Only a woman of enormous spirit could have spread the word of freedom with such boldness; only such a woman would have devoted her life to helping those slaves who made it North adjust to their new status, teaching them to be economical and to develop a cooperative community life.

SOJOURNER TRUTH[12]

She adopted the name herself, believing she was "sojourning" through the Lord's land, spreading the "truth." It was part of a religious conversion following her escape from a Dutch owner. Her mysticism may have been self-styled, but her preaching was so moving, her tongue so sharp, and she proved to be so charismatic that she became one of the most popular orators on the abolitionist circuit.

As she was tall and gaunt, with a deeply resonant voice, some of her detractors spread the rumor that Sojourner was really a man disguised as a woman. While she was addressing a group in Indiana, they challenged her to prove her sex by retiring to the vestibule of the hall and showing her breasts to some of the women. Sojourner stepped close to the edge of the stage and indignantly shouted: "Oh no! I will show my breasts to the entire congregation!" Then, standing, breasts bared, she calmly said to a hushed audience: "It is not my shame but yours that I should do this. Here, then." She was not so challenged again.

Like most freed slaves, Sojourner thought President Lincoln to be The Great Emancipator. She extolled him in her speeches, reminding people that he deserved their love, insisting on going to Washington personally to thank him. Her white friends raised the necessary money and one of them, Lucy Coleman, accompanied her to the capital.

After many weeks of attempting to see the President they were finally granted an 8.00 A.M. appointment, only to be admitted at 11:30. Even then, according to Mrs. Coleman, President Lincoln delayed them another half hour, gossiping with a group of merchants. When he acknowledged Lucy Coleman at last, she said: "I am happy to say, Sir, that I have not come for any personal favors. I have come to present my friend, Mrs. Sojourner Truth, a woman widely known not only in our country but abroad. She will say to you what she wishes to say."

President Lincoln had no polite small talk for Sojourner, calling her "aunty," as if, according to Mrs. Coleman, "she was his washerwoman." When she complimented him on being the first anti-slavery President, he is alleged to have said: "I'm not an abolitionist. I wouldn't free the slaves if I could save the Union any other way. I am obliged to do it."

Sensing the President's discomfort, Mrs. Coleman concluded the appointment in short order. "We are not sure what Sojourner thought or said; for the first time in her life, she was speechless."[13]

After Lincoln's assassination, Sojourner wanted to see the new President, Andrew Johnson. This time she was treated with dignity. The President stood, shook hands, and called her "Mrs. Truth." As they both kept standing, Sojourner said to Mr. Johnson: "Sit yourself down, Mr. President. I have been standing on my feet lecturing for fifty years. I don't know what the United States would have done had it not been for my lecturing."

The President seemed to enjoy the visit, inviting Sojourner to stay longer and asking her to call again.

THE GUNS OF APPOMATTOX

When the guns of Appomattox were finally silenced, four million black people were freed from 250 years of slavery, and suddenly there was nothing significant for them to do and no place for them to go.

The dismantling of the slave system had really begun in earnest during the years of the Civil War, from 1861 to 1865:

> . . .Some slaves, 179,000, had fought in the Civil War. Most of them fought on the Union side, as military laborers, but some fought alongside their masters, as slaves. They had seen new vistas of opportunities, unknown in the close confinement of slavery. And they were not about to go back to slavery.
>
> . . . Some had taken advantage of the absence of warring slave-

> holders from the plantation and run away. They were beginning to congregate in large refugee encampments all along the warpath. They were awaiting freedom.
>
> . . . Some were freed as early as the winning of the first Union battle.
>
> . . . But most did not gain freedom until the end of the war in 1865— although the Emancipation Proclamation carries an 1863 date.[14]

In fact, some did not really gain freedom for many years following emancipation. Many slaves heard rumors of freedom but were afraid of retaliation and did not dare to test its truth. Many were so isolated from civilization that their masters were able to keep the facts a secret.

> . . . Mother said her master didn't tell them it was freedom. Other folks got told in August. They passed it round secretly. Some Yankees come, asked if they was getting paid for picking cotton in September. They told the Yankees, "Yes," 'cause they was afraid they would be run off and no place to go. They said Master Hood paid them well for their work at cotton-selling time. He never promised them nothing. She said he never told one of them to leave or to stay. He let 'em be. I reckon they got fed. . . .[15]

Even when told, some were reluctant to "be free." Slavery, bad as it was, lulled many of the victims into a false sense of security. They either feared freedom, or adopted the negative attitudes of their masters. Some refused to leave even when told they were no longer obliged to stay, demanding that their masters take care of them.

> . . . I suppose them Yankees was allright in their place . . . but they never belong in the South. Why, one of them ax me what was them white flowers in the field. You'd think that a gentleman with all them decorations on hisself would a'knowed a field of cotton! And, as for they a-setting me free! . . . us niggers on the Bennett Place was free as soon as we was born. I always been free. . . .[16]

Most of the slaves heard the news as an answer to a lifelong ambition, a release from oppression. In joyous anticipation, they danced in the fields, held celebrations, and dreamed of sharing the goods of a land they knew to be rich.

> . . . My mistress said to me when I got back home, "You're free. Go on out in the orchard and git yourself some peaches." They had a yard full of peaches. Baby, did I git me some peaches. I pulled a bushel of 'em.[17]

> . . . When the war ended, white man come to the field and tell my mother-in-law she free as he is. She dropped her hoe and danced right up into Old Master's parlor. She went so fast a bird coulda sot on her dress tail. That was in June. That night she sent and got all the neighbors and they danced all night long.[18]

However "freedom" was neither "dancing in the fields" nor a "bushel of peaches." After the rejoicing was over, the less adventurous ones, believing that their new status would bring them security in their home country, cast about for a livelihood. There was no "forty acres and a mule"; there was not one acre and only the muscles of their own bodies to see them through the trials of freedom. In fact, even as they had tilled another man's land as slaves, they tilled now—sometimes for the same master—only in a new system: tenant farming, destined to bind generations of freedmen to the same cruelties and insecurities of their fathers. The only difference was that they were "free."

But there were adventurers who started out—to taste, feel, see, touch *freedom*! This great desire to leave, to walk away from the plantation, to go in search of a place to live, away from the old reminders of their former status, overwhelmed them as they hoed in the field, and they simply left the tools of their enslavement in the cotton rows. They left the meager possessions of a lifetime in the cabins they once called home. They went by foot mostly—singly, in pairs, in groups of strangers that soon became lifelong friends bound together in common cause, as they fought the weather and vindictive "patroller" Southerners, and as they camped and scrounged for food. With no compasses to guide them, they went in search of places that they had heard of in snatches of conversation with Yankees. Mostly they just headed North. But, "which way North?"

In the novel *Miss Jane Pittman* by Ernest J. Gaines, recently televised with Cicely Tyson in the starring role, fourteen- or fifteen-year-old Jane Pittman—a name given her by a Yankee from Ohio, headed for that state. "Soon as you point that way."

> "I don't know too much 'bout Ohio," Unc Isom said, coming out in the road. "Where it at or where it s'pose to be. I ain't for sure." He turned toward the swamps, then raised his hand and pointed. "North is that way. Sun on your right in the morning, your left in the evening. North Star point that way at night. If you stay in the swamps, the moss is on the north side of the tree root."
>
> "I'm heading out," Jane Pittman said, "soon as I get me few of them apples and my other dress. Anybody else going?"[19]

Like the companions who joined her, most of these travelers wandered aimlessly in circles, looking for these places. Jane Pittman, and most of the others, never reached the North; they grew tired and frustrated and they, too, settled into tenant farming in the South, living out their natural lives very near the places of their enslavement.

Out of this aimless wandering without the help of a blueprint for social change, searching for places to build a life, spurred by government promises and hindered by its blunders, came the great black upheaval associated with Reconstruction.

What was reasonable to expect of millions of black people suddenly uprooted from a highly organized aristocratic-paternalistic slave system, who now were unwelcome everywhere and had no place to go and nothing to do?

No immigrants entering America have been promised so much or rejected so bitterly. No wave of immigrants has been dumped into America in such large numbers and been given so little opportunity to find jobs or homes. No immigrant group entered America's labor market with centuries of unpaid bills for services already rendered as slaves.

And no group had less grounds to expect such ill treatment—for this group of blacks had helped build the American economy as slaves, for no pay. They had a right to expect some help; and with no help forthcoming, they had a right to become embittered about Freedom!

They had marketable skills. They could farm and work as domestics. They were carpenters, artisans, and seamstresses. During early Reconstruction days Booker T. Washington abhorred the idea that vast numbers of black people "were not able to perfect themselves in the industries at their doors and in securing property."[20] It was his belief that an agrarian people who had tilled the soil for generations, as slaves, should build a foundation based on marketing these skills. The soil and Mother Nature, as Washington reasons, had given every nation and race of people its start toward financial independence.[21]

Booker T. Washington sought to build an educational blueprint for further developing skills by founding Tuskegee Institute in Alabama. He was bitterly denounced by those who thought his views too narrow and "Uncle Tommish." History has proven that his detractors were too harsh. These skills were indeed marketable and could have provided an economic base for a "new" immigrant group.

But more important was the fact that blacks were never

allowed to own land. They had no money to purchase land, and so they had to survive in occupations entitled "common laborer," "tenant farmer" and "domestic," those traditional black occupations of history. Starting out at the bitter bottom of the occupational ladder as freedmen, they entered at an income level that has still bound us to the edges of poverty and kept us outside the economic mainstream.

Black women focused their energies on the grim reality of freedom and went on sewing, cooking, hoeing, birthing, and plowing, as they attempted to mold this Freedom into something manageable, workable, practical. Men, women, and children soon found that Freedom was nothing tangible; it had little relationship to one's life style. It brought no bread and board.

Out of their dashed hopes and beliefs in Mr. Lincoln and their government came a rude awakening to the fact that nobody was going to give them anything and that they were as destitute as their forebears, forcibly brought here in chains. Though the chains were gone, they still were bound as a people, to a government that did not respond to their needs, to white Southerners who exploited them as mercilessly in tenant farming as they did in slavery, and to each other as the purest sources of help and companionship. And in this dilemma sex differences were of a secondary nature. They were one people—all needed, if they were to attain the only viable goal: survival.

FREEDOM VISITING AWHILE

Julius Lester put it this way: "Freedom did not come to the slaves. It just visited awhile."

Blacks were free but owned nothing except spiritual hope and faith. Eleven million white people in the South nursed their wounds and held an ambivalent attitude concerning the war they fought, for they had not been slaveholders, they were simple ordinary white people, referred to all too often as "po' white trash."

It soon became clear that the South was reconstructed to fit the needs of a mere quarter of a million, the old oligarchy of slaveholders. They had ruled Congress for two generations, and Lincoln and other powerful interests were bound and determined not to incur their alienation.

What to do with the freed slaves was never a question seriously debated as a life and death matter. "To bind up the nation's wounds" was the first order of business for Lincoln, and he was determined to be merciful toward the vanquished property owners of the South. Those who spoke about a social plan for former slaves were not only few in number, but generally ignored, silenced, or thought demented.

Horace Greeley was convinced that Negroes would be citizens by a kind of "natural process"—industry on their part balanced by white acceptance of them as political equals. Senator Thaddeus Stevens, leader of the Radical Republicans, when he heard people say: "Preserve the Union!" asked, "What but slavery has ever threatened the Union?" As he introduced numerous bills that failed time and time again, he surely became a realist about the political intentions of his colleagues. He respected Lincoln, but saw him as a gradualist at best, and at worst, a man influenced by those who had vested interests in slavery.[22]

Lincoln wanted slavery abolished in the border states by 1900. He not only wanted a constitutional amendment abolishing slavery to be ratified state by state, but favored shipping blacks out of the country. He was not committed to emancipation at once, but preferred to emancipate the slaves gradually. He tried to devise plans whereby the freed slaves could settle in South America cheaply, hoping that when numbers of them were large enough to be company and encouragement for one another, others would follow.[23]

The historical fact that black scholars stress so urgently is that the need for land lay at the heart of emancipation. Thaddeus Stevens introduced a bill in 1867 to confiscate the large estates and divide them among the tillers of the soil. Each freedman would receive 40 acres and $50 for a homestead. But, only a few of the abolitionists and the Radical Republican Party led by Stevens saw this. Stevens had said:

> . . . I would seize every foot of land and every dollar of property as our armies go along and put it to the uses of the war and the payment of our debts. . . . I would sell Confederate lands to the soldiers of independence; I would send those soldiers with arms in their hands to occupy the heritage of traitors and build up there a land of free men and of freedom which, fifty years hence, could swarm with its hundreds of millions without a slave upon its soil.[24]

Abolitionist Wendell Phillips shared Stevens' concern:

> "While those large estates remain in the hands of the defeated slave oligarchy, its power is not destroyed. But let me confiscate the land in the South and put it into the hands of the Negroes and white men who have fought for it and you may go to sleep with your parchments. I have planted a Union as sure to grow as an acorn to

> become an oak. You do not build governments like a clapboard house; you plant them like an oak. Plant a hundred thousand Negro farmers and by their side a hundred thousand white soldiers and I will risk the South."[25]

But Lincoln would not hear of this. Lincoln never really moved beyond his original idea of paying owners of slaves the full value if they freed their slaves. "In a certain sense," he said, "the liberation of slaves is the destruction of property—property acquired by descent, or by purchase, the same as any other property." Later he threatened to veto a bill unless it was made clear that the rebel owner did not lose his title to the land.

Finally, the Freedmen's Bureau was instituted. Its purpose was to restore order to the South. Much has been written about the value of this bureau. Some critics thought it doomed to failure for several reasons. (1) It was the political tool of the Radical Republicans. (2) It was run by carpetbaggers from the North, many of whom were corrupt and insensitive to the needs of Southern whites. (3) These carpetbaggers worked in cahoots with the scalawags, former non-slaveholding whites, from whom the overseer group had been drawn.

Others have harshly judged the Freedmen's Bureau because it was run by the military. The Bureau set out to register voters, hold elections, and choose delegates for conventions to adopt the Fourteenth Amendment and the new state constitutions. Justice William O. Douglas' criticism was that "the voters registered by the Army were largely Negroes, carpetbaggers and scalawags. Elections became corrupt. Negroes were marched from precinct to precinct, voting many times."[26] Justice Douglas blamed the corrupt and exploitive practices of the carpetbaggers and scalawags for creating resentment among Southern peoples. "The Ku Klux Klan was formed . . . to frighten blacks away from the polls and to threaten carpetbaggers and scalawags."[27]

While the Ku Klux Klan organized and terrorized blacks, creating also a false sense of superiority among poor whites, some whites would have liked to reconstruct a New South; mostly white women from the North.

THE NEW ENGLAND SCHOOLMARMS

The work of the white female abolitionists, sometimes called "New England schoolmarms," was especially helpful during Reconstruction. They were mistreated by soldiers, ridiculed by southern white women, and taunted as "nigger-lovers." Many were driven away, but still others kept coming South to replace the intimidated ones. They established schools for freed blacks and regularly sent letters to their church congregations to be read each Sunday.

Through the eyes of these women the picture of black women and their families becomes sharply focused. One schoolmarm, Miss Brock, worked in South Carolina from 1866 through 1869 and her letters tell of the daily struggles, and how the emancipated blacks coped with life, sickness and death. She wrote:

> Their dwellings generally have an air of cleanliness about them. They seem to be very industrious people, doing all in their power to maintain their families. Some of the women support themselves by washing and ironing, others by baking pies and cakes. . . . They wear no bonnets, simply a bandana, carrying all their burdens upon their heads, which gives them a very erect carriage. It is no uncommon occurrence to see a woman pass along with quite a load of wood upon her head, another with a barrel of flour, etc. They are very poorly and thinly clad, requiring all they can earn to feed their families, I suppose. Some of the men are employed by the government, others are soldiers in the army, whose families live here. They all have gardens, mostly cultivated by the women, in which they raise sweet potatoes, peanuts, and various kinds of vegetables. . . ."[28]

Another white woman, Elizabeth Botume, noticed that the women had learned to take a few handfuls of cotton from the field, spin it in a tin basin, and make knitting needles out of reeds found in the swamps. "It was not an unusual thing to meet a woman coming from the field where she had been hoeing cotton, with a small bucket or cup on her head, and a hoe over her shoulder, contentedly smoking a pipe and briskly knitting as she strode along. I have seen, added to this, a baby strapped on her back. The patient devotion of these Negro women was most admirable."[29]

I'M LOOKING FOR MY FAMILY

In addition to describing the general conditions of the camps provided for ex-slaves, and noting the industriousness of these freed women, the accounts of those New England schoolmarms tell of the poignant search for "husbands," "wives," and "children" among the freedmen. Miss Brock wrote that "the taking of Savannah caused great rejoicing among the colored people—husband and wives, parents and children, brothers and sisters, who had been separated for years and now have been permitted to meet each other on free soil."[30]

General John Eaton, superintendent in charge of freedmen for the Department of Tennessee, sought to make the Negro a self-supporting unit of society. Negro men were provided with arms to guard the camps. Each man was made responsible for his own family.

Family stability became a primary objective of Reconstruction. Marriage choices were frequently difficult to make. One day an army chaplain married 119 couples in over an hour.[31] Often when husbands and wives were sold from each other they were forced to choose other mates. When the war ended some of them ended up with two spouses. Sometimes when two men claimed the same wife, the woman played a game of coquetry, choosing the highest bidder. Some worked out polygamous relationships. One woman, a second wife, lived with her husband and stepdaughter. When the war ended, she shared both with wife number one! Some of the reunions were happy, some awkward. While freedom brought new opportunities for black men, for most women it augmented old problems. Their husbands had scattered in every direction, for they either joined the armies of the Union or would travel to distant points, unhindered by small children. Therefore most black women were actually on their own.

"AIN'T MUCH ON THE NEEDLE, BUT GREAT ON THE HOE"

Observers of black women at work were unanimous in their description of them as hard working. "Most of the women around us had always been field hands, and they know nothing of any other kind of work," many said. The New England schoolmarms taught them to sew and do other jobs. But even then one man said of his wife, she's "not much on the needle, but . . . great on the hoe."[32]

> Most of the fieldwork was done by women and girls; their lords and masters were much interrupted in agricultural pursuits by their political and religious duties. When the days of "conventions" came, men were rarely at home; but women kept steadily at work in the field. . . .
>
> We could not help wishing that since so much of the work was done by women—raising the provisions for their families, besides making and selling their own cotton, they might also hold some of the offices held by men.[33]

Black men, consumed by an interest in politics, tended to leave book learning to the women. And it appears that few black women desired to hold office. They were preoccupied with wanting to learn to read and write. Sewing classes were also popular everywhere. White women didn't have the vote, so there was hardly a thought among freedwomen that voting and office holding were things women could enjoy. But white women were teachers . . . and soon black women began to entertain ideas about becoming teachers.

At first old and young were eager to learn. "Us ain't know nothing and you is to learn us," they said to the schoolmarms. Then they began to come to the school houses at all hours and there weren't enough teachers. As fast as literate black students were produced, they were placed in teaching posts. However, because the freedmen, both male and female, had to work so hard in the fields, adult pupils tapered off in their school attendance. But this never was a reflection of waning enthusiasm. It was sheer fatigue. Botume tells that the women were eager to learn but they thought they could go through a book as they did a task. "Please read me quick and let me go," was usually their first exclamation. "It took time to make them understand that learning was not given by weight or measure."[34]

One of the most constructive accomplishments of Reconstruction was the contact and interaction between the whites who came to the South as teachers and blacks who were so eager to learn from them. As these schoolmarms taught blacks and observed their daily struggles, the letters sent back home were read in the pulpits of the North and thousands of congregations heard the intimate details of the Reconstruction years. It was not an uncommon thing for the Northern churches to have at least one of their congregation teaching among the freedmen.

Most of these New England schoolmarm accounts are unpublished and scattered, awaiting some scholar's interest. These women were highly emancipated for their time and it was fortunate for all concerned that this was considered missionary work and was an acceptable task for white women. Furthermore, they provided a new, healthy role model for black girls. Now, in addition to working in the fields or becoming domestics, a growing number of black girls could aspire to teach.

For many freedmen the picture of a white woman enduring so many hardships and living so independently was unusual: they were used to white Southern belles. The combination of gentility, religiosity, and work skills combined to produce a model that black parents and young girls came to admire. Beyond the hoe and the washpot and kitchen was the schoolroom, and the same zeal that produced good cotton pickers and domestics took some ex-slaves into the schoolrooms of the nation.

THE ROLE OF EDUCATION

Though attendance by adults with family and work responsibilities tapered off, there was much encouragement for the young to become educated. In 1850 there were 13,864 males and 12,597 females attending school. By 1860 there were 16,594 males and 16,035 females enrolled.[35] The numbers among females grew larger in succeeding years, and the position of schoolteacher emerged as an "elitist" position for Negro girls to hold.

Thus, it is not surprising that a white woman and a black woman each established the first two schools for freedmen that were administered by women.

Myrtilla Minor, a young white woman, founded a seminary in 1851 in Washington, D.C., for training Negro girls as teachers. She taught them Latin and Greek as well as other conventional subjects taught to young women in those days, and she lectured on scientific and literary subjects.[36]

The first day school for blacks was established in 1861 in the town of Hampton, Virginia, by Mary Peake, who was born a free woman. She had gone around among the slaves before emancipation teaching them to read and write. Then she founded her school—the first of its kind in the South. It was the first step toward the establishment of Hampton Institute.[37]

But what did they learn?

After stating that the character of the Negro woman had been defamed in the institution of slavery because of the role many of them had played as concubines to men of the white race, one Negro educator proposed this kind of curriculum for Negro women:

> . . . Let us state here definitely what I want for the black girls of the South. . . . I wish the intellectual training . . . limited to reading, writing, arithmetic and geography . . . they should be taught accurately all domestic work. . . .[38]

He also believed that the Negro woman should be "educated to be the helper of poor men."[39]

Thomas Baker, a Negro, set forth the following ideas of college education for Negro women:

> 1. She must not be educated away from being a mother; slavery days degraded motherhood and made merchandise of it. This fact is dependent on her giving her best to her children.
>
> 2. She needs for the sake of the race to be better educated than the men.

3. Her education should be rooted in Christian education.[40]

Jack Thorne put a plea for moral education of Negro women. He believed Negro women were susceptible to the white men's desire to sow wild oats among them—even though these same white men were compulsively concerned with protecting the white woman from the Negro man. He thought education should train the Negro woman to appreciate and help to promote the men of her race.[41]

And so the argument waged. The black woman was safe as long as she desired to teach. But as she learned, there always lingered a strong morality-based education which somehow suggested that unless she were carefully taught Christian virtues and rigidly supervised, she would revert to the sins of her mother—become a concubine. This moral overtone was to influence the founding of her schools and her education for many years to come. As a college coed she was the last to be emancipated—or liberated, as might be said today.

The rules and regulations surrounding her dormitory life in the boarding schools, the chapel services, all would constantly remind her of her grandmother's fate, not so much as a slave, but as a concubine. And education, above all else, was to keep her a virgin, give her a practical way to make a living, and help her maintain a model family life. If she was to put her mind to a career, it was to be a career that would allow her to be a family member first. Thus, teaching as a goal served both needs.

STILL A' CLIMBING

Reconstruction was a chapter of failure. Opportunists made fortunes. There was widespread corruption during and following the Civil War and this was, of course, dreadful for all concerned. Yet, as one pores over the volumes of literature on this period in American history, it is difficult not to be trapped into oversympathizing with the "poor ole South" and its pitiful white families who lost so much of their grand old life. Still, black scholars knew, as did every black person, that ex-slaves were the most tragic victims. They were ill-equipped for an effective life of freedom. Nothing in slavery prepared them for an immediate introduction into American institutions. There was a need for rehabilitation. This was clear.

That any American could have hoped for anything better than utter confusion displays a naiveté that nations seldom exhibit when dealing in foreign wars. It is inconceivable that any military victor would fail to present an occupation plan for the vanquished, or to provide for the refugees made homeless by that war. And it is also a strange aftermath of war that not only restored "the losers" to power after seven years, but so ensconced white Southerners in power that to this very day they dominate the seats of economic and political power in the same territory in which they had chained blacks as slaves. The enemy—in this case the Southern oligarchy—out of power only six years, rode off with more than the horse the government allowed them to keep. They galloped to power with such finality that they immediately began to terrorize blacks in the name of white womanhood, to enslave them further in the name of segregation and discrimination, and to mete out a peculiar justice of their own called "separate but equal."

Despite reams of scholarly attempts to tell the Southern story, one fact must never be forgotten. Blacks not whites—Southern or Northern—inherited the bitterest aftermath of slavery.

The Southern oligarchy, returned to power, have never lost their grip on the destiny of white supremacy in America. The ex-slaves knew better than anyone else that they needed education, political power, land, and jobs. Yet, on every turn, the Southern oligarchy blocked their attempts to become truly free. They first pitted poor whites against blacks. For when it became clear that a new occupational ordering was to emerge and blacks were receiving pay for labor, the propaganda mills ground out the message: "Look out, 'poor whitey,' the nigger will get your job and your status. Let's keep him on the bottom." There emerged then the cruelest pecking order of all times. The landed aristocracy whites robed poor whites in Ku Klux Klan uniforms to do their dirty work. When the idea of "top dog, low dog," took hold among the poor whites, there emerged an unwritten law which assured the working class white that he would be favored and excused if he "kept the nigger in his place." That meant lynching him and harassing him. And it meant lynching black women also. Few know of the thirty-four women lynched during Reconstruction—and not for whistling at or raping white women; they were lynched mostly for "sassiness" and organizing resistance movements.[42]

All the white oligarchy had to do was sit back and reap the benefits of racism, playing the role of the genteel Southerner.

While black legislators were in some of the Southern courthouses, they pushed for social reform and for a strong school system. Southern whites not only drove these black men out of political power but established the school systems as separate and unequal. As the white schoolmarms left, thousands of black women became teachers—and then more and more. Finally, it became a fact that more black women than men had earned college degrees. Teaching in America had become a female occupation and non-threatening to white men. Black men also came to see teaching as woman's work and they naturally wanted the diversification of occupations that they knew to be available to white men. Through these circumstances, there emerged a group of black women who set the style of life for the middle class Negro woman—the black bourgeoisie. Later, they might marry doctors, preachers, taxi drivers, or unskilled laborers—still there was that air about them that made them feel "on top of the heap." To be a black school-teacher for many years was to be an upper class Negro!

The black man's strong agricultural and artisan skills, however, were a threat to white men. The result was despair and frustration for the black man. The manhood that the abolitionists spoke of and black men yearned for, which the white Southern male strutted in front of their faces, soon became unreachable.

Manhood in America means power. It also, unfortunately, means domination and exploitation. So overwhelming is male chauvinism in America, so exaggerated was it in the South and so tied to a "clinging vine Southern belle syndrome," that for centuries the black man had before him only one image of true manhood. So uptight have Americans been about clearly defining "man" as the chief economic provider and decision-maker in the family, complete with a wife as housewife, that the black man could scarcely have escaped an insidious comparison of himself with the white man. As he assessed himself and saw himself in the eyes of the white male, he forgot the heroism of his past, his own valiant efforts to gain freedom, his invincibility in troubled times, and he began to know himself wrongly. He knew frustration and failure as no other men in history have known.

With his self-hatred and lack of resources he could not build a carbon copy of the intact nuclear American white family. As John Galbraith said, "To some extent family life is a function of an adequate income." And the black man was already too far from his African heritage to exercise the option of building alternative family patterns that would gain him respect. He was indeed building it in many ways without knowing it, for he was father to more than the sons and daughters he sired; but America had no place for the extended family concept of fatherhood. And pushed by spiritual impoverishment and economic necessity, far too many escaped from the embarrassment of failure and left the family-building roles to black women.

Out of this despairing situation came the mother-oriented

families—families of children who are reared without a man in the home on a full-time basis.

Only one of the foundational social institutions of America was ever readily available to blacks, in slavery or in Reconstruction. Though they could not copy the intact family pattern, could hardly get an education or a job, black people *were* allowed to seek salvation in the Christian church. They had in common with the white slave owner the fact that they "loved the Savior." Black people could worship God, pray, sing, and a few learned to read and write in the name of Jesus Christ. With a head start in religiosity, they quickly parlayed religion into the single most influential black institution in America. More than any other people, they took the white man's religion and embellished it, acted on it, believed and practiced it. Their leaders were preachers. Their gathering place was the church. Their first teachers were religious ones. Their philosophy of life was Christian.

The church was also a political base. And it grew stronger each year. During slavery a vision of "pie in the sky" tranquilized their rage so that they could survive; religion provided this escape. Later it sustained their hurt when abandoned by Mr. Lincoln's government. It taught them to be patient, to be grateful for freedom. All this time the church grew stronger in their lives.

They did not consciously choose the church as a political force for social change and freedom. But when at last they came to see: "Who would be free, himself must strike the blow," they converted this old tried and true institution into a political instrument that shook American white supremacy at its roots. Men such as Martin Luther King, born of generations of preachers, plus millions of black churchgoers, took the one institution that the white man allowed the black to enter and made it work on behalf of freedom. What a shock it must have been for white racists to realize that a perfectly harmless thing like religion, something the slaveholders had used to lull the slaves into submission, could be used against them in a bold play for justice!

The church was also the cornerstone of black people's aesthetic and recreational life. Our music, like that of Africa, was an expression of spiritual yearnings. Out of religiosity, we created the gospel music of slavery and Reconstruction, the spirituals and the songs of liberation we sing today. From "Steal Away to Jesus" to "Free at Last," this religious music served us well. From here there was only one step to make: for the beat remained the same; the lyrics just changed to "we shall overcome."

Amid the sounds of the tambourines, guitars, the drums, and

the shouts of their churches, there rose the black woman as singer. Rising like a phoenix from the ashes of dead and stolen children, lost husbands, hunger, pain, and hopelessness came the sounds of black femininity. The Blues! A hundred thousand Mahalias, Arethas, and Leontynes, with names like April, Cirly, and Rose, began to weave into American music the special suffering and caring and coping of the black woman.

Many became superstars but still they paid obeisance to the music of their church. Others would improvise on it and stylize these sounds in the sophisticated artistry of a Lena Horne. Yet, there is an historical thread which binds them all, from pure Soul to the Metropolitan Opera, and it makes them sisters together and "expresses us all."

Out of the past they came: the black female singer, the black woman domestic, the black woman who rears her family without a husband, and the black woman teacher, or intellectual—the middle class model. They became the prototypes of the present black woman in America and the foundation of our future. Out of their struggles, failures, and triumphs come our pride and respect for self, our faith in our beauty and strength.

CHAPTER 3 NOTES

[1]W. E. B. DuBois, *Black Reconstruction in America 1860–1880* (New York: Harcourt Brace and Co., 1935), p. 124. By permission of Shirley Graham DuBois. Not to be reproduced without written consent of Shirley Graham DuBois.

[2]See John Hope Franklin, *Reconstruction After the Civil War* (Chicago: University of Chicago Press, 1961); and Henrietta Buckmaster, *Freedom Bound* (New York: Macmillan & Company, 1965).

[3]E. Franklin Flazier, *The Free Negro Family* (New York: Arno Press, 1932), p. 14.

[4]*Ibid.*, p. 16.

[5]*Ibid.*, p. 18.

[6]Elizabeth Keckley, *Behind the Scenes* (New York: Arno Press, 1968).

[7]*Ibid.*, p. 19.

[8]*Ibid.*, p. 78.

[9]*Ibid.*, p. 193.

[10]*Ibid.*, p. 201.

[11]*Ibid.*, p. 262.

[12]See Arthur Huff Fauset, *Sojourner Truth: God's Faithful Pilgrim* (Durham, N.C.: University of North Carolina Press, 1938); Hertha Pauli, *Her Name Was Sojourner Truth* (New York: Appleton-Century-Crofts, Inc., 1962); and in the Sophie Smith Collection at Smith College, Northampton, Mass., a booklet by Lucy Coleman entitled *Reminiscence,* pp. 66–67.

[13]Coleman, *Reminiscense,* pp. 66–67.

[14]See Franklin, *Reconstruction.*

[15]B. A. Botkin, *Lay My Burden Down* (The University of Chicago Press, 1945), p. 227.

[16]*Ibid.,* p. 206.

[17]*Ibid.,* p. 226.

[18]*Ibid.,* p. 226.

[19]Ernest J. Gaines, *Miss Jane Pittman* (New York: The Dial Press, 1971), p. 14. Reprinted by permission of the Dial Press.

[20]Booker T. Washington, *Up from Slavery* (Doubleday Company, Inc., 1963), p. 60.

[21]*Ibid.,* p. 64.

[22]Buckmaster, *Freedom Bound,* pp. 5–7.

[23]DuBois, *Black Reconstruction,* pp. 145–149.

[24]Buckmaster, *Freedom Bound,* p. 5.

[25]*Ibid.,* pp. 5–6.

[26]William O. Douglas, *Mr. Lincoln and The Negroes* (New York: Atheneum, 1963), p. 83.

[27]*Ibid,* p. 86.

[28]Papers in the Sophie Smith Collection, Smith College, Northampton, Mass.

[29]Elizabeth Hyde Botume, *First Days Among the Contrabands* (New York: Arno Press, New York Times), p. 58.

[30]Elizabeth Brock, A Collection of Papers at Smith College, Northampton, Mass.

[31]Buckmaster, *Freedom Bound,* p. 9.

[32]Botume, *First Days,* p. 221.

[33]*Ibid.,* p. 273.

[34]*Ibid,* p. 273.

[35]Jeanne Noble, *The Negro College Woman Graduate* (New York: Teachers College, Columbia University Press, 1954), pp. 28–30.

[36]John Hope Franklin, *From Slavery to Freedom* (New York: Alfred A. Knopf, 1967), p. 231.

[37]*Ibid,* p. 275.

[38]Noble, *Negro College Woman,* p. 156.

[39]*Ibid,* p. 156.

[40]Thomas Nelson Baker, "The Negro Woman," *Alexanders Magazine,* II (December 15, 1906), 77 (quoted in Noble, *Negro College Woman*).

[41]Jack Thorne, "A Plea for Social Justice for the Negro Woman," New York Occasional Papers No. 2, Negro Society for Historical Research, Lincoln Press Association, 1912, pp. 2–6 (quoted in Noble, *Negro College Woman*).

[42]James Weldon Johnson, *Along This Way* (New York: The Viking Press, 1965), p. 330.

PART II

THE CRUCIBLES OF STRENGTH

She does not know
her beauty
She thinks her body
Has no glory

If she could dance
Naked
Under palm trees
And see her image in the river
She would know

But there are no palm trees
On the street
And dishwater gives back no images.

WARING CUNEY[1]

Dishwater Images

The idea of "dancing naked under palm trees" would strike black domestics as a "put-on." Few see themselves as beautiful. "Black women get old fast," says Helen, Lillian Hellman's domestic. "Yes," answers Miss Hellman, "watching white women stay young."[2]

Most black domestics see their work as unattractive. Reflecting the feelings of their society, they look upon their job as requiring little skill, and they believe that nobody would do this work if they could do anything else. "There is nothing to this job," they often say. And skilled as they are, they also think, "Anybody can do this!"[3] They have little sense of their beauty and rarely realize their worth.

During Reconstruction, domestic work was the black woman's principal occupation. It is the image of the black woman as a domestic that emerges most clearly in the mind of Americans. And ever since the earliest days of "freedom," it has been the earnings of domestics that kept so many black families surviving.

Among all black women who were in the labor market in 1973, 25.5 percent of us worked in the service occupations (a census description for women who work in hospitals, hotels, and commercial institutions washing, scrubbing, cleaning) and among this group 17.9 percent worked exclusively in private households—in other words, as domestics. Among these, 1.5 million domestics, 98 percent are women, 64 percent are black women.[4]

The long shadow of slavery may be fading for some, but over one fourth of all black sisters are still marketing the skills of our ancestors who washed, scrubbed, and hoed in the mansions, yards, and cotton fields of Southern plantations, and whose daughters entered the census pages of the twentieth century with little choice except to do the same.

Elizabeth Duncan Koontz, former Director of the Women's Bureau, spoke from the vantage point of experience: "Today's household worker does not, by and large, work under decent conditions for a decent reward. It is not always that conditions are uniformly bad; they are not. But at worst, household employees must endure not only a continuation of the master-servant relationship—a humiliation we must eliminate as rapidly as possible—but also low wages, long or irregular work hours, and heavy workloads."[5]

While it is true that the numbers of black female domestics are diminishing (the percentage decrease of those in service occupations fell from 59 percent in 1966 to 44 percent in 1970), the image of the black domestic is still woven in the very fabric of America, especially in the South, where the role was perfected. As she made her way in weary steps along country roads and city streets, carrying always the determination, the foresight, the strength and constancy of the black woman, few Americans have failed to recognize her and her shopping bag. Most black women know her intimately.

> . . . Lutie . . . glanced . . . at the women coming toward her. . . . Their shoulders sagged from the weight of the heavy shopping bags they carried. And she thought, "That's what's wrong: We don't have time enough or money enough to live like other people. . . . The women work till they become drudges. . . ." She had no way of knowing that at fifty she [too] would be misshapen, walking on the sides of her shoes because her feet hurt so badly . . . [going to] church on Sunday and . . . the rest of the week slaving in somebody's kitchen.[6]

That kitchen might belong to a family that is "well-to-do" or, if in the South, to a family with a relatively small income; for the South has long been the "housewife's Utopia": not only was black labor cheap, but until the civil rights movement, most white families employed some kind of black domestic help. In other regions it required twice as high a family income as in the South to hire a domestic.

Few white Southern families have developed a concept about blacks that is free of a black domestic's influence. Southern writers have woven her ideas, attitudes, actions, throughout the pages of fiction. And, far too many stereotypes about black women have come from contacts whites have had with domestics.

Wherever blacks are, north or south, eating "high off the hog" or eating hardly at all, the influence and contribution of these domestics is a very important part of our heritage. Mordecai Johnson, long-time President of Howard University, used to admonish the graduating classes to respect and revere "that woman who washed and ironed and slaved in the white folks' kitchen to put you through college." And since for generations Howard University produced the majority of all black professionals, the scope of the domestics' influence is vast.

For blacks and whites, "dishwater" images of Afro-American women exist. And while often projected through fiction, they do have bases in reality. Most pervasive of all these images is the domestic as "Mammy" to the white family.

Many of the traits and qualities whites associated with the "Mammy" image, however, are more fictional than factual. Certainly, survival meant that "what white folks expected" became internalized in the minds of blacks as necessary for the job. So showing affection, love, and loyalty, actually felt or faked, soon became generic to job performance.

How a servant class comes to share their deepest feelings of concern and warmth with those who oppress them defines an unhealthy aspect of the maid-mistress relationship. What fantasies these "Mammies" must have contrived in order to love those who suppressed them!

It would surely be impossible to refer to this particular image without acknowledging the character that codified all those qualities most whites came to accept as standard for all such nurturing paragons—a character whose only name was "Mammy."

MAMMY: THE "TAKE CHARGE" IMAGE

There is irony in the fact that for her portrayal of Mammy in the film version of *Gone With the Wind,* Hattie McDaniel became the first, and still the only, black woman to win an Academy Award. She brought to life the character unsurpassed in fiction as the role model of what whites perceived to be the perfect Mammy. She is martinet, confidante, and also a loving haven of comfort and solace. There is little more anyone could add to the descriptive tribute paid Mammy by Margaret Mitchell, the white woman who created her image. Though Mammy was a pure black African, she felt close kinship to the O'Haras. She expected a high code of conduct that exceeded the expectations even white owners had of themselves and their children.

A Mammy was always expected to be an affectionate woman who loved unstintingly. This love was expected to be there, through thick and thin. In order to make sure there was enough bosom and lap, Mammies were most often depicted as fat.

In *Gone With the Wind*, Mammy embodies all the stereotypes. There is the disciplinarian, the companion, plus the love and welcoming comfort. There is in her character a faithfulness as well, that quality which the city of Charleston glorifies in the Old Slave Mart Museum with a plaque which reads: "Dedicated to the loyal and faithful servants who did not desert their mistresses during the Civil War."[7]

Before and even during the Civil War, Mammies may well have been able to function as expected within the system that created them, but what about afterward? As "house niggers" they were often black snobs, too "uppity" and backward looking to participate in building unity with other blacks who had served in the fields and yards, and they hated poor whites too much to trust an alliance with them. They could not even respect "free issue" blacks, as was the case with Miss Mitchell's Mammy. From such an estrangement between household slaves and field slaves came the label "handkerchief head," which is the feminine version of an "Uncle Tom." Blacks as well as whites fell victim to the stereotypes born of fiction and of the myths that it pleased owners and, later, employers, to believe.

As could be predicted, this stereotyping resulted in deep and destructive "self-hatred" among blacks. Not wanting to be compared with just one particular black group, many freedmen thought that if Mammy would leave the white folk's kitchen, whites would see other qualities in us. How mistaken we were—to lay the blame of stereotyping at Mammy's feet! Actually, those black women who worked closely with whites performed many roles—some helpful.

There are whites who claim they really understand blacks, simply because they employed them as domestics and servants. Some blacks are quite sure that the Mammies of white folks' kitchens understand white people better than whites do blacks. Lorraine Hansberry declared: "Anytime we have washed and ironed your dirty clothes, we get to know you pretty well." We have had to develop empathy while working for simple survival reasons. "Negroes—especially servants and intellectuals—can enter into the lives of whites and see them as they really are. When someone is serving your coffee in the morning you forget to be other than yourself. The servant is just part of the furniture. There is no restraint."[8]

There are some white people who seem to have a genuine realization of the workings of that black world so foreign to their own. William Faulkner, whose attitudes toward blacks may not always have been ideal, did display a rare and incisive comprehension of black domestics, enabling him to create several plausible black female characters. They may well be larger than life, but sometimes reading Faulkner seems like reading the inside of a black domestic's mind. His own personal attachment to his own Mammy, Caroline Barr, might account for his perception, for so highly did he regard her that he dedicated a book to her.[9]

Faulkner also recognized the line of thinking which rendered domestics invisible and inaudible to so many whites, not because of their behavior or inadequacies, but because of the inhumanity which clouds the understanding where domestics are concerned. He illustrates this perfectly in *The Sound and the Fury*, when he notes that for as long as Dilsey had worked for her, Mrs. Compson "could not see her except as a blobby shape without depth." And later in the same novel, Quentin, another member of the white family, sums it up: "I realized that a nigger is not a person so much as a form of behavior; a sort of obverse reflection of the white people he lives among."[10]

"THE ROCK OF GIBRALTER" DOMESTIC

To some whites, one quality associated with "a good black" is the unquestioning of the servile status assigned to them. When they accept their fate with dignity and show affection and concern as human beings, they are perceived as even better domestics. But mostly it is strength that marks their great contribution.

Dilsey, one of the few strong, sane, and admirable characters in *The Sound and the Fury,* is such a symbol. Though she was hired as a cook, her duties and influence reach far beyond the kitchen. She is a surrogate mother for the children and provides what emotional stability there is for the family's retarded son. Dilsey is the personification of strength, loyalty, and endurance. She may well be the living embodiment of a statement made by Irving Howe: "He [Faulkner] places a tremendous perhaps intolerable weight of responsibility on the Negroes . . . nothing less than the salvation of the whites."[11]

Against Dilsey's strength, the strength of a woman who has

known nothing but physical toil all her life, he pits the weakness of Mrs. Compson. There is no medical diagnosis for the illness that keeps Mrs. Compson in bed and complaining most of the time. But Faulkner, who usually projects white Southern women unfavorably, implies that Mrs. Compson has what might be called the white Southern woman's disease—"non-facing-up-itis," "loss of gumption," and "simpering idiocy." The children of the household tiptoe around whispering, "Be quiet, Mother is sick." On the other hand, Dilsey is expected to endure. She expects herself to endure. In fact, the entire household acknowledges Dilsey's age, even makes jokes about it, and indeed, she herself sees her own physical strength declining after 50 years of being a Compson domestic. But that is that! She endures!

Mrs. Compson sees herself as weak and unable to cope with the daily problems of her household—not to mention Christmas: "Nobody knows how I dread Christmas. Nobody knows. I am not one of those women who can stand things. I wish . . . for the children's sake I was stronger."[12] Dilsey's authority is never questioned by her own family, no matter what their ages, but they know she cares about them. "Mammy always talks about hit gwine rain," says Luster. "If I don't worry about y'all, I don't know who is," says Dilsey.

Faulkner pits Dilsey also against the titular head of the Compson family, Jason, a man who struggles with her for control of the family, a man whose intrinsic meanness the older woman knew would one day be turned against her. When the way is finally clear for him to discharge Dilsey after fifty years of service, he declares: "Abe Lincoln freed the niggers from the Compsons. In 1933, Jason Compson freed the Compsons from the niggers."[13]

Throughout the years Dilsey had held the family together, but once Jason gained the upper hand, she knew the family name and honor had come to an end. Yet in typical Faulkner fashion, the black woman wins in the long run, for it is her progeny that live to build another day—proof of the rewards of endurance.

American literature offers a number of examples of black women in the role of mother surrogate. Perhaps two of the best known examples are Calpurnia in Harper Lee's novel, *To Kill a Mockingbird* and Berenice in the play *A Member of the Wedding* by Carson McCullers,[14] both works created by white women. They draw portraits of domestics who not only express a maternal drive but humanize the work situation so that the essential qualities of caring, concern, and sharing were continuously present. These domestics felt needed and rewarded by the close observaton of a generation of white children whose moral virtues they had helped develop, and this was a definite plus factor for both blacks and whites. In one of the best statements regarding human isolation in general, and the black version of that condition in particular, Berenice says to Frankie, her young charge who finds it painful to deal with growing from childhood into adolescence:

> ". . . We all of us somehow caught. We born this way or that way and we don't know why. . . . We each one of us somehow caught all by ourself. . . . I'm caught worse than you is. . . . Because I am colored . . . they done drawn completely extra bounds around all colored people. They done squeezed us off in one corner by ourself. So we caught that first way I was telling you, as all human beings is caught. And we caught as colored people also."[15]

It's those "extra bounds" we want to be free of!

THE DOMESTIC WHO WORKS TO ENSURE HER CHILDREN'S FUTURE

Still another motivating factor illuminated through the pages of fiction is the force which caused black women to fight and scratch and sacrifice so their children or grandchildren might have a better life. DuBose Heyward has given us a poignant novel built on such a struggle, *Mamba's Daughters.*[16]

Mamba schemed to become a domestic in order to gain respectability in Negro circles for Lissa, her granddaughter. She had already seen the waterfront claim her hard-working, but fun-loving daughter, Hagar. Mamba selected a very prestigious white family, the Wentworths, and ingratiated herself into their employment. She knew that it was important for an ambitious black to have connections with "quality whites," and she wanted this protection for Lissa. Also, the Wentworth's black cook, Maum Netta, was a descendant of a long line of Wentworth slaves. Mamba needed social position but required a highly competent instructor; true, she knew the old servant would treat her with contempt and condescension, but in the true spirit of the social climber, Mamba was prepared to pocket her pride "until it could be worn with dignity." The Wentworths paid Mamba very little, but Hagar earned good money doing very heavy manual labor, for long hours. It was important that Mamba identify herself, and thus Lissa, with white aristocracy, so she suffered any and all humiliations and deprivations.

In this tragic story, no sacrifice was too great for either Mamba or Hagar, and in the end Hagar commits suicide to avoid the possibility that a scandal might touch Lissa.

From Mamba, to Hagar, to Lissa, came a continuity of strength. In the end Lissa becomes a singer, carrying some of her grandmother's hard-won respectabilty working in "white folks' kitchen," and her mother's earthiness, into a prestigious life, bought at such a high price.

It is rare for a white employer to be aware of the emotional problems endured by black domestics, so much can be taken for granted when a pay envelope is handed out at the end of each week. Lillian Hellman is apparently able to see beyond the mask, and even with her perception, Ms. Hellman cites problems in her autobiographical work, *An Unfinished Woman*:

> . . . these two black women you loved more than any other women. . . . How often Helen had made me mad . . . but with Sophronia nothing had ever been bad . . . Sophronia was the anchor for a little girl . . . but by the time I had met the other, years had brought acid to a nature that hadn't begun that way. . . . Our bad times came almost always on the themes of Negroes and whites. The white liberal attitude is, mostly, a well-intentioned fake, and black people do and should think it is a sell. But, our bad times . . . come . . . I think, because she did not think white people capable of dealing with trouble."[17]

THE DOMESTIC: AT WIT'S END

The picture of most white employers as set down by black authors is quite different from the ones described by their white counterparts, especially when those who write have served as "domestics" themselves. In Maya Angelou's fine autobiography, *I Know Why the Caged Bird Sings,*[18] is to be found some of the most stylishly accurate observations of this mistress-servant relationship. One incident brings into sharp focus the stupidly insensitive attitude of some white employers which enables them to ignore a black woman's actual name because it may be a bit off the beaten Anglo-Saxon path. In Ms. Angelou's case, her employer didn't even have the excuse of coping with an African name, she simply refused to call her "Margaret," a name Maya had adopted. The name "Mary" was her choice as somehow easier and more appropriate. But this sort of gratuitous insult can prove dangerous; for too long black people have suffered this loss of identity in relative silence—young Maya one day reached the breaking point!

One afternoon while serving tea to her employer and her guests, Maya carefully considered the china most favored by the lady of the house, and in front of her friends, dropped it, smashing the service into hundreds of useless bits. When one of the guests asked, "Who did it, was it Mary?" the woman replied through hysteria and grief at the loss of her fine "Virginia dishes," "Her name's Margaret, her name's Margaret," and threw a wedge of a broken dish at Maya who, fortunately, ducked in time as she scampered away from her domestic job forever.

DOMESTICS: ON THE TAKE

Douglas Turner Ward gives us a comic look at one brand of self-preservation fostered by meager pay and lack of white understanding. It's stealing! In "Happy Ending,"[19] Vi and Ellie explain their distress at the breakup of their white employers' marriage. When Junie finds such concern inconsistent with the reality of their situation as servants, his Aunt Ellie reminds him that:

> . . . from top to bottom, I cook the food, scrub the floor, open the door, serve the tables, answer the phones, dust the furniture, raise the children, lay out the clothes, greet the guests, fix the drinks and dump the garbage—all for bad pay . . . [the] money I git in my envelope ain't worth the tim'n'the headache. . . . But—God helps those who help themselves. . . . I also *order* the food, estimate the credit, *pay* the bills and *balance* the budget. . . . Every once in a full moon they git so goodhearted and tell me take some leftovers home, but by that time my freezer and pantry is already fuller than theirs. . . . And all our bills I add on to their bills, weekly prescriptions filled on their tab, tons of laundry cleaned along wit' theirs and a thousand other services and I'm earning me quite a bonus along with my bad pay. It's the *bonus* that counts. . . . So, when me and Vi saw our pigeins scampering out the window for good today, tears started flowing like rain.[20]

A DREAM DEFERRED

The tone is more serious in Lorraine Hansberry's award-winning play, *A Raisin in the Sun.*[21] As the years go by, the Younger family is no closer to their dream of getting a house out of the slums. Yet the fire of ambition still flares up, still warms their hearts, sustains them in the face of defeat. Eventually, after many years of scrubbing and serving in white kitchens, the dream is nearly realized, but there is a need for more money. Ruth cries out: I'll work twenty hours a day in all the kitchens in Chicago. . . . I'll strap my baby on my back if I have to and scrub all the floors in America and wash all the sheets in America if I have to . . . but we got to move. . . . We got to get out of here. . . ."[22]

Ruth expressed feelings many black women have known: when there are no jobs, a mop, a broom, and a dustrag will see you through.

It should be clearly understood that hard domestic labor is not always an "uplifting" force in the lives of those who perform such work. Ann Petry has written two striking novels in which the despair and pain of the principals prove how eroding domestic service can be for all too many women.

In *The Street* we watch as Lutie is pulled away from her family, earning $75 a week as a sleep-in maid. We see the irreparable damage done to her self-respect as she overhears guests in her employer's house state flatly that because she's black she's "like all the rest," an easy and eager mark for any white man. We see how the protracted time away from her husband destroys her marriage, and so another black woman is set adrift to fend for herself and her child alone.

The same author proves she understands the true nature and cause of violence when she writes of William and Pink, in "In Darkness and Confusion."[23] The couple had but one goal: to give their son all those precious advantages they never had. Pink, like her mother before her, was a "good" domestic—gentle, noncomplaining. On a quiet Sunday morning, at the news of their son's "legalized" murder in the army, Pink launches a wave of violence that surges and smashes through the streets, destroying everything in her path, collecting hoards of followers as she goes along. Just as her heart was destroyed by the violence done her as a human being, so did she lead a crowd to riot. This is a work whites would do well to read, especially those who shake their heads at reports of riots and wonder why things have come to this!

Most blacks can identify with Pink's recourse into senseless destruction. Somehow the disappointment of those who labor at society's least compensated jobs, who keep all its rules, has the existential sting of Frantz Fanon, black revolutionary author of *The Wretched of the Earth*, a primer for black militants in the sixties, in his admonishment: ". . . sometimes violence itself is the only cleansing, purifying agent against oppression."

THE FADING "MAMMY" IMAGE

While fiction presents the opportunity to look deeply into its characters' minds and hearts, what we see is always filtered through the creative mind and heart of the author. There is another kind of writing which offers great insight into the problems black women have had with the image and the reality of their lives as domestics, and it is to be found in journals—in their published statistics as well as in the half-truths they have represented.

Beginning in the early 1900's and increasingly ever since, articles have appeared decrying the diminishing number of women available for domestic work. They range in character from a piece published in 1917 by *Printer's Ink* which encouraged manufacturers to invent labor-saving devices, because the war had not only "spoiled" women who ordinarily served as domestics but may indeed "have driven them out of this work entirely," to the following excerpt from a YWCA Conference in that same year of 1917.

> . . . When employers adopt for their households a business basis, systematizing the work, regulating hours, granting the worker sufficient time and freedom to live a normal life among her own people, then both educators and girls will be more than glad to do their part in meeting the demand for trained service.[24]

An article, properly placed in the *Journal of Home Economics* by Mary Anderson, Director of the Women's Bureau, said in 1928 that "the servant question" involved two factors: first, the perception that a person engaged in domestic service is regarded with the inferiority and social stigma of the job, and second, the conditions under which domestics work. The conditions most often mentioned were low pay, long hours, the incredible demands for "round the clock" hours of a sleep-in maid, and lack of fringe benefits. Miss Anderson predicted that whites would continue to leave the occupation, but "the great bulk of Negro women will have to depend upon it as a means of maintenance." Miss Anderson also advised better conditions in order to retard the rate at which women—black and white—were being lost to the profession.[25]

Other articles began to appear that raised questions concerning the relationships between the domestic and the members of the household. In 1928 in *Parents* magazine, Ruth Sapin said: "For Better or Worse—Servants Influence Children." She gave several cases of unhealthy influences of black domestics on children: "A Negro laundress . . . told her three-year-old boy the dentist always pulled out your teeth and hurt something awful." She told of another woman who had no help "because she can't leave her high-spirited son alone with a young female servant." Miss Sapin made a case for teaching children to respect the domestics. But she also suggested that relationships were becoming serious enough for "training programs."[26]

Fortune magazine concluded that domestic help was overpaid!

They even suspected that some schoolteachers and stenographers would make "ideal second maids." The statistics pointed out that while housemaids might earn up to $1,586, a figure which included their actual wages plus food and lodging, schoolteachers were receiving only approximately $1,000 exclusive of those necessities.[27] Perhaps it was only the prospect of loss of dignity that prevented the nation's schoolteachers from defecting en masse to the ranks of domestic service. Perhaps they saw more than just the money, for the emotional output required to keep up an image of friendly warmth and hard physical labor combined with daily insults to one's humanity, one's race, and one's sex was, and is, too poignant a reminder that the system remains a first cousin to slavery.

What is the domestic scene today? Though some may think there have been improvements, the facts offer little encouragement. Pay is still far below the effort expended and the skills demanded. Domestics are not protected by the Federal Fair Labor Standards Act, nor do the majority of them receive unemployment insurance, paid vacations, or paid sick leave. And, unless they work for household help agencies, domestics seldom receive Social Security coverage. Little wonder that, with the domestics' having lived so long in the shadow of despair and near poverty, it was from their ranks that the nation's civil rebellions drew their forces. On a positive level, Marcus Garvey, Malcolm X, and other civil rights leaders found their largest following among female domestics.

So what is to be the future of this traditional work role for black women? Some would like to see it go. Others, like the National Council of Negro Women and the Women's Bureau of the Department of Labor, argue for better working conditions. The most aggressive organization in upgrading domestics is the National Committee on Household Employment, which is supported by several national voluntary organizations, including the National Council of Negro Women, and which operates with funds from the Ford Foundation.

Their goals include:

> . . . Raising household wages to at least the minimum set forth by the federal Fair Labor Standards Act.
>
> . . . Providing household workers with common working benefits, including paid vacations and holidays, sick leave, and workmen's unemployment compensation.
>
> . . . Developing realistic attitudes toward the occupation and its members on the part of employers and the public.
>
> . . . Creating among the workers an awareness of the value of their

> labor. Only when this has been done will the workers begin expecting the benefits, wages, and respect to which they are entitled.

The methods by which they hope to achieve these goals are:

> . . . Assisting the individual and organizational development of cooperatively and privately owned household service enterprises which act as intermediaries between housewives and workers.
>
> . . . Assisting in the organization of concerned household workers and private citizens at a local level throughout the United States.
>
> . . . Encouraging the development of training programs designed to raise the quality, status, and economic value of household services.
>
> . . . Increasing public awareness of the household employment problem and the efforts being made to solve it.
>
> . . . Promulgating a "Code of Standards" upon which employers and employees can base their working relationship.[28]

Once the status and conditions surrounding domestic work are changed, it can become a decent occupation, even a profitable one. Edith Sloan, former Executive Director of NCHE, said of domestics at a recent convention, "They have been the invisible technicians, the ghosts around the house." She called for better wages, improved working hours, and a recognition that being a domestic is no low business.[29] And with more unity among domestics, these things will come.

Again, we come face to face with a desperate need to change attitudes, perhaps the most important change to be made, and certainly the most difficult. It is through our attitudes that we shape reality, so we must be concerned and cautious of the thought patterns we encourage. It may be too easy to make Hollywood the whipping boy, but negative notions about domestics and blacks in general have been communicated to both blacks and whites through the film medium. It has taken too many years to move from Hattie McDaniel's Academy Award for her fine performance in *Gone With the Wind* to Cicely Tyson's nomination for her sensitive and brilliant acting in *Sounder.*

Television drama, because of its relative immediacy, may prove to be more realistic. In the Seventies, the popular TV show *Maude* introduced Florida, a day worker, ably played by veteran actress Esther Rolle. Florida was presented as a no-nonsense woman who was strictly concerned about business. In one episode, the determinedly "liberal" Maude told her maid, "I want you to feel like *this* is your home." Florida quickly replied, "I *have* a home." What a breakthrough! At last we were given a working black woman we could recognize and be proud of.

That the character of Florida became popular enough to spin off a series of her own, *Good Times,* is a tribute to Esther Rolle's artistic ability in projecting a positive image of a domestic. Still, though producer Norman Lear had originally intended for "Florida" to continue as a domestic in the popular *Good Times,* she became a housewife and an occasional worker in a variety of jobs. Why *not* a domestic? In any event, the National Council of Negro Women presented Lear with a plaque for "a positive portrayal of a black domestic," and it was disappointing to some that the character was not further explored in *Good Times.* There are parallels connecting this basic comedy to the drama of *Sounder.* In both we see a black woman balancing many relationships with dignity. Both women work to keep their children cared for and motivated to achieve better lives for themselves. None of these things have ever been easy for black women, and no simplistic characterization has ever really done justice to their struggles. But here and there we do have a few honest attempts to deal realistically with the black woman and her family.

Domestics are no kinder or meaner, no smarter or dumber than any other humans. They can be sad or uproariously funny, not because they are stupid but because sometimes, just sometimes, in the balancing of the human drama of relationships, domestics do have the upper hand—the last laugh. They hold the ace.

Dishwater may at last be sending back positive images!

CHAPTER 4
NOTES

[1]Waring Cuney, "No Images," as the poem appears in *The Poetry of the Negro, 1746–1949,* edited by Langston Hughes and Anna Bontemps (Garden City, N.Y.: Doubleday and Company, Inc., 1949), p. 145.

[2]Lillian Hellman, *An Unfinished Woman* (New York: Bantam Books, 1970); reprinted by permission of Little, Brown and Company, 1969), p. 212.

[3]Jeanne Noble, "Domestics View Their Work Roles," U.S. Department of Labor Research Government Report #91-34-67-06, pp. 101–105. (Unpublished)

[4]Tables 39 and 70, Occupations of Employed Women: 1970, in *The Social and Economic Status of the Black Population in the United States, 1973,* Special Studies Series #48, U.S. Department of Commerce, Bureau of the Census, p. 23.

[5]Elizabeth Duncan Koontz, speech before the Northern Virginia Conference on Household Employment, Alexandria, Virginia, April 14, 1969.

[6]Ann Petry, *The Street* (New York: A Pyramid Book, published by arrangement with Houghton Mifflin Company, 1961), p. 118.

[7]Margaret Mitchell, *Gone With the Wind* (New York: Avon Books, 1936/1973), p. 25. (Originally published by The Macmillan Company, 1936).

[8]Interview with Lorraine Hansberry, *New York Herald Tribune,* March 13, 1960.

[9]The following dedication appeared in one of William Faulkner's books:

To Mammy
CAROLINE BARR
Mississippi
(1840–1940)
Who was born in slavery and who gave
to my family a fidelity without stint or
calculation of recompense and to my
childhood an immeasurable devotion and
love.

[10]William Faulkner, *The Sound and the Fury* (New York: Vintage Books, Random House, 1946), p. 106.

[11]Irving Howe, *William Faulkner: A Critical Study* (New York: Random House, 1952), p. 133.

[12]Faulkner, *Sound and the Fury,* p. 130.

[13]*Ibid.,* p. 422.

[14]See Harper Lee, *To Kill a Mockingbird* (New York, Philadelphia: J. B. Lippincott and Company, 1960); and Carson McCullers, *A Member of the Wedding* (New York: Bantam Books, published by arrangement with Houghton Mifflin Company, 1946, 1950).

[15]McCullers, *Member*, pp. 113–114.

[16]DuBose Heyward, *Mamba's Daughters* (Garden City, N.Y.: Doubleday and Company, Inc., 1929).

[17]Lillian Hellman, *Unfinished Woman,* p. 214.

[18]Maya Angelou, *I Know Why the Caged Bird Sings* (New York: Random House, 1970).

[19]Douglas Turner Ward, *Happy Ending,* one-act play as it appears in *New Black Playwrights,* ed. William Couch, Jr. (New York: Avon Books, 1970), pp. 27–46. Copyright © 1966, by Douglas Turner Ward. Reprinted by permission of the author and of Dramatist's Play Service, Inc.

[21]*Ibid.,* pp. 39–41.

[22]Lorraine Hansberry, *A Raisin in the Sun* (New York: A Signet Book, by permission of Random House, 1959).

[22]*Ibid.,* pp. 119–120.

[23]Ann Petry, "In Darkness and Confusion," *Black Voices,* ed. Abraham Chapman (New York: A Mentor Book, 1968), pp. 161–204.

[24]Proceedings of YWCA Conference on Domestics, New York City, 1917.

[25]Mary Anderson, "The Servant Question," *Journal of Home Economics,* January 1928, pp. 7–12.

[26]Ruth Sapin, "For Better or Worse—Servants Influence Children," *Parents* magazine, January 1928, pp. 20–21.

[27]*Fortune* magazine, December 1931, pp. 44–47.

[28]See *Goals of the National Committee on Household Employment,* 7705 Georgia Avenue N.W., Washington, D.C. 20012, Anita Bellamy Shelton, Executive Director.

[29]*The New York Times,* October 10, 1972.

Color him father
Color him love . . .

There is a man in my house
He's so big and strong
He goes to work each day
And stays all day long
Comes home at night, looking tired and beat . . .

I think I'll color him Father
Think I'll color this man Love . . .

"O.C. SMITH AT HOME"[1]
COLUMBIA RECORDS CS9908

Color Him Father

Many black children would envy a boy singing about a man who works hard every day and comes home to share with his woman and children the economic and emotional support of a family. What child would not like to grow up in an intact family? The image of "Mother, Father, Dick, Jane, and a dog named Spot" are well set in our minds, from the first grade primer to television's *Little House on the Prairie.* That particular primer is obsolete, but the image of the ideal family remains. Moreover, the extent to which a child's family fits the ideal "intact family" can greatly influence a person's growth and development.

Nearly 30 percent of all black children live in families that don't fit the American Ideal Family norm. Not only is how they feel about themselves important, but just as important are the coping strategies of the women who inevitably have to rear children without the consistent supportive presence of a father.

There is the reality of more and more black children being reared in female-headed homes than ever before, and this situation will probably change very little considering the worsening economic conditions blacks face in the Seventies.[2]

In addition to the economic situation are also social realities. Black women of marriageable age outnumber black men by about one million. Even if it were possible to declare every black male eligible for marriage, that is, none in jail, on hard drugs, or dead in some war grave as was the case during the Vietnam War, many black women would still have to choose to bear and rear children outside of marriage. There simply are not enough black men available for marriage. Many black women have to make the choice of either getting pregnant and rearing a child alone, or remaining unmarried and childless.

But for many black women, rearing children alone is not a choice. It is a consequence of many economic and social factors that prevent them from realizing the traditional intact nuclear family model. By 1974, one-third of all black families were headed by women,[3] a trend that not only continues, but is highlighted by the large percentage of black low-income families who are headed by women. And much larger proportions, compared with whites, have two or more children to support. How these women cope with the economic and social pressures, how they and their children create a life, has long been a subject for songs, poems, and novels. Whatever the medium, the message is not a simple one.

Take O. C. Smith's song "Color Him Father." A "father substitute" has moved into the father role in such a postive way that he is colored *love.* Perhaps he moved into the boy's house as a "common law" husband, as his mother's lover. It would not be surprising if the boy's teacher, psychologist, and social worker looked at his coloring book and asked: "Who is the male figure introduced into these drawings?" There is no father noted on the record! Has a man moved into his home? Is this the mother's lover? Carried to its logical ending, the boy's drawing in years past might have precipitated an investigation, even a welfare raid. How did regulating an individual's most intimate choices come to be society's business? The secret word is "welfare."

Sexual choices and living arrangements are one's private business. Yet, it somehow becomes everybody's business when a mother is on welfare. For generations, the very presence of a male who "lives in" jeopardized the welfare support system which controls the lives of so many black children. Few reasonable people would make a case for sexual abstinence, loneliness, or rearing children in isolation from strong males who can and will form close relationships with them. Yet, for welfare mothers there have always been such unreal expectations! John Kenneth Galbraith writes: "To some extent family life is itself a luxury of an adequate income."[4] It should be added that privacy is also a luxury of an adequate income. So much of welfare mothers' "business," which middle-class people might well hide, is in public view. Those women, who reputedly benefit from the welfare system and are variously labeled "welfare cheaters," "eaters," or some other negative epithet, are expected to pay a price in self-denial of companionship and sex that few of their critics would long tolerate for themselves.

THE "WELFARE"

"Let's play Welfare," Mary suggested. "Okay," replied Doris, "I'll be the mother." "Knock Knock" "Who's there?" "Miss Smith." (Pause.) "Who you? . . . the social worker?" Doris pantomimes locking doors and pulling curtains, sealing every possible entry while screaming, "Ain't nobody home."

Contrary to what many white people believe, "going on welfare" is considered a fearful last resort, a dead end for many black families. It barely provides enough for a meager subsistence. The price one pays is endless harassment, bureaucratic red tape, and constant frustration. Welfare brands a woman as an American failure and signifies to a man that he is unable to provide for his family. Although regulations are changing, welfare rules for too long forced a man out of the family picture until and unless he could get a job that paid more than the welfare check. This is a difficult task for a man with few skills and a shoddy education; most find it impossible, and few escape the stigma of "separated father."

As painful as it may be for him, at least a man can walk away from the mirror of his disappointment; indeed, he is often forced to leave wife and children if they are to benefit from welfare. But what is the black woman left with? Far too many psychologists and social workers are insensitive to the coping strategies these women have had to devise in order to rear children in a male-oriented, father-dominated society without such a strong force in their own homes. The mother has been left with the responsibilities of caring for her children at a bare subsistence level, but with her own needs for companionship and sex totally ignored. She is expected to be the mainstay for the next black generation, and yet what sort of healthy example can she project when vital areas of her emotional and physical responses have been virtually legislated away.

Most black women know "the domestic sister" intimately, as a relative or friend. We may even have spent some time in this category ourselves. Most of us can identify with those sisters soloing through life with children but no man. Gladys Knight singing "Help Me Make It Through the Night" gains a response from any of us—from Ph.D. to welfare mother. We need, perhaps, to carry this emphathy over to those sisters with children who break "welfare rules" in order to establish male-female relationships even if they are not sanctioned by society.

In October 1972 the Senate explored welfare reform legislation. The two dominant themes which emerged were that runaway fathers should be tracked down, and welfare mothers be put to work.

As for the first solution proposed, what kind of emotional and economic support can a man provide if he is unemployed or underemployed? Men are conditioned to care deeply about their role as "breadwinners," so few are able to withstand the pressure of a needing wife and begging children. The distinguished senators should also remember a man is measured *first* by his place in the occupational/income order, with his family status assuming secondary importance; fatherhood, unfortunately, has never been valued above manhood in this country. Even so, it is interesting to note that while 50 percent of all white families on relief in New York City were shown to be suffering from marital breakdown, only 44 percent of the Negro families were reported to be in the same situation. According to these statistics, black men may value family life more than their white counterparts and may be willing to settle for less in order to stay with their wives and children.[5]

Family desertion is not a black genetic deficiency; look for its roots in the economic plight of the male. Repressive legislation which fails to attack rising unemployment and massive underemployment will increase the numbers of women who make up the statistics of solo mothers, not eliminate them. It will place greater strain on male-female relationships, and make of marriage, not a joy, but a threat. If black men come to see marriage to a black wife as a potential liability, a black husband will become a luxury fewer and fewer black women will ever be able to have.

There should and must be financial help for those families in need, but it should and must be designed to recognize and strengthen the humanity of the recipients. Some people are trying to make the facts and struggles known. Johnnie Tillman, welfare rights leader, summed up the frustrations of black women on welfare with these words:

> I'm a woman. I'm a black woman. I'm a poor woman. I'm a fat woman. I'm a middle-aged woman. And I'm on welfare.
>
> In this country, if you're any one of those things—poor, black, fat, female, middle-aged, on welfare—you count less as a human being. If you're *all* those things, you don't count at all. Except as a statistic.
>
> I am a statistic.
>
> I am 45 years old. I have raised six children.[6]

THE "TYPICAL" BLACK FAMILY

The black family structure is a richly varied and complex network of relationships and shared resources. To analyze black family life against such oversimplified classifications as "male-headed" or "female-headed" obscures the resourcefulness of black families and ignores their strong drive to survive.

The *nuclear family* structure which consists of mother, father, and offspring, is regarded as ideal, but is not always possible in black communities. Other common family patterns which have evolved to give support to black women and children are: *the extended family,* consisting of two or more kinfolk living under one roof; and *the augmented family,* consisting of kinfolk and unrelated people who share resources and companionship under one roof.[7]

In 1971 Robert B. Hill, in a study entitled *The Strength of Black Families,* struck down many of the myths surrounding black families. The central findings of this study were: that most black families are two-parent rather than one-parent households; that men are the primary breadwinners in the overwhelming majority of black families; that most black women who head their own families work and are not dependent on welfare; that most black families have a strong work ethic and achievement orientation; and that most families among blacks are characterized by equalitarian roles rather than by a matriarchy.[8]

Black people have fit into the American system in remarkably imaginative ways. A less sturdy and determined people, given the historic odds and scant current resources, might have failed miserably. A brief look at some statistics proves how well blacks have managed their lives, in spite of economic factors and the fact that black women outnumber black men significantly.

In 1975 the National Urban League summarized Dr. Hill's findings in a pamphlet identifying five strengths and stating relevant statistics:

1. *Strong Kinship Bonds*

The strong kinship bonds in black families are demonstrated by the absorption of other relatives into black households. There is a high rate of informal adoption of children. For example, only about 7% of the black babies born out of wedlock each year are given away for formal adoption, while close to 90% of them are informally adopted or retained by already existing families. About two thirds of the white babies born out of wedlock each year are given up for formal adoption, while less than 10% of them are kept by already existing families.

2. *Strong Work Orientations*

The majority of black families place a strong emphasis on self-reliance and ambition: three-fifths of the black poor work, compared to about half of the white poor. Only about half of the people entitled to welfare assistance receive it. Sixty percent of the women heading black families work and are not completely dependent on public assistance.

The husband is the primary breadwinner in the overwhelming majority of black families and is not "peripheral" or "weak." In fact, the Bureau of Labor Statistics data reveal that in 85% of low-income black families with working wives, the husband's earnings far exceed the wife's.

3. *Adaptability of Family Roles*

Black families have a high degree of role flexibility and adaptability of family patterns. In many families with working wives, for example, the wife often has to act as the father and the husband as the mother. Contrary to the widespread belief in a matriarchy among blacks, most black families (whether low-income or not) are characterized by an "equalitarian" family pattern in which neither spouse dominates, but shares decision-making and the performance of expected tasks.

The fact that a family is headed by a woman is no justification for morally prejudging it as "maladaptive" or "pathological." A number of studies, in fact, have found many one-parent families to be more functional and adaptive than many two-parent families. This is particularly true for those one-parent families that have the support of other relatives, which is especially evident among black families.

4. *High Achievement Orientations*

The overwhelming majority of low-income families in general, and black families in particular, have high achievement orientations. One indicator of this is the high proportion of black college students from lower socio-economic backgrounds. For example, three fourths of the blacks presently enrolled in college come from homes in which the family heads never went to college. Moreover, many studies have consistently found black students to have high educational aspirations and achievement orientations—often higher than that of similar status white students.

5. *Strong Religious Orientations*

The black church has historically been in the vanguard of the black man's struggle for freedom in America. It was a major source of strength, not only during slavery, but during the civil rights movement of the '50's and '60's as well.[9]

When traditional patterns cannot be sustained, it is clear that the black community still respects the family unit. These alternate family life styles deserve attention so that the intrinsic value of "fatherless" homes can be more fully understood and supportive plans formulated which will enable us to build on existing strengths. And surely, understanding the true problems facing black families as put forth in the so-called "Moynihan Report" must be avoided.

DANIEL PATRICK MOYNIHAN'S "NEW FANGLE TANGLE"[10]

Entitled "The Negro Family—The Case for National Action," such a study might have been expected to offer practical solutions, to provide encouragement and support for those who have worked so hard to nourish their children emotionally as well as physically. Instead, Mr. Moynihan kindled the flames of righteous anger that swept through our black communities from welfare mothers to the wealthy. There was shock that a white liberal would suggest that Negroes have no unique values and culture to guard and protect.[11] Mr. Moynihan over-idealized the white family as "achieving a high degree of stability," while stating that "at the heart of the deterioration of the fabric of Negro society is the deterioration of the Negro family. . . . It is the fundamental source of weakness of the Negro."[12] The report went on to explain that the "fearful price" blacks pay as a result of mistreatment over the centuries is a matriarchy. Over and over he stressed the importance of a "society in which males are dominant in family relationships" not because of the intrinsic value he sees in such male-female order, but because society presumes male leadership in private and public affairs and rewards this kind of structure. "After all, the very essence of the male animal, from the bantam rooster to the four-star general, is to strut."[13]

Not content with that, Moynihan stated: "When Jim Crow made its appearance—it was the Negro male who was most humiliated—the male was more likely to use public facilities—segregation, and the submissiveness it exacts, is surely more destructive to the male than to the female personality."[14]

Little wonder few social documents have equaled "The Negro Family—The Case for National Action" in social impact. Certainly none has provoked such widespread black outrage. Mr. Moynihan's report contained something to offend everybody!

He minimized the fact that the core problem of black "so-called-family-instability" is the lack of or low income, joblessness, and he surely did not cite the need to support families until such time as black family unity was magically achieved.

By suggesting that the black female was less traumatized by

slavery, Moynihan was not only derisive but blind. Black women generally felt that he was making them a party to the oppression of black males, when in fact, they were also victims. How did domestics get to work, except on segregated transportation? Where did they shop except in places where they could not use public facilities? Who took the children to segregated toilets?

It was not mere male chauvinism for Moynihan to dismiss the black female situation as less serious than the black male's, but blatant ignorance about the plight of black women. His insensitivity to the crushing burden borne by numbers of us who rear children alone, and who struggle through the humiliations visited upon us by white society, is unforgivable.

The black woman has never had an economic advantage in this country. Being able to get a job as a domestic is not necessarily an advantage; and yet, that is the outlet so often referred to as the black woman's economic opportunity denied black men.

Mary Keyserling, an economist and former Director of the Women's Bureau during the Kennedy years, came across a statement which indicated that in the perspective of the underemployment of the Negro father, the Negro mother is *overemployed*!

She found this "very puzzling," since her statistics showed that unemployment among nonwhite women was 19 percent higher than among nonwhite men, that their income was lower, and that nonwhite women who work year round and full-time were decidedly in the minority. Moreover, the rate of unemployment among black women, particularly adolescent females, was then and is now appallingly high. Moynihan's thinking was dangerous inasmuch as it risked giving support to those who have always believed that we solve unemployment problems by taking jobs away from women and giving them to men.

Moynihan influenced many social planners, some not as perceptive and wise as Dr. Keyserling. He also gave fuel to some black men who also feel that the best way to develop a strong family unit is to give the best social and economic opportunities to males.

Such would be disastrous. Some shoring up of existing family structure is imperative, and it cannot be done without increasing income-producing opportunities for women in these homes. Black women are already deeply mired in the obligations of family responsibilities—and a decade of poverty programs has not helped.

Moynihan at first had support from Whitney Young of the Urban League, but even Young was eventually forced to denounce him. Before the report was officially published, all the civil rights organizations protested its conclusions and implications.

Moynihan's conclusions appeared in President Johnson's Howard University June 1964 Commencement address. Almost at once black leaders became distressed, believing attention focused on the black family would detract from civil rights and economic problems of blacks, the root causes of whatever family problems existed among us.

Moynihan advised President Johnson to call a conference on *The Negro Family.* A *New Yorker* magazine article thought it would be "a conference aimed at developing the Ego of the Negro Male in the United States,"[15] President Johnson heeded black protests, particularly a pre-conference held in November 1965, called by Benjamin Payton and attended by one hundred prominent leaders, who "resolved that the question of 'family stability' be stricken from the agenda." He changed the conference to a White House Conference, To Fulfill These Rights, at which jobs, housing, education, and other problems were discussed and "the black family" seldom mentioned.

Moynihan ended up, as reporter Mary McGrory stated, as "The Non-Person at the Rights Parley, copiously ignored." Many, according to Ms. McGrory, "wanted to see him, but few wanted to talk to him."[16]

E. Franklin Frazier, noted Howard University sociologist and expert on the Negro family, was one of those who had long called the nation's attention to the depressing statistics concerning broken homes and the large number of children who are being reared in "fatherless homes." Frazier never dealt with black family statistics in such an arrogant way as did Moynihan, nor did he feel that family breakdown was a Case for National Action—something the government should attempt to change by law and social engineering. He saw its primary cure in economic strength for the total black community, both men and women. The Case for National Action is *jobs* and adequate income, not tinkering with family life!

THE WELFARE MOTHER: COLOR HER FATHER?

The black woman solo parent is neither irresponsible nor lazy, according to recent studies, including the Hill one. We would conclude from all the evidence that she is more likely to work than her white counterpart, and though qualified, the majority of poor black women do not even receive welfare. Actually a disproportionate share of welfare money comes to poor black women, considering the large numbers who qualify.

A great amount of self-reliance and strength are apparent in the Hill study, as well as others. But "self-reliance" is not the same as self-sufficiency. Black women on welfare rolls are not there because they prefer this status. They do not connive and improvise to care for children out of an urge to be domineering or matriarchal. There is no cultural historical foundation which supports a preference for solo parenthood. We have only to recall the far-reaching web of protection which traditional African tribes wove about all its members to have a real, workable model for a welfare system worthy of the name.

Though she is referred to as a "solo parent," the black woman with a child in her care is more. With one mind, one heart, one frame of reference, she must be not only mother but father as well. The black woman's reputation as a strong mother figure is a matter of historical fact; even her owners during slavery days entrusted their children to her care. Her maternal credentials well established, white society now forces her to assume the doubly difficult role of father to her children by dealing her man a losing hand in the welfare game. A boy's best friend may well be his mother, but who would deny that a boy needs a male role model for proper psychological growth and development? Cobbs and Grier in *Black Rage* certainly seem right in saying that black men when describing their relations with black women look back and see their mothers as having been contradictory. "She may have been permissive in some areas and punitive and rigid in others. . . . The black mother shares a burden with her soul sisters of three centuries ago. She must produce and shape and mould a unique kind of man. She must intuitively cut off and blunt the masculinity, assertiveness, and aggression lest these put the boy's life in jeopardy . . . the child must know that the white world is dangerous and that if he does not understand its rules it may kill him."[17]

Perhaps this cautious upbringing leads black men to an exaggerated feeling toward the women they deal with as adults.

MOTHERHOOD VERSUS MANHOOD: WHICH DOES "THE WELFARE" HELP?

In an essay on motherhood in *The Black Woman,* Joanne Clark illustrates the difficulties she and other black women face in seeking welfare when their husbands feel their manhood is compromised by such an act. She had a job, but couldn't get baby sitters. With only one semester to go at CCNY she attempted to find a day care center for her two children. The waiting lists were too long and she was told by the day care authorities to seek welfare so she could rear her children. Friends of her husband, whom she nicknamed Peter Pan, talked him into saying, if anyone asked, that he couldn't support us. "It was the truth, but I wasn't sure that he knew it."[18]

The pain of admitting his inability to support his family was just too much for Joanne Clark's husband, no matter how much good accepting state funds would ultimately be. When asked for verification by an investigator, he said "he didn't see why his family was on welfare since he was able to care for it." Since the Welfare Department would do nothing to help establish her right to their financial aid, Joanne was forced to take her husband to court. The monumental unfairness of that body was established by arranging for her husband to contribute the grand sum of $15 a week, which would even then be delayed due to some debts he had to clear up first. The insanity of it all washed over this woman whose only crime was to finish college and become a productive member of the community. With the pittance allowed her by the probation officer, she couldn't support her two children, nor would they allow her to turn them over to their father, because that would be desertion. Her husband even thwarted an attempt to place the children in a foster home, and when asked by the social worker what his wife was supposed to do, he answered: "She's an intelligent woman. I'm sure she'll think of something." Whatever else this man was doing, he felt compelled to maintain a front; he could not appear to be "less than a man" in the eyes of white authorities.

The inequities of welfare became obvious through Joanne's eyes. A man who chooses to rear his children alone, on welfare, is entitled to a housekeeper, paid for by welfare. Foster home parents are given more resources to cope with children than their natural parents. It is impossible not to have contempt for a system that fails to support a mother with only one semester left to finish college, knowing full well that such an investment will "pay off," not only for the person, but for society. Welfare foes speak often about "welfare loafers," few bother to know thousands of victims who need just temporary help, or help of a kind not recognized in the rules or regulations—like Joanne—that could mean the difference between prolonged struggle and success.

The treatment of welfare mothers as statistics and "welfare eaters" have so radicalized many of the mothers that the emergence of organizations such as National Welfare Rights should not have surprised America.

Johnnie Tillman, the first chairperson of the National Welfare Rights organization says: "Welfare is all about dependence.

Welfare is the most prejudiced institution in this country, even more than marriage, which it tries to imitate. . . ."

Aid to Families with Dependent Children, according to Ms. Tillman, is not about families, "since 99 percent of them are headed by women." Speaking against the "able-bodied man around the house" rule, which automatically cuts a woman off welfare even though the man cannot find work or works for less than welfare payments, she says: "AFDC is like a super-sexist marriage. You trade in a man for *the* man . . . *the* man runs everything. In ordinary marriage, sex is supposed to be for your husband. On AFDC you're not supposed to have any sex at all."

> . . . You give up control of your own body. It's a condition of aid. You may even have to agree to get your tubes tied so you can never have more children, just to avoid being cut off welfare.
>
> *The* man, the welfare system, controls your money.
>
> . . . *The* man can break into your house any time he wants and poke into your things . . . you've got no right to privacy.[19]

Mothers on welfare are generally eager to accept opportunities for further education and job training, if day care facilities are adequate. But repressive welfare proposals that force recipients to accept public and "private" work and to leave their children with a friend or relative (custodial care) if a day care center is not available is another burden heaped upon black women, further grinding their strength against impossible odds.

DON'T NEED A MAN!

Douglas Turner Ward wrote *Happy Ending* as a satire, poking fun at the domestic's advantage in a white home. The two domestics in the play, Ellie and Vi, do fit the stereotype of matriarchs.

Ellie and Vi enjoy their breadwinner role at home, including pampering their playboy nephew Junie as long as he recognizes his dependence on them. They also enjoy running their "white folks" house, with their employers also dependent on them.

Junie is clearly "wise" to them and knows intuitively that he is an "item of conspicuous consumption," and that his aunts not only have a low opinion of men but have developed a survival life style that excludes dependency on men.

One day both aunts come home upset that their employer is dead and they will no longer run the "Big White House." Junie gets angry and says:

> I never heard you shedding such tragic tears when your own li'l crumbcrushers suffered through fatherless periods! All you grumbled was "good riddance, they better off wit'out the sons-a-bitches!" Maybe Harrison tots will make out just as well. They got puny li'l advantages of millions of dollars and slightly less parched skins![20]

Junie had evaluated them right. Vi and Ellie are representative of some black women who, having shouldered the responsibilities of large families over long periods of time, become so wrapped up in their "breadwinning" role that they express little concern or patience with the struggle to get a man. They simply say, "Don't need one"! This is hardly the most desirable solution.

THE MISSING MALE ROLE MODEL AND PROTECTOR

On the other hand many black women, so lauded for their strength, have never claimed that they could play all the roles necessary in bringing up children. But when faced with a "missing man," as Maya Angelou's mother was, what is there to do except the very best one can. In her moving, sensitive book *I Know Why the Caged Bird Sings,* Maya Angelou describes her mother as "the original do-it-yourself" girl.[21] As always, her major concern was to live the life given to her, and her children were expected to do the same. She was a good provider and friend to Maya and Bailey, but she could not protect Maya from her stepfather's sexual advances and eventual rape. So, like so many black girls growing up in poverty or on the edges of it, Maya had a negative introduction to sex. For such girls, there is always sex to look at, listen to, and deal with. Not all grow up traumatized by its force and influence on themselves and others, but many do. Joyce Ladner writes:

> . . . an eight-year-old girl has a good chance of being exposed to rape and violenceand neither parents nor community leaders have the power to eliminate this antisocial behavior."[22]
>
> . . . All of these influences superimpose emotional precocity on the girl that often exceeds her chronological years.[23]

Though it is quite true, as Ladner suggests, that these children react to antisocial behavior with fright and displeasure, as do children anywhere, they are socialized early to defend themselves. Naturally, the ability to defend oneself, to escape "the rape man," as one of Ladner's subjects said, is a positive value. But truly, what is often forgotten in applauding this ability to cope is the fact that too many Maya Angelou's grow up unprotected from violence and seldom live out a childhood free of anxieties and problems that can carry over to adulthood and male-female relationships.

TO SOME EXTENT FAMILY LIFE IS . . . A LUXURY OF ADEQUATE INCOME

So says John Kenneth Galbraith, the eminent economist and author. It is an unavoidable truth that not all the love in the world, nor all attempts to imitate the standard American way of life, can keep a family intact when there is no money.

In 1966 a Task Force on the Disadvantaged Family, at the request of the Citizens Advisory Council on the Status of Women, filed a statement on behalf of black women in the proceedings of the 1966 White House Conference, "To Fulfill These Rights." (This was the conference which originally Moynihan and other Presidential advisers had sought to have President Johnson call on the Negro family and its pathology.) The paper stated the main cause of disadvantaged black families as lack of income. The basic disadvantage continues to be economic powerlessness.

The sole fact of poverty, whatever its source, creates a burden and a disadvantage for the woman who must meet the daily needs of herself and her family. Whatever may be its additional effects, and these are many, poverty in and of itself stands in the way of the development of her full potential and that of the children for whom she is responsible.

The rate of separation and desertion and the percentage of children living with a solo parent decrease as the family income increases. When the income reaches as little as $4,000 to $5,999, 82 percent of the children are found living with their families. Only as the income sinks below $2,000 do we get the Moynihan "tangle of pathology," *and even then* over one half of the children still live with both parents!

WHAT OF THE SPIRIT?

The most significant impoverishment faced by black women attempting to rear children alone is perhaps not the bureaucratic red tape of welfare, but the poverty of the spirit which threatens to undermine the will to forge an adequate family system.

This lethargy of the spirit begins with the pregnant girl. (There are more youthful mothers among the poor.) To be poor while "in the family way" is to begin a seemingly endless cycle of social and personal dependency. A young black mother often depends on her mother to rear the child while she attempts to recapture some of her lost youth.

Tender loving care is often replaced by frustration and agitation. Sometimes the young mother sees the child as a doll, a toy. Though motherhood marks entry into womanhood, for poor black girls it does not always mean that young mothers are able to shoulder the responsibilities. Once she is dependent on the "grandmother/mother" relationship and the agencies attached to welfare recipients, the web of dependency is spun.

What of their fathers? If one is a single victim of poverty there is at least a freedom from the sense of failing others. But to be poor and responsible for a family too is to have one's chances for failure and frustration multiplied. A deadened will to go on, to try something else, or even to hope for better days, often results. For many young poor males there is simply no will to take on a consistent father role. They seldom try. And since the girls know this, but need their companionship, the fathering of several children in the same neighborhood is not unusual.

Though welfare regulations for many years encouraged the flight of non-income-producing fathers, many also seem to flee because they cannot face this steady cycle of frustration. Society may well point out that it is more noble to face problems than to run from them. But even if society were able to produce all the training and jobs these fathers needed, there is still psychological damage. Many no longer *believe* they can succeed. Even in the best of families some take flight from pain and anguish; some take to alcohol or drugs. The defeated poor father often takes flight physically.

But for the women of poor families there is no way out. Whether one is a mother, grandmother, or some other female in the house, one stays and tries to cope.

There is a correlation between how a family lives and its income. Certainly, the one family in thirteen that has less than a thousand dollars a year is suffering from a limited diet and insufficient clothing, shelter, and health care—not to mention loss of self-esteem when it measures itself against its neighbors in an affluent society. In cases where the husband is the breadwinner and the family still falls beneath the poverty line, the fabric of family life is already threadbare. When one considers "financial worries" as a chief reason stated for youthful middle-class divorce, the plight of the poor couple can be seen as even more acute.

When children are born into poor families—and some 16

million children are suffering this plight—they become the statistics of defeat in health, education, and even crime. When families with women as the head of the houehold constitute as much as 70 percent of all nonwhite families, it is possible to conclude that among the poor, poor women are the poorest.

Many children of poor families have "copped out." Nothing "turns them on." And contrary to the widespread notion that sex brings satisfaction to the poor, few of the girls in poverty express hedonism. Joyce Ladner's classic study of poor black girls teaches us that a sense of belonging, of feeling needed, a sense of identity and usefulness, forces many black girls into premarital sex.[24] And the revolving door of poverty gives one more turn.

A corrosion of the spirit can do more to undermine the values of family life or any cherished institution than can physical deprivation. For when the spirit is killed, we are at the mercy of baser instincts. We begin to deal with words like "survive" instead of "thrive."

When we operate on a level of mere personal survival, we can hardly be expected to care enough to socialize subsequent generations into "the American Way of Life," including the intact monogamous family.

The Moynihan report gave the nation a view of social pathology as it affects the black male. From his view, Negro males need to be "bantam roosters and to strut." He dealt with the outward appearance of things. But the black community does not need "strutters," it needs doers—it needs jobs for both men and women. And surely the black community deserves a better social structure than the henhouse pecking order! Would he add that the bantam rooster needs a hen to cackle?

Everybody, male and female, black and white, needs to feel worthwhile, competent, and capable of enjoying autonomy in a balanced sense. That is not the way of the rooster. Furthermore, there are humanistic values that should order human relations: concern, compassion, caring, and sharing.

Neither Hylan Lewis, Franklin Edwards, William Billingsley, nor Robert B. Hill, all experts on the black family, accept the premise that the American white family is chock full of lofty patterns to emulate, except the fact that more white children than black are living with both parents—a function of an adequate income.

They have said: "The black family is not falling apart, it is adapting itself to a hostile system." They have said: "The black woman has played a necessary role essential for survival."

The question that needs to be posed by students of family life, black and white, is an existential one: What kind of rearing patterns and social structures best produce the kind of people with whom we want to populate this earth?

Few of us know the models we want.

Do we want war-makers, violence-prone children? Do we want insensitive, selfish offspring?

There is a vision many of us have of a New Society, a new America. It would be one that is more expressive, more emotional, more intuitive, possessing some of those characteristics now ascribed to women. In such a society we will have to redefine male aggressiveness. Already there is a great debate in our country concerning the need to humanize people. Urie Bronfenbrenner writes about changing patterns of childrearing and tells us that in paternalistic families we get the academic achievement gains so desirable to us all, but in return there is the likelihood that these "high achievers" will be aggressive, tense, dominating, and cruel.[25]

Kenneth Kenniston in *Young Radicals*[26] pointed out that activist mothers, those engaged in causes related to a better life for minorities and to peace, for example, seemed to develop among their offspring an unusual capacity for nurturant behavior. Concern for others—the oppressed, the needy—was associated with activist motherhood. This certainly gives us hope for those black children whose mothers are actively involved in community change, often the case with mother-oriented families.

The point here is that the America some of us envision—one that is nurturant, caring and dedicated to human concerns—will have to reject the old values associated with paternalism and masculine dominance and aggressiveness. We need to substitute sympathy, compassion, love, and tenderness, values most often associated with women.

It may well be that the black family can more readily adapt itself to a shared equalitarian relationship which would be more humanistic than current paternalistic models seem to suggest.

Certainly, Moynihan is correct in implying that "it is possible to right whatever perceived imbalance there might be toward a matriarchy in favor of a paternalistic, masculine-dominated America." All of the institutions of society are geared toward supporting paternalism. But it would be inimical to black history and its best interests to tip the balance toward *total* masculine dominance in the black community. Not only can we not afford the "strutting," but that type of structure imitates the worst of America's values: male chauvinism.

What is also difficult, but needed, is for white feminists to tip the balance toward more feminine qualities among whites. When this is achieved, the roles black women have played in solo parenthood may not be all negative. In fact, they may be instructive for all who desire a New American.

CHAPTER 5 NOTES

[1]"Color Him Father," BMI, Holly Bee Music Co.; Richard Spencer, writer; Johnny Bee, publisher.

[2]*The State of Black America 1977,* National Urban League, 500 East 62 Street, New York, N.Y. 10021.

[3]U.S. Bureau of the Census, Current Population Reports Special Studies, Series P-23, No. 54, *The Social and Economic Status of the Black Population in the United States, 1974,* p. 106.

[4]John Kenneth Galbraith, *The Affluent Society* (Boston: Houghton Mifflin Company, 1958), p. 324.

[5]"Marriage or Relief: A Statistical Study," *New York Times,* March 11, 1972.

[6]Johnnie Tillman, "Welfare Is a Woman's Issue," *Ms. Magazine,* I (Spring 1972), pp. 110–112.

[7]Andrew Billingsley, *Black Families in White America* (Englewood Cliffs, N.J.: Prentice-Hall, Inc., 1968), pp. 15–21.

[8]Robert B. Hill, *The Strength of Black Families* (New York: Emerson Hall Publishers, Inc., 1972), p. 6.

[9]*The Strength of Black Families,* National Urban League and National Council of YMCAs, 1975 (National Urban League, Inc., 500 East 62nd Street, New York, N.Y. 10021), pp. 5–6.

[10]*The Negro Family, The Case for National Action,* Office of Policy Planning and Research, United States Department of Labor, March 1965.

[11]*Ibid.*

[12]*Ibid.,* p. 5.

[13]*Ibid.,* pp. 16, 29.

[14]*Ibid.,* p. 16.

[15]Richard H. Rovere, "Letter from Washington," *New Yorker* magazine, September 11, 1965, pp. 116–130.

[16]Mary McGrory, "The Non-Person at the Rights Parley," *Washington Evening Star,* November 19, 1965.

[17]William H. Grier and Price M. Cobbs, *Black Rage,* (New York: Basic Books, Inc., 1968), pp. 61–62.

[18]Joanne Clark, "Motherhood," in Toni Cade, ed., *The Black Woman* (New York: Signet Books, 1970), p. 65.

[19]Tillman, *Welfare,* p. 111.

[20]Douglas Turner Ward, *Happy Ending,* in *New Black Playwrights,* ed. William Couch, Jr. (New York: Avon Books, 1970), p. 34.

[21]Maya Angelou, *I Know Why the Caged Bird Sings* (New York: Random House, 1970).

[22]Joyce A. Ladner, *Tomorrow's Tomorrow,* (Garden City, N.Y.: Doubleday and Company, Inc., 1971), pp. 51–52.

[23]*Ibid.*, p. 52.

[24]*Ibid.*, p. 212.

[25]Urie Bronfenbrenner, "The Changing American Child: A Speculative Analysis," *Journal of Social Issues,* 17 (1961), 6–18.

[26]Kenneth Kenniston, *Young Radicals* (New York: Harcourt, Brace & World, Inc., 1968).

We wear the mask that grins and lies
It hides our cheeks and shades our eyes—
This debt we pay to human guile;
With torn and bleeding hearts we smile,
And mouth a myriad subtleties.

We smile, but O great Christ, our cries
To Thee from tortured souls arise,
We sing, but oh, the clay is vile
Beneath our feet, and long the mile;
But let the world dream otherwise,
We wear the masks.

PAUL LAURENCE DUNBAR[1]

We Wear the Masks

"She made it!" "I made it!" "Why can't you?"

When blacks take up this Horatio Alger theme, sexual identity makes no difference. Black women who "make it" do so because they are motivated by the need to achieve success. Throughout the years black women have sought a college education and job opportunities, particularly teaching, because they wanted to escape working in a white woman's kitchen. For many years even those marginal jobs like clerking in Woolworth's were for "whites only." So, a black woman's choice was to teach or become a domestic.

Now that discrimination in jobs is illegal, black women are entering professions other than teaching. They pursue better and better jobs with the attitude that nothing in their future, neither marriage nor children, will change the likelihood that they will need to work.

The choice is minimal. If they expect to share in the American way of life and enjoy some of its economic and social benefits, they will have to earn these in the occupational world. Most often in partnership with a mate, most probably alone at some time in their lives, but as certain as the ancient African mother's admonition to her daughters, "You are beautiful, but you cannot eat your looks, you must learn to work," American black sisters will have to work for what they get.

White women have usually evaluated their self-worth through their husband's occupation and status (isn't this what the women's liberation movement seeks to change?). Still other white women hold the purse strings to fortunes left by deceased husbands—

money which earns money while they sit idly by, or make a career of volunteering for various causes. Although more and more white women are entering the labor force, especially those in the highest educational brackets, this phenomenon is so recent that their participation is still considered by many to be a search for a more interesting life outside the home.[2] For black women a job has always been an economic necessity, even though some of us gain self-fulfillment as well.[3]

Black women strike out to "make it"—enter school, get a good job, gain a promotion—because there are few alternatives to self-worth and security outside the job market. Even in marriage, it's the black wife's earnings which provides that margin of income that enables her family to be categorized as middle class. In fact, income parity among young (under 35) blacks with white families is made possible *only* when the black wife works.[4]

That good job a black sister gets, however, is not taken without "paying dues." Her college degree and job, one or both, place her in a category called "middle class" and expose her to a life style that sets her apart from 70 percent of all other blacks. She is likely to be tracked across sociological tables, pictured in *Time* magazine and other publications as one of a growing number of blacks who "made it," thus winning the disdain of a growing number of whites who feel blacks somehow have it easier than they. Furthermore, that tenacity of spirit, that strength and sheer grit which motivates her into J. Walter Thompson, Exxon, and the high councils of government will all too often earn her the label "matriarch," with all the negative attitudes and "put-downs" Americans associate with that description.

The life of the college-educated, achievement-oriented black woman, married or single, is not only based on a long history of participation in the labor force, but includes as well leadership in family and community affairs. While the woman's income has consistently raised the financial base of the black family, black women have also carried the traditional role prescribed for all women in our society. They are volunteers in community affairs. They mold the character of children. And, unfortunately, some of them act out certain negative attitudes and values associated with social status and class distinctions.

Among this group are those who fantasize that they are specially privileged and turn against poor blacks—the group from which they narrowly escaped—viewing their lot with little empathy and sometimes overt antipathy. The "put-down" of welfare mothers at the bridge table, the snide contempt for "shiftless lazy Negroes" who "make it bad for the rest of us" is heard all too often. Such an attitude is unfortunate within an oppressed group whose destiny in America demands a group solidarity that cannot tolerate class warfare.

THE TYPICAL MASKS

Some who make it "up and out"—up from the ranks of the poor and out of the ghetto—wear masks of pretension which hide their real selves. Such masks enable some of us to be acceptable to whites, the masks of too many Aunt Jemimas who spend their lives preening and pleasing whites for personal advantage. They somehow believe it is a compliment when whites single them out as unusual or special. They seldom see that for every black who makes it in America, many more could also, were it not for systematic racism. This does not take anything away from those blacks who have made it; certainly, most have worked hard and diligently and deserve any advantage they enjoy. Other blacks, however, also have talents and drive, but the system allows for only a small black middle class (some 35 percent of all blacks as compared to 69 percent of whites made over $10,000 in 1973).[5] This kind of "making it" demands behavior and attitudes acceptable to whites because it is likely they control the opportunities for financial success. In contrast are those blacks who are visibly angry or nonconforming and unable to mask their true feelings about racism and injustice. The fact that they are seldom successful ought to call upon the greatest understanding from achieving blacks.

But, some blacks have worn the mask of conformity so long that the real face of anger and frustration lies repressed. Rage is rarely expressed. "To be a Negro in this country," wrote James Baldwin, "and to be relatively conscious is to be in a rage almost all of the time."

"One thing that whites need knowing," echo psychiatrists Cobbs and Grier, "is that all blacks are angry."

But to admit anger, much less rage, is to risk too much. And those of us who play out this role of pretense become what we act out. We forget that we repressed our own anger and denied our rage in order to achieve. So, the angry black who tells it like it is becomes a threat—especially to us.

There are also masks worn by blacks to impress other blacks. African mothers first used the mask as a scarecrow. They painted frightening faces on the bottom of water gourds in order to discourage their children from following village women to the waterholes.

Our in-group masks say: "Keep away while I do my thing." "If you come near me you'll get in my way." Attempts to avoid or scare off one's own people who are considered "lazy," "loud" and "ill-mannered" can be seen in the attitudes of some successful blacks. The achieving group often puts on airs and develops snobbish attitudes. Some have spent so much time emulating the outward mannerisms of successful whites and establishing a "Negro Society" that real communication problems now stand between those who have achieved middle-class status and the poor black masses.

Learning to affect certain attitudes, to strike certain poses, to deny our real feelings, likes, and dislikes stemming from common black experiences, has become par for the success course. Certainly, many may claim that they are bright, hard-working, and deserving of their status, but who will deny that a little bit of luck and the proper mask did not also contribute to success?

THE "CLOSE PROXIMITY" SYNDROME

It's difficult to assume life styles that make the middle-class group distinct or distant from poor blacks. The social system of America structures our lives in close proximity.

The middle class expanded from 9 percent making $10,000 and above in 1960 to 24 percent in 1969. Yet every possible social index—employment, education, housing, income, and family pathology—points to a growing poor black population.[6]

It is difficult to be black in America and hide from these facts. Residential patterns protect middle-class whites from the visible sight of poor whites. There are few such "hiding places" for comparable blacks. All too often the sheer struggle to move away from the ghetto saps all the resources and energies of this group. It has long been established that a middle-class style of living, particularly housing, costs more for blacks than whites in the same income bracket. Racist housing and employment patterns bind most blacks together in the same neighborhood, regardless of income. Poor blacks observe "better off" blacks from close quarters.

Furthermore, blacks who "make it" most often do so within a job context of administering, servicing, or teaching poor blacks. Most black teachers still teach black children, black social workers carry mostly black case loads. Poor blacks are visibly present, their struggles and setbacks a constant reminder that "there, but for the grace of God, go I."

Unfortunately, close proximity seldom develops empathy

among middle-class blacks. On the contrary, the situation often exaggerates negative attitudes toward blacks who haven't made it. One social worker was heard saying, "I think black women with too many children ought to be sterilized." Self-hatred is a constant stalking companion for all too many. Whether or not planned parenthood is desirable is not the point in this context. To be an agent of social control because too many black babies threaten and embarrass your position is questionable, when one has not faced the real economic issues of the "haves and have nots," and has failed to learn this from one's own reference group.

MASKS AND THE BLACK STRUGGLE

Masked behavior and pretense constantly threaten to undermine the major objectives of black liberation: group solidarity, planning and action. It is impossible to develop such solidarity when one segment of an oppressed group pretends that things are much better than they really are. It is impossible to eliminate "self-hatred" and work in a spirit of togetherness when a minority within an oppressed group resents the majority of its members and desires social distance.

In the Sixties many blacks began to shed some of the masks worn for white approval. Poor blacks openly challenged middle-class phoniness, especially if middle-class workers serviced or represented a poor black constituency. Many successful blacks learned during the War on Poverty days that they had become so alienated from blacks in the ghettos that communication was impossible. Imagine the shock when poor blacks threw many black leaders and professionals out of poverty programs, exhibiting more distrust of this group than of whites, and expressing a sense of being betrayed by their so-called leaders in words and reprisals more vitriolic than ever used with whites.

Almost irreconcilable are the ground rules for acceptance into white middle-class America and acceptance by poor black groups. The centers of action for black Americans are the ghettos of the land—the Harlems, Watts, and Buttermilk Bottoms! The issues there are very basic: unemployment, poor housing, poor schools, violence, and crime. It is hard to operate as a "phony" in the face of such life and death issues. The need for bold acknowledgement of injustices and their causes, and a commitment to change institutions, not "patch up" a few clients, demands an honesty that can be costly to the ambitious individual. It is always easier to administer to the victims than attack the institutions that created them.

The center of middle-class American values is the suburb. There, negotiation is polite, problem-solving is carefully structured, and the rules of the game are set by the power elite. Masking feelings so that they are acceptable to others is not only tolerated but encouraged. In the ghetto masks are torn away and labeled a pretentious nuisance. It is not inconsequential that "Tell it like it is," or "Right on" entered the language of communications during the Sixties. Contrast this with the Watergate "cover-up" language!

The black student revolt of the Sixties sought to avoid the "alienation anxiety" expressed by older generations. They feared that total immersion in white college life styles socialized them into a carbon copy of a white person, made them a "print-out sheet" representing something whites programmed, designed, and fed into a giant computer, somehow transforming blacks into something whites like, or at least can tolerate. Certainly changing institutions so that racism is eliminated is not a top American priority! Containing individual black troublemakers and a growing black lower class is!

Young blacks now say, "We will not wear masks!" We will "tell it like it is." And the continued existence of the black middle class as we have seen it is not only threatened by poor blacks, but rejected by those whom we normally expect to induct into the black middle class upon "coming of age"—the young sons and daughters of those "who made it."

THE VISIBILITY OF THE BLACK FEMALE MIDDLE CLASS

No group is more prone to "identity crises" than black women who have traditionally carried the onus of black snobbery. Therefore, black co-eds would perhaps be the first group to recognize that a college education might cause alienation from the masses of black people. Their fears are well founded.

The most visible symbol of black middle-class status and style of life comes to the ghetto as a female. She, not the black male, is most often the hated social worker, the insensitive teacher, and more recently, the indifferent nurse. She represents the bourgeoisie in the slums. The census has traditionally enumerated more black women than men in those occupational categories sociologists designate as "middle class." Though the income level of black male workers as a group is higher than that of females, more black women than men are in white-collar occupations.

Furthermore, the middle-class black woman, unlike the black

man, has no common meeting place—a bar, a poolroom, the racetrack, which provides informal and nonthreatening opportunities for different social classes to come together. She is locked into a social system that formalizes her relationships with poor black women. Neither can she easily cross class lines for sexual experiences and expect to keep her reputation. She has to move with the right people.

Finally, the style of living one desires for one's children is most often managed by the woman. Visible to the poor black is not the father's demand that his child not play with this or that child, but the mother's intercession in fights, or appearances in school to see that her child socializes with "proper" people. Class differences are always more rigid for girl than boy children and are usually enforced by mothers. So, the slum mother comes to see the middle-class mother as snobbish, rejecting, and uptight.

Hence, in all visible matters and noticeable ways, it is unfortunately the black middle-class woman who is the brunt of the poor black's epithets about those "dickty" Negroes.

BLACK CLASS STRUCTURE

All people everywhere, despite the circumstances, tend to sort themselves into categories that define some as better than others. Black people are no exception.

Africa recognized different statuses, and class differences accompanied the slaves across the middle passage. Aboard those ships were queens, some of whom the Spanish and Portuguese freed when their status was discovered. But not in America. Here the lust for black labor threw all sanity to the winds; the only marks of distinction important on the auction block were descriptions like "strong," and "a good breeder."

The "plantation aristocracy," with its division of labor, as discussed earlier, further contributed toward a status system. A kind of reciprocity between whites and blacks evolved. And in that complex tangle of relationships those of both races who traversed the fine line of social demarcation were punished.

From a plantation aristocracy there emerged black families who indeed started their freedom days better off than the field blacks. Many who worked for white aristocracy continued to do so after freedom came. Though they received little in the way of wages, many, like Mamba, had the protection of the white power structure.

As recently as the Sixties, teachers in many parts of the South were given jobs upon recommendation of some "good white family." Jobs as postal clerks—all of the jobs that paved the way for the emerging black middle class—were controlled by whites and available to those blacks who were sponsored by them. White connections and paternalism were as much the foundation of the black middle class as was "mixed blood."

That house blacks were snobbish and privileged is no idle talk. And domestics, the last group "in service" to white families after the Civil War, did indeed use their privileged status to give subsequent generations of their children a chance to get educated, to gain entry into white-collar jobs, to become doctors, teachers, and other professionals.

It is not only to the house slave group, however, or their descendants who worked in white homes of the South after the Civil War, that any notion of a black privileged class has come. There were those Negroes freed prior to the Civil War who formed a "mulatto aristocracy" and established itself as the so-called upper class.

THE MULATTO ARISTOCRACY*

Essential to the establishment of the first free families was the founding member—usually a woman whose sexual relationship to a white man made it possible for her to gain freedom and set up a dwelling apart from both blacks and whites. These mulatto women were in most cases the offspring of white slaveholders and female slaves. In some instances the slavemasters freed their mistresses, often when their wives were cruel to them and the man wanted to continue the relationship indefinitely. Most of these relationships, however, were exploitative and fleeting, and only a few led to freedom.

Some white slavemasters, by no means the majority, freed their mulatto offspring. And, some established plans to ensure the education and future of these children.[7]

Where the freedman was male, he was able to establish a paternalistic family patterned after those of whites. But, since most of those freed persons were females, left to fend for themselves or dependent on a white male benefactor for sustenance, the life style of freedmen was greatly influenced by black women. "A woman's work" became an essential factor in social status designations, continuing an unbroken tradition of placing high value on a black woman's earning capacity. In the early days, as in the example of

*While the correct definition of a mulatto includes the first generation offspring of a white and a black person and of persons of mixed white and black ancestry, over the years blacks include those who are light skinned and whose features are similar to whites.

Elizabeth Keckley (see Chapter 3) freed women marketed domestic skills, particularly needlework, and little else.

These freed mulatto women were no pampered lot, not even the concubines. Who but the latter knew so well the transitory nature of their love relationships? They were unprotected by law and subject to the whims of their mates. There have always been new problems (as well as new hopes) created when an unmarried woman is faced with rearing a child. While some might have been able to live isolated from both white and black worlds in order to please their white lovers, few women are willing to subject their children to a life of isolation. Whereas a freed man had the advantage of mobility and the independence to consider only his own welfare, the woman always had to make decisions about her children that limited her mobility.

These black concubines learned early to develop skills and to work. Black men have traditionally resented white men having sexual access to black women while they were lynched for simply glancing at a white woman. All too often, however, this resentment has led to a mistaken belief that black women preferred white men to black men. Moreover, the benefits to black women involved in such liaisons were exaggerated, even mythicized.

In the first novel published by a black man, James Wells Brown wrote that "most of the slave women have no higher aspiration than that of becoming the finely dressed mistress of some white man."[8] The theme of *Clotel* is that of a "tragic mulatto" whose mother, Currer, allegedly bore her by Thomas Jefferson. Apart from furthering the misconception of black women's preference for white men, Brown constructed a fascinating picture of what life was like for those suspended between the black and white worlds, not entirely trusted by either group.

While Brown goes to great lengths to detail the plight of one who is "as white as any Anglo-Saxon," the distinguished writer and author Sterling Brown points to the "tragic octoroon mulatto" theme as a favorite one for white writers, as well, implying that sympathy could more easily be aroused for mulattos than pure blacks. With some sarcasm Sterling Brown could detect that whites would take the position "how could such dastardly things be done to people who, but for a legal technicality, are really white!"[9]

George Cable, a white writer, embellishes the tragic quadroon (a person with more white blood than a mulatto) theme in *Madam Delphine*:

> During the first quarter of the present century, the free quadroon

> caste of New Orleans was in its golden age. Old travellers spare no terms to tell their praises, their faultlessness of feature, their perfection of form, their varied styles of beauty—for there were even pure Caucasian blondes among them—their fascinating manners, their sparkling vivacity, their chaste and pretty wit, their grace in the dance . . . their taste and elegance in dress . . . they were indeed the sirens of the land, where it seems always afternoon . . . the balls that were got up for them . . . were to that day what the carnival is to the present.[10]

Cable went on to say that it was useless for whites to hold society balls on the night of these quadroon balls since all the leading white males were at the latter.

Madam Delphine, a quadroon, was established in a home by a Creole of aristocratic family. A child Olive was born of this union. After years of separation and mistreatment, the daughter comes to live once more with Delphine.

"Does she look like you, Madam Delphine?" asks a priest when told of the child's coming.

"Oh thank God, no! You would never believe she was my daughter; she is white and beautiful!"[11]

The tragic mulatto theme! And again, self-hatred.

The first black female novelists dealt also with the tragic mulatto theme. Their choice of this theme leaves little doubt that the mulatto woman was occupying a highly visible place in the social class structure of blacks. These writers, however, focused on the inability of the black heroine to identify successfully with black society and pointed up the conflicts inherent in identifying with one or the other race.

The first of these novels, published in 1892 and written by Francis Walker Harper,[12] describes the conflicts inherent in her heroine Iola's near-white status. There is no question that Mrs. Walker is convinced that near-white blacks must totally identify with their black brothers or suffer continuous conflicts and ambivalence.

Nella Larsen, one of the writers who helped create the Harlem Renaissance, wrote two books, *Quicksand* and *Passing,* published in the late Twenties, describing the inner conflicts between "primitive jungle feelings" as represented by black blood, and the pull of a white world.[13] The author, a mulatto, gives no prescription for solving the "mixed blood" conflict. She simply describes the pull of two opposites, highlighting the attractiveness and negative conditions of both, leaving the lives of both heroines tragically unresolved at the end.

Jessie Fauset wrote four novels during the same period, but, like Francis Walker's, her heroines resolve their mulatto tragedy through total identification with black people. One of her novels, *The Chinaberry Tree,* is typical of her fictional approach to the emotional trials borne by those of mixed blood.[14]

The image of the mulatto woman as a desirable part of the aristocracy of that time became well established in the minds of blacks over several generations. What black writers had done by the time the description "black bourgeoisie" became a term of derisiveness was to put the mulatto status in some perspective. Those who passed for white were seldom allowed to do so comfortably, as we see from the novels of Fauset and Larsen. There was always an eventual intermingling of "mixed blood" mulattos with an evolving respectable black-skinned enterprising group. The near-white complexion and white features of a mulatto became negotiable for an esteemed place among blacks, especially for mulatto women who married black-skinned men. Those blacks with African features, however, soon discovered that they had best get a good education and job or they would fail to make it at all.

Neither blacks nor whites have accepted a mulatto ancestral claim to hereditary status. Such claims are contrary to the American ethos, "to gain status by virtue of family descent has been an uneasy practice . . . never touching more than a small fraction of the population."[15] Furthermore, opinion and prejudice enshrined in the saying "three generations from shirt sleeves to shirt sleeves" has largely discredited the idea of inherited status as being "either foolish, non-existent, obsolete, or nefarious."[16] Disrespect for class distinctions, coupled with a belief among whites that blacks are genetically inferior, did not cause the nation to seriously accept mulatto claims to superiority.

Their own disdain for class distinction, however, did not keep whites from making class distinctions among blacks—after all, the small amount of white blood had to make some difference—and so they favored those who looked most like them.

Margaret Just Butcher, a descendant of a mulatto "first family" and a distinguished scholar, noted that "there was a deferential treatment of the mulatto in an effort to develop a . . . buffer class. Such privileges granted them more opportunity and recognition than was given to other blacks, but always something less than was a standard for privileged whites."[17] In this case, opportunity meant a chance, through education, to become a professional, and recognition meant that other blacks came to see this group as brokers for a white system that was oppressive for all blacks regardless of background.

Slavery and then later legal segregation followed by the racism of the Seventies have now labeled *all* blacks as "have-nots" and make status pretentions divisive and distracting.

Moreover, no hereditary status has given any black family of mulatto background the usual things associated with "first family," namely power and wealth. Even when black families with well-documented evidence of kinship with luminaries like Martha Washington and Thomas Jefferson[18] laid claim to white kinship, there was never a payoff in actual power and wealth.

For those with a need for self-affirmation, the recognition of prestigious white blood might make them feel that this somehow brings them closer to power, to white acceptance. But unless there is tangible evidence of some kind of superior status, specifically the power to make one's will felt through sanctions, negative or positive, to demonstrate some control over institutions of power, then one's so-called inferiors are rarely persuaded to confirm such pretentious claims.

Yet the "mulatto claim to superiority" continued in some subtle forms throughout the generations, and in some instances continues today. For a long period of time, before the emergence of the "black consciousness" era of the Sixties, there was more truth than joke to the often chanted rhymes of black childhood:

> If you're black, stay back
> If you're brown, stick around
> If you're white, everything is right!

MIDDLE-CLASS STATUS AND THE "BLACK BOURGEOISIE"

There are few terms associated with black people that raise as much in-group anger as "black bourgeoisie." Always a definition is demanded, always an argument at hand. "Middle class" can be defined sociologically and dutifully documented with facts from a large body of social class theory. Various indices including occupation, income, education, social status, and place of residence are scientifically balanced in order to distribute Americans up and down a social pyramid ranging from upper class to lower class, with the upper class being the smallest and the most powerful class. Middle-class standing in this sense describes a sociological phenomenon which places a class between the upper and lower class.

To apply social class theory to the black population, however, without understanding the ramifications of in-group class structure is to greatly misunderstand the ordering of social positions among blacks.

Soon after slavery there was a recognized black "upper class" whose characteristics were unlike those in the white society. It consisted of mulattos who gained free status during slavery and were able to gain a small economic advantage in the job market before emancipation. Such a head start established their claim to black aristocracy and gave them the title of "old families."

E. Franklin Frazier believed that this class had higher standards of morality and a superior culture to that of the great mass of blacks,[19] though they were distributed among several occupations usually associated with lower-class jobs. "There was a class of caterers, clerks, teachers, professional men, small merchants . . . who constituted the aristocracy of the Negroes,[20] and even "carpenters, barbers, waiters and Pullman porters."[21]

One hardly finds clerks and waiters among a white upper class. But the occupations open to freedmen were limited, and the ability to get and keep any job was remarkable enough to win esteem among other blacks.

The "old" mulatto families had always shown contempt for the black immigrants who came from the plantations, but they accepted a few into their ranks when their behavior and enterprising ways merited it. Inevitably, mulattos had to mate outside their circle. It became a mark of distinction for achieving black males to win a "light-skinned lady." Not only did this mulatto status contribute toward self-hatred among black-skinned people, but it established an attraction-repulsion tenseness in relationships among all.

The mulatto aristocracy's preoccupation with pride of white ancestry, as well as their powerlessness, contributed toward a distaste for class distinctions among poor blacks. Certainly the "old mulatto families" produced the largest number of professional Negroes for several decades, but not enough to continue a mulatto aristocracy for too many generations.

So-called "society" women contributed toward the perpetuation of a class structure as the "chief sticklers and arbiters."[22] They set the style for acceptable behavior and morals. A rigid morality code and a genteel tradition of culture and refinement of manners were ideals they sought to further among themselves and the masses. This included imitating the uncorrupted language of the cultured whites, the best literature (white), and love of the classics. Their pattern of behavior was copied from the life styles of Southern white ladies and as James Weldon Johnson put it "a replica of all the pettiness of 'society' in general."

By 1900 the "mulatto aristocracy" had been diluted by intermarriage with black-skinned Negroes. Those who had no near-white complexion to offer negotiated for entrance into black society by industriousness and good jobs.

A middle class now evolved which included men and women in business enterprises and white-collar occupations, those engaged in professional pursuits, and those employed in responsible positions in public service. Though this newly accepted group sloughed off some of the traditions of the old mulatto families, they too were uncomfortable with the black masses. Personal success and economic advancement ordered their lives.

During this period dark-skinned blacks accumulated enough money (though very little compared with whites) to compete with the old mulatto families for leadership positions and in educating their children.

Unlike white aristocracy, black upper-class status did not help any of them to accumulate wealth—surely not enough to control jobs and opportunities for other blacks. Neither did their status keep them from constant humiliation by whites. They had no land, little money, and no clout. Black aristocracy rested its laurels on mixed blood, fancy behavior, and a rigid moral code. None of this equaled power, and lower-class blacks seldom hesitated to tell them so. The black masses never developed a genuine respect for upper-class Negroes and had nothing to lose or fear by laughing at them.

By the Fifties, the old mulatto families and the black-skinned middle class had lost all rigid distinctions along color lines and had become amalgamated into the "black bourgeoisie." The term, most often identified with the eminent sociologist E. Franklin Frazier, had come to define a group with the usual middle-class jobs and incomes in the occupational dictionary, but with a certain style of life and set of aspirations and attitudes. Frazier was quite specific in describing the characteristics of the black bourgeoisie.

> . . . a group without cultural roots in either the Negro world with which it refuses to identify or the white world which refuses to accept it.
>
> . . . a deep-seated sense of inferiority as a result of rejection by whites.
>
> . . . because of feeling inferior, compensation by living in a world of make believe. In this world there are "socialites" and "a

society." All of this is an escape from the reality of their subordinate status in America.

> . . . great confusion and considerable personality conflict caused by constant striving for status both within the Negro world and the white world.
>
> . . . an unconditional acceptance of the values of the white world.
>
> . . . extreme self-hatred; disdain for things that remind them of the black folk culture.
>
> . . . education that has been shaped by bourgeoisie ideals based on Puritan morality.
>
> . . . extreme sensitivity to the slights and discrimination Negroes suffer because of a feeling that they, as individuals, have paid all of the dues America has demanded, plus more, and are above discrimination . . .[23]

Such descriptions are powerful indictments against any group, especially one that claims race pride and upliftment as cardinal virtues and cannot overcome racial discrimination along class lines. Even if Professor Frazier's assessment could be dismissed, the Poverty Program's philosophy of the Sixties—maximum feasible participation of the poor—gave poor blacks the power to act on Frazier's concepts, and in city after city they rejected the participation of middle-class blacks in key policy positions, or forced them to develop skills in working with them.

A disavowal of the traditional leadership of the middle-class has raised many unresolved questions. What is the function of educated blacks in a racist society? Of what functional use is an "elite" group when the caste status of blackness relegates all blacks throughout the world to a common inferior status?

And more significant to this book, what role do black women play in the perpetuation of both "good" and "bad" elements of middle-class behavior?

THE MIDDLE-CLASS WOMAN'S JOB AND INCOME

Unlike the case with many white women, the claim to middle-class status for black women is seldom solely a function of one's identity as "Mrs. Doctor So and So" whose prestige is a reflection of a husband's social standing and occupation. For us, the American housewife syndrome where "Diaries of A Mad Housewife" intone the frustrations and idleness of Friedan's *Feminine Mystique* is a rarity, confined to the upper reaches of black income where black men's occupations do not require the woman to be employed outside the home. Some wives of civil rights leaders, of public officials of national prominence, of the giants of the "Black Enterprise/100 Most Successful Black Businesses," and of doctors, perhaps, would be a group from which "housewife only" designations would be found.

Most black families considered middle class are so designated because both husband and wife are wage earners. They are families that have fewer children on the average than whites in similar circumstances and they are likely to have a female wage earner who is a college graduate.

In 1972 the median income of black families in which both husbands and wives worked was $11,566, compared to $6,949 where only the husbands worked. Among couples under 35 years old, 70 percent were joint wage earners, compared to 57 percent of comparable white couples, and young black families in the North and South had achieved income parity with their white counterparts. The black woman's earnings comprised 43 percent of the mean income of the black husband-wife earners, compared to 36 percent contributed by white wives.

These women certainly are not working for pocket money. And yet, the kind of jobs held by black women with their academic degrees, which enable them to fight for "good jobs," also contribute toward the matriarchy myth which is so divisive and destructive in black male-female relationships.

In 1973 approximately 29 percent of all employed black women, compared to 27 percent of all employed black men, were considered professional, technical, managers and administrators (except farm), as compared to 40 percent of white females and 57 percent of all white men.[24]

However, the extent to which the working environment called "white collar," with all of its assumed benefits, establishes any sense of superiority is tempered by the fact that most of the so-called white-collar jobs held by women, both white and black, are clerical. This category accounted in 1973 for over one third of all white women and nearly one fourth of all black women. Furthermore, since legal job discrimination ended, the fastest growing occupation for black women is clerical.

Blue-collar workers accounted for 58 percent of all black men who worked, yet this group has accumulated median earnings of $6,338, while no specific occupation within the clerical field, where 24 percent of black women worked, accounted for more than a median income of $5,000 for black women. In no category of blue-collar work did black men have such a low median income.

A better index of middle class presence is participation in the professional, technical, and managerial positions, the prestigious and most financially rewarding categories in America. Even here, white and black women are doing "women's work." Nearly 50 percent of black women in this category were teachers, below the college and university level, and nearly 25 percent were nurses. The occupations in the white-collar category held by black men were clearly more highly paid and prestigious than those held by black women.

In 1972, however, black women had moved slightly ahead of professional white women in median income ($7,181, compared to $6,307) among all workers.[25] This is due largely to black women's reaching income parity with white women in the traditional female fields of teaching and nursing, and the presence of more part-time white women in the labor force. Even so, among college graduate women and those holding higher degrees (see Table 2), the black woman is never more than $1,000 behind white women in median income.

This is not to say that black women have "made it." They are under-represented in medicine, law, and engineering; in teaching they are under-represented in university administrative posts and as college and university full professors. Their most recent occupational breakthroughs are as managers and administrators. While this group represents only one percent of all black female workers, compared to 5 percent of white females and 3 percent of the black males; at least one black woman, Ernesta Procope, was listed as owner of one of the 100 top black businesses. Those black female managers and administrators with a college education had just about reached parity with white women who earned $8,335 in 1969 as compared to $8,285 earned by black women. The median income for black men was $9,843. Of course, white men were considerably ahead with median earnings of $15,030 in this category.[26]

The number of black women holding public office has doubled, since 1969 from 131 to 337. Four black congresswomen serve in the House of Representatives. The first one elected, Shirley Chisholm of New York, also ran for the Presidency of the United States. Congresswoman Barbara Jordan of Texas won great public acclaim as a brilliant and articulate member of the Judiciary Committee during the Nixon impeachment hearings and, as the polls clearly indicate, is surely headed for higher political office, maybe even the Vice Presidency!

TABLE 1

WHITE-COLLAR OCCUPATIONS (MEN/WOMEN) 1973

	White Men	*White Women*	*Black Men*	*Black Women*
Total number employed (thousands)	46,830	28,448	3,999	5,133
White-collar workers	41.7%	63.3%	22.9%	41.5%
Professional and technical	14.2	14.9	8.2	12.0
Medical and other health	1.4	3.8	1.0	3.4
Teachers (except college)	1.7	6.5	1.4	5.0
Other professional and technical	11.0	4.6	5.8	3.7
Managers and administrators (except farm)	14.5	5.2	5.2	2.6
Salaried workers	11.5	4.0	3.7	1.9
Self-employed	2.9	1.2	1.5	0.8
Sales workers	6.5	7.5	2.1	2.5
Retail trade	2.4	6.3	1.2	2.2
Other industries	4.1	1.2	0.9	0.3
Clerical workers	6.5	35.7	7.4	24.4

Source: Tables 38, 39: *The Social and Economic Status of the Black Population in the United States,* 1973, Special Studies Series P-23, No. 48. U.S. Department of Commerce.

TABLE 2

Earnings and Education of Professional, Technical and Kindred Workers: Worked 50 to 52 Weeks in 1969

	Total Number of Workers	*Median Income*	*$10,000 to $14,999*	*$15,000 and more*
Professional, Technical, and Kindred Workers				
White Males				
Total, 25 to 64 years old	4,729,074	12,237	1,736,992	1,404,683
College: 4 years	1,130,243	12,987	454,376	382,221
5 years or more	1,599,751	14,110	497,235	711,334
Black Males				
Total, 25 to 64 years old	131,332	9,095	37,159	15,637
College: 4 years	30,880	9,496	10,287	3,417
5 years or more	33,774	11,684	11,770	9,082
White Females				
Total, 25 to 64 years old	1,561,751	7,172	226,815	47,559
College: 4 years	365,885	7,775	58,196	10,329
5 years or more	298,124	9,056	89,948	29,532
Black Females				
Total, 25 to 64 years old	138,712	6,771	17,396	2,388
College: 4 years	34,796	7,460	4,712	314
5 years or more	21,792	8,971	6,455	1,351

Source: *Earnings by Occupation and Education,* Subject Reports, 1970 Census, U.S. Department of Commerce, Bureau of the Census (PC 2)–8B, Tables 1, 2, 3, 7 and 8.

In diplomacy, Patricia Roberts Harris had the distinction of serving as the first black woman ambassador to a foreign country and has been appointed Secretary of Housing and Urban Development—another first. At the supergrade level of government, GS 16–18, there were thirteen black women, actually 11 percent of all women in those grades and 10 percent among blacks. Again, black women are more likely than black men to achieve parity with their white counterparts in most fields, but racial barriers still brake rapid progress. In 1973, black women represented 22 percent of all full-time people working as federal employees. Whenever the government is the employer, the median income of black women is twice as high as that of her sisters who are self-employed or who work in the private sector. Higher earnings appear to be more possible in government, since 5.2 percent of government workers make $10,000 or more, compared to 2 percent or less of those otherwise employed.

Though the black professional male with a college degree has a median income of $9,496 (Table 2), which is about $2,000 more than both white and black women, it is precisely this close proximity in status and income—first to black women who are competing quite favorably with white women as new opportunities unfold, and then to white women—that perhaps accounts for his fear that women will outdistance him and are gaining more opportunities than he. This often makes black men feel competitive with these two groups. (In a sexist society, who wants to compete with women?) The black male measures himself against white men, and as he sees his position economically, "much like women's," he often forgets who his real competitor is—white men!

The distance between the $12,236 median income of the white professional male and the $9,095 of the black male is still a great distance to overcome, almost as great as the gap between black and white male managers and administrators (Table 2). Table 3 shows that again black men run neck and neck with black and white women, but there is a $6,000 gap between the college educated black manager and his white male counterpart.

Probably the theory of a "close proximity" to women's economic status explains the black man's frustration in the competition for jobs and income, not the black woman's "bossiness" or tendency to be matriarchal. Here, in the statistics of jobs comes a story of black women having milked the economy for all it offers *women,* rather than of their emergence in jobs that black men desire. It is a proud legacy of their having competed quite successfully with white women, proving that opportunity gains a positive response from them. Particularly in the newly evolving careers in management do we see that black women may even move ahead of white women in median income.

While there are, in fact, more college-educated black women than men in the general population, black men with the same degrees have a higher median income than do the women (Table 2). While there are numerically more black women in the white-collar and professional categories and even managerial occupations, black men, again, exceed them in median income.

Though black men are doing better than black women economically, they are running "nip and tuck" in a close competitive game with women in a society where men are supposed to be clearly superior to women. Like it or not, the measure of a man is how much money he can make, what he can do with it, and whether or not his job attracts esteem. White men are so clearly outdistancing the rest of society in occupations and income that it should be obvious that it is a piece of Charley's action that the "have-nots" desire, not a "close proximity" fight for what women and blacks hack out of society for their own survival.

Hence, the black middle class woman emerges in the marketplace as a necessary participant of black economic life, though not appreciated enough for this by black men, and as a fierce competitor with white women for jobs and status. Doubtlessly she feels she's caught in the middle, likely at any time to be the target of both groups.

BLACK WOMEN'S ORGANIZATIONS

For every individual black woman who makes it in the career world, there is probably another badge of identification—that of the organizational woman—which distinguishes her life and is a part of her life style.

For some, club and organizational affiliation is an index of social position.

"There is yet no large Negro 'jet set,' " wrote Hyman in *Look* magazine some time ago. "But the Negro first families of Washington hold a strategic position in American Negro society. At the junior level are the Jack and Jill clubs, which introduce proper young boys to proper young girls. Next comes the December Cotillion, where twenty carefully screened girls are presented during the Christmas season to their social peers. Feeder lines reach out to Alpha Kappa Alpha and Alpha Phi Alpha, the most prestigious Negro sorority and fraternity. Later, the chosen move up to women's

TABLE 3

Earnings and Education of Managers and Administrators (Except Farm) by Work Experience in 1969 Worked 50 to 52 Weeks in 1969

	White Men	*Black Men*	*Black Women*	*White Women*
Median earnings (all levels of education) 25 to 64 years old)	**$12,101**	**$8,382**	**$6,085**	**$6,246**
College: 4 years	**15,030**	**9,843**	**8,285**	**8,335**
5 years or more	**16,736**	**13,055**	**12,129**	**11,121**

clubs like the Links and Girl Friends, sponsors of the December Cotillion."[27]

Prior to the organization of the Links, Moles, Girl Friends, and a few others, the college-based sororities were considered the reigning elitists. For many years at Howard University, for example, few other than light-skinned girls with "brains" and "family connections" could join Delta Sigma Theta. This sorority, and possibly others, democratized their ranks when the state colleges and the land grant rural-based universities were credentialized to establish sorority chapters. Shortly after World War II the rush of poor, bright, first-generation co-eds from these colleges simply changed the color and style of the sororities.

Yet the "color and style" issue surfaced as recently as 1971, when Delta Sigma Theta elected Lillian Benbow, a dark-skinned woman with an Afro, as its fifteenth President. Some of the "old-timers" were quite vocal about her hair not being acceptable and expressed a fear of her militancy.

We do wear masks!

Ironically, Lillian Benbow became the first national president of any black women's organization in history to challenge her membership of 85,000 women to "break new ground" by moving beyond social services to economic ownership and institutional change. She established a corporate entity, DST Telecommunications, Inc., an outgrowth of Delta Sigma Theta through which members and nonmembers invested financially in a record and movie designed to change negative media images of black women, and present positive ones.

Clubs, lodges, societies, organizations, and sororities have been strongest in providing a training ground for individual talents, as in the cases of Congresswoman Barbara Jordan and HUD Secretary Patricia Robert Harris, both of whom developed strong leadership skills in Delta Sigma Theta. Like white women who developed a parallel organizational system for themselves as an expression of their need to be involved outside the home and to avoid forcing the issue of joining men's groups, black women channeled their energies and interests into various organizations. Perhaps parallel male-female structures started in Reconstruction, when black men for a short while had the vote and spent much time in political activity while women tended school activities.

For some women, these organizations have always represented a potential for collective power. "Men always underestimate women," wrote Shirley Chisholm. "They underestimated me and they underestimated women like me. . . . The women are always organizing for something, even if it's only a bridge club . . . they are the backbone of the social clubs and civic clubs, even more than the men. So the organization was always there. All I had to do was get its help. I went to the presidents and the leaders and asked, 'Can you help me?' If I succeeded in convincing them, they were ready to help . . and able."[28] Looking back at her Presidential campaign failings, however, she acknowledged the potential power of organizations: "I tell you what was lacking. I had no support from the black female organizations. Where was the National Council of Negro Women? Where were the Deltas? They simply never turned on to my campaign."[29]

That their support might have made a difference in the outcome of her campaign is doubtful. That they failed to see the political implications of demonstrating such power by uniting around Shirley Chisholm is, perhaps, an example of their political immaturity. Women's organizations have a tremendous potential for collective action on behalf of black people, but rarely have they moved beyond the safest "feminine" course of action. They pass resolutions which eloquently express their outrage against injustice. When institutions fail, they minister to the victims in service projects. There is scarcely an American middle-class virtue that they have not extolled in constituency after constituency. But to move as an aggregate group to bring about institutional change has been difficult for them. Like white women's organizations, they have had a history of serving as "the conscience" for the nation. Very few risks have brought them into the social change arena, where unpopularity might result. And while raising the consciousness level of the nation about what is wrong is admirable, moving boldly to right these wrongs requires a tenacity of spirit and effort, and such collective strength has yet to be fully demonstrated. And this is a pity considering the number of strong, skilled black women who excel as individuals, but as one young sister said, "can't get it together organizationally."

Early Organizational Efforts

While the pioneering leaders of black women's clubs were in the top financial and educational strata, their prime motivating force was social betterment through recognition and destruction of racial and social inequities suffered by all blacks. Local clubs sprang up, usually connected with churches, where caring for the sick and needy and support of the preacher and the church in general were of the highest priority. There were even some literary clubs formed by black women, whose objectives were to improve cultural and educational opportunities for their children.

There is considerable disagreement concerning the founding of the first national organization for black women. Exactly where and by whom it was founded is perhaps not as important as identifying the reasons that prompted the women to organize in the first place.

Between 1892 and 1897 a confluence of activities led to the organization of the National Association of Colored Women, of which Mary Church Terrell was the first president.

Early in 1892 a few women had begun to respond to the speeches and writings of Ida B. Wells, surely one of the most militant of the early organizers. That same year, Victoria Matthews of New York and Maritcha Lyons of Brooklyn organized a committee of 250 women to raise enough money to enable Ida Wells to continue her publishing and lecturing campaign against the common practice of lynching.[30]

Another active organizational woman of that time was Josephine St. Pierre Ruffin of Boston, through whose efforts Ida Wells met Mary Church Terrell. Thus, the paths of these three organizational pioneers converged, each bringing to their common cause different backgrounds and somewhat different ideas concerning the priorities and means of accomplishing goals. And yet, out of their lives and struggles, each in her turn left a definite imprint on the development and growth of the earliest national organizations, shaping their initial aims and influencing the direction of organizational life even today.

Ida B. Wells Barnett

One of the most active and forceful women on the early organizational scene was Ida B. Wells. Born of slave parents in Holly Springs, Mississippi, just six months before the Emancipation Proclamation was declared, Ida Wells was marked to be a fighter early in life. Orphaned by a yellow fever epidemic, young Ida was left to rear her five younger siblings, and at the age of fifteen she was able to pass the test which enabled her to start teaching in a local rural school.

When she was 22, a better teaching job opened up in Memphis. Her trip to Tennessee opened up another path, one which was to lead Ida Wells from rural teaching to a life dedicated to the struggle of humanizing white society and extending justice to those left outside its doors.

While traveling to her new job, a conductor attempted to move her from the ladies' car to a smoker. Laws had not been passed to segregate blacks into "Jim Crow" cars at that time and each conductor set up his own coercive tactics to handle black passengers. Ida, of course, refused to move and was forced to get off the train rather than face physical abuse.[31]

Filing a suit against the railroad, she was awarded damages of $500 and her first newspaper headline, "A Darky Damsel Obtains a Verdict for Damages. . . ." Though the State Supreme Court reversed the findings, Ida was already launched on a long crusade in which disappointments and reversals were to become frequent grist for the mill.

Ida Wells could never have won a popularity contest. She attacked blacks for their lack of courageous leadership and preachers for failing to "lead people into practical consideration of their plight." She irritated both blacks and whites, who for different reasons did not want to rock the social boat. Clearly, she was too controversial for teaching.

She started writing and was later offered part ownership of the *Memphis Free Press.* She became the first black to write an exposé on lynching, making this her cause célèbre. She took the lynching issue to Europe. She cajoled black women to organize and lend their good names to this cause. The women not only rejected her ideas, but ended up rejecting her.

She helped organize a boycott of Memphis businesses that may have become the model for the boycotts of the sixties.

The combination of Ida's organizing talents and penmanship was too much for Memphis whites. A mob destroyed the offices of her paper and she was warned not to come home after attending a meeting out of the state. Relocating in New York, she began writing for *The New York Age* and came into contact with other black women just beginning to organize into formal groups. She met and influenced Victoria Matthews, Maritcha Lyons, and Josephine St. Pierre Ruffin, founders of the New York Women's Legal Union and the New Era Club of Boston. Even they steered clear of Ida's "lynching issue."

Within the ranks of groups dedicated to bettering black life, Ida Wells was just too outspoken for their tastes. Her stormy battles with Mary Church Terrell, President of the National Association of Colored Women's Clubs; Francis Willard, President of the Women's Christian Temperance Union of America, even Susan B. Anthony, are painfully detailed in her autobiography. Yet nothing stopped her. In 1895 she married a Chicago attorney, Ferdinand Lee Barnett, adding family responsibilities and the rearing of their son to her other duties. She was one of the group that conceived and organized the NAACP. She fought for prison reforms. One of her last courses was an investigation of that city's race riots just before her death in 1931. She was never far from the fiercest battles; she was aggressive and verbal, and she made many enemies, but her shadow still stretches over the continuing fight for black justice. Black women's organizations might indeed have emerged more courageously today had Mrs. Terrell and Mrs. Ruffin accepted Ida *and* her "lynching issue."

Josephine St. Pierre Ruffin[32]

Josephine St. Pierre Ruffin brought to the organizational movement an air of elegance possible only from one born to an aristocratic New England mulatto family. There was nothing in her immediate past to bind this woman to the great masses of her people, and yet she was to start a movement which would ultimately cross her own rigid social boundaries.

Her early married years were spent in England, so she was removed from the crippling effects of American discrimination. Returning after the Civil War, she and her husband, George Ruffin, a graduate of Harvard Law School and the first black man named to a judgeship in Boston, settled in that city.

Before she joined forces with the black women's organizations, Mrs. Ruffin was already well established in club life through associations with distinguished white women like Julia Ward Howe, Susan B. Anthony, and Elizabeth Stanton.

Perhaps it was Mrs. Ruffin's aristocratic background combined with her refined circle of friends that made her concern center not so much on Ida Wells' lynching issue but rather on attacks in the press on the moral character of Negro women. "One of the pressing needs of our cause is the attention of the public to a just appreciation of us," she said in an address to representatives of some twenty black clubs who had answered her "Call to Meeting" in July of 1897.

While Ida Wells wanted confrontation with the real issues affecting the lives of all blacks, it was clear that Mrs. Ruffin wanted respectability for those "well off" black women who had measured up to the model of sacred womanhood established by white society.

Nevertheless, through Josephine St. Pierre Ruffin's efforts to show the world the virtues of quality black women, the wheels were set in motion for the organization of the National Association of Colored Women's Clubs (NACW), a group in which she served as vice-president and remained active until her death in 1895.

Mary Church Terrell

Mary Church Terrell was seen at age 82 hobbling across a busy Washington intersection. When offered a lift she said, "Oh no, son, I don't have time to ride. You get out and join me on the picket line."

According to her biographer, Gladys Shepperd, "At eighty-five, she set her hand to the greatest task of her career and wrung from destiny one of the most revolutionary social changes that the nation and the nation's capital had ever witnessed: The Supreme Court Decision on June 8, 1953, in the John R. Thompson Restaurant Case, which rang the death knell of rampant social segregation in the city of Washington."[33]

Mary Church was born in Tennessee in 1863 into mulatto aristocracy. Her parents were slaves; her white paternal grandfather, however, made it possible for her father to inherit valuable real estate which brought him great wealth during Reconstruction. Reared in the lap of luxury. Mary led a fairy-tale existence, but it was not an idle one.

In 1884 she graduated from Oberlin College at the head of her class, but her father, believing a woman's education was strictly for adornment, forbade her to work. Certainly, he thought no wealthy woman should work and thus possibly deprive some less fortunate person of a job.

She said of herself: "I was introduced to Washington society with a capital 'S.' " She attended the presidential inauguration festivities after the Civil War, with no way of knowing that Washington soon would become the world capital of racism and segregation, and that she would not see such happy social intermingling again until she was 85!

After a brief teaching career, Mary Church spent two years studying and traveling in Europe, a rare opportunity for blacks. Upon her return home in 1891, she married Robert Terrell, a man she knew from her school; he eventually became a judge.

After her marriage, Mrs. Terrell devoted her life to club and civic activities, which included her appointment as the first black woman to serve on the Board of Education of Washington, D.C., a post she held for eleven years.

After her election to the presidency of NACW, her national and international fame skyrocketed. Certainly her background and life style set her apart from the masses of black women—most of whom were poor, ignorant, and disenfranchised. An electrifying orator, fluent in several foreign languages, she was an image of scholarliness and crusading zeal. We can easily recognize her charisma, yet today her priorities would certainly be challenged by many young militants. It's hard to communicate to a present generation the work of an organizer of the past. Present critics of earlier leaders are not necessarily wiser, only later!

The NACW established kindergartens and day nurseries all over the United States, but the real contribution made by these women was the organization of nonpoor (later to be labeled "middle class") women into a national network. Mary Church Terrell especially helped Negro women to see the importance of group solidarity, the values of group pressure, and the importance of organizational skills.

Black Greeks[34]

Mary Church Terrell was to extend her influence beyond the realm of women's clubs when in 1913, twenty-two young Howard University co-eds decided to seek her help in organizing a Greek letter sorority—Delta Sigma Theta. This would have been an innocent enough move had it not been for the fact that the young women were already members of Alpha Kappa Alpha, the first Negro sorority established at Howard five years earlier.

In proposing a new name, new symbols and standards, they could not know that they were attempting to abolish a group destined to grow into a distinguished national sorority. They were also unaware of the strong alumnae group that AKA had developed in just four short years which moved quickly to assure Alpha Kappa Alpha's perpetuity through the legal act of incorporation.

Delta Sigma Theta was formed, followed later by two more college sororities, Zeta Phi Beta and Sigma Gamma Rho. That Howard University was the common root for all four did not lessen the fierce competiton that exists among them. There is no absolute answer to the questions: Who has the finest principles? the best programs? the most illustrious members?

Practically all black sororities have similar goals: educational, civic, and moral excellence. They have all fought and worked for civil rights, they have all drawn from a small pool of college students who are noted for their leadership and scholastic standing. Until recently, most black female leaders could claim that much of their leadership talent had been developed in one of the four sororities.

For all their positive action on a social level, there are still detractors who accuse them of snobbery and preoccupation with social frivolities. Perhaps in the past most bright girls, caught between the ugly world of segregation and the struggle to internalize their own expectations of what a cultured, refined college girl should be, needed an organizational format that would creatively mix the social and the serious. This may also have been a necessary process in the increasing politicizing of the middle class.

The real issues with sororities are more challenging than their history and past programs. How can they now move quickly to eradicate class differences between poor black women and college women? What special skills and programs should be rightly expected from college-educated women? Can they help work out a responsible coalition between black women and the white women's liberation movement? They are in the best position to move vertically to establish strong ties with poor black women, and horizontally to develop an effective coalition with the women's liberation movement whose leaders are mostly college oriented.

Perhaps there is one saving point in favor of the college sororities. They are still almost evenly divided between undergraduates and alumnae. In each of them the "old guard" is constantly faced with widespread revolt or inactivity by young college women who insist on a more "black community" based program and feel that the sororities siphon off too much talent and place it at the disposal of "integrationist schemes." Somewhere in the resolution of these conflicts lies the future of the Big Four.

The Fist With the Mighty Blow: Mary McLeod Bethune[35]

More than any other black American woman, with the exception, perhaps, of Marian Anderson, Mary McLeod Bethune has become one of history's black women heroines. In 1974 an impressive statue of her was fittingly unveiled in Lincoln Park, Washington, D.C. Like everything else connected with this woman, it was realized only after great struggle and effort.

Born in 1875 in Maysville, South Carolina, Mary was the last of seventeen children, the first to be born in freedom. Her mother was of royal African blood. Mary once wrote she was her father's champion cotton picker, able to pick 250 pounds a day when she was nine, but Mary McLeod was to be the harvester of something more valuable than "white gold": she was to nurture and help to maturity untold numbers of black children.

Like Ida B. Wells, Mary came up the hard way. An enterprising student, she won scholarships and was easily placed in teaching posts as a "domestic" missionary for the Presbyterian Church. Her ambition in those early days was to join the missionary service in

Africa, but on several occasions church authorities felt she was not sufficiently mature for such work! She soon came to realize she could do the most good right in the South, where education for black children was severely limited.

She was obsessed with the idea of founding a school for girls and in 1904, when she was 29, she realized her dream by setting up meager facilities in Daytona Beach, Florida, where she taught five little girls and her own young son. For many years she weathered crisis after crisis through ingenious fund raising, often getting money from vacationing whites who had come to that resort area. Over a period of years she upgraded the school into a college, Bethune-Cookman of Daytona Beach, Florida. Her interests soon extended beyond that state to encompass the national plight of blacks, especially the concerns of black women.

In 1909 she attended a meeting of the National Association of Colored Women at Hampton Institute, Virginia. There, she met others, Mary Church Terrell and Mrs. Booker T. Washington, who, by her own admission, had long been her role models. After listening to their speeches detailing their interests in "homemaking, health and morals," she asked permission to address the group.

Mrs. Bethune was a persuasive speaker with obvious boundless energy. After appealing to the NACW for funds to help support her school, Mrs. Booker T. Washington made a motion that they take up a collection for that purpose. Mary Church Terrell heard something else in her words, and said, "She will some day be president of the National Association of Colored Women."

By 1927 Mary Bethune had fulfilled Mrs. Terrell's prophecy and was president of that group, but she held a different dream for an organization of black women and that was destined to cause a rift in the relationship of these two women.

During Mary Bethune's term of office she advanced the fight against school segregation and for prison reform. She was especially effective in persuading white women to join efforts with black women to work on racial problems, winning the lifelong friendship of Eleanor Roosevelt and establishing the credentials which were to bring her to several federal appointments, being the first black to serve at that governmental level.

Mary Bethune understood the necessity for an amalgamation of clubs on local and state levels, which NACW represented, but she also recognized the need for a national coalition of organizations which could work with federal agencies and the government itself in a concerted effort to gain progress for all blacks. Hers was a brilliant move to create a council of national presidents: "If I touch you with one finger," she said, "you will scarcely notice it. If I tap you with two fingers, you will feel a light pressure. But if I pull all my fingers together into a fist, you will feel a mighty blow."[36]

So in 1935, five years after her presidency of NACW ended, she founded the National Council of Negro Women. Here at last was an attempt to form a powerful coalition of black women who, if convinced and properly led, could really move mountains.

Mary Church Terrell, then 73, was never to see this move as anything but Mary Bethune's struggle for a personal political base and an effort to weaken the NACW. In some ways she was right. Mrs. Bethune's personal charisma and power, coupled with NCNW as a base, soon brought her into national prominence; and lacking similar leadership, NACW was never again a force for national recognition.

Whether or not NCNW was actually to realize the power she envisioned, she succeeded in making it front runner for the role of spokesman for black women and, at least to whites, the legitimate voice of black women.

And today it stands as the best potential vehicle for the unification of often dissident and disparate black female organizations.

The National Council of Negro Women

The conceptualization of the National Council of Negro Women not only was brilliant, but it served to refocus the sorority groups on their responsibilities to the black masses. Though it would take years to effectively harness all the diverse interests and concerns of twenty-two women's organizations, the very plans to do so helped them to take the first steps. So, when students began to sit in, freedom riders met with Southern violence, and four little girls were bombed in a Birmingham church, the organization was strong enough to translate outrage into the mobilization of thousands of women. The NCNW was in the right place at the right time during the civil rights days.

Mrs. Bethune was the first female leader to work on an equal basis with her black male counterparts. There is evidence of strong ties and mutual interdependence between Mrs. Bethune and Walter White and other race leaders. Women leaders who followed her would be given token recognition and perhaps be nominally involved in decision-making, but never since then were they to be a seriously respected part of the black power structure. By the time of the March on Washington in 1963, the only nationally recognized black women acceptable to the civil rights coalition were the distinguished roster of black singers!

Dorothy Ferebee and Vivian Carter Mason followed Mary Bethune as presidents of the NCNW. Intelligent and skilled as they were, and in spite of the work they did to keep the idea of a united coalition of women's organizations alive, they were both handicapped by lack of funds and by the long shadow of their predecessor. It was left to Dorothy Height to utilize the growing science of groups—how they function, and what motivates them—to build a firm foundation of organizational strength under Mrs. Bethune's idea.

With a quiet, understated, scholarly style of leadership, Dorothy Height was able to do what Mrs. Bethune never accomplished. She built a financial and administrative capability that for the first time in black women's history attracted grants from Ford, Rockefeller, and other prestigious foundations. And she made the national program more relevant to the needs of the black community. Without antagonizing white liberals who are always attracted to black groups as long as they are not too militant, she has steered the course of the organization to a middle-of-the-road movement.

Within a few years, a bankrupt organization became a million dollar business with a staff of ninety, thus giving recognition to the fact that volunteers, especially black full-time working women, cannot administer a national program without budget, structure, and staff.

Among this staff were young black militant women, and women without formal educational degrees. In Mississippi, the late Fannie Lou Hamer worked as a Field Specialist, utilizing indigenous community organizational skills to help NCNW develop a Hunger Project in rural areas. Over in Issaquena County, Mississippi, another school dropout, Uneida Blackwell, worked as a Staff Specialist to help NCNW organize rural communities and build housing units. From "pig banks" to Career Development, NCNW has a history of distinguished national programs, including food cooperatives in the South, a franchise enterprise to protect domestics, and leadership training for Africans.

So rapidly has the national program grown that it now faces a problem of moving ahead of its local constituency. With the aid of Ford and Rockefeller grants in recent years, NCNW has begun to strengthen its national affiliate involvement, especially at the state level. Still, its most critical problem is the inability to harness the energies of the national sororities and college-educated women in a coalition with the masses of women.

Though Dorothy Height has often been criticized for holding on to "too much power," as both national president and executive director for nearly twenty years, her organizational genius remains indisputable. And yet the greatest challenge—to actually unite twenty-two national groups—has lain unrealized as the organization competes in local communities with the locals of its own national constituents.

Thus, while NCNW has been legitimized by whites as spokesman for 3.5 million black women, it is a claim of mere illusionary power, for few of the leaders among the twenty-two nationals are actively involved in setting its goals.

With a slow demise of the National Association of Colored Women's organizations as a national force, though it is strong in its organization of local clubs, there is a need, perhaps, for another Ruffin "Call to Action" with a merger of NACW and NCNW as an agenda item for the Seventies. There is also a need for NCNW to build more effective coalition power shared among the twenty-two national organizations, to realize Mrs. Bethune's dream of "bringing all the fingers together in a mighty fist" so that there is collective action stemming from a valid power base.

A more urgent problem for this "highly visible" black women's organization, however, is the lack of young women in leadership positions, which raises a question of continuity and validity.

Among the young there began to grow in the Sixties a new group of black female leaders forging new styles of black female revolutionary activities. Angela Davis is a child of the black bourgeoisie. Kathleen Cleaver is a product of a middle-class home, and so were numerous women of the Black Panther party. At work on many college campuses were young sisters who learned how to deal with a new feminine model based on shared leadership with black men—models they fashioned for themselves without the help of organizational efforts. They learned to work more effectively with poor black women. As they now move more and more in the Seventies into prestigious new careers, there is a feeling that many are becoming individuated and unconcerned with group solidarity. Many are turned off by the old guard NCNW and sororities, and it's evident the elitist Links and others are clearly not their style. Some have moved toward the new Black Women's Feminist Organization, in an effort to define their relationship to black men, white women, and black issues. But most still hope that the old guard will flex and share power with them. Such sharing is essential if these organizations are to survive.

The poet Margaret Walker, in her classic poem "For My

People," saw a "new generation" coming forth. Maybe she expressed a kind of tiredness as a black woman trying to motivate other middle-class black women:

> For my people standing staring trying to fashion a better way from confusion, from hypocrisy and misunderstanding, trying to fashion a world that will hold all of the people, all the faces, all the Adams and Eves and their countless generations;
>
> Let a new earth rise. Let another world be born. Let a bloody peace be written in the sky. Let a second generation full of courage issue forth; let a people loving freedom come to growth. Let a beauty full of healing and a strength of final clenching be the pulsing in our spirits and our blood. Let the martial songs be written, let the dirges disappear. Let a race of men now rise and take control.[37]

Perhaps, there is need for a "second generation" of black women to "rise and take control" of the organizations run by the "Old Guard." If not control, shared power!

CHAPTER 6
NOTES

[1]"We Wear the Mask," Paul Laurence Dunbar, in *The Complete Poems of Paul Laurence Dunbar* (New York: Dodd, Mead & Company, 1968), pp. 112–113. Reprinted by permission of Dodd, Mead & Company, Inc.

[2]Women, including blacks, comprised 27 percent of the work force in 1947 and 39 percent in 1971. Fifty-six percent of all female college graduates and 71 percent of all women with one or more years of college and beyond were unemployed. About 63 percent are believed to work for strong economic reasons. (Presentation by Dr. Jennifer McCleod to Exxon managers and professionals in Affirmative Action Program, Fall and Spring, 1975 and 1976, based on Bureau of the Census Statistics.)

See also "Why Women Work," U.S. Department of Labor, Employment Standards Administration, Women's Bureau, Washington, D.C., May 1974 (revised).

[3]Among the young husband-wife families, black wives were more likely than white wives to have participated in the employed labor force and as year-round workers in 1970. Nationally, about 68 percent of the young black wives contributed to the family income by working, compared to 56 percent for young white wives. In the North and West, a larger percentage of young black wives worked year round. These black wives earned approximately 30 percent more and also made a larger contribution to the family income than did their white counterparts. For the North and West, the ratio of young wives' earnings to the family income was 35 percent for blacks and 27 percent for whites. U.S. Department of Commerce, Bueau of the Census, "The Social and Economic Status of the Black Population in the United States," 1971, Special Studies, Current Population Report, Series P-23, No. 42, p. 2. See Tables 14 and 15 in Special Series P-23, No. 48 (1973).

[4]U.S. Bureau of the Census, Current Population Reports, Special Studies Series P-23, No. 48, 1973, Tables 14 and 15.

[5]*Ibid.,* Table 8, p. 19.

[6]*Ibid.,* pp. 1–2.

[7]See Robert Samuel Fletcher, *History of Oberlin College* (Oberlin, Ohio: Oberlin College, 1943).

[8]James Wells Brown, *Clotel* (London, New York: Charles Scribner & Sons, 1853).

[9]Sterling A. Brown, *The Negro in American Fiction* (Washington, D.C.: Associates in Negro Folk Education, 1937; Arno, 1969). (Also in combination with *Negro Poetry and Drama,* New York: Atheneum, 1968).

[10]George Gable, *Madam Delphine* (New York: Charles Scribner & Sons, 1881), pp. 8–9.

[11]*Ibid.,* p. 44.

[12]Francis Walker Harper, *Iola Leroy* (published in Boston by James H. Earle, c. 1892, Schomberg Collection).

[13]See footnotes in Chapter 7, Nella Larsen.

[14]See notes in Chapter 7, Jessie Fauset.

[15]C. Wright Mills, *The Power Elite* (London, Oxford, New York: Oxford University Press, 1956), p. 50.

[16]Nathaniel Burt, *First Families* (Boston: Little, Brown and Company, 1970), p. 3.

[17]Margaret Just Butcher, *The Negro in the American Culture* (New York: Alfred Knopf), p. 18.

[18]Sidney Hyman, "Washington Negro Elite," *Look* magazine, April 6, 1965, p. 60.

[19]E. Franklin Frazier, *The Negro Family in the United States* (University of Chicago Press, 1937), p. 296.

[20]W. E. B. Dubois, *The Philadelphia Negro* (Published for the University of Pennsylvania, 1899, Schomberg Collection), p. 7.

[21]James Weldon Johnson, *Along This Way* (New York: The Viking Press, 1965), p. 131.

[22]*Ibid.*

[23]See E. Franklin Frazier, *Black Bourgeoisie* (New York: The Free Press, The Macmillan Company, 1957). See also Nathan Hare, *The Black Anglo-Saxons* (New York: Manzini and Munsell, Publishers, Inc., 1965).

[24]Tables 38 and 39 in *The Social and Economic Status of the Black Population in the United States,* 1973.

[25]*Ibid.,* Table 43, p. 59.

[26]"Earnings by Occupation and Education" (U.S. Department of Commerce, Bureau of the Census, 1970), (2)-8B Tables 1, 2, 6, 7.

[27]Hyman, "Washington Negro Elite," p. 16.

[28]Shirley Chisholm, *Unbought and Unbossed* (Boston: Houghton Mifflin Co., 1970), p. 75.

[29]As told to Marcia Ann Gillespie, *Essence,* November 1972.

[30]Alfreda M. Duster ed. "Crusade for Justice," *The Autobiography of Ida B. Wells* (Chicago and London: University of Chicago Press, 1976), pp. 78–80.

[31]*Ibid.,* p. 19.

[32]Papers on Josephine St. Pierre Ruffin are in the Sophia Smith Collection, Smith College, Northampton, Mass.

[33]Gladys Byram Shepperd, *Mary Church Terrell, Respectable Person* (Baltimore: Human Relations Press, 1959), p. 19.

[34]See Marjorie H. Parker, *Alpha Kappa Alpha 1908–1958* (Alpha Kappa Alpha, Inc., 1958); and Mary Elizabeth Vroman, *Shaped to Its Purpose: Delta Sigma Theta, The First Fifty Years* (New York: Random House, 1964).

[35]Rackham Holt, *Mary McLeod Bethune* (New York: Doubleday and Company, Inc., 1964).

[36]Filmstrip on *The National Council of Negro Women,* as narrated by Ruby Dee, National Council of Negro Women.

[37]Margaret Walker, "For My People" (New Haven: Yale University Press, 1942). "For My People" first appeared in *Poetry* magazine, 1942.

Speak the truth to the people
Talk sense to the people
Free them with reason
Free them with honesty
Free the people with Love and Courage and Care
for their Being

Spare them the fantasy
Fantasy enslaves
A slave is enslaved
Can be enslaved by unwisdom
Can be enslaved by black unwisdom. . . .

MARI EVANS[1]

Speak the Truth to the People

A young poet told Langston Hughes, black Poet Laureate extraordinaire, "I want to be a poet, not a Negro poet." Hughes advised that running away spiritually from his race would never help the young man become a great poet. In his opinion ". . . standing in the way of any true Negro art in America is the racial mountain . . . this urge within the race toward whiteness, the desire to pour racial individuality into the mold of American standardization and to be as little Negro and as much American as possible."[2]

Langston Hughes is dead, yet his works survive as testimony of a particular artistic genius which flourished during the Harlem Renaissance of the Twenties. Hughes and other artists expressed significant black experience themes so eloquently that for the first time in history there emerged an artistic synergism that appealed to masses of blacks. They fermented the first black consciousness era and intensified interest in race pride and solidarity. These themes and artistic expressions flourished during the Twenties, only to lose their grip on the hearts and minds of blacks for decades.

Indeed, the course of Negro art might be likened to the fairy tale path to Sleeping Beauty's castle. It was well traveled during those brief but vibrant years of the Twenties; later, most of it lay hidden from view, sadly overgrown with the weeds of forgetfulness. Decades passed and the wealth of black literature, largely untaught in our public schools, waited until the Sixties to be reclaimed by blacks and discovered by whites. Then in the midst of the black revolution of the Sixties another explosion of leadership among young writers and artists emerged with slogans like "Black Is

Beautiful" and "Black Power," and they built new works upon the foundation of those Renaissance writers.

Some of the literary trailblazers were black women writers. They not only contributed much to that Renaissance genre, but revealed important insights into the inner world of black women.

Some believe the Harlem Renaissance was killed by the Great Depression. But it was also sucked of its vitality by whites who either co-opted its ideas and style in a desperate attempt to transfuse their own Lost Generation with new and vigorous creativity,[3] or who deliberately repressed the literary movement when the reality struck that the Renaissance was not all fun and games. Like the drums of our ancient forebears, the words of poets and writers were beating out messages of liberation. These new voices, sounds, words, at first considered "quaint and exotic" coming from "the coloreds," when really understood had to be perceived as weapons sharpened to match a martial cadence.

Countee Cullen wrote:

> We shall not always plant while others reap
> The golden increment of bursting fruit,
> Not always countenance, abject and mute
> That lesser men should hold their brothers cheap,
> Not everlastingly, while others sleep
> Shall we beguile their limbs with mellow flute,
> Not always bend to some more subtle brute;
> We were not made eternally to weep.

In the closing lines there is a subtle militancy:

> So in the dark we hide the heart that bleeds,
> And wait, and plant our agonizing seeds. . . .[4]

No less militant, even to the point of pitting one's body against oppressors, were Claude McKay's words:

> If we must die, let it not be like hogs
> Hunted and penned in an inglorious spot
> While round us bark the mad and hungry dogs,
> Making their mock at our accursed lot.
>
> Like men we'll face the murderous, cowardly pack,
> Pressed to the wall, dying, but fighting back![5]

Words, drumming resistance to the point of violence? Surely in a nation that had choked blacks in racist laws and denied their humanity there would be little encouragement for writers whose pens had the power to someday move beyond the college-educated blacks and reach into the minds of the masses of unschooled blacks. The ability to grab this proletariat mass—not as intellectuals speaking some esoteric ideology but as warriors whose words would incite, exhort, and galvanize poor blacks to action that would one day demand freedom—was a thrust whose promise was only dimly seen in the Twenties. These seeds would see their ripe red harvest of revolution in the Sixties.

Before then, in the Twenties, Thirties, Forties, and Fifties, blacks owned nothing, neither publishing houses nor monies for helping young struggling writers. Black authors were almost completely dependent on whites for public exposure and financial help, though their creativity grew out of the black experience.

Painful conflict would always attend the choice of material and audiences so long as financial dependence rested with whites. The racial mountain was there for Phillis Wheatley to face and is still there for Nikki Giovanni to leap!

The black revolution of the Sixties brought sharpened sensitivities and black awareness stimulated first by preachers and congregations singing gospel songs and spirituals. It also provided the first black foundation and an acceptance of a nourishing black literature. Poets and preachers, organizers and writers joined hands and spoke directly to the masses of unschooled churchgoers. Angered black youth leaped into the "we shall overcome" fray with words of such literary impact that it is impossible to disassociate the bursting cultural revolution of the Sixties from the black struggle for liberation in the streets, on campuses, and everywhere.

Certainly most would agree with Harold Cruse, who sees black intellectuals (including creative and performing artists and writers) caught between, on one hand, the pull of a white world that largely rejects black aspirations while controlling the institutions that produce and distribute literary and artistic works, and on the other hand, by the push of black "inner realities" that offer the richest source of creativity.

Certainly there has been a traditional belief among some black artists and intellectuals that they do indeed comprise a special class who are well integrated into an artistic and literary world that is a "truly open society." While some might delude themselves that there is such a favored status for artists, and that intellectual and cultural activity is above class, race, and national divisions, it would be folly to conclude that social intermingling and integration into the power structure of America are the same. Garnering the power to create and produce ideas and artistic products without facing co-option by whites whose values and tastes by necessity intrude upon creativity is a real crisis. What usually happens is that blacks become "detached from their own Negro ethnic world," and alienated from the black masses. It then becomes apparent to the masses, who feel no need to be supportive of people who write, sing, dance, or act out themes that are alien to their struggles and interests that they are not considered. Thus, the black intellectual "must deal intimately with the white power structure and America's cultural institutions while dealing as spokesperson for the inner realities of the black world at one and the same time."[6]

Elizabeth Catlett in *The Black Scholar* adds to Cruse's concerns still another problem—the how-to and whereby of reaching the mass of black people, "This is the principal preoccupation of all artists who consider themselves first black and then artists."[7] Certainly, the growth of a large black audience is necessary for the survival of writers who write from the black perspective.

The use of literature as a weapon for black liberation and words as ammunition, according to John O. Killens, has been a preference for most black writers. W. E. B. DuBois himself said, "I stand in utter shamelessness and say that whatever art I have for writing has been used for propaganda. . . ."[8] Killens adds: "All art is propaganda; all art is politics."[9] And John Williams agrees: ". . . black writers with some exception, of course, tend to believe that a man and his art do not stand separately, that one is conceived from the experiences and sensibilities of the other."[10]

Intellectuals, of course, come with varied roles to perform, and scientists, professors, and teachers have certainly made great contributions to the advancement of black people. But few would deny that the black writer's contribution is unique, because it is the "imaging" which, according to Ralph Ellison, mirrors "an internality of Negro American life that poses its own attractions and mysteries, . . . that captures the imagination of the masses."[11]

Ellison believes writers are able to probe more deeply into the internality of the black experience than is usually expected of social scientists. Certainly, sociologists, among others, categorize, label, and theorize in compartments, using confining terms that often lack human feelings. Ellison, like others, believes that ruling out the subjective dimensions of black people's lives—how they feel about life, death, love, and struggle—blocks a true understanding of the inner world of blacks. It is this internal "something else" which is difficult for social scientists to describe. Therefore an affirmation of black humanity which goes beyond scientific labels and theories becomes the proper province of writers and artists. There is, according to Ellison, a revelation of truth in art that "transcends narrow definitions while proving pleasure and insight . . . affirmation and a sense of direction."[12]

From Hughes to Cruse and to Ellison, all speak of the need to draw upon the interiority/internality of the black experience. Fiction and poetry are essential as protest weapons, but there is also something else. "Revelation is what is called for," says Ellison, "not argument."

To abstract and enlarge life, to go beyond narrow sociological theories and rigid psychological labels, to break out beyond cognitive definitions which, for blacks, are all too often negative and seldom deal with the affective dimensions of a vibrant, resilient, living, black people—all this is the work of the creative artist, the major domain of black writers. The choice of subject matter for each individual writer is, of course, a birthright that none would deny. But without writers to "tell it like it is" with blacks, we would be scripted in history with little true human understanding.

Throughout the ages, those black writers who have chosen to write from and of the black experience have made their marks on the black profile of history. Many of these writers have been women, and their expressive themes a product of the black experience as viewed through female eyes. From Phillis Wheatley to Carolyn Rodgers, one traces protest and revelation; one sees also the conflict of being spokesman for the black masses and the pull of the white world—and, here also, again and again, the self-hatred that Langston Hughes believes so inhibiting to creative expression.

PHILLIS WHEATLEY AND THE EARLY LITERARY PIONEERS

Throughout black communities more schools, YWCA's, and dormitories carry the name of Phillis Wheatley (1753?–1784), than perhaps that of any other black woman. She is honored not only for the content of her poems, but because she was the first black American to write a poem that received national recognition and established her as the Mother of Black Literature in North America.[13]

"Considering her slave status, even though a pampered favorite in the home of the Wheatley family who bought her on the auction block in Boston, it is remarkable that a few years after her arrival in America, judged in the light of the day in which she wrote . . . she was an important poet."[14]

There were many remarkable things about Phillis Wheatley. She was bought at age seven, probably to be trained as a servant and companion for the Wheatley women. She soon mastered English and Latin and by fourteen was a published poet. Her talents made her an intellectual adornment in the Wheatley household.

While she was never really family in that she associated with the Wheatleys as an equal, neither was she allowed to fraternize with other slaves. She was given freedom to study and write at her own pace, freed of most household chores. Mary Wheatley, the daughter of the household, taught her to read as much as she could, but New England white women of that time were not very educated themselves. Yet the Wheatleys basked in their prize possession—a black, young female poet and fascinating conversationalist! She was an exotic curiosity in Boston salons and appeared in their homes as a dazzling entertainer as well as a poet. Actually, critics who have found it difficult to rate her poems as great have grudgingly (with the notable exception of the definitive biography of Wheatley by Richmond) simply missed the gestalt effect on people of all that Phillis represented—youth, slave, female, literate, outgoing, writer! It is the summation of the various roles and parts that adds up to *greatness.*

But we must ask why, if in fact good writers draw upon their most intimate experiences, did Phillis either block out or ignore her slave status, speaking little of the faint remembrance of being kidnapped in Africa (probably Senegal). Why, some ask today, did she not make of her pen a sword to cut away the untruths and lies of slavery?

Perhaps because she was "marginal" in her life style—neither white nor slave, an ambiguous identity too tenuous and full of conflicts and hardly likely to provide a rich source of feelings which would impel Phillis's pen to write: Freedom! Being also a poet "who entertained," let us not forget the applause of the audience which for any entertainer influences the choice of material and style. In the chronicling of her life there is mention of only one slave friend, and their relationship was built not around literary interests, "but Puritan piety."[15] There was no black audience.

At age 23, Phillis Wheatley sent a letter to George Washington, after having written a very flattering poem to him in which she wished for him, a slave owner:

> A crown, a mansion and a throne that shine
> With gold unfading, Washington, be thine!

In 1776 she visited Washington at his headquarters in Cambridge. The poem, "To His Excellency General Washington" was published in April 1776 in the *Pennsylvania Magazine,* edited by Thomas Paine.

Phillis Wheatley's poems are deeply religious and deal almost exclusively with "otherworldly" themes. When she spoke of slavery it was as something better than being African:

> Father of mercy; t'was thy gracious hand
> Brought me in safely from those dark abodes . . .[16]

And yet, there was nostalgia in one poem for her native land:

> Should you, my lord, while you peruse my song
> Wonder from whence my love of freedom sprung,
> Whence flow these wishes for the common good,
> By feeling hearts alone best understood,
> I, young in life, by seeming cruel fate
> Was snatched from Afric's fancied happy seat.[17]

She appeared more interested in life after death than in the justice of a better life in the daily struggles of her slave brethren. Though everywhere slavery was a topic of discussion, there is no evidence that Phillis was moved to write about the slave experience. When she speaks of freedom, one has to struggle to relate the words to the system. Though many critics speak of her imitation of Alexander Pope's literary style, she stopped short, claims Richmond, of Pope's "literary sensitivity to white prejudice" and the "employment of satire."

But then, as Richmond concludes, whites were willing to accept piety elegies and hymns of praise to famous men from a slave poet, but would scarcely have endured satire at their expense, much less protest.

Phillis's slave status ended in 1778. By this time all the Wheatley family was dead or in England. Times were difficult for whites, and doubly difficult for a freedwoman who knew very little about blacks and had only one skill, the writing of poetry. Unprepared to cope with life or marriage, she failed at both.

Was her husband Peters "shiftless," as some, including her one black friend, described him? He was unable to be a good provider, but we have no way of knowing whether circumstances or "shiftlessness" was the reason. Could any black man of her time have been a suitable mate for a woman reared as Phillis had been?

As Richmond states, "What might have been good about the

marriage is buried. The only certainties that endure are its poverty and tragedy. She bore three children, and all died in infancy. . . ."[18] She had always been physically frail, and the menial labor she was forced to do in order to survive finally depleted her physical strength; she died alone in the process of bearing the last child. "From an unmarked village in Africa she finally arrived at an unmarked grave in America. All that remains now is her literary work, an indistinct image of her, and a poor legacy of critical appraisals.[19] According to Richmond: "She was permitted to cultivate her intelligence . . . her language and her facility in its use, but one thing she was not permitted to develop: the sense of her own distinct identity as a black poet. And without this there could be no personal distinction in style or the choice of themes that make for greater poetry."[20]

Certainly Phillis Wheatley's poems must have been an inspiration to Frances E. W. Harper (1825–1911). This woman, however, wrote clearly about the injustices of slavery as a member of an anti-slavery literary group.

Mrs. Harper may have been "the most popular American Negro poet of her time." It is asserted that 50,000 copies of Mrs. Harper's two volumes were sold. Not a bad record in any day![21]

She was an outstanding orator, and many of her poems were best suited for the lecture platform. As Mrs. Harper traveled throughout the North speaking for the abolitionist movements, her poems became standard parts of her message. And the message was about the cruelty and immorality of slavery—hers were clearly protest poems. One very popular one, usually quoted in Negro anthologies, "Bury Me in a Free Land," has the cadence and swing of stirring prose, designed to bring an audience to its feet (and possibily to elicit financial contributions for the movements).

> Make me a grave wher'er you will,
> In a lowly plain, or a lofty hill;
> Make it among earth's humblest graves,
> But not in a land where men are slaves.
>
> I ask no monument, proud and high
> To arrest the gaze of the passers-by,
> All that my yearning spirit craves,
> Is bury me not in a land of slaves.[22]

After the Civil War she traveled in the South as a representative of the Women's Christian Temperance Union. While there she published *Sketches of Southern Life.*[23]

Mrs. Harper brought into literature "the woman's theme"—how women felt about slavery. Her poem "Elisa Harris" could well have been the inspiration for Mrs. Stowe's character in *Uncle Tom's Cabin.* Unlike Phillis Wheatley, who spoke of lofty dreams, Mrs. Harper gives a "blow by blow" description of the impact of slavery on women.

> The sale began—young girls were there
> Defenseless in their wretchedness
> Whose stifled sobs of deep despair
> Revealed their anguish and distress.
>
> And mothers stood with streaming eyes
> And saw their dearest children sold;
> Unheeded rose their bitter cries
> While tyrants bartered them for gold.[24]

Several other female poets followed in the years after Mrs. Harper's publications: Angelina Grimke, Anne Spencer, Lucy Ariel Williams, Clarissa Scott Delany, Helene Johnson, Alice Dunbar-Nelson (wife of the early poet Paul Laurence Dunbar). Others are listed in various anthologies. Most of these writers were teachers who wrote poetry at their leisure and they are generally considered minor writers.[25] Their works dealt with the injustices of slavery and segregation, also with love and temporal matters.

One among them—Georgia Douglass Johnson—is perhaps representative of those who received acclaim years before the Harlem Renaissance. Born into "mulatto aristocracy," educated at Atlanta University and Oberlin College, Georgia Douglass studied to become a composer. Believing the "double handicap" of race and sex unsurmountable in realizing this dream, she entered teaching.

Her artistic talents found expression in poetry, volumes of which were published before she died. She married Henry Lincoln Johnson, a Republican Party official active in Reconstruction politics. Her poems speak mostly of love and dreams.

> I want to die while you love me
> While yet you hold me fair
> While laughter lies upon my lips
> And lights are in my hair.[26]

Whenever she used her pen to tell of black oppression it was within the content of broken dreams. Perhaps her own dashed hope of becoming a composer came through in this poignant understanding of *Old Black Men*.

They have dreamed as young men dream
  Of glory, love and power,
They have hoped as youth will hope
  Of love sun-minted hours.

They have seen as others saw
  Their bubbles burst in air,
And they have learned to live it down
  As though they did not care.[27]

Yet there comes forth a definite social protest and a weariness of asking, requesting, and begging. Hers is surely not the strong protest of Margaret Walker, and nowhere near the bold revolutionary statements of Nikki Giovanni, but a toughness resonant of the black struggles of her day is here!

Long have I beat with timid hands upon life's leaden door,
Soft over the threshold of the years there comes
  this counsel cool:
The strong demand, contend, prevail; the beggar is a fool![28]

When the Harlem Renaissance assumed literary importance, its major figures would draw upon their ancestors' literary contributions for motivation, and upon their lives as role models. And at least one, Georgia Douglass Johnson, lived to give personal encouragement to those who were the first fruits of the Negro Renaissance—Jessie Fauset, Nella Larsen and Zora Neale Hurston.

THE BLACK FEMALE LITERATI OF THE HARLEM RENAISSANCE

Sun-baked lips will kiss the earth.
Throats of bronze will burst with mirth.
Sing a little faster,
Sing a little faster!
Sing![29]

Singing! Dancing! Writing! Faster and faster! Living! More openly, freely, and honestly. All of this characterized the golden days of the Twenties, those all too brief years of literary and artistic excitement which appeared to end with the Great Depression.[30]

The Twenties was a glittering, gay time for white intellectuals, marked perhaps by their quest for a new intellectual excitement and new reasons for existence. The key words were modern, different, new. The search turned its range from eternity to the moment, "symbolized . . . by the sophisticates' ceaseless quest throughout the Prohibition era for an unholy grail," in the words of one critic of the times.[31]

Gertrude Stein labeled the white intellectuals, and authors of the Twenties, "The Lost Generation"; she believed them "lost as a person who cannot find his way and lives in confusion, . . . lost to salvation, abandoned to sin."

Out of the social and intellectual revolt of the times came the New Negro, a new movement of artistic and intellectual activity never before so focused on the literary institutions of America. The movement found its home in Manhattan's Harlem and took the descriptive title: the Harlem Renaissance.

Langston Hughes described it best:

> It began with *Shuffle Along, Running Wild,* and the Charleston. . . . But certainly it was the musical revue *Shuffle Along* that gave a scintillating sendoff to the Negro vogue in Manhattan which reached its peak just before the crash in 1929, the crash that sent Negroes, white folks, and all rolling down the hill towards the Works Progress Administration. . . . Put down the 1920's for the rise of Roland Hayes . . . Paul Robeson . . . Florence Mills . . . Rose McClendon . . . Bessie Smith . . . Ethel Waters . . . Gladys Bentley . . . Josephine Baker. . . . White people began to come to Harlem in droves; . . . It was a period when, at almost every . . . upper-crust dance or party, one would be introduced to various distinguished white celebrities there as guests . . . when the parties of Alelia Walker, the Negro heiress, were filled with guests whose names would turn any Nordic social climber green with envy—It was a period when every season there was at least one hit play on Broadway acted by a Negro cast. And when books by Negro authors were being published with much greater frequency and much more publicity than ever before or since in history. . . . It was a period when white writers wrote about Negroes more successfully (commercially speaking) than Negroes did about themselves. . . . It was a period when the Negro was in vogue.[32]

Alain Locke, patron of young artists and writers, observing the Harlem scenes from his teaching post at Howard University, called the writers and advocates "the New Negroes."

> In the last decade something beyond the watch and guard of statistics has happened in the life of the American Negro and the

three names who have traditionally presided over the Negro problem have a changeling in their laps. The Sociologist, the Philanthropist, the Race-leader are not unaware of the New Negro, but they are at a loss to account for him. He simply cannot be swathed in their formulae. For the younger generation is vibrant with a new psychology; the new spirit is awake in the masses, and under the very eyes of the professional observers is transforming what has been a perennial problem into the progressive phases of contemporary Negro life. . . .

. . . By shedding the old chrysalis of the Negro problem we are achieving something like a spiritual emancipation. Until recently, lacking self-understanding, we have been almost as much of a problem to ourselves as we still are to others. . . .

. . . The days of "aunties," "uncles," and "mammies" is equally gone. Uncle Tom and Sambo have passed on, and even the "Colonel" and "George" play barnstorm roles from which they escape with relief when the public spotlight is off. The popular melodrama has about played itself out, and it is time to scrap the fictions, garret the bogeys and settle down to a realistic facing of facts."[33]

Alain Locke acknowledging Harlem as the center of this "New Negro" mood saw the New Negro substituting self-direction for the old notion of being an object of philanthropy.

. . . Up to the present one may adequately describe the Negro's "inner objectives" as an attempt to repair a damaged group psychology and reshape a warped social perspective. Their realization has required a new mentality for the American Negro. And as it matures we begin to see its effects; at first, negative, iconoclastic, and then positive and constructive. In this new group psychology we note the development of a more positive self-respect and self-reliance; the repudiation of social dependence . . . the rise from social disillusionment to race pride, from the sense of social debt to the responsibilities of social contribution, and offsetting the necessary working and commonsense acceptance of restricted conditions, the belief in ultimate esteem and recognition. Therefore the Negro today wishes to be known for what he is, even in his faults and shortcomings, and scorns a craven and precarious survival at the price of seeming to be what he is not. He resents being spoken to as a social ward or minor, even by his own, and to being regarded a chronic patient for the sociological clinic, the sick man of American democracy. For the same reasons, he himself is through with those social nostrums and panaceas, the so-called "solutions" of his "problem," . . . Religion, freedom, education, money—in turn, he has ardently hoped for and peculiarly trusted

> these things; he still believes in them, but not in blind trust that they alone will solve his life-problem.
>
> Each generation, however, will have its creed, and that of the present is the belief in the efficacy of collective effort, in race cooperation. This deep feeling of race seems to be the outcome of the reaction to proscription and prejudice; an attempt, fairly successful on the whole, to convert a defensive into an offensive position, a handicap into an incentive. It is radical in tone, but not in purpose and only the most stupid forms of opposition, misunderstanding or persecution could make it otherwise.[34]

James Weldon Johnson, from his position as "older intellectual," as the young artists put it,[35] said: ". . . this was the era in which was achieved the Harlem of story and song; the era in which Harlem's fame for the exotic flavor and colorful sensuousness was spread to all parts of the world.[36] Johnson was certain that Harlem was the center of this new Negro literature and art, and that designation made Harlem famous among cities—thanks to black writers.

But why Harlem? What led to the conclusion that manna from heaven descended on a part of Manhattan that whites had begun abandoning to black newcomers? It was not simply an influx of black migrants from the South and the West Indies in the post World War I era. Strangely, few of the men and women writers of this time were born and reared in the South, so the Renaissance writings did not reflect the richness of black Southern life. Many thought that important factors were the publication of the poems of Countee Cullen and Langston Hughes, and the Broadway production of the all-black musical comedy *Shuffle Along* by Eubie Blake and Noble Sissle, with its popular songs and dazzling performers like Florence Mills. The NAACP publication *Crisis,* as well as *Opportunity,* the Urban League's publication edited by sociologist Charles S. Johnson, believed artistic labor was also important in achieving the aims of their organizations. Both gave exposure and cash prizes to writers. Within this decade, Claude McKay's *Dark Shadows* was published and a few influential whites like Carl Van Vechten became enamoured with black writers and performers and helped to forward their careers. There were new musical sounds like those of Jelly Roll Morton. It was a period when Marcus Garvey astonished the nation, particularly the black intelligentsia, by organizing masses of poor blacks around an "I'm black and I'm proud" theme. Proclaiming Africa as the black man's homeland was no longer a laughable matter, it was an idea masses of blacks found attractive. Garvey was a potent force!

The writers absorbed all these new faces, ideas, sounds; sought them out, made friends with these "new" men and women. Zora Neale Hurston cultivated a friendship with Ethel Waters. Langston Hughes sat night after night enthralled with *Shuffle Along*. And, while it would take over forty years for leaders of masses of blacks like Martin Luther King to reach for the music of an Aretha Franklin in a united appeal for black solidarity, or for a Nikki Giovanni to recite poems in front of a gospel choir and ask Reverend Ike to introduce her thirtieth birthday party performance, this formula born in the Twenties, the bringing together of intellectuals, artists, writers, performers, and leaders, greatly influenced the cultural revolution of the Sixties. If there is to be further blossoming of literary and artistic creativity in the future, one would hope that the same formula might be implemented. For although the Twenties showed the way toward artistic emancipation from white tastes, the Harlem Renaissance was still stymied by a dependence on white patrons and publishers, and their means of exposure and communication. This artistic movement never really connected with Marcus Garvey or other "mass" leaders and their followers. It was still "elitist" and as such grazed over the sensitivities of poor blacks rather superficially.

It was not until the Sixties that the civil rights movement brought writers, singers, and schooled and unschooled blacks into a united movement.

The challenge of the future is to move toward more closeness between writers, artists, and black audiences who because of economic conditions continue to be poor and uneducated.

Jessie Fauset

Jessie Fauset was one of the most productive authors of the Harlem Renaissance. She was also literary editor of *Crisis* and a patron of younger writers such as Langston Hughes and Countee Cullen. She was well educated, at Cornell and the Collège de France. Her writings reflected an interest in characters and situations that people of her cultivated tastes and life style would enjoy. All of her heroines were cultured and beautiful, even if they were morally flawed. The colorful women of Harlem cabarets and speakeasies skitted about the outer edges of her books, but never were heroines. Domestics and other black women whose daily struggles for existence were being enacted in Harlem did not find their lives dramatized in her books.

All of her books, from *Plum Bun* to *Comedy, American Style,*[37] dealt with problems faced by light-skinned Negroes who were well educated, enterprising, and desirous only of being accepted into the institutions of America.

Langston Hughes was able to understand Jessie Fauset's popularity with their contemporary critics, even those who were not enthusiastic about his own works.

> Negro critics and many intellectuals were very sensitive about their race in books. . . . In anything that white people were likely to read, they wanted to put their best foot forward, their politely polished and cultured foot—and only that foot. There was a reason for that, of course. They had seen their race laughed at . . . maligned and abused . . . made a servant and clown . . . and forever defeated . . . when Negroes wrote books they wanted them to be books in which only good Negroes, clean, cultured and not funny Negroes, beautiful and nice and upper-class were presented. Jessie Fauset's novels they loved, because they were always about the educated Negro . . . but my poems . . . they did not like . . . sincere though they might be. . . .[38]

While Langston Hughes moved freely among older intellectuals and his own "radical" contemporaries, he was well able to write about house-rent parties, fried fish and pig's feet, meeting "ladies," maids and truck drivers, the ring of their laughter in his ears, the soft slow music and floor shaking as the dancers danced, but none of this touched the pages of Jessie Fauset's books. She attended neither A'Lelia Walker's nor Carl Van Vechten's parties. Her own parties had quite a different atmosphere.

> At Miss Fauset's, a good time was shared by talking literature and reading poetry aloud and perhaps enjoying some conversation in French. White people were seldom present there unless they were very distinguished white people, because Jessie Fauset did not feel like opening her home to mere sightseers, or faddists momentarily in love with Negro life. At her house, one would usually meet editors and students, writers and social workers, and serious people who liked books and the British Museum, and had perhaps been to Florence (Italy, not Alabama).[39]

Although she was not the first black woman to have a novel published, in 1924 with the appearance of *There Is Confusion,* Jessie Fauset became the first Negro woman to be publicly recognized as an accomplished writer of this form.

The most important contribution she made is perhaps best seen in her portrayal of intraracial cast distinctions among Negroes.

Robert Bone, white critic of black writers, rated all four of

Jessie Fauset's novels poor. He did not like her "passing for white" themes or her efforts to apprise educated whites of the existence of respectable Negroes and to call their attention to racial injustice. She was considered part of the rear guard who were criticized for drawing their characters from the middle class rather than lower income blacks and for suppressing "racial differences rather than emphasizing them."[40] He lists Walter White and Nella Larsen along with Jessie Fauset in this category.

It is true that Jessie Fauset maintained a traditional social distance from the Negro masses. Yet she wrote of "that oneness which colored people feel in a colored crowd, even though so many of its members are people whom one does not want ever to know."[41]

Bone's arrogance shows! One is tempted to restate the views of those who say white critics are too insensitive to review fairly the works of black writers. Suffice it to say that Bone might have explored more fully the life of Negro women during that period. No other writer, surely not Nella Larsen, whom he praises, deals more directly and sensitively with the inner conflicts and turmoils of the "mulatto aristocracy" than Jessie Fauset.

The concerns, anxieties, and hangups of the middle class, especially the women, are an authentic part of the black experience, and they needed also to be revealed, if not protested. There *is* an exploration of interiority in Fauset's works.

Color preferences and differences have seriously divided black people in the past and much of this division continues even today. This is a history we must know and analyze in order to avoid the same mistakes and prevent the painful consequences of a divided group. Many light-skinned Negroes were holding leadership positions in the race at the time of Fauset's writing. How they thought, felt, behaved, what their aspirations were, even what rejections they faced while abiding by all the rules of white America provide this continuing valuable lesson: When the chips are down, all blacks, regardless of status, can quickly become "niggers" to too many whites in this land.

Miss Fauset wrote about the Negroes she knew. She never pretended to delve into areas unfamiliar to her. And yet, the theme of black self-acceptance runs through all her novels. In this respect she satisfies Alain Locke's criteria for the New Negro Mood; she spoke directly to the theme of cultural black nationalism—Black Is Beautiful! With the large numbers of mulattos in the Twenties, the issue was one of light-skinned Negroes accepting themselves as Negroes and not as a group apart from the black masses and deserving special consideration. She handles this theme well.

Her last book, *Comedy, American Style,* published in 1933, describes the effect of one Negro woman's self-hatred on the lives of her three children.

Married to a doctor who could pass for white if he so chose, Olivia spends all her energies trying to force their two oldest children into pseudo-white lives; their youngest son, she despises because of his disappointing brown color. The daughter suffers a loveless marriage to an ill-tempered bigot from whom her true racial identity must remain hidden, the older son manages to thwart his mother's lily-white drive, and the younger son, after futile years of trying to win his mother's affection, finds his only solace in suicide. *Comedy, American Style,* provides some stinging truths of how one woman's hatred of her race and herself destroys all but one of the lives she should have nurtured and enriched.

Dramatic? Yes, of course. Real? Ask any "over thirty" bourgeoisie black. Color differences have made serious inroads into our self-concept. Jessie Fauset makes no appeal to whites to accept Negroes. Rather, she asks that we blacks accept ourselves.

Her portrayal of black professionals acknowledges the presence of a respectable middle class that is very much caught up in its own affairs. Though they may be considered elitist, they exhibit little concern for white institutions and values. In fact, she almost makes a case for middle-class separatism. Those of her characters who favor white meet with tragic endings. The heroes are those who have a healthy regard for a Negro identity.

Even though Jessie Fauset had a limited constituency, she was an ardent advocate of Langston Hughes, Countee Cullen, and other "young radicals." "We all liked Jessie Fauset," said Countee Cullen, "though she held different social views." Bone seems puzzled by this inconsistency. Whites often make the mistake of believing that blacks have the same generation gaps that they have or that our professional jealousies and divisions are more serious than they appear. As literary editor of the *Crisis,* she was openly supportive of the young Renaissance writers. Being actively involved in the NAACP, it would have been inconsistent for her to reject the new Negro disciples and to consider their work unimportant. Rather, she championed them and still wrote about the themes closest to her.

Nella Larsen

Nella Larsen wrote two books that placed her in the Renaissance period.[42] Unlike Jessie Fauset, who was right in the middle of the excitement, Nella Larsen was unheard of until the publication of her book *Quicksand* in 1928.

Born in Chicago, she moved to Tuskegee, where she taught nursing. She was married to a physicist, had been a social worker, Assistant Superintendent of Nursing at Lincoln Hospital, and an assistant librarian.

It was alleged that Carl Van Vechten discovered her and probably introduced her to publisher Alfred Knopf. But there is no mention of her in any of his biographies, though his association with other Negroes is a substantial part of his life story. Nor do any of the other Renaissance writers mention her in their autobiographies.

Quicksand won the Harmon Award for distinguished achievement among Negroes. Later a second novel, *Passing*, was published. Knopf had agreed to publish three novels in all, but only those two were ever completed.

Quicksand is probably part autobiography. Helga Crane, the heroine, like Nella Larsen herself, was the daughter of a Danish mother and West Indian Negro father. Also like the author, her heroine spent several years in Copenhagen. Miss Larsen went to college there.

Quicksand and *Passing* deal with the problems of adjustment faced by two women who are products of interracial marriages. *Passing* is a story about a "tragic mulatto who lived as a white woman then tried to resume life again as a black woman." *Quicksand* presents an emotional suicide brought about by an intelligent, talented black woman taking up life among poor blacks in the South. The modern black reader, if not those of the past, will surely find the description of her life among the poor blacks in Alabama offensive. The stories are so overdrawn that one finds it difficult to understand Robert Bone's put-down of Jessie Fauset's completely plausible characters and his enthusiasm for Nella Larsen's works. He considered her the only successful writer among the rear guard group. Margaret Just Butcher's assessment was more nearly an accurate one. She indicated that Nella Larsen's novels fail somehow to "overcome a self-conscious effort to convince the reader that the leading characters are really caught between two worlds or two cultures."[43] White is really preferred.

And certainly the heroines' solutions in both books are all tragic failures. Unlike Miss Fauset's novel, in these we never see a constructive solution to these color hangups.

Somewhat like the heroine Helga, Nella Larsen just disappeared after 1930. That year a short story of hers appeared in *Forum*

Magazine entitled "Sanctuary." Many readers wrote the magazine suggesting that the story had been plagiarized from one published in 1922. She rebutted the claims to the satisfaction of the publishers of *Forum,* but never published another piece. A former friend of hers said: "After that, she just passed on over and disappeared into Greenwich Village." Neither she nor Helga accepted blackness.

Zora Neale Hurston[44]

If the Harlem Renaissance was characterized by an iconoclastic spirit, experimentation in life styles, and accent on the new and untried, then Zora Neale Hurston was the living embodiment of it all.

If the New Negro searched through African ancestral arts seeking a particular source of inspiration, as Alain Locke claims, then Zora Neale Hurston was their High Priestess.

If the New Negroes were differentiated from other intellectuals by their race consciousness, group awareness, and sense of common purpose, then Zora Neale Hurston was surely one of the intimate circle. But, with it all, she was an individualist, doing her own thing in her own way.

The New Movement for Negro artists and creators is said by some to have been marked by show-offism and an uninhibited display of one's significance. In this, Zora Neale Hurston was a superstar! Wallace Thurman called the Harlem literati the "niggerati," and of this "niggerati," says Langston Hughes, Zora Neale Hurston was "certainly the most amusing." She was part of the "we" about whom Arna Bontemps, poet and novelist of that time, wrote: "When we were not too busy having fun, we were shown off and exhibited and presented in scores of places to all kinds of people. And we heard the sighs of wonder, amazement and sometimes admiration when it was whispered or announced that here was one of the 'New Negroes.' "[45]

Here indeed was not only a New Negro, but absolutely and forthrightly a New Negro Woman. Zora Neale Hurston, anthropologist and writer, not only broke the bonds of bourgeoisie respectability, but defied the rigid expectations of educated, gifted black females and strutted across the pages of the black Renaissance as its Amazon!

Exciting, unconventional Zora was really the first black female scholar and writer to cut loose from the typical bourgeoisie pattern of living and writing which characterized all female writers before her. Unlike most of them, she never spent a day teaching in a schoolroom. In fact, when she couldn't get funds to write and pursue her anthropological field studies, she worked as a domestic!

She got just close enough to club and sorority activities of the middle class to get membership cards, but Zora never really fitted into this area of black female life.

Always the individual, in her writings she departed drastically from every other literary woman. There was none of the emotional and racial protest appeal of Frances Harper in her writings. The gentility and wistfulness of Georgia Douglass Johnson's poems never touched her stories. And unlike Nella Larsen and Jessie Fauset—the towering figures of her day—she never wrote about the mulatto aristocacy. She wrote about Southern sharecroppers and laborers, black and struggling to survive. She is, perhaps, the most outstanding black folklorist of that time, though acknowledged as such only by black writers. She wrote of the hates, loves, and daily grinding struggles of poor marginal blacks. Child of the masses, she lived and wrote of their humanity as a soul sister who had been there.

In the end she died in poverty and obscurity, unnoticed and almost forgotten by both blacks and whites. Even today the mention of her name brings the sad query: "Zora Neale Hurston, what ever happened to her?"

Maybe the current quest for authentic material for black studies will resurrect her work from such undeserving obscurity. Her concern with the female intelligentsia was not matched again until Gwendolyn Brooks became poet laureate of Chicago.

Her fierce determination to shock and avoid the usual safe, pretty protest themes of polite, gentle-bred Negro women and to deal with the violence, terror, and humanity of the proletariat paves an independent way for a growing number of young black female writers of today. Surely, from somewhere Zora smiles upon Nikki Giovanni, Maya Angelou, and Carolyn Rodgers, to mention only a few of the beautiful "home free" sensitive writers now among us. Were she alive she'd say again: "Grab the broom of anger and drive off the beast of fear."

She grew up in one of those near-poverty all-Negro towns, Eatonton, Florida, one of eight children whose mother died early. While her mother was in labor, a white man wandered by and cut the umbilical cord. Thus began a friendship which lasted until the man died, while Zora was still a child. Her family considered her "not like anybody they knew" and it was this white man who listened to her and responded to her intellectual curiosity. He also advised her to "grow guts as you go along," helping to instill a value system that included courage and fight, two things she was never without.

In spite of her large family, she was to say, "Nothing and nobody touched me." She loved books, but was seldom able to remain in school. She knew poverty firsthand: "There is something about poverty that smells like death. Dead dreams dropping off the heart like leaves in a dry season and rotting around the feet; impulses smothered too long in the fetid air of underground caves. The soul lives in a sickly air. People can be slave-ships in shoes."[46]

Another white friend entered her life at a critical moment, this time in the person of a poor white woman. Seeing Zora mistreated by the woman's physician brother, knowing she was unable to go to school, she recommended Zora to a singer from up North who was appearing in a Gilbert and Sullivan Company in a local theater. Zora lied about her age, and was hired as a maid; she traveled for several months with the troupe. She was at home with this gay, witty group and soon became a "play-pretty" to them. This observation of how whites saw her was to last with her always.

The actress for whom she worked insisted that Zora continue her education. Eventually she went to Morgan College and received a scholarship to Howard University, where she met Alain Locke, Charles S. Johnson, and other Negro scholars. She joined a literary society, and one of her stories, "Spunk," received an award. At Howard she was stimulated by black intellectuals. In a short time she won a scholarship to Barnard College and a job as Fannie Hurst's resident companion-secretary. "The Social Register crowd at Barnard soon took me up, and I became Barnard's sacred cow."[47]

She was interested in anthropology and became Franz Boaz's protégé. Upon her graduation from Barnard, Professor Boaz secured for her a fellowship, one of several she received during her life, to go South and collect Negro folklore. Though her friend Langston Hughes thought Zora was a fine folklore collector, "able to go among the people and never act as if she had been to school at all," she felt her Barnard education had alienated her from the masses. "My first six weeks were a failure. The glamor of Barnard College was still upon me. I dwelt in marble halls . . . I went about in carefully accented Barnardese, 'Pardon me, but do you know any folk songs?' " She had to unlearn some of her cultured ways in order to get material, and this took time and effort.

During this period, Mrs. R. Osgood Mason became Zora's godmother and patron. A $200 a month stipend and other gifts from her made it possible for Zora to study and work. Mrs. Mason was also the patroness of Miguel Covarrubias, Max Eastman, and Langston Hughes.

Zora Neale Hurston and Langston Hughes used the same words in describing Mrs. Mason: "amazing, brilliant, rich, and demanding." They both thought she tried to control people's lives. Both speak of glamorous evenings in her Park Avenue apartment. Both spoke of her impatience with any dissipation of their energies in projects which did not meet with her approval. She was "eager to hear every word on every phase of life on a saw mill 'job,'" said Zora. "I must tell the tales, sing the songs, do the dances, and repeat the raucous sayings and doings of the Negro farthest down. She is altogether in sympathy with them, because she says truthfully they are utterly sincere in living."[48]

Yet one gets the feeling that Zora chafed under the demands made on her. Langston Hughes also saw their patroness's drive in the same light.

"Concerning Negroes," he stated, "she felt that they were America's great link with the primitive, and that they had something very precious to give to the Western world. She felt that there was a mystery and mysticism and spontaneous harmony in their souls, but that many of them had let the white world pollute and contaminate that mystery and harmony, and make it something cheap and ugly, commercial and, as she said, 'white.' She felt that we had a deep well of the spirit within us and that we should keep it pure and deep."[49]

He did agree with Zora's description of Mrs. Mason's famous tongue: "cutting off your outer pretenses, and bleeding your vanity like a rusty nail."

After his book went to press, he grew tired of the grind and pressure of writing. "I felt she knew," he said, "that sometimes for months a writer doesn't feel like writing." Then he grew restive in New York as the Depression began its erosion. "I got so I didn't like to go to dinner on luxurious Park Avenue . . . and come out and see people hungry on the street, huddled in subway entrances. . . . I knew I could very easily and quickly be there too, hungry and homeless on a cold floor, anytime Park Avenue got tired of supporting me. I had no job, and no way of making a living."[50]

During the Depression Zora went to Westfield, New Jersey, and rented a house near Langston's writing retreat; together they worked on *Mule Bones,* a Negro folk comedy.

Zora, according to Langston, "was seriously hemmed in in the village-like Westfield." But their mutual patroness felt Zora should not be running about New York while preparing her folk material for publication, "so she was restless and moody, working in a nervous manner." This may account for her eventual falling out with Hughes and the termination of their working partnership. Or perhaps she became enraged with him because he terminated his relationship with Mrs. Mason. "More and more tangled that winter became the skein of poet and patron, youth and age, poverty and wealth—one day it broke! Quickly and quietly in the Park Avenue drawingroom it broke. . . ."[51]

The rift between Zora and Hughes was perhaps to prove even more painful. Discovering that the Gilpin Players of Cleveland had agreed to stage a trial run of *Mule Bones,* Hughes tried desperately to get in touch with Zora. However, according to Hughes, she had developed an insane jealousy over Hughes' relationship with an unnamed woman, which led her not only to deny permission for the production of the play, but to render her break with Hughes beyond repair.[52]

Langston never heard from her again. She never mentions him in her own autobiography beyond the most casual notice. It was never known what happened to Zora's growing annoyance at Mrs. Mason's demands.

Perhaps she was better able to fit the "primitive category" so needed to satisfy Mrs. Mason. Unlike Langston Hughes, who was digging into Harlem culture for his literary expression, Zora spent several years in the turpentine camps of Florida writing in vibrant imagery of life there. Barely escaping being cut to death by a turpentine worker's lady friend, she hurriedly packed her clothes and went on to study voodoo in New Orleans.

Picture Zora lying naked for three days and nights on a couch, with a rattle snake on her navel and a pitcher of water—that's all—at the head of her couch! As a student of Frizzly Rooster, the voodoo priest, she became a High Priestess of Voodoo. Her study of this ancient art took her to Nassau. There she collected over 100 songs which she meant to show the world. *Voodoo Gods* was published after further intensive study of the subject in Haiti and the British West Indies.

Then, taking to the concert stage, she introduced West Indian songs and dances to American audiences, but it was not until Pearl Primus and Harry Belafonte popularized Caribbean dance and music that we came to appreciate Zora's pioneer research into the folk music and art of the Caribbean.

In *Jonah's Gourd* she wrote about poor whites, saying she was so fed up with the race problem she wanted to prove that she could write about whites. In all, Zora wrote five books, several stories, and, with Langston Hughes, one play, and she held two Guggenheim Fellowships.

Though her novel *Their Eyes Were Watching God* was written in Haiti, it is about a black woman who chafed under the yoke of middle class respectability and who lived freely and uninhibitedly among the migrant Florida Everglades cane pickers. Some of Zora's personal determination to enjoy life comes through in the characterization of the novel's heroine, Janie.

This is a work which deserves reading by anyone interested in a well-told story, a well-drawn portrait of the emotional compromises struck by all too many blacks determined to make it in America, and it will be enjoyed as well by those who appreciate finely drawn characterization. There is Janie, whose joy of life was stifled through marriages to two men whose expectations of her did not deal with her sexuality. There is Tea Cake, twelve years her junior, who finally frees Janie's spirit and body, and eventually, with whom she has a positive love relationship.

Zora Neale Hurston's deep understanding of human nature enabled her to report with sharp accuracy the moods and modes of her female characters, but she also had a marvelous capacity to see the meaning of black manhood in the lives of the male characters she created.

People remember Zora Neale Hurston as colorful and unorthodox.

> . . . Zora on Lenox Avenue is measuring the heads of passing Harlemites with a strong-looking anthropological device.
>
> . . . Zora, needing a nickle to go downtown, approaches a blind man who is calling out, "Please help the blind." "I need the money worse than you do today," she says, taking five cents out of his cup. "Lend me this. Next time I'll give it back."

Like Langston Hughes and others, she was a friend of Carl Van Vechten. "If Carl was a people instead of a person, I could then say, these are my people."

Yet it was precisely her relationship with white patrons and other white persons that detracted from her popularity among blacks. She had been befriended by whites at critical moments in her life and was convinced of their sincerity. On the other hand, she suffered some of the snobbishness from the Negro bourgeoisie who did not see her as did writer Fannie Hurst, who later was to say, "Regardless of race, Zora had the gift of walking into hearts." At a time when a college education was proof of a person's ability to live a respectable middle-class black style of life, Zora was breaking all the rules. Those who valued safety and security viewed her as raffish, unpredictable, and irresponsible.

The final break with the black community came in 1950, just ten years before her death. She became a domestic on the Florida Gold Coast. When reporters discovered her, she said: "You can use your mind only so long. Then you have to use your hands. It's just the natural thing. I was born with a skillet in my hands. I like to cook and keep house."[53]

She was severely criticized for working as a domestic as well as for her refusal to become militant on racial matters. Quoted *Time* magazine: "The race question, she said, always left her completely unmoved. She died without succumbing to bitterness [meaning racial matters]."[54]

That may well have been the understatement of the year.

She died without opening herself to white people. Zora may not have been as pro-white and anti-Negro as some felt. In a speech before a white audience in Washington, D.C., she said: "We are a polite people. We do not say to the questioner, 'Get out of here.' We smile and tell him something that satisfies him. . . . The white person doesn't know what he is missing. The Indian resists curiosity by silence. The Negro offers a featherbed resistance. That is, we let a little slip out. The white man is always trying to know into somebody else's business. 'All right,' we say, 'I'll leave something outside the door of my mind for him to play with and handle. He can read my writing but he sho can't read my mind.' "[55]

Zora saw herself as a showcase Negro, and perhaps she held back the "inner Zora" from them, despite her pretense at *not being* a race woman. Though she worked in many literary mediums, she may well go down in history as a superb folklorist. Indeed, much of her material is still waiting for future scholars and writers to harvest.

A'Lelia Walker: The Harlem Renaissance Salon Lady

Throughout history women have been vitally involved in the search for better ways of conducting human affairs, of humanizing the life of mankind. Their prescribed "behind the scenes" roles have forced them to express themselves mainly through organizational efforts; instead of dealing with females as individuals, society has had to deal with collectives, numbers of women united under a club or society banner.

One notable exception was the Salon.

Most of the early European salons flourished at a time when

censorship prohibited freedom of speech. Notable women, a few creative themselves, provided protection for those who espoused unpopular causes like representative government, liberty, and equality by offering a place and climate for discussion.

Into the Harlem Renaissance came just the right hostess to create a black salon—A'Lelia Walker. "A'Lelia an intellectual? You must be kidding! Why, she was as intellectual as my left shoe." So spoke a distinguished woman upon hearing her described as an important figure of the Renaissance period.

She was not a writer, a composer, a dancer, or a painter, nor was she an organizational woman, and though her mother, Madam Walker, left her the first million dollar fortune created within the race—a hair-straightening empire—she never used any of it to become a race leader. In fact, she hated clubs and organizations and only nominally ran the Walker enterprises. She attended Fisk University for a while but never graduated. Many would claim that she was not a beauty, at least by white standards held so sacred by many Negroes of that time. But Langston Hughes thought her a "gorgeous dark Amazon."[56]

A'Lelia grew up in an opulence made possible by her mother's vast wealth. There was a fine townhouse at 80 Edgecomb Avenue, New York City, plus a mansion called Villa Lewaro on the Hudson River, resplendent with gold-plated piano, Flemish billiard table, Japanese prayer rugs, bronze statues by Rodin, a library of more than 600 volumes (many never opened but bound in the best leather), including the complete works of Rabelais, Balzac, and Plato. There were spacious sunken gardens, a swimming pool, and a completely equipped gymnasium. It was a $600,000 investment which later sold under the hammer of the auctioneer at less than $100,000. Her mother died at the age of fifty and left it all to A'Lelia.

Madam Walker, as she was called, was a philanthropist and race-conscious woman, and shortly before her death she had completed plans for a Tuskegee-type school in Africa. A'Lelia never carried this out, for she took no interest in civic affairs, though the company maintained a responsible role in the black community throughout its productive life.

A'Lelia Walker was a colorful person. She was married and divorced three times, and escorted about town by many prominent men. One of them, Caska Bonds, introduced her to Carl Van Vechten.

A'Lelia's name was closely associated with Van Vechten's and some believed that she provided the inspiration for Adora Boniface in *Nigger Heaven.*[57] He depicted Adora as beautiful, witty, restless, and cosmopolitan—at least this much of Adora resembled A'Lelia. And since she attended many of his parties (and he hers), many blacks who hated *Nigger Heaven* accused her of betraying her race by giving Van Vechten opportunities to intimately observe Negroes at play. She refused even to discuss the book.

It is hard to assign a "serious" role to the A'Lelia Walker of the society pages. Her standard of living was dazzling by any measure, but it was incredible to poverty-stricken blacks. When her daughter reached debutante age, A'Lelia gathered a group of young girls and founded the Debutantes Club, thereby launching the first Negro debutante ball. When her daughter married it was a $42,000 affair—unheard of in Negro life.

If A'Lelia provided the material for Adora Boniface, then Carl Van Vechten painted only a part of her life. Hughes observed:

> At her at-homes, Negro poets and Negro numbers bankers mingled with downtown poets and seat-on-the-stock-exchange racketeers. Countee Cullen would be there and Witter Bynner, Muriel Draper and Nora Holt, Andy Razaf and Taylor Gordon. And a good time was had by all.[58]

They came to A'Lelia's Thursdays as often as they could—not because she was an intellectual, for she made no such pretense—but because she knew how to put people at ease and help them relate to each other.

In 1927 a group of young artists and writers were invited to discuss and plan a meeting place for members of the arts. A'Lelia was anxious to turn over a portion of a family house for this purpose. The name Dark Tower, which she named the meeting place, was taken from a Countee Cullen poem. She decorated the quarters and it was to have been maintained through subscription of 50 members. The club flourished for a period in the Twenties, but failed during the Depression and was eventually sold to the city.

The Dark Tower, however, did not take the place of her weekly gatherings. As she traveled around the world, the exciting people she met were always invited to meet the talents who came regularly to her salon. The mixture of old and young, the odd and the established respectables created a brew of intellectual and artistic ferment that marked the Harlem Renaissance and established her role in it.

A'Lelia was the first and last black Salon Lady. Only one white woman, Mabel Dodge, was to take on this role in America, creating a salon for white intellectuals in Greenwich Village.

Curiously, Mabel Dodge and A'Lelia Walker drew some of the same people, at least the white ones. Carl Van Vechten frequented both salons. Some of the white intellectuals seen at A'Lelia's are to be "remembered for their close personal relationships with certain individuals from the Harlem Renaissance."[59]

One has to understand the emergence and growth of the Harlem Renaissance within the framework of Negro-white relations in New York and the reality of New York City as the intellectual and cultural capital of the white world of America. "Historically there was an ethnic or aesthetic interaction between those two racial movements."[60]

By studying the development and life of Mabel Dodge's salon, one can understand something of the intellectual and cultural ferment of the times; also one can gain some insight into the personality and temperament needed to hostess such an affair by reading Mrs. Dodge's *Memoirs.* But it is clear that Mabel Dodge had no inclination to entertain blacks. In fact, she made a point of declaring that only two blacks ever attended her salon.

A'Lelia's gatherings, on the other hand, were open to all with something to add to the group.

> Once a Scandinavian Prince tried to get through the crowd in the hallway but gave up, sent a message to A'Lelia that His Highness was waiting outside. A'Lelia sent word that she saw no way of getting His Highness in either, nor could she get through the crowd to greet him. But she offered to send down refreshments to the Prince's car![61]

A'Lelia had all that it took to be a Salon Lady. But all that she stood for faded with her death at age 46. Later there would be superb party givers and sensitive hostesses, some of whom would display the gift of occasionally gathering together the new and established intellectuals and artists. Marietta Dockery, Marian Logan, and Mollie Moon could qualify as successors. But, for one reason or another—lack of money or time, the need to pursue professional lives of their own—no black woman has really filled the role of Salon Lady as A'Lelia Walker did.

A'Lelia was stricken at a party in New Jersey with what her friends described as "nervousness" and retired to her cottage early. In the night she called her friend Mamie: "Mamie, I can't see, get me some ice." She then slipped into a coma. A doctor was called and pronounced her dead of a stroke.

Langston Hughes wrote: "When A'Lelia died in 1931, she had a grand funeral. . . . That was really the end of the gay times of the New Negro era in Harlem, the period that had begun to reach its end when the crash came in 1929 and the white people had much less money to spend on themselves, and practically none to spend on Negroes, for the Depression brought everybody down a peg or two. And the Negroes had but few pegs to fall."[62]

THE TRANSITIONAL WRITERS[63]

What was the "continuing tradition" of the New Negro movement among black female writers between the end of "the generous 1920's" and the time of the black revolution of the Sixties, a span of thirty years? "It started as a Black Depression indeed—we were no longer in vogue. Colored actors began to go hungry, publishers politely rejected new manuscripts and patrons found other uses for their money. . . ."[64]

Jessie Fauset was the exception; she was acknowledged as a leader of the Negro Renaissance and held a position as editor of *Opportunity* as well as being a patron of young Negro writers. The two major women writers of the Negro Renaissance, Nella Larsen and Zora Neale Hurston, disappeared into oblivion; Zora Neale died broke and, like Bessie Smith, was buried in an unmarked grave.

Nella Larsen simply passed over the color line . . . being and living black was probably too painful for her. With her passage went her literary continuity, for little of the struggle of Helga, heroine of *Quicksand,* relates to the female black experience in America today.

There are lessons for all black women to learn in recognizing the loneliness of the two lives—Nella Larsen's and Zora Neale Hurston's—and even in the widespread acceptance of Jessie Fauset's contribution much can be understood. Black women's organizations have a special obligation to literary and artistic women in whose hands rest the brush strokes and printed images of black womanhood—how black women lived, loved, and endured. This talent must be encouraged if black female personality is not to be totally defined by whites and men. It should be unthinkable that an artist would suffer rejection from her black sisters.

Davis believed that one of the reasons Zora Neale did not enjoy popularity was her "writing counter to the protest themes"; yet, she was ahead of her time, for she clearly wrote "revelation" themes, Janie's interaction with three different black husbands is as relevant today as yesterday. While, as Davis says, the theme to emerge from the pens of black male writers as they moved to intergroup conflicts were "attacks concerning the Negro woman," Zora is accused of "emasculating her husbands and lovers by insisting that they conform to middle-class standards."[65] On the other hand, the interiority theme, so important to Ralph Ellison, is surely seen through Zora Neale's eyes, and her ideas about black female-male conflicts are as instructive to black women today as any other black theme. Janie is the first literary female model whose struggle to "make it" with black men remains true to life.

Jessie Fauset and Georgia Douglass Johnson were "establishment" blacks. They had the support of distinguished families and well-to-do husbands. And the Negro literary establishment accepted them as peers. Zora faced snobbishness.

What comes through from the Harlem Renaissance is a camaraderie of kindred literary figures whose lives intertwined and bouyed each others' efforts. Yet little of this togetherness is associated with women writers, either as peers of the men in their time or as a "we are women together trying to make it" sisterhood.

Osceola Adams, actress and founder of the Harlem Actors School which was supported during the Great Depression by WPA funds, speaks often of other women artists and writers who disappeared from the public eye, discouraged because the racism and sexism in literature were too much to bear.

One of Miss Adams' favorites, Gwendolyn Bennett, did, in fact, in the summer of 1926, help start a literary magazine called *Fire.* According to Hughes, the young artists founded the magazine to abolish "conventional 'Negro-white' ideas of the past" and to force the black literary power structure to recognize the younger Negro writers and artists, and provide them with an outlet for publication not available in the established journals.

Fire, according to Hughes, was rejected by "Negro intellectuals, DuBois, the Negro Press, and went largely unnoticed by whites."[66] With the exception of a few poems appearing in a few anthologies, Gwendolyn Bennett became a "whatever happened to . . . ."

And yet, whatever their lives had been, or whatever the evaluation of their literary contributions, there was motivation enough and encouragement aplenty for the emergence during the transitional years of four major black women writers; they bridged the twenty-year period before the black revolution of the Sixties produced the New Breed.

Ann Petry: The Richard Wright Tradition[67]

Like Zora Neale Hurston, Ann Petry also attempted to express her versatility by writing a novel about whites. Of all the black female writers she was probably in the best position to do so. Zora Neale Hurston did not move among whites until she entered Barnard, where, by her own admission, she was the "showcase Negro." For twelve years she wrote about Southern blacks. When she finally did write about poor white Southerners, in *Seraph on the Swanee,* it was her very last literary contribution.

Ann Petry, however, was born and raised in Old Saybrook, Connecticut. Her father was the local druggist and she herself a product of integrated education, from grade school through the University of Connecticut School of Pharmacy. For a short while she worked in her family's drugstore, but growing restless to write and live among Negroes, she moved to New York. There, among other jobs, she served as a reporter for the *People's Voice.*

Her first novel, *The Street* (1946), was considered by some as a worthy successor to Richard Wright's *Native Son.* Her thesis was simply to "show that environment can change the course of a person's life." The character of Lutie is immediately recognizable to us. In 1946 we were all able to identify numerous Luties among our family and friends. The novel is about a black woman's struggle to (1) get a decent job "other than that of a domestic," (2) make an attractive home out of a rundown inadequate apartment, and (3) rear a boy to be a decent, ordinary citizen, without the help of husband and funds. They are basic black female struggles, and as such serve an important function in literary expression.

Bone justifies his "poor" rating of this novel with these words: "The trouble with *The Street* is that it tries to make racial discrimination responsible for slums . . . a larger frame of reference is required."[68]

What larger frame of reference? Was Lutie lacking in will power? Did she lack physical strength? Was she lazy? Immoral? The reader tests these character demands on page after page. But it is precisely The Street with its opportunity structure girded by institutional racism that beats Lutie in the end. It is this plus a mixture of black pathology that ruins her. Just as Jessie Fauset brought us face to face with the mulatto-black theme among Negro women, showing the divisiveness and sickness it bred among black people, so Petry wastes little time creating white characters for us to blame. *The Street* was the first novel written by a black woman that characterized a black woman struggling to exist in institutional racism of which slums are a direct result.

The interpretation of slum life in terms of institutional racism was an important undertaking for writers in the Richard Wright school. How else would a people cease believing that something in their genes doomed them to everlasting injustice? How else would they one day rise from their knees "taking everything to

God in prayer" and shout "We shall overcome." How else without writers who could focus attention on the institutions and structures of society that perform so well the function of oppression; how else, until writers, artists, and leaders turned our sights away from self-hatred and toward institutional racism?

Bone considered Ann Petry's *Country Place* an excellent novel. He appears to like the idea of black writers writing about whites. Perhaps the novel is superior. But, for blacks at least, it has little meaning. It may have served to mark Miss Petry as a superior novelist to white critics, but it scarcely added to the need for a strong literature on the black experience.

Paula Marshall should be considered in this transitional period. *Brown Girl, Brownstones* (1959),[69] like most of Marshall's work, deals with West Indian Negroes and their struggles in New York. *A Timeless Place, a Chosen People*[70] (1969) is actually centered in the West Indies.

There are two exceptional women writers, however, who dominated the Fifties and who continue to influence black literature in many ways—Margaret Walker and Gwendolyn Brooks. In many ways, both retain a close commitment to young people and are always given recognition by younger poets as models whose works influenced their own.

Margaret Walker[71]

Margaret Walker, poet, novelist, and Professor of English at Jackson State College, Mississippi, took the mulatto theme and placed it within a Southern context.

The scene of her prize-winning novel *Jubilee* opens with Vyry's mother, Sister Hetta, dying. She is 29 years old and had given birth to fifteen children, most of them by Master John Marston. Sis Hetta had been given to the young master by his father, who thought it better for a young man of quality to "learn life by breaking in a young nigger wench than it was for him to spoil a pure white virgin girl."[72] Vyry was Sis Hetta's last child.

Through the pages of this book, any student of history will recognize the background and landmarks of slavery and Reconstruction. *Jubilee* is a Civil War and Reconstruction novel. What is unique about it is the view from the inner world of a black woman as written by a black woman. It speaks to the mythology of the "matriarchy," male-female relationships, color differences, and slave versus free Negroes, and develops the character of Vyry as a model of female strength.

Margaret Walker creates no mysterious special status for mulattos; rather she shows the commonality of the brotherhood of slavery and gives a view of slavery from the Big House.

Vyry, in a moment of anger with a man she loved, gives her view of her place in the scheme of things: "You done called me a white folks nigger and throed up my color in my face because my daddy was a white man. He wasn't no father to me, he was just my master. . . . I ain't had nothing to do with my looking white no more'n you had nothing to do with your looking black. Big Missy was mighty mean to me from the first day I went in the Big House . . . she emptied Miss Lillian's pee pot in my face. She hung me up by my thumbs . . . worked me like a dog. They stripped me naked and put me on the auction block for sale. And worsted of all they kept me ignorant so I can't read and write my name. . . . Old Marster was my own daddy and he never did own me for his child. I begged him to let me marry you and go free and he say no. He ain't punish nobody when he stand to see them beat me. . . .[73]

Through obstacles, tragedies, and carefully designed plans for survival, we plot our way with Vyry. Which was worse for Vyry, slavery or Reconstruction? Both demanded all of her talents, energies, and fortitude. Through it all, she carries a firm, quiet determination to help her family survive.

The reader gets an excellent opportunity to test the matriarchal stereotype. Vyry never nags or dominates her husband, but is quick to intervene in decisions about the welfare of the family.

As we watch Vyry at work, the casual reader might say that Vyry is in the tradition of all the frontier women of America. They helped settle the West. Certainly, these pioneer women did play a variety of roles; some even assumed masculine roles. But the roles played out by Vyry were never to be temporary ones in America. There never has been a time of settlement for black people when black women could assume any other role. And the strength that Vyry manifested in working side by side with her husband needed also to be passed on to her daughter and great granddaughters. And no matter where they are found today, it is likely that Vyry's model would be relevant to them.

Margaret Walker's contributions to literature are probably best known through her poetry. Just as Vyry emerges strong and sure, so does the strength of protest come swiftly from Margaret Walker's pen. Two of her poems that are very popular among black college students take us a long way from the gentle poems of Georgia Douglass Johnson and the piteous appeal to the heartstrings sometimes associated with Mrs. Harper's protest poetry.

In *We Have Been Believers* she is "turned off" from the "American Dream" and both African and Western religions.

We have been believers in the black gods of an old land,
believing the secrets of the seeress and the magic of the charmers
and the power of the devil's evil one.

Neither the slavers' whip nor the lynchers' rope nor the bayonet could
kill our black belief. In our hunger, we beheld the welcome table,
in our nakedness the glory of a long white robe. We have been
believers in the new Jerusalem.

We have been believers believing in our burdens and our demigods
too long.
Now the needy no longer weep and pray; the long suffering arise,
and our fists bleed against the bars with a strange insistency.[74]

This "strange insistency" she feels will be fulfilled in a "second generation full of courage coming to growth." The militancy of *For My People,* probably one of the most popular of all black poems, gives us a kind of soul shout.

Let a new earth rise. Let another world be born. Let a bloody
peace be written in the sky. Let a second generation full
of courage issue forth, let a people loving freedom come
to growth, let a beauty full of healing and a strength of
final clenching be the pulsing in our spirits and our blood.
Let the martial songs be written, let the dirges disappear.
Let a race of men now rise and take control![75]

Gwendolyn Brooks: Poet Laureate of Bronzeville[76]

Arthur Davis rightly described Gwendolyn Brooks as the "Poet of the Unheroic." She celebrates the life of garbagemen, domestics, Blackstone Rangers, and other ordinary poor folks who live in any black ghetto in America. They are "things of dry hours and the involuntary plan" who are caught up with "rent," "feeding of wife," "satisfying a man."

Bronzeville, or the Mecca—places where Miss Brooks' characters act out their lives—could be Watts, Hough, or Harlem, but are drawn from Chicago, Miss Brooks' long-time home. (After Carl Sandburg's death she was made Poet Laureate of Illinois.) The streets of Bronzeville are everywhere. There, in crowded tenement houses people get drunk, die, are raped and killed. But they also live!

All about are the cold places,
all about are the pushmen and jeopardy, theft—

all about are the stormers and scramblers but
what must our Season be, which starts from fear?
Live and go out.
Define and
medicate the whirlwind.[77]

It is the summation of little moments, unheroic actions, that bring such vitality of black people before us.

Exhaust the little moment. Soon it dies
And be it gash or gold it will not come
Again in this identical disguise.[78]

These are not the heroes who change the direction of history, or lead groups to momentous decisions. They are domestics like Hattie Scott who comes to the end of the day and says:

If she don't hurry up and let me out of here.
Keeps pilin' up stuff for me to do.
I ain't goin' to finish that ironin'.
She got another think comin'. Hey you.
Whatcha mean talkin' about cleanin' silver?
It's eight o'clock now, you fool.
I'm leavin'. Got somethin' interestin' on my mind.
Don't mean night school.[79]

In Bronzeville, "bad" and "good" girls cross each other's paths. A good girl may "stay in the front yard all my life. I want to peek at the back where it's rough and untended and hungry weeds grow. A girl gets sick of a rose."[80]

The women in Bronzeville are hard working, strong, and loving. They have hurt feet, loud voices, and fighting spirits. Loving men and children is their consuming concern, even the children lost in abortions.

Abortions will not let you forget.
You remember the children you got that you did not
get.[81]

One finds very little bitterness and defiance in the racial protest themes in this poetry. Before the publication of *In the Mecca,* her poetry reflected the goals of the integration period. Negroes were knocking on doors asking to be let in, appealing to justice as a source of racial progress. A typical low-key protest appeal comes at the end of *Annie Allen,* winner of the 1950 Pulitzer prize.

Open my rooms, let in the light and air.
Reserve my service at the human fest.
And let the joy continue. Do not hoard silence
For the moment when I enter, tardily,
To enjoy my height among you.[82]

But if the protest lacks outrage and anger, there is plenty of racial wisdom which stems from Miss Brooks' belief in group strength. At the conclusion of *Annie Allen,* she writes:

Rise
Let us combine. There are no magics or elves
or timely godmothers to guide us. We are lost, must
Wizard a track through our own screaming weed.[83]

Not enough can be said for Gwendolyn Brooks' involvement as mentor and editor of the works of young poets. Having won the coveted Pulitzer Prize in 1950, she might have joined the safe, conservative black literary establishment. But her life took a turn toward militancy, and evidently for at least one critic this caused her work to be seen in a lesser light. Davis writes: ". . . never a simple poet, Gwendolyn Brooks has grown more difficult with the years . . . she changed her style as well as her viewpoint in mid-career."[84] Though she was labeled by Davis as an integrationist in the mid-forties, he acknowledges that now Miss Brooks writes from "a very strong affirmation of blackness." Davis also believes that as Miss Brooks became "more black," there has been an increase in the obscurity of her verse. Davis is a respected scholar and critic of black writers, so his choice of the word "obscurity" must mean something very significant in the literary world. Gwendolyn Brooks, as an interpreter of the black experience through her existential position of being a black woman, perhaps more than any other black female writer has been a bridge, a foundational support, which encouraged the young "new breed" to "tell it like it is" and to move straight out of the academic chapels into the streets and places that touch the hearts and minds of black masses. And as these young writers moved, she moved.

By Miss Brooks' own account, she became involved with the Blackstone Rangers, a large group of Chicago ghetto youth, in 1967. After seeing these talented, so-called "teen gangsters" in a musical show, she offered to work with those who might be poets and prose writers. "With the arrival of these people my neatly paced life altered almost with a jerk. Never did they tell me to 'change' my hair to 'natural.' But soon I did. Never did they tell me to open my eyes to look about me. But soon I did. . . ."[85]

She not only nurtured many of the "new breed" poets and writers, through friendship or tutorship, but she made a commitment to publish her works through Dudley Randall of Broadside Press at a time when she was in demand by white publishers. This relationship is a very important one. Dudley Randall, himself a poet, was the first and sometimes only publisher of black poets. She and Randall together share, perhaps like no other literary figures, the designation of "Assistant to the Progress of Most Black Poet-Stars of the Day."

For Gwendolyn Brooks the connecting thread which runs through all her works is a commitment to human dignity. At the end of *In the Mecca* we see the majesty of common ordinary blacks.

> A garbageman is dignified
> As any diplomat.
> Big Bessie's feet hurt like nobody's business,
> but she stands—bigly—under the unruly scrutiny, stands in the wild weed.
>
> In the wild weed
> she is a citizen,
> and is a monument of highest quality; admirable.
>
> It is lonesome, yes. For we are the last of the loud,
> Nevertheless, live.
>
> Conduct your blooming in the noise and whip of the whirlwind.[86]

That's where Gwendolyn Brooks is, "in the noise and whip of the whirlwind," where many of us find also a reaffirmation of our black womanhood.

Young, Gifted, and Black: Lorraine Hansberry[87]

Lorraine Hansberry died too young—an obvious fact—but surely too young to be pigeonholed in Harold Cruse's "safe accommodationist black bourgeoisie box."

True she was a product of a well-to-do middle-class black family. One thing about being black, at least until recently, is the likelihood that all black classes mix constantly because of segregated housing in America. The suburban black child who never interacts with poor blacks is a phenomenon of hardly more than a decade.

Her play *A Raisin in the Sun* achieved unprecedented critical acclaim. Winner of the New York Drama Critics Circle Award for the Best American Play of 1959, it was an immediate hit. Never before had a black female playwright, black director, and star-studded cast of black actors and actresses come together on Broadway with such success. Its performers who were already gaining fame—Sidney Poitier (Ossie Davis followed him), Ruby Dee, Claudia McNeil—went on to greater success. And a young actress named Diana Sands got started on an equally successful career which, like Lorraine's, ended in a young and painful death.

Cruse felt that Americans accepted the play because it was "a good old-fashioned homespun saga of some working-class folk in pursuit of the American Dream—in their fashion." He thought the play glorified soap opera and took Miss Hansberry to task for "emerging like a Saint Joan of black cultural revival sounding off in journalistic and television debates like a prophetess who had suddenly appeared carrying messages from the 'soul' of the people."[88] Cruse considered the play simply one about a Negro family.

But integration is not the theme of "Raisin." It is about "Walter Lee coming into his manhood," as his mother aptly puts it. What blacks usually find in this play is a crisis of black male identity played out in a house full of women. Lorraine Hansberry chose to lead Walter Lee into a dilemma around the issue of a white man telling him he couldn't move his family into a white neighborhood when Walter Lee wanted to buy a house using his father's insurance money. Eldridge Cleaver's cry, "We shall have our manhood," was not yet the major demand of black militants in the year Lorraine Hansberry chose to deal with the theme of integration.

In the role of Walter Lee Younger, she created a character that was hammered out on the anvil of black intra-family struggles. The integration theme was a minor one; were it not, how could we account for the long run of the musical adaptation, *Raisin,* still so popular in the mid-Seventies. There was yet to come Ossie Davis's character Pearlie Victorious, who could look at the women in his family and say, "stay out of my struggle for power." For in Hansberry's time, Walter Lee was desperately coping with women who worked in "white folks' kitchens" to gain safety and security in home ownership. Walter Lee's need to make money fast and discard his chauffeur's cap for the significant job which would give him the dignity he craved led him to gamble his father's money away and jeopardized the purchase of the house—a house whites didn't want the Youngers to occupy. He almost succumbs to white pressure. In the end he dons the chauffeur's cap, acts courageously, and moves his family into the house, knowing the economic struggle would continue and he would only make it by hard work.

Lorraine Hansberry, like Ann Petry and others, wrote about

whites. The play *The Sign in Sidney Brustein's Window*, written in the Sixties, was based on characters she knew in Greenwich Village, most of them white. This play closed on the day of her death in 1965.

Cruse thought Miss Hansberry should have dealt with black middle-class themes, or emerging black militancy, or the subterranean world of black Negro life. She certainly could and probably would have done so had she lived. There were signs that pointed to future directions Miss Hansberry may have taken: In a letter to the editor of *The New York Times* in 1964: "I now read that some Negroes my own age and younger say that we must now lie down in the streets, tie up traffic, take to the hills with guns if necessary . . . and fight back. Fatuous people remark these days on our 'bitterness.' Why, of course we are bitter."[89]

Later she wrote, "I think . . . that Negroes must concern themselves with every single means of struggle: legal, illegal, passive, active, violent and non-violent. They must harrass, debate, petition . . . sit-in, sing hymns . . . and shoot from their windows when the racists come cruising through their communities. . . . The acceptance of our present condition is the only form of extremism which discredits us before our children."[90]

We cannot say where Lorraine Hansberry might be today on a political continuum and in comparison with the new breed writers, though her work is still very much alive. *To Be Young, Gifted and Black*, a collection of her works, some unfinished, enjoyed a long off-Broadway run. The theme prompted Nina Simone to write a song of the same name.

Certainly for her works to leave a continuing legacy—though she died at age 35, just before the fiercest testing period of the black revolution—is itself monumental. And we will always ponder these among her last words: "I think when I get my health back I shall go into the South to find out what kind of revolutionary I am. . . ."[91]

THE NEW BLACK RENAISSANCE AND ITS NEW BREED

It is commonly stated that following the wake of the civil rights movement of the Sixties, a new breed of revolutionary young black writers emerged. Davis, among others, credits the foregoing black writers with having prepared the ground and seeded the ideas for this current crop of writers. With Davis and others there is the strong suggestion that the new young writers have broken with their predecessors who wanted to be considered American writers and "a part of the mainstream of Western literary tradition." The new breed appeared more interested in a separatist black nationalist movement than in becoming carbon copies of the white mainstream American writers. The new black arts movement came to fruition as a "spiritual sister of the Black Power concept" with "a separate symbolism, mythology, critique, and iconology."[92]

This description, especially the use of the word "separatist" seems unrealistic, even repulsive, and is surely an inadequate assessment. These "new breed writers" have made constructive contributions to the literature of the black revolution. Any mass movement that requires courage and action needs literary and artistic support. While leaders have their place in calling the people to action, it is the artist's ability to engage the spirit and minds of the people which sustains their hopes and dreams.

The black women writers, for example, come close to Lerone Bennett's statement on the special role of black artist:

> . . . an artist in the situation of a Negro (i.e., a situation of oppression and injustice) in a segregated society which questions the humanity of all Negroes, whether they peel potatoes or write poems, has special responsibilities and special tasks . . . to break through to authenticity as a [person] to hack away through the dense underground of myths . . . to come to terms with [herself] and [her] history, to accept [herself], to accept the color of [her] skin and accept the ambiguity and tension of [her] experience: to see with [her] own eyes and to hear with [her] own ears and to find new language and new forms to express what [she] sees and hears, to see Negro experience within a wider context, to relate that experience to the great human themes of liberation and oppression, struggle and growth, victory and defeat, to express [herself] directly, openly, honestly, and if necessary, brutally without a prior check with the white Other; to emancipate [herself] from the limitation of the white culture structure and the subtle tyranny of white audiences. . . ."[93]

Among the prominent women writers, particularly among the youngest of them, there is a denial of a drastically "new" literary beginning. In a rap between Nikki Giovanni and Margaret Walker, who won the Yale Young Poets Award for *For My People* the year Nikki was born, Margaret Walker says: "Black literature is connected like a chain, with people who are influential in one period knowing and influencing folks in the next." Nikki agreed and added: "I have not seen the flames [of the Harlem Renaissance] die to be rekindled. . . . I think the terms we are using when we say Black Renaissance or the explosion of the poets or whatever in the Sixties are commercial terms and not scholastic or intellectual terms. . . ."[94]

Conversely, if "new language and new moods and ideology"

are characteristics of these writings and associated only with young writers, the women, at least, have displayed little of a generation gap, if by that we mean "the inability to communicate with those over 30."

Gwendolyn Brooks, who is not a "new young poet," was herself renewed and changed by the "new breed," especially Don I. Lee who, as her principal stimulus, wrote a poem that greatly influenced her.

> I
> seek
> integration
> of
> Negroes
> with
> black
> people.[95]

There are definitions and phrases that best differentiate "black revolutionary writers" from other poets who are black. Nikki Giovanni wrote: "Many people have asked what makes this different from the previous 'renaissance' . . . the difference is that there is no intellectual vanguard, there is no difference between the warrior, the poet and the people . . . no more movement that all the people aren't a part of. . . ."[96]

This is not easy. Sometimes the intellectuals feel that in this effort to relate to all the masses of blacks, there is a denigration of standards. Note the exchange between Margaret Walker and Nikki Giovanni.

> WALKER: Well, now you have asked a real aesthetic question and I think a good one. Sometimes a work of art is popular. Rarely is that true, because for something to be popular it must appeal to the taste of the masses, and in many instances the taste of the masses is not what we call a cultivated taste.
>
> GIOVANNI: (raises her voice) But that is *nothing but arrogance*!
>
> WALKER: (vehemently) I disagree, I disagree!
>
> GIOVANNI: Nothing but arrogance!
>
> WALKER: You are knocking down everything that's serious—art, music, literature. A person like Paula Marshall, for example, that's not ordinary writing that she does. It's exceptionally good writing. And you're saying it's arrogant if everybody doesn't appreciate it.
>
> GIOVANNI: No, I'm saying that the fact of it's being fine means if I took *Brown Girl, Brownstones* down to my little unwed mothers in

> Brooklyn and read it to them, they could relate to it. They should be able to relate to anything that Paula writes.
>
> WALKER: Well, now you're saying that they don't have to have a cultivated taste?
>
> GIOVANNI: I'm saying that art is not for the cultivated taste. It is to cultivate taste.
>
> WALKER: Well, I agree with that. But I'm saying to cultivate a taste is one thing, and not having it another.
>
> GIOVANNI: No, I'm saying that if we are indeed as great as sometimes we like to think we are, then we should be able to be heard by whomever chooses to become involved.[97]

"The black struggle," writes Toni Morrison, is "extricating oneself from an obsession with whiteness . . . the definition of one's self, life, art, experience, consciousness as black (and other things as white) must be understood as the effort of the psyche to free itself of its demons. So the deluge of writing . . . is not just the consequence of fashion. . . . It is a part of a monumental struggle for psychic liberation. The canon of black writing that is emerging is the result of an organic process of becoming, a process of establishing criteria and determining authenticity."[98]

From Phillis Wheatley's flight away from slave identity poetry to Nikki Giovanni and contemporary other "new breed" women poets and writers, there is not one rude, abrupt leap, but a progressive movement. All along, and surely by the time Gwendolyn Brooks and Margaret Walker gained popularity, black female writers were steadily becoming more iconoclastic, more power oriented, and therefore, some would say, "more violence prone."[99]

Margaret Walker predicted the coming of this new breed and joyfully wrote: "Let a new race of men now rise and take control," and Nikki reminded her, "We *are*."

About Gwendolyn Brooks, one of the young poets said: "Her writing might not be as loud as that of someone like Le Roi Jones, but she is the foundation on which a lot of black writers had to stand in order to get where they are. Her statements might seem quiet, in a way, but if you look closely, you'll see that she has been dealing with things the way they really are, that she has had her knuckles on all the time. That is why we think of her as a bridge."[100]

That, to say the least, she is.

> I am proud of these young people [wrote Gwendolyn Brooks]. They scratch out roads for themselves, are trying *be* themselves.

> They do not mind making "mistakes." In a new nation, what are mistakes, anyhow? . . . They are blacking English. . . . True, black writers speak as blacks, about blacks, to blacks. . . . These black writers do not care if you call their products Art or Peanuts. Artistic Survival . . . appointment to glory among the anointed elders, is neither their crevice nor creed. They give to the Ghetto gut. Ghetto gut receives. . . .[101]

This generational continuity is important. It is perhaps too painful or risky to acknowledge Stokely Carmichael's words: "Every Negro is a potential Black," or Cobbs and Grier's, "What needs knowing is that all Blacks are angry." If one can say that the new breed of poets represent "only a few Negroes," or dismiss them as a "bunch of radical misfits," then we reject reality. We pretend—wear masks that hide any identification with these words or images. Black women writers are simply expressing the anger, frustration, and yearnings of all but the most copped out, rejecting, and "hung-up" black women.

BLACK WOMEN WRITERS OF THE NEW RENAISSANCE

Maya Angelou (*I Know Why the Caged Bird Sings*), Louise Merriweather (*Daddy Was a Number Runner*), Toni Morrison (*The Bluest Eye*), and Alice Walker (*The Third Life of Grange Copeland*)[102] are all writers whose novels must be considered outstanding examples of the new breed who have probed Ralph Ellison's concept: "The interiority of the Black Experience."

Each of the novels deals with intragroup problems that focus on the "growing up" process of becoming a woman and the struggle it takes to be a whole person. They bypass the popular theme of black reactions to a racist society. Their books, as Gwendolyn Brooks says, express "blacks talking to blacks."

More important, these books were all published around the time when black male leaders of the black revolution were preoccupied with the need for black manhood and were relegating black women to secondary behind-the-scenes positions in the civil rights movement. These four writers, in particular, are responsible for pulling the black male/female problem/question/partnership out of the closet, enabling us to examine dimensions of the black female experience seldom before explored in print.

Alice Walker wrote recently: ". . . No matter what anyone says, it is the black woman's words that have the most meaning for us, her daughters, because she, like us, has experienced life not only as a black person but as a woman. . . . How simple a thing it seems to me, that to know ourselves as we are, we must know our mothers' names."[103] We have names here.

The Bluest Eye traces the tortuous development of a young girl's self-hatred; we see young Pecola's obsession with white standards of beauty eventually contributing toward her insanity—"best of all is ask God for a Blue Eye, settling even for one." We see her mother Pauline's preoccupation with acquiring virtues which she deems necessary for respectability: no drinking, no smoking, no sex. Pauline's obsession with such "goodness" leads to a rejection of fun and sexuality and eventually her vitality and humanity are stripped away. The total picture of self-denial, of not sharing a natural sexuality with her husband, leaves her a tragic victim. Virtue without natural human expression is too costly a price to pay for respectability. To cut off one's naturalness is corrosion of the human spirit. Yet, distinguishing between that which is respectable and healthy, and that which is irresponsible and excessive has always been a dilemma for all black women who feel we must live down that old stereotype of being oversexed!

Toni Morrison triggers words across the pages like bullets. She forces the reader sometimes unwillingly but always honestly to examine all the myths of those "thou shall not do's" that are perceived of as pleasing whites. Toni Morrison helps us question whether accepting phony "do's and don'ts" might not lay a foundation for neurotic repressions that negate self-affirmation—joy, laughter, sharing, and a natural sensuousness which justifies living.

Margaret in Maya Angelou's *I Know Why the Caged Bird Sings* and Francee in Louise Merriweather's *Daddy Was a Number Runner* are two girls who grow from childhood to adolescence in black ghettos. We see the maturing process black girls often go through as they develop into young women strong and competent enough to cope with life in spite of hostile environments. All the sordidness of life is documented—rape, incest, violence, hunger, pain. Both books help us understand the role of strong males in the development of healthy black females. One surely concludes from these works that homes where the father is either absent or powerless are just as detrimental to girls as to boys.

In Alice Walker's novel *The Third Life of Grange Copeland,* one black woman who faced life with "a certain inventiveness" is Sister Madelaine, a poor woman who became a fortune teller in order to put her son through Morehouse College. Her reward is a respectable civil rights fighter son who grew to love and respect her. But Sister Madelaine is a minor character, and Sister Madelaine has no visible husband. The rest of Walker's women fall victim to the problems their men face in their inability to share love and support with them.

It is a tragic story about men and women who fall in love and marry. As each of their love stories and passions unfold, the reader might cry out, Hold on to *that,* for God's sake, hold on to *that*! One by one, however, these women are destroyed—sadly, through the violence of men. This is a story about intragroup self-destruction attenuated by the injustice of the sharecropper system. Black women and children are equally victimized by any negative treatment of black men. When a man's selfhood is threatened, outraged, hacked away by oppression, he all too often turns against the woman and children he loves. He beats them, abuses them, and in some cases, even kills them.

Alice Walker writes about those themes; in that way she is closest in spirit to her predecessor Zora Neale Hurston. Zora grew up among poor Southern blacks; Alice Walker worked among them as a SNIK worker during the civil righs movement.

The message we face through *The Third Life of Grange Copeland* is best stated by one character as he watches Martin Luther King on TV during the early Montgomery movement days ". . . even with them crackers spitting all over him, he's gentle with his wife and children."

Here Alice Walker points toward the interiority of the black experience, the desperate, urgent problems of rage all too often turned inward, against one's own group, indeed, toward the persons one loves most. Through this book we also gain an understanding of men who just walk away from family life, and the women who yank themselves up, like Sister Madelaine, and draw upon their "strength constancy" and forge a way for themselves and their children.

As we live with Alice Walker's characters in the early Fifties, we are helped to face the vindication of the black rage turning outward to whites and away from ourselves—a phenomenon of the Sixties. We surely helped to put behind us those long years of self-hatred and in-group violence, almost too painful to read about.

THE NEW BREED POETS

Few would dispute that at the forefront of this New Literary Renaissance is poetry. One day, for example, over one hundred copies of Nikki Giovanni's *Poem for Angela Davis* sold out in twenty minutes on a corner adjacent to New York University. Much of the national interest in the new poets, especially the women, is credited to Dudley Randall, a poet and founder of Broadside Press in Detroit. He distributed poems first as mimeographed pamphlets, then as

"Broadsides," and today as well-designed and attractive books. Randall's poets did not hold out for being published by a "prestigeous publishing house"; they opted to take the poems to the people, "by any means necessary." By underground, by word of mouth, like the drums of ancient Africa, the poems began to reach black people.

Ellis Haizlip, as producer and director of the WNET/TV show *Soul,* was the first television producer to present a group of women poets reading their own works. During the Sixties the show was widely acclaimed and rerun many times. A deluge of requests for copies of the poems showed clearly that poetry had struck a responsive chord among a large mass audience of blacks who did not associate poems with "highbrow culture." Later, Ellis Haizlip persuaded Nikki Giovanni to read her poems backed by a gospel choir. Nikki recorded *Truth Is on Its Way*; disc jockeys played it on rhythm and blues stations, and people and poets were at last "moving as one." The art of poetry had shifted from the grips of the elite into the hearts of domestics, welfare mothers, and *everybody.*

The roots and sources of these black women's poems are not new with this generation. There is, however, a style, a direct openness and explicit language, which sometimes takes listening to as well as reading in order to be fully experienced. That's what television exposure contributes. A thirst for a multi-media experiencing of poetry, a desire to be taken beyond print into the meanings inherent in the presence of the person—her voice, even her "asides"—all these have contributed mightily to the fact that the women poets, especially Nikki Giovanni, are the hottest stars on the campus speaking circuit.

The most common themes are universal—love, sex, nature—but markedly and decided the most popular poets deal specifically with love between black men and women, with a few sideswipes at black men who chase white women.

Sonia Sanchez waits for the chase to end.

yea.
        they
hang you up
those grey chicks
parading their
tight asses
in front of you.
some will say out
right
        baby i want

to ball you
while smoother
ones will in
tegrate your
blackness
yeah.
brother.
this Sister knows
and waits[104]

On the other hand, Sonia Sanchez speaks of a black woman's need for a black man's love, believing this important in a black revolution.

an u got a
re vo lu tion
goin'
like. man. program
us in blk/
ness & u'll
have warrior
sons & young
sistuhs who will take
what we just rapped
bout doin'.
read us midnite
poems of Elijahs fanons
nkrumahs karengas
and then
make us sing they music/
wisdom by heart
to our children
but. above all.
LOVE US.
LOVE US.
LooooooooOOOVE US
yo/stereotyped/blk/woman
& u got a win![105]

All poets write of love, and especially do women, black or white, speak of loneliness and unrequited love. Yet black women poets express an unusual loneliness which is the result of too few positive relationships between black men and women. Sonia Sanchez writes about it: "I am what I am/woman/alone/amid all this noise."[106]

And Carolyn Rodgers expresses this theme in her poem:

We are lonely women
who spend time waiting for occasional flings

We live with fear
We are lonely
We are talented
dedicated, well read BLACK, COMMITTED
We are lonely
We understand the world problems
Black women's problems with Black men
But all we really understand is lonely.[107]

In "Marrow of My Bone" by Mari Evans, there is the same desire.

Fondle me
caress
and cradle
me
with your lips
withdraw
the nectar from
me
teach me there
is
someone[108]

Carolyn Rodgers would relieve the oppressive conditions of living with the healing balm of love.

and while we are waiting
    for the ashes of the evil

to kiss the soles of our feet
and caress our eyes in pyramids of dust

    yes, while we are waiting,

        for the sun to cover kiss the night
        our faces and limbs sweating honey

and while we are waiting and
            wishing and
            needing and
            dying and
            living in spite of

oh, while we are waiting
let us work and build and lasso
the universe with our spirit and
above all things,
while we are waiting . . .

let us love[109]

In addition to the love theme, most of the women poets write about middle-class bourgeoisie pretensions; they criticize black leadership in their poems, even the colleges they attended, and certainly life styles that set them apart from the masses. In "Sepia Fashion Show," Maya Angelou writes:

The black Bourgeois, who all say "yah"
When yeah is what they're meaning
Should look around, both up and down
before they set out preening.

"Indeed," they swear, "that's what I'll wear
When I go country-clubbing,"
I'd remind them please, look at those knees
you got at Miss Ann's scrubbing.[110]

Nikki Giovanni writes about token Negroes:

I am the token negro
I sit in the colored section with Fanon in hand
(to demonstrate my militancy)[111]

In a poem entitled, "Concerning One Responsible Negro with Too Much Power," she reinforces the theme:

i only want to reclaim myself
i even want you
to reclaim yourself
but more and more i'm being convinced
that your death
responsible negro
is the first step
toward my reclamation.[112]

Mae Jackson strikes a similar yet stinging critical note in a poem entitled, "To the Negro Intellectuals":

What can you tell me
now that i know
you,
the negro philosopher
who wrote the answer to life in ten short essays?[113]

In "Blackjam for Dr. Negro" Mari Evans writes, "Ancient eyes see your thang baby and it ain't shit," and then writes in "Status Symbol":

i
have arrived
i
am the
New Negro

they
gave me my
status symbol
the
key
to the
white . . . locked . . .
john[114]

There is also ribaldry, laughing at oneself and others. "Where have you gone," writes Mari Evans, "with your confident walk/your crooked smile/the rent money in one pocket/ and my heart in another. . . ."[115]

And always the theme of abandonment is present:

They went home and told their wives
that never once in all their lives
had they known a girl like me,
But . . . They went home[116]

Most have written poems to singers like Nina Simone, Lena Horne, Billie Holiday, and Aretha Franklin, recognizing the common bond of communication between writer and singer. Picture Nikki Giovanni, backed by a choir singing "Nobody Knows the Trouble I've Seen," reciting, "Aretha was the riot/was the leader/if she had said 'Come let's do it'/it would have been done."[117]

What emerges as a powerful theme in these poems is the demand for action. There are questions raised and solutions offered for the liberation of black people. With Sonia Sanchez, intragroup destruction will not be tolerated:

blk/people
are we C I A
agents is that why we killing
each
other with re/gu/la/rity
if we so angry
why not kill
that wite
motha/fucka

laughing at
us while we shoot
down our brothers
on our/nigguh/streets in
our nigguh/dreams
        blk/people
we suicidal
      or something
or are we all bugalooers
of death:
    our own???[118]

For Sharon Scott, simply to write a poem, publish it, recite it, is not enough.

nor, will anyone dare say to
her face more than once what
a boss black writer she is—
or otherwise

for there can be no recognition
for me nor my poems through
more words and more paper.
only by your

yes sister *I can feel*
yes sister *I can hear*
yes sister *we will move*

Here sister, is our lives.

there can be no poems to
gratify my poems.
only changes
    action, and steady pulses.

    then, maybe someone
    can say
    here was
    a
heavy sister!
        Salaam[119]

Nikki Giovanni softens the demand for such relentless effort to organize blacks for concerted group effort, with the theme of human relationships.

and if ever i touched a life
I hope that life knows

that i know that touching was
and still is and will always
be
the true revolution[120]

But then, Nikki Giovanni herself is perhaps a new breed poet whose contributions personally and intellectually are deserving of special notice.

Nikki Giovanni

Nikki once wrote: "I am always lonely/for things I never had/and people I've never seen.[121]

Certainly this whirling dynamo, thirtyish young sister has seemed alone (there is that feeling when one is in the forefront, the vanguard) in forging new platforms and directions for black writers. Speaking on countless campuses year in and year out, inspiring college students to work hard at their studies and come to the revolution with tools and skills is not easy. In refusing to be categorized and limited to those strict definitions that could rigidly describe her creative genius, and in creating a life style that has won her widespread respect while defying bourgeoisie defintions of Puritan respectability—there were lonely times.

But not too much loneliness! She can go "Ego Tripping" and become many people, past and present.

I was born in the congo
I walked to the fertile crescent and built
the sphinx
I designed a pyramid so tough that a star
that only glows every one hundred years falls
into the center giving divine perfect light
I am bad

. . .

I am so perfect so divine so ethereal so surreal
I cannot be comprehended
except by my permission

I mean . . . I . . . can fly
like a bird in the sky . . .[122]

Nikki's winning the Ladies' Home Journal Woman of the Year Award in 1974 meant to some young revolutionaries that she was joining forces with the very people she often considered foes. But, she does not shun confrontation or even violence if whites provoke it. As recently as 1974, in her rap with Margaret Walker about violence, she said:

> . . . violence hurled against us will be met and if you want to say with violence, I am going to say, yes, because I cannot take the weight of a constant degradation. . . . it is too much, I do not value seeing my contemporaries, the men that I've known . . . I don't like to see their riddled bodies. And I don't like the fact even that they're in jail, I don't like the way that they are being attacked and I am proud that they respond. And they must respond because otherwise they would be unhealthy. Black people, whether any of us like it, have given up on trying to reform white people.[123]

Like most of the New Breed, she rejects a one-dimensional description of herself: "People are always calling me a hater, and I'm really a lover."[124] Hers is indeed a philosophical struggle to achieve altruistic humane goals and there is no inconsistency in resorting to battle with those who perpetuate hate and racism while advocating peace and love. After all, as Nikki says, "I run the kitchen and i can stand the heat." After all, her life is hers.

> i'm saying it's my house
> and i'll make fudge and call
> it love and touch my lips
> to the chocolate warmth
> 'cause it's my house
> and i plan to live in it.[125]

THE INCOMPLETE TRUTH

No effort to "talk sense to the people" is complete without drama, the presence of black actors and actresses on our stages, TV sets, and movie screens. The artistic power of black actresses has yet to be fully realized. Ironically, their underutilization comes at a time when there are many superior black actresses whose talents surface only enough to whet our appetites and increase our sense of loss. How much more of an impact Janie, Pink, Lutie, and Mem would have on our imaginations if they moved from the pages of novels as "live images" with messages and characterizations acted out by a Ruby Dee, Ellen Holly, or Cicely Tyson. For a people whose self-concept is still overlaid with self hatred there is a need for redefinition of stereotyped images of black women. Poems and novels do much to inform our minds, but dramatization of concepts and characters increases our sensitivities and intensifies our thought patterns. Only when the reclamation of our images becomes as much of a priority as a Right to Read program, and when black organizations and institutions find ways of funding films, television, and stage productions, will we move the Renaissance of the Sixties into the Seventies. For what makes this time different from that of the Twenties is the desperate need to "come across" in media other than that of print. And just as the earlier pioneers found it difficult to get their material published, so it is that our current challenge is to move from print to stage and screen. In a multi-media, audio-tactile world, "the medium is the message."

A Nikki Giovanni can write a poem and feel a creative release. An actress needs more complex support. She needs writers, directors, and producers, and that takes money. Since whites own the media industries, what we see is what whites want and tolerate. And few deny that what comes through is distorted to please whites and protect sponsors. "We seldom appear in media as who we say we are," writes actress Ellen Holly, "but as whites say we are."[126]

Lenin once said: "Give me your filmmakers and I will make my revolution." He knew well that how people are pictured soon comes to be perceived as the truth. "Any form of art is a form of power," says Ossie Davis; "it has impact, it can affect change—it not only moves us, it makes us move." "Television," adds Eugenia Collier, "is one of the most potent weapons this nation has for keeping blacks lulled, deceived, and impotent." There we have it! The need to project the talent of black actresses through whom we can change negative images and project real ones is critical.

We have seen only a small part of Cicely Tyson's talent in *Sounder,* or of Ruby Dee's in *Wedding Band,* or of Gloria Foster's in *The Cherry Orchard.* One marvels at how Rosalind Cash, with all that talent, just misses coming across as a "blackploitation sister" in a film like *Melinda.* A whole group of experienced actresses who work off-Broadway, many in the outstanding Negro Ensemble Company productions, rarely make it to Broadway, television, or films. And yet, in 1976 Broadway would have been a financial disaster area had it not been for *The Wiz, Guys and Dolls, Bubbling Brown Sugar,* and others, all selling tickets in theaters that now boast of large numbers of black theatergoers.

We need more scripts from Micki Grant, J. B. Phillips and Alice Childress, to mention a few playwrights. And there are director-producers like Vinette Carroll, Novella Nelson, and Barbara Ann Teer who have proven their talent. Surely the newest young poet/dancer/actress Ntozake Shange, whose play *For Colored Girls Who Have Considered Suicide/When the Rainbow Is Enuf* opened in

May 1976 to critical acclaim, points toward the emergence perhaps of excellent young black female writer/director/producers.

From domestics to tragic mulattos to sexpots, the limitation of material capable of calling forth the great dramatic talents of these women is apparent. Even as we acknowledge the large numbers of blacks filing into theaters to enjoy "blackploitation" films, there is more black women need to say in these films than "we hate them." Whites have a range of female images, while there are few available to black women. "White films range at will over the full spectrum of human possibility from *Deep Throat* to *War and Peace*; most black films have been mired in the rut of a single formula: the so-called action film which deals with marginal anti-social elements in the Northern Urban ghetto," writes Ellen Holly. Black women who have lived such varied and rich lives in this nation, are locked into a one-dimensional image.[127]

Here and there one reads that the "new image" of women created for blacksploitation films is a step in the right direction. Certainly the new heroines are neither sexpots nor Mammies, but "pistol packing mamas." They handle a gun better than a dishmop, exchange cowering before Whitey for blasting off the heads and genitals of "bad guys" and generally karate kick their way to fame and fortune. They are not victims, but tough, shrill and unreal conquerors who would put Bionic Woman to shame!

That step forward might have made some few black actresses "bankable stars," but the above description of what they did to qualify as such is pitiful. A large number of distinguished white actresses such as Katharine Hepburn never demeaned themselves by playing similar roles. Rather, they came onto our screen as images of admirable and valid women, women we would want to emulate. There is a similar need for black actresses to project a variety of authentic roles.

To do so, as Davis and Holly say, we must gain control over the means: scriptwriting, producing, and directing. Or at the very least, as Holly says:

> While I fervently hope that more black films will be made and controlled by black people, I suspect that it is a lot closer to the point to hope that more black films will be made and controlled by people of any color whatsoever who CARE about black people. That, in the final analysis, is really the point.[128]

There is still another void in our incompleteness—dance. "Movements don't lie," said Martha Graham. Dance movements extend our vocabulary of artistic expression and add their special truth to the black experience. Generations of blacks grew up being sensitive to the epithet "all blacks have rhythm" as a put-down. This stigma certainly discouraged middle-class families from seeing the dance as a respectable field for their daughters. And yet perhaps more than any other artistic form, dance demands an awesome combination of arduous technical training and a life style of austerity and rigid discipline. There are for dancers, except for a few white superstars, less financial renumeration and fewer opportunities for sustained work than in any other of the performing arts.

Martha Graham recently said, "Civilization is at its height when you see a great dancer. Then you see the human race in its potential."[129] It is therefore not surprising that Mary Hinkson's rise to stardom as a principal dancer in Miss Graham's company did the most to make dance respectable to blacks and establish its artistic form as one of incredible beauty and depth. She, Carmen de Lavallade, and Matt Turney blazed a glorious historic trail of dance and made it possible for a Judith Jamison to emerge in the Seventies as the first black female dance superstar.[130] Pearl Primus, Katherine Dunham, and Janet Collins were the first pioneers. And yet, Judith with all her stupendous talent and beauty could never have emerged as such had Alvin Ailey's choreography not produced "Cry," the dance that expresses so eloquently through movement the inner emotions experienced by millions of black women as they have struggled to survive. Dancers need choreographers like actresses need writers.

It is an impact upon the emotions to see dance movements which express our deepest feelings in relation to our history as this is experienced in *The Mooche,* for example, a dance again choreographed by Ailey. One hears the sounds of Bessie Smith's singing while Judith Jamison moves to express how Bessie might have dealt with people. Serita Allen dancing the spirit of the Cotton Club chorus girl helps us imagine what life might have been for a chorus girl at that time. And since there are no films to help us fix Florence Mills in our minds, it's good to have Estelle Spurlock recapture some of the elusiveness associated with the "Mills Legend." And we surely feel the spirit moving with Mahalia Jackson as Enid Britten dances as Mahalia might have, "making a joyful noise unto the Lord." Billie Holiday's agony and vulnerability come home as Donna Woods and Sarah Yarborough dance John Butler's *Billie.* Through movement the songs we love and the images we cherish take on a life of the spirit and body that become stamped in our memory forever.

And yet the Alvin Ailey Company, where *The Mooche* and its interpreters are seen, is the only dance institution with a large national audience appeal in which black dancers can express through movement the interiority of the black experience. When the hours are totaled and the persons who dance as a livelihood are counted, fewer than twenty black women, most of them dancing in this company, can claim a decent salary as a full-time dancer! How fragile are the plights of even those few institutions whose mission is to "speak the truth to the people," for the demise of any one artistic institution such as Alvin Ailey's Company, which greatly deprive blacks of a cultural outlet.

Wanted! A new chapter in the history of black actresses and dancers who have ample opportunity to realize their potential! We need them, as well as writers and poets, to

Speak the truth to the people
To identify the enemy is to free the mind
Free the mind of the people
Speak to the mind of the people
Speak Truth.[131]

CHAPTER 7 NOTES

[1]"Speak the Truth to the People" (excerpts), Mari Evans, *I Am a Black Woman* (New York: William Morrow & Company, Inc., 1970), p. 91. Reprinted by permission of the author.

[2]Langston Hughes, "The Negro Artist and the Racial Mountain," *The Nation,* June 23, 1926.

[3]John A. Williams, "The Crisis in American Letters," *Black Scholar,* June 1975, pp. 68–69.

[4]Countee Cullen, "From the Dark Tower," in *On These I Stand* by Countee Cullen, Copyright 1927 by Harper & Row, Publishers, Inc., renewed 1955 by Ida M. Cullen. By permission of Harper & Row, Publishers, Inc.

[5]Claude McKay, "If We Must Die," from "Harlem Shadows" by Claude McKay, in *The Poetry of the Negro,* ed. Langston Hughes and Anna Bontemps (New York: Doubleday & Company, Inc., 1949), p. 333.

[6]See Harold Cruse, *The Crisis of the Negro Intellectual* (New York: William Morrow & Company, Inc., 1967), pp. 9–10 and 451–475.

[7]Elizabeth Catlett, "The Role of the Black Artist," in *The Black Scholar, Arts and Literature,* 6, No. 9 (June 1975), 10.

[8]W. E. B. DuBois, quoted by John O. Killens in "The Image of Black Folk in American Literature," in *The Black Scholar,* p. 46.

[9]John Oliver Killens, "The Image of Black Folk in American Literature," in *The Black Scholar, Arts and Literature,* p. 46.

[10]John A. Williams, "The Crisis in American Letters," in *The Black Scholar,* p. 70.

[11]Ralph Ellison, "A Very Stern Discipline," interview with Ralph Ellison, *Harper's Magazine,* 234, No. 1402 (March 1967), 76–95.

[12]*Ibid.*

[13]M. A. Richmond, *Bid the Vassals Soar* (Washington, D.C.: Howard University Press, 1974), p. 4. Reprinted by permission of Howard University Press. Copyright © 1974 by Merle A. Richmond. Richmond gives an interesting account of Lucy Terry, a contemporary of Phillis Wheatley, also a slave in Massachusetts, who wrote verse before Jupiter Hammer who has long been considered the first Afro-American to write poetry. By Richmond's account, Terry was more of a raconteur and orator than a poet.

[14]J. Saunders Redding, *To Make a Poet Black* (College Park, Md.: McGrath Publishing Company, 1939), p. 12.

[15]Richmond, *Bid the Vassals Soar*, p. 43.

[16]Phillis Wheatley, "To the University of Cambridge in New England," in *The Negro Caravan: The American Negro, His History and Literature,* ed. Sterling A. Brown, Arthur P. Davis, and Ulysses Lee (New York: Arno Press and *The New York Times,* 1969), p. 283.

[17]*Ibid.,* p. 284.

[18]Richmond, *Bid the Vassals Soar,* p. 47.

[19]*Ibid.,* p. 52.

[20]*Ibid.,* pp. 64–65.

[21]Sterling A. Brown, Arthur P. Davis, and Ulysses Lee, eds., *The Negro Caravan* (New York: Arno Press and *The New York Times,* 1969), p. 293.

[22]Frances E. W. Harper, "Bury Me in a Free Land," in *The Negro Caravan,* p. 296.

[23]See *The Negro Caravan: The American Negro, His History and Literature,* p. 293, where reference is made to Frances E. W. Harper's book *Sketches of Southern Life* (published in 1872).

[24]Frances E. W. Harper, "The Slave Question," in *The Negro Caravan,* p. 295.

[25]Arthur P. Davis, *From the Dark Tower, Afro-American Writers, 1900–1960* (Washington, D.C.: Howard University Press, 1974). Reprinted by permission of Howard University Press. Copyright © 1974 by Arthur P. Davis.

[26]Georgia Douglass Johnson, "I Want to Die While You Love Me," in *The Negro Caravan,* p. 340.

[27]Georgia Douglass Johnson, "Old Black Men," in *The Poetry of the Negro,* ed. Langston Hughes and Anna Bontemps, p. 58.

[28]Georgia Douglass Johnson, "The Suppliant," in *The Negro Caravan,* p. 340.

[29]Gwendolyn Bennett. This poem appears in a Negro Quarterly of the Arts named *Fire,* which Wallace Thurman, Zora Neale Hurston, Aaron Douglass, John P. Davis, Bruce Nugent, Gwendolyn Bennett, and Langston Hughes published with their own funds in 1926. It met with instant failure though the young writers and artists became famous (See Hughes, *The Big Sea,* pp. 236–337). A copy is available at the Schomberg Collection, 103 West 135th Street, New York, N. Y.

[30]For a further discussion of the dates of the Harlem Renaissance see Arthur B. Davis, *Dark Tower,* pp. 1–13; and Anna Bontemps, *The Harlem Renaissance Remembered* (New York: Dodd, Mead and Company, 1972), pp. 1–26. Both speak of earlier literary beginnings of great impact on black literature that had been building in the mid-Twenties and gained public recognition as the Harlem Renaissance.

[31]Edward Luedens, *Carl Van Vechten and the Twenties* (Albuquerque, N.M.: University of New Mexico Press, 1955), p. 9.

[32]Langston Hughes, *The Big Sea* (New York: Hill and Wang, 1940). Reprinted with the permission of Farrar, Straus & Giroux, Inc. from *The Big Sea* by Langston Hughes, pp. 223–228. Copyright © 1940 by Langston Hughes.

[33]Alain Locke, *The New Negro: An Interpretation* (New York: Boni and Liveright, 1925; Atheneum, 1968), p. 5.

[34]*Ibid.*, p. 11.

[35]Davis places James Weldon Johnson in historic perspective with the designation of planter; one among five, including Locke whose writings influenced the Harlem Renaissance writers; Davis, *Dark Tower,* pp. 4–5.

[36]James Weldon Johnson, *Along This Way* (New York: The Viking Press, 1965), p. 380.

[37]See Jessie [Redmond] Fauset (1882–1961): *There Is Confusion* (New York: Boni and Liveright, 1924). *Plum Bun, a Novel Without a Moral* (London: Matthews and Marrot, 1928; New York: Stokes, 1929). *The Chinaberry Tree: a Novel of American Life* (New York: Stokes, 1931; New York: AMS Press, 1969; New York: Negro Universities Press, 1969; College Park, Md.: McGrath, 1969). *Comedy American Style* (New York: Stokes, 1933; New York: AMS Press, 1969; College Park, Md.: McGrath, 1969; New York: Negro Universities Press, 1969).

[38]Hughes, *The Big Sea,* p. 267.

[39]Hughes, *The Big Sea,* p. 247.

[40]Robert A. Bone, *The Negro Novel in America,* rev. ed. (New Haven: Yale University Press, 1965), p. 97.

[41]*Ibid.*, p. 98.

[42]See Nella Larsen (1893?–1960?): *Quicksand* (New York and London: Knopf, 1928); New York: Negro Universities Press, 1969). *Passing* (New York and London: Knopf, 1929; New York: Arno, 1969; New York: Negro Universities Press, 1969; New York: Collier Books, 1971).

[43]Margaret Just Butcher, *The Negro in the American Culture* (New York: Knopf, 1956).

[44]See Zora Neale Hurston (1903–1960): *Jonah's Gourd Vine* (Philadelphia: Lippincott 1935 [introduction by Fannie Hurst], 1971). *Mules and Men* (Philadelphia and London: Lippincott, 1935, [introduction by Franz Boas]). *Their Eyes Were Watching God* (Philadelphia and London: Lippincott, 1937; New York: Negro Universities Press, 1969). *Tell My Horse* (Philadelphia and New York: Lippincott, 1938); British version is titled *Voodoo Gods; an Inquiry into Native Myths and Magic in Jamaica and Haiti* (London: Dent and Sons, 1939). *Moses, Man of the Mountain* (Philadelphia and New York: Lippincott, 1939). *Dust Tracks on a Road: An Autobiography* (Philadelphia and London: Lippincott, 1942; London and New York: Hutchinson and Co., 1944; New York: Arno, 1969, 1970; Philadelphia: Lippincott, 1971 [introduction by Larry Neal]). *Seraph on the Suwanee* (New York: Scribner's Sons, 1948).

[45]Hughes, *The Big Sea,* p. 238.

[46]Zora Neale Hurston, *Dust Tracks on a Road,* p. 124. Copyright © 1942 by Zora Neale Hurston. Copyright © renewed 1970 by John C. Hurston. Reprinted by permission of J. B. Lippincott Company.

[47]*Ibid.*, p. 177.

[48]*Ibid.*, p. 185.

[49]Hughes, *The Big Sea,* p. 316.

[50]*Ibid.*, pp. 319–320.

[51]*Ibid.*, p. 324.

[52]*Ibid.*, pp. 331–334.

[53]See Zora Neale Hurston newspaper clippings and other literary materials file in the Schomburg Collection.

[54]*Ibid.*

[55]*Ibid.*

[56]Hughes, *The Big Sea,* pp. 243–249.

[57]Carl Van Vechten, *Nigger Heaven* (New York: Alfred A. Knopf, 1926).

[58]Hughes, *The Big Sea,* p. 244.

[59]Cruse, *The Crisis,* pp. 21–29.

[60]*Ibid.*

[61]Hughes, *The Big Sea,* p. 245.

[62]*Ibid.,* p. 247.

[63]Arthur P. Davis, writer and distinguished professor of literature at Howard University, fixes the period dating from 1942–1960 as being influenced by two crises: the integration movement (which was climaxed by the 1954 Supreme Court decision), and the civil rights revolution which began around 1960. Davis thought that up to the fifties Negro literature had been predominantly a protest literature . . . there was a common enemy, there was a common purpose and a strong urge to transform into artistic terms the deep-rooted feelings of bitterness and scorn. Hope that integration was possible in the not-too distant future tended to destroy during the fifties the protest element in Negro writing. Davis acknowledges that while there was no actual integration in the fifties, "the Negro literary artist recognized and acknowledged that the climate had changed, and resolved to work with it at all costs." In the meantime, he had to live between the two worlds and that for any artist is a disturbing experience. ". . . the integration movement influenced Negro writing in the following ways: It forced the black creative artist to play down [protest themes]. It sent him in search of new themes, it made him abandon, at least on occasion, the Negro character and background; and it possibly silenced a few of the older writers then living." (Davis, *Dark Tower,* pp. 138–141.)

[64]Hughes, *op. cit.,* p. 339.

[65]Davis, *op. cit.,* p. 142.

[66]See footnote number 30.

[67]See: Ann Petry: *The Street* (Boston: Houghton Mifflin, 1946) (novel). *Country Place* (Houghton Mifflin, 1947); Chatham, New Jersey: Chatham Bookseller, 1971). *The Drugstore Cat* (New York: Crowell, 1949) (juvenile). *The Narrows* (Boston: Houghton Mifflin, 1953) (novel). *Harriet Tubman, Conductor on the Underground Railroad* (New York: Crowell, 1955). *Tituba of Salem Village* (New York: Crowell, 1970) (young adults). *Legends of the Saints* (New York: Crowell, 1970) (juvenile). *Miss Muriel and Other Stories* (Boston: Houghton Mifflin, 1971). (Other short stories and articles not listed).

[68]Bone, *op. cit.,* p. 180.

[69]Paula Marshall, *The Brown Girl, Brownstones* (New York: Random, 1959).

[70]Paula Marshall, *The Chosen People, The Timeless Place,* (New York: Harcourt Brace, 1969).

[71]See Margaret Walker (1915–): *For My People* (New Haven: Yale University Press, 1942; New York: Arno, 1968) (poetry). *Jubilee* (Boston: Houghton Mifflin, 1966). *Prophets for a New Day* (Detroit: Broadside, 1970) (poetry). *Poems published separately:* "Dark Blood," *Opportunity,* XVI, no. 6 (June 1938), 171. "Ex-Slave," *Opportunity,* XVI, no. 11 (November 1938), 330. "Palmettos," *Opportunity,* XVII, no. 1 (January 1939), 14. (Other articles and publications not cited).

[72]Walker, *Jubilee,* p. 9.

[73]*Ibid.,* p. 484.

[74]Walker, "We Have Been Believers."

[75]Walker, "For My People."

[76]See Gwendolyn Brooks: *A Street in Bronzeville* (New York: Harper, 1945).

Annie Allen (New York: Harper, 1949; Westport, Conn.: Greenwood Press, 1971). (poems). *Maud Martha* (New York: Harper, 1953). *Bronzeville Boys and Girls* (New York: Harper, 1956). *The Bean Eaters* (New York: Harper, 1960). (poems). *Selected Poems* (New York: Harper and Row, 1963). *A Portion of That Field: The Centennial of the Burial of Lincoln* (Urbana, Ill.: University of Illinois Press, 1967). *In the Mecca* (New York: Harper and Row, 1968), (poems). *Riot* (Detroit: Broadside Press, 1969). *Family Pictures* (Detroit: Broadside Press, 1970). *Aloneness,* illustrated by Leroy Foster (Detroit: Broadside Press, 1971). Ed., *A Broadside Treasury* (Detroit: Broadside Press, 1971). Ed., *Jump Bad: A New Chicago Anthology* (Detroit: Broadside Press, 1971). *The World of Gwendolyn Brooks* (New York: Harper and Row, 1971). (*A Street in Bronzeville, Annie Allen, Maud Martha, The Bean Eaters, In the Mecca*). "They Call It Bronzeville," *Holiday,* X (October 1951), 60–64. "We're the Only Colored People Here," from *Maud Martha,* 1953, in *The Best Short Stories by Negro Writers,* ed. Langston Hughes, 1967, p. 204. "Paul Robeson," *Freedomways,* XI, no. 1 (First Quarter, 1971), p. 104, (poem). (Other writings not cited).

[77]Brooks, "The Sermon on the Warpland" from *In the Mecca* in *The World of Gwendolyn Brooks,* p. 425.

[78]Brooks, "The Womanhood" from *Annie Allen* in *The World of Gwendolyn Brooks,* p. 115.

[79]Brooks, "Hattie Scott" from *A Street in Bronzeville* in *Gwendolyn Brooks,* p. 36.

[80]Brooks, "A Song in the Front Yard" in *Gwendolyn Brooks,* p. 12.

[81]Brooks, "The Mother" in *Gwendolyn Brooks,* p. 5.

[82]Brooks, "The Womanhood" from *Annie Allen* in *Gwendolyn Brooks,* p. 123.

[83]*Ibid.,* p. 124.

[84]Davis, *Dark Tower,* p. 185.

[85]Brooks, "Introduction" in *Jump Bad,* p. 11.

[86]Brooks, "The Sermon on the Warpland" in *Gwendolyn Brooks,* p. 426.

[87]Robert Nemiroff, *To Be Young, Gifted and Black: Lorraine Hansberry in Her Own Words,* adapted by Robert Nemiroff. Copyright © Robert Nemiroff and Robert Nemiroff as executor of the estate of Lorraine Hansberry. (Englewood Cliffs: Prentice-Hall, Inc., 1969).

[88]Cruse, *The Crisis,* p. 278.

[89]Nemiroff, *To Be Young, Gifted and Black,* p. 21.

[90]*Ibid.,* p. 213–214.

[91]*Ibid.,* p. 250.

[92]Davis, *Dark Tower,* pp. 227–228.

[93]Lerone Bennett, Jr., *The Challenge of Blackness* (Chicago: Johnson Publishing Company, Inc., 1972), pp. 191–192.

[94]Nikki Giovanni and Margaret Walker, *A Poetic Equation: Conversations Between Nikki Giovanni and Margaret Walker* (Washington, D.C.: Howard University Press, 1974), pp. 41–42. Reprinted by permission of Howard University Press. Copyright © 1974 by Nikki Giovanni and Margaret Walker.

[95]Don L. Lee, "The New Integrationist," from *Black Pride* (Detroit: Broadside Press, 1965, Old Mill Place, 1972), p. 11. Reprinted by permission of Broadside Press. Copyright © 1968, by Don L. Lee.

[96]Mae Jackson, *Can I Poet With You* (New York: Black Dialogue Publishers, P.O. Box 1019, Manhattanville Station). See Introduction by Nikki Giovanni, April 4, 1969, p. 2.

[97]Giovanni and Walker, *Poetic Equation,* pp. 76–77.

[98]Toni Morrison, Book Review of "Amistad 2," *New York Times,* February 28,

1971; copyright © 1971 by The New York Times Company; reprinted by permission. Also see *Amistad 2,* ed. John A. Williams and Charles F. Harris.

[99]LeRoy Jones and Larry Neal, *Black Fire* (New York: William Morrow and Company, Inc., 1968), p. 75.

[100]Lee, *Black Pride.*

[101]Brooks, *Jump Bad,* p. 12.

[102]See Maya Angelou, *I Know Why the Caged Bird Sings* (New York: Random House, 1969, 1970); Louise Merriweather, *Daddy Was a Number Runner* (Englewood Cliffs, N.J.: Prentice-Hall, 1970); Toni Morrison, *The Bluest Eye* (New York: Holt, Rinehart & Winston, Inc., 1970); Alice Walker, *The Third Life of Grange Copeland* (New York: Harcourt, Brace, Jovanovich, 1970).

[103]Alice Walker, letter to the editor, *Ms. Magazine,* III, no. 2 (August 1, 1974, p. 4. Reprinted with permission.

[104]Sonia Sanchez, "To All Brothers," from *Home Coming* (Detroit: Broadside Press, 1969). Copyright © 1969 by Sonia Sanchez.

[105]Sonia Sanchez, "Change Us," from *We a BaddDDD People* (Detroit: Broadside Press, 1970), p. 68. Copyright © 1970 by Sonia Sanchez.

[106]Sanchez, *Home Coming,* p. 32.

[107]Carolyn M. Rodgers, from "Poem for some Black Women," copyright © 1971 by Carolyn M. Rodgers in *How I Got Ovah* by Carolyn M. Rodgers. Reprinted by permission of Doubleday & Company, Inc.

[108]Mari Evans, "Marrow of My Bone," in *I Am a Black Woman* (New York: William Morrow & Company, Inc., 1970), p. 32. Reprinted by permission of the author.

[109]Rodgers, "And While We Are Waiting," in *Jump Bad,* ed. Gwendolyn Brooks, p. 127.

[110]Maya Angelou, "Sepia Fashion Show," in *Just Give Me a Cool Drink of Water 'fore I Diiie* (New York: Bantam Books, published by arrangement with Random House, Inc., 1973), p. 49. Reprinted by permission of Hirt Music Inc.

[111]Nikki Giovanni, "The Dance Committee," *Black Judgement* (Detroit: Broadside Press, 1968), pp. 3–68. Copyright © 1968 by Nikki Giovanni.

[112]*Ibid.,* p. 6.

[113]Jackson, *Can I Poet With You,* p. 5.

[114]Evans, "Status Symbol," in *I Am a Black Woman,* pp. 68–69.

[115]*Ibid.,* p. 35.

[116]Angelou, "They Went Home," from *Just Give Me a Cool Drink,* p. 4.

[117]Nikki Giovanni, "Poem for Aretha," from *A Broadside Treasury*, ed. Gwendolyn Brooks, copyright © 1971 by Broadside Press.

[118]Sonia Sanchez, "Question 1," in *We a BaddDDD People,* p. 19. Copyright © 1970 by Sonia Sanchez.

[119]Sharon Scott, "Sharon Will Be No/Where on Nobody's Best-Selling List," in *Jump Bad,* ed. Gwendolyn Brooks, p. 177.

[120]Nikki Giovanni, "When I Die," from *My House* (New York: William Morrow and Company, Inc., 1972), p. 37. Reprinted by permission of William Morrow & Co., Inc. Copyright © 1972 by Nikki Giovanni.

[121]Giovanni, *Black Judgement.*

[122]Nikki Giovanni, "Ego Tripping," from *Re: Creation,* Copyright © 1970 by Nikki Giovanni. (Detroit: Broadside Press, 1970), p. 37.

[123]Giovanni and Walker, *Poetic Equation,* p. 30.

[124]Giovanni, *Gemini* (New York: The Viking Press, 1971), p. 25.

[125]Giovanni, *My House,* "My House," p. 67.

[126]Ellen Holly, speech at the Delta Sigma Theta Convention, Seattle, Washington, August 1975.

[127]Holly, "Where Are the Films About Real Black Men and Women?" *The New York Times,* June 2, 1974.

[128]Holly, "Where Are the Films."

[129]"Martha Graham," *The New York Times,* May 15, 1977, pp. 1 and 15.

[130]Deborah Jowitt, "Call Me a Dancer," *The New York Times Magazine,* December 5, 1976, p. 40.

[131]Evans, "Speak the Truth to the People," *I Am a Black Woman,* p. 92.

G'way an' quit dat noise, Miss Lucy—
Put dat music book away;
What's de use to keep on tryin'?
Ef you practise twell you're gray,
You cain't sta't no notes a-flyin'
Lak de ones dat rants and rings
F'm the kitchen to de big woods
When Malindy sings.

She jes' spreads huh mouf and hollahs,
"Come to Jesus," twell you hyeah
Sinnahs' tremblin' steps and voices,
Timid-lak a-drawin' neah
Den she tu'ns to "Rock of Ages,"
Simply to de cross she clings,
An' you fin' yo' teahs a-drappin'
When Malindy sings.

PAUL LAURENCE DUNBAR[1]

When Malindy Sings

Is it really that black Malindys simply "got de natural organ fu' to make de soun' come right"?* Have the "turns and twistins" of sorrow, joy, disappointment and triumph contributed uniquely to the presence of so many outstanding black women singers in American history? Surely the most visible symbol of black women's claim to greatness, in a land that has traditionally viewed us as inferior, is an extraordinarily brilliant honor roll of black women who "Spread their moufs" and sing.

Down through the ages, we sisters have sung in some strange places; in the cramped quarters of slave ships, in the fields as we picked cotton, in jails, on chain gangs, on freedom marches. Black women were largely responsible for making the black church a musical institution as they led in singing the Lord's songs in a strange land.

Whether draped in silks and satins, propped against Hollywood's phony stage pillars and directed to sing something sexy and exotic for white audiences, or huddled in the freezing cold in front of the Lincoln Memorial (singing there because the Daughters of

*This and the following quotes are also from "When Malindy Sings" by Paul Laurence Dunbar.

the American Revolution barred one of us from Constitution Hall), we have sung gloriously. Whether poised on a horse, singing in "The Girl of the Golden West" (an operatic role surely foreign to the black experience) or sending "notes a-flyin' " in church choirs, singing "*good*" has continuously headed the list of black female achievements.

While many might prefer opera to blues or lieder to jazz, a single thread of music identity weaves through the style and substance of the greatest of all our singers, creating for them a common shared kinship.

"Miss Price," an interviewer asked the opera star, "if centuries from now you wanted future men to unearth a time capsule symbolizing the greatest achievements of modern life, what would you include?"

Without hesitation, Leontyne Price replied, "An Aretha Franklin record."

"There is an Aretha Franklin in every black woman, screaming to come out," remarked Lena Horne.

Music has forever been touched and shaped by black female singers. In voices that opened opera seasons throughout the world, inaugurated presidents, opened fairs, exhibits, and meetings, the sound of these singers has become as American as apple pie. In spirituals, gospel music, blues, ballads, arias, black singers have tinted the complexion of American music and added a permanent kink to the interpretation of the most sacred songs. Since Aretha Franklin sang "The Star Spangled Banner" at the 1968 Democratic Convention, it might be argued that even this hallowed song may well rock forever with the beat of a black sound.

If by chance (or plan?) black women were to vanish from the earth, what would history record of us? Surely, that we cleaned and scrubbed a lot of white folks' kitchens, perhaps that many of us were regarded as welfare burdens to the American taxpayer, but that is surely not all. We will be remembered for our dancers, actresses, and, of course, those who struggled up from the ranks of the poor and out into "the mainstream of American opportunity" claiming individual fame. But the image of black women that is most indelible is a moving montage of a black woman singing!

SELF HATRED—AGAIN

Like most things distinct about ourselves as blacks, neither the style nor substance of singing was considered worthwhile until the "black consciousness era of the Sixties" reclaimed a surrendered identity. Until the Sixties, self-hatred had twisted its ugliness into the very source of black people's spirituality and soul—music!

At the most, "black music"—blues, gospel, shouts—were private pleasures. At the very least, many educated blacks throughout the years thought such music lowbrow and uncultured.

Aspiration toward acceptance by whites and a need to be respectable members of the "cultured and refined" middle class encouraged certain attitudes and tastes: (1) hate or merely tolerate gospel music, spirituals and blues, but love Bach and Beethoven; (2) avoid night clubs and people in show business because they lack respectability; (3) stop tapping one's foot and moving one's body rhythmically because white folks might think Negroes too passionate and emotional.

THE AFRICAN PAST

Singing, like everything else black, has an African past. As the coffles wound their way from the African inlands down to Whydah Beach where the great slave ships lay, the sons and daughters of Africa chanted:

> Take our songs
> but not our singers' voices;
> Take our speech
> but not our drummers' hands.[2]

When the winds howled and the sea threatened to capsize the boat, they rattled their chains in unison, chanting and singing.

Sometimes it pleased the captain, somehow justifying his traffic in human life, to have them baptized. "I conjure you," said the Christian priest, "every unclean spirit, in the name of the Father, Son and Holy Ghost, depart from all these creatures, from this violent savage whom our Lord has called to his Holy Ark. Begone I say, depart. . . . Think no more of your native land, think only of the eternal life to come. Foreswear your savage practices."[3]

Then the priest took a bucket and ladled out a few drops of water on each head, and placed salt on each tongue. And that was it. Many of these new black Christians must have thought: "Is that the end of the ceremony? What is this joylessness? No tambor? No songs, dances?"[4] They soon found out that the God of white Christians was stern and demanding, giving them little in return.

African songs, then considered heathen, were sometimes tolerated by the slave traders. The impact of vigor and strength in the combination of dancing and singing frightened them and the slaves were soon limited to singing alone. It was the drum, however, that the captors feared most. They recognized its power of communication and its intoxicating hold on the people. And so it was soon banned. The drum was to remain a feared object as the slaves came to America, for the white man soon learned that the drum could be used to encode messages, some of which did indeed incite revolts as well as accompany dances.

At first African slaves sang African chants and litanies in the cotton and rice fields. But soon their songs and chants reflected American experiences. Slaves were not allowed to sing about African gods, and their African litanies soon lost relevance. How could they sing about fishing and weaving and hunting as they worked white men's fields. How could they sing about ceremonies when every living act of theirs was reduced to haste and subjugated to a work ethic? How could they celebrate birth when children were often born in fear and threat of separation? How could they celebrate name-giving when the newborn child was often sold away from its mother's breast?

Fannie Kemble once enjoyed a group of slaves singing, "Fare you well, and good-by, oh, oh! I'm goin' away to leave you, oh, oh!" She was amazed when they "went off into nonsense verses about gentlemen in the parlor drinking wine and cordial, and ladies in the drawing room drinking tea and coffee." Kemble attributed this abrupt change to a prohibition of slaves' singing melancholy tunes and words and an encouragement to sing cheerful music. She thought this a judicious precaution since "poor slaves are just the sort of people over whom a popular musical appeal to their feelings and passions would have an immense power."[5]

What did endure from African music? The "basic rhythmic, harmonic and melodic devices," says LeRoi Jones. Also the "use of polyphonic, or contrapuntal rhythmic effects. Melodic diversity in African music came . . . also in the singer's vocal interpretation. [The] tense, slightly hoarse-sounding vocal technique of the work songs and the blues . . . a combination of pitch and timbre used to produce changes of meaning in words . . . the antiphonal singing technique. A leader sings a theme and a chorus answers him. The answers are usually comments on the leader's theme or comments on the answers themselves in improvised verses. Improvisation not only survived in the first work songs but also in jazz."[6] A distinctive way of projecting lyrics also survived in the work songs and the blues. "The shouts and 'field hollers,' " Jones points out, "were primarily 'rythmic lyrics.' "[7]

Until recently, however, most Americans, including educated blacks, considered these products of African heritage and American adaptation crude and unimaginative. When at last whites began to comprehend the beauty of the spirituals, blues and jazz (doubtlessly influenced by Europeans, who appreciated these sounds first), black music was taken over by those who had the financial resources to popularize it. Those "capitalizing" whites reaped the greatest economic benefits from these natural resources. Agents, publishers, record companies, club owners, and all the other attending figures and institutions who are barnacled to the giant bulk of the music world seized upon the music, its creators, its interpreters, and parlayed it all into a multimillion dollar business. Thus our music, like everything else about us, was mortgaged for its survival. Only in limited ways would we receive the belated acknowledgement of having given birth to this purely original American music and be recognized for setting styles that also shaped white artists.

In terms of fame and money, white performers who imitate black sounds soon surpassed authentic black musicians. This constantly changing "offshoot" music, owing its existence to the blues and jazz, has gained a huge white audience, as well as white interpreters who outsell black artists. Music publishers and recording centers have made and broken thousands of young black aspirants and molded others to images they preferred. Even those black singers who have made it big with the American public never really match the profits made by whites.

But a new generation of singers has now emerged who "make it" with black audiences first, and survive as long as the financial base of the black community supports record buying and tickets. These singers recognize the dues paid by their choir sisters, gospel singers, tent blues singers, and others long gone—all who sang their hearts out and built a musical base for them. And above all, they respect the fact that it all began in the church.

THE CHRISTIANIZED SLAVE AND HIS MUSIC

The slaves found solace and a means of expression in the religion of the white man. The white man found slave participation consistent with his design to keep them meek and subdued, so the slaves were encouraged to worship God.

The other-world-oriented songs they sang seemed innocent enough. "By and by I'm gonna try on my long white robe," and "soon I will be donna wid de trobles of de world" or "in that great gittin' up mornin," while "rocked in the bosom of Abraham," did not sound like themes of revolution or insurrection. The slaves found palliatives in the sheer emotionalism of songs and in their minds the lyrics could symbolically mean freedom from slavery.

The militantly oriented spirituals were about suffering. "Go down Moses, Tell Ole Pharaoh to let my people go," "Marching to Zion," and "Joshua Fit de Battle of Jericho" were martial songs, but they seemed safe enough. Moses didn't mean a Martin Luther King, and the battle lines had not been drawn in Watts, Harlem, and Hough.

These slaves molded their church to fit their needs. The emotionalism of the Methodist and Baptist denomination, especially the Baptist, seemed more akin to their African religions, and since the religions of West Africa endowed the river gods and priests with great power, they considered "going down to the river to be baptized" a powerful religious ritual. In fervent religiosity, thousands and thousands laid their "burdens down by the riverside."

The congregation brought with them a vast reservoir of feelings, repressed in their daily grinds. In the church they could sing and shout. The sisters were the real "shouters." Sitting by Brother Pastor's side in the "Amen" corner, where those who had "been called by the Lord" presided, it was most often some sister, rocking and humming and fanning, who would oblige the minister by "raising a song." And from a deep well of feeling, a female voice would bellow, "In that Sweet By and By." In rhythmic call and response pattern, these songs, evoking total group participation, constituted the major portion of those long-ago religious services. But then the people were living true, worshipping according to the old African dictum: "The spirit will not descend without song."

THE SPIRITUALS

While spirituals are generally associated with blacks, neither their origin nor worth were free of early controversy. LeRoi Jones and others believed "the spirituals themselves were probably the first completely native American music the slaves made."[8]

When abolitionists, New England schoolmarms, and others took notice of these songs and suggested they were original creations by black slaves, there were those who declared the songs merely English folk tunes which the slaves had heard and tried to imitate.

Nevertheless, the spirituals were noticed, and much credit must go to Lucy McKim, Jeanette Robinson Murphy, and other abolitionist women who generated a reading and listening audience for this "new music," giving credit to the slaves as the originators of an exciting musical form, even if at first the music defied definition and categorization.[9]

As blacks gained understanding of white church music and customs, however, the intense emotionalism associated with "gospel" singing was neutralized in the accepted spirituals.

It was prestigious to sing in a church choir, and choir meetings became an important training ground for young singers. Moreover, since pastors dared not eliminate altogether "the old-time religion" for fear of losing members, the choir selections were drawn from the "old time" spirituals and gospel music as well as anthems and other general church hymns. Thank heavens, thousands of young girls sang all of this—old and new. For from just such Baptist and Methodist choirs emerged Marian Anderson, Leontyne Price, Dionne Warwick, Aretha Franklin and countless other stellar singers. Though these other women were destined to gain fame in non-church music, they were born into and nourished on spirituals and gospel songs.

GOSPEL MUSIC

Though gospel music differs from spirituals, it too is based on religious impulses. There is a zest and "shout" component, not necessarily witnessed in spirituals. One usually expects a tender or even doleful rendition of spirituals, perhaps with piano, string, or later even a symphony orchestra in accompaniment. But in gospel singing the organ pumps with all the stops out. The tambourines and the drums beat. One hums and cries from somewhere hurting when most spirituals are heard, but with gospel music it's ecstatic hand-clapping and foot-stomping time. Gospel music, indeed, sprang from the soul of the enslaved field blacks.

It is the gospel circuit more than the spiritual trail that generally leads a singer from church music to the secular rhythm and the blues halls of music. While Marian Anderson and Leontyne Price would take the spirituals into the prestigious concert halls as serious music, many singers who preferred gospel singing became cabaret and supper club singers. Dorothy Dandridge traveled for a while in a family gospel singing group. The circuits for her, as for many others, were the churches in given areas. The "big time" was an invitation to sing at the National Baptist Convention. Once one started there, invitations to give concerts at churches were assured. Aretha Franklin and Dionne Warwick took to such a gospel circuit before moving into rhythm and blues.

The Clara Ward Singers began their rise to fame in a choir in Philadelphia and performed at the National Baptist Convention in 1943. Sister Rosetta Thorpe started out as a gospel singer, worked the Cotton Club and other night spots for a while, and eventually returned to the gospel singing circuit.

Mahalia Jackson: Gospel Queen

Among all the others, Mahalia Jackson stood as a Rock of Ages. Everything about her attested to the durability and majesty of gospel music.

Mahalia Jackson did not sing "the devil's music" which she heard others were singing in nightclubs. "Anybody that sings the blues," she says, "is in a deep pit, yelling for help. It always gives me joy to sing gospel music."[10]

Though pressured by many friends and by her first husband, Mahalia never accepted night club work even though the supper clubs and cabarets in her hometown of New Orleans were filled with such music when she was growing up. Jelly Roll Morton and King Oliver were local musicians. She heard the New Orleans brass bands and played the records of Bessie Smith and Mamie Smith. Some of her relatives worked in Ma Rainey's Tent Show and even tried to lure her into this troupe. But a strict aunt who raised her was determined that Mahalia remain committed to religion.

Actually, Mahalia preferred to sing with the congregation rather than the choir of her hometown Baptist Church.

> All around me I could hear the foot-tapping and hand-clapping. That gave me bounce. I liked it much better than being up in the choir singing the anthem. I liked to sing the songs which testify to the glory of the Lord—those anthems are too dead and cold for me. As David said in the Bible—"Make a joyous noise unto the Lord!"—that's me. . . . Those people had no choir and no organ. They [gospel singers] used the drum, the cymbal, the tambourine, and the steel triangle. Everybody in there sang and they clapped and stomped their feet and sang with their whole bodies. They had a beat, a powerful beat, a rhythm we held on to from slavery days, and their music was so strong and expressive it used to bring the tears to my eyes. . . .
>
> . . . We Baptists sang sweet, and we had the long and short meter on beautiful songs like "Amazing Grace, How Sweet It Sounds," but when those holiness people tore into "I'm So Glad Jesus Lifted Me Up!" they came out with real jubilation.
>
> . . . First you've got to get the rhythm until, through the music, you have the freedom to interpret it. Perhaps that's why white folks just never do clap in time with my music the right way. I tell them, "Honey, I know you're enjoying yourself but please don't clap along with me."[11]

Actually by the time Mahalia was recognized by whites, she had enjoyed many years of acclaim by her own people. And by sticking close to church folk, she diminished the likelihood of being insulted and demeaned by whites. Although blues singers were paid more money, they constantly faced "Jim Crow" hotels and restaurants. She, like other gospel singers, was a "fish and bread" singer, especially during the Depression. They always ate well and were housed in the homes of local ministers.

As a child, she worked as a domestic; as a young woman, she was a laundress and hotel maid in Chicago. She began singing in the choir of the Greater Salem Baptist Church and soon after joined several other members of the choir who formed the Johnson Gospel Singers. This group gained considerable popularity in local churches, but soon Mahalia received invitations to give church concerts alone.

Many of the gospel songs in Mahalia's repertoire were written by her accompanist, "Georgia Tom" Dorsey, former piano player for Ma Rainey. Though Dorsey was "saved by the Lord," his "happy beat," as Mahalia called it, did much to popularize gospel music, but it also got Mahalia into trouble with "colored" ministers who spoke out against her hand-clapping, stomping style. She had an answer for this criticism:

> I told him [a preacher] I was born to sing gospel music. Nobody had to teach me. I was serving God. I told him I had been reading the Bible every day most of my life and there was a Psalm that said: "Oh, clap your hands, all ye people! Shout unto the Lord with the voice of a trumpet." If it was undignified, it was what the Bible told me to do.[12]

She had her knocks too from "high-up society Negroes," among whom was a music teacher who told her:

> You've got to learn to stop hollering. The way you sing is not a credit to the Negro race. You've got to learn to sing songs so that white people can understand them.[13]

Then, as her story goes, Mahalia was discovered by whites. Until then she had lived in an all-Negro world, hardly giving a thought to whites from one day to the next. But in 1950 Marshall Stearns, the music critic, heard some of her records and invited her to take part in a symposium on the origins of jazz to be held in the Berkshires in Massachusetts. Of course, once they discovered her, whites either wanted to "market" her in ways she resented, or offered legal and professional advice that she rejected.

Nevertheless, after 1950 Mahalia was "movin' on up," to Carnegie Hall, to Europe, to guest appearances on TV shows. She had her own successful TV program in Chicago, but was told there was no possibility of network shows since sponsors could not risk offending Southern white customers.

Thus, after winning acclaim and affection all over the world, Mahalia came to know the special kind of prejudice that greets blacks "who have made it." Now a famous black woman, she, too, faced institutional racism which levels all blacks and causes even the famous to conclude that—rich or poor, famous or infamous—when the chips are down, blacks are seen by whites as inferior.

As Mahalia said: "It's gotten so I spend part of almost every day with a white person, yet when I come from off that concert stage they're still likely to treat me as if I had leprosy." Perhaps this daily battle with "the Man" led her to a greater involvement in civil rights, especially while Martin Luther King lived.

Until the end of her life in 1972, Mahalia Jackson stood firm and proud in her choice to sing the Lord's music in a joyous manner. She proved that it is possible to earn a living by singing black folks' music to blacks. Like Ma Rainey and Bessie Smith, she was confirmed in her musicianship by the people whose social conditions produced the music itself, and like gospel singer Shirley Caesar, she gloried in combining evangelism with singing, "working only for the Lord."

Finally acclaimed by "upper-class Negroes" who had first rejected her, welcomed in Big Churches that had thought her music unworthy, and ecstatically accepted by whites, Mahalia Jackson exemplified African-Christian music at its zenith. "I want my hands . . . my feet . . . my whole body to say all that is in me. I say, 'Don't let the devil steal the beat from the Lord! The Lord doesn't like us to act dead. If you feel it, tap your feet a little—dance to the glory of the Lord!' "[14]

THE BLUES

The blues is a state of mind and a music which gives voice to it.[15] That simple and accurate definition needs no further interpretation.

The primitive blues singers projected a very special state of mind. They were mostly men who accompanied themselves on instruments such as the guitar, banjo, jug, and washboard. They sang mostly about leaving the South for Northern opportunities, hard times, and other dissatisfactions. Women were especially popular themes, but mostly in saloons where "barrelhouse" pianists copied the guitar rhythms and created their own version of the blues.

Classic Blues Singers

Names of the earliest blues singers have long since been forgotten, but remembering Ma Rainey, Bessie Smith, Mamie, Clara, and Trixie Smith, Bertha "Chippie" Hill, Sippie Wallace, Ida Cox, Lucile Hegamin, Rosa Henderson, Victoria Spivey brings images of the classic female blues singers. LeRoi Jones wrote:

> . . . the classic blues took on a certain degree of professionalism. It was no longer strictly the group singing to ease their labors or the casual expression of personal deliberations on the world. It became a music that could be used to entertain others formally. The artisan, the professional blues singer, appeared; blues-singing no longer had to be merely a passionately felt avocation, it could now become a way of making a living. An external and sophisticated idea of performance had come to the blues, moving it past the casualness of the "folk" to the conditional emotional gesture of the "public."[16]

Richard Wright thought the blues to be a feminine mode of expression while LeRoi Jones considered the great classic blues singers women. "There is a certain degree of passivity, almost masochistic in quality and seemingly allied to sex in origin, that appears as part of the meaning of the blues."[17] This is a classic female psychological, masochistic-passive interpretation of the blues. One striking example of the femininity, or feminization, of the blues through vocalization (certainly not instrumentation) is seen in *St. Louis Woman,* the one film Bessie Smith made. She played the submissive, "need to be loved and cared for" role. But her man gives only enough affection to soften her so he can hustle her money, then beats her and exits triumphantly waving the money over his head. She has "the St. Louis Blues, just as blue as I can be."

This is masochism of classic dimensions—the inability to love without hurt and pain, most of it self-inflicted.

In Bessie Smith's "Empty Bed Blues," for example, we go deeper and deeper into psychologist Erik Erikson's concept of "the inner space of women."[18] One phrase expresses and inflicts on the listener new pain, recalls and reactivates old hurts, disappointments, and aches. Down, down, down—where is the release? It does appear that this is a woman's thing, this singing the blues. The professionalism that LeRoi Jones talks about, wooing of the public, might be associated with another so-called feminine quality—narcissism. In the case of female blues singers, it does seem to take the form of a kind of "mirror, mirror on the wall" syndrome—who's the most miserable of them all?

Carrying this feminine symbolism further, but not too far, musical instruments became dominant blues vehicles for men. One can readily identify instruments like the trumpet, saxophone, even piano, as outward extensions of inner feelings. Though Willie the Lion Smith, Fletcher Henderson, and Louis Armstrong often accompanied the great blues singers, all of them preferred to "go for themselves." As the Lion said: "The blues a musician plays depends a great deal on the mood he is in at the time. A man's blues come from the hard work . . . they sing and play what their heart tells them to express. If one is in trouble, sad and downhearted, he can really express the blues."[19]

The Minstrel Tradition

Ma Rainey, Bessie Smith, and all the other classic blues singers served their professional apprenticeships in traveling minstrel shows, circus sideshows, and tent shows.

Since 1830, Americans had fed upon a steady diet of blackface minstrels. Of course, there had been Negro character delineations, on stage at least, since Othello, but the institution of black minstrels was a form unto itself.[20] Character stereotypes formed from superficial observations of blackface minstrels, showing blacks poking fun at other blacks seemed to entertain mass audiences. This "art" is said to have reached its zenith when Thomas D. Rich (Daddy Rice) invented the figure of an old Southern Negro, complete with tattered clothes and shuffling gait. Rich had been inspired to produce this comic caricature from a passing observation of a black man he saw in Cincinnati.[21]

Soon his Old Black Joe character was immortalized along with the song he heard the man sing:

> First on de heel tap, den on de toe,
> Ebery time I wheel about I jump Jim Crow
> Wheel about and turn about and do jis so,
> And every time I wheel about, I jump Jim Crow.

By the 1850's and 1860's, all the minstrel groups followed the same pattern: jokes by "end men," or burlesque on one of the legitimate operas or dramas of the day, and, of course, songs of humor and pathos.

These shows did not ordinarily employ women, though a few female minstrels were performing as early as 1850. The stars of the average minstrel show were female impersonators such as Bobby Newcomb, who became famous for playing Topsy. Either the public did not like the idea of women in burnt cork, or their concept of feminine purity precluded the idea of white women playing the roles of blacks. Indeed, when white women brought over the can can from France and appeared before the footlights as themselves, they helped to change the public's taste from minstrelsy to vaudeville.

Most of the minstrel sketches used such objectionable titles as "The Coon Rehearsal." They showed bossy black women with henpecked husbands, stupid-lazy slow-reacting men, or dealt with themes of violence like "Love and the Carving Knife."

This was probably American entertainment in its most flagrantly racist period.

Americans idealized minstrelsy and kept it alive until vaudeville became established. So ingrained in show business was the burnt cork mimicry of blacks that blacks started imitating whites imitating blacks! Callender's Colored Minstrels was established in 1877. In 1880 a group of Negro waiters appeared in a Saratoga hotel in a minstrel show, covering up their own black skin with burnt cork![22]

Emerging as a part of the all-black show format was the female blues singer. She emerged, however, as clearly unique and unimitative either of whites or of blacks imitating whites. She was herself—a black woman singing the blues. Without the aid of microphones and shunning megaphones, she and her sisters stood in front of gasoline mantle lights in Southern tents and belted out their songs. Blackface comics, of course, met the fate of history. Future generations of young blacks would discredit them and deride their jokes. But the women who passed through the tough initiation rites of the tent shows, barnstorming from Georgia to Houston to New Orleans and from settlement to township all over the South, created the indomitable image of the black woman as singer. And one would hear something of that woman, perhaps Ma or Bessie, in Aretha, Nina, Lena, Novella, and even in Leontyne.

"Ma" Rainey[23]

Gertrude Pridgett, "Ma" Rainey, was born in Columbus, Georgia, in

April 1886. Her family was neither exceptionally poor nor well-off—just ordinary black folks. A few people in Columbus remember that some of her kinfolk "may have been in tent shows from way back." Red-hilled Columbus, Georgia, has always been a sporting town, and Gertrude, at age fourteen, began her stage career in *The Bunch of Blackberries,* a local show. She soon became "local talent," someone to be shown off to visiting showmen. When she was sixteen, Will Rainey came through town in the Rabbit Foot Minstrels, married her, and changed his act to a husband and wife team called The Assassinators of the Blues. Their routine, especially Ma's singing, became one of the most popular acts on the minstrel and circus sideshow circuits of the South.

Ma wrote many of her own songs and was accompanied by a jug band or a small group of five or six musicians. Her songs depicted the trials, tribulations, and joys of Southern black life. In "Cell-Bound Blues," she convinces us that she knows firsthand the terror of a Southern jail. But Ma Rainey was really at her best when singing about broken-hearted women having man trouble.

Like Mahalia Jackson much later, Ma Rainey achieved fame by performing before poor black audiences. People walked, rode mules, and came crowded on wagons for miles and miles to hear Ma sing. "I'm jus' a common ole rollin' stone," she sang, "just got the blues for home sweet home." And, though she became rich, compared to those who sat on the hard seats of the tent shows, her audience believed she sang about them and their lives because she was one of them. Now and then she sang before Northern audiences, usually while she was in Chicago for recording sessions. But she preferred Southern audiences and they, of course, adored her until the end.

Nobody dared call her "Ma" to her face. She preferred to be called "Madam," having acquired all of the temperamental characteristics of great artists. Some have described her as ugly, expressing little taste for her short, "squat and dumpy" figure, gleaming gold-toothed grin, and loud and flashy clothes. Her favorite trademarks were a headband and a huge necklace of gold coins. She could display a volcanic temper at times, but was also generous and warmhearted.

After several years of marriage, Ma separated from Will Rainey and gained notoriety from her love affairs, some say with young men, even boys.

In a taped interview, one writer gave his impressions: "Ma Rainey was a tremendous figure. She wouldn't have to sing any words; she would moan, and the audience would moan with her.

She had them in the palm of her hand. I heard Bessie Smith also, but Ma Rainey was the greatest mistress of an audience. Bessie was the greater blues singer, but Ma really *knew* these people; she was a person of the folks; she was very simple and direct. That night when we saw her, she was having boy trouble. You see, she liked these young musicians, and in comes John Work and I—we were young to her . . . we just wanted to talk, but she was interested in other things. She was that direct. She was the tops for my money."[24]

A professional trouper till the end, Ma Rainey retired from the stage in 1935; she spent the last four years of her life running the two theaters she bought with her earnings and working in her brother's church.

Bessie Smith: Empress of the Blues[25]

It is either truth or legend that Ma discovered Bessie Smith while appearing in the Rabbit Foot Minstrel in Chattanooga in 1910.

Bessie had attracted local notice at the age of nine when she won a prize of $18 in a singing contest at a local theatre. As the story goes, Ma Rainey secured a job for Bessie in the Rabbit Foot Minstrel, featured her as a child singer, and proceeded to teach her the art of blues singing.

There is no record to assure us that Bessie Smith ever acknowledged Ma Rainey's influence and little truth can be claimed for Ma Rainey's role as mentor to Bessie. Bessie credits a minor blues singer with having inspired her. Nonetheless, Bessie must have been influenced by a day-in, day-out association with a superstar like Ma Rainey. Moreover, some musicologists hear the influence of Ma Rainey in Bessie's style and technique, whether Bessie admitted it or not.

After a few years with the Rabbit Foot Minstrel, Bessie started moving out on her own, from tent show to levee camps and waterfront dives. Her artistry matured in this bitter school of show business.

Unlike Ma, however, who worked under a tent most of her career, Bessie preferred the TOBA circuit (Theatre Owners Booking Agency), or as black performers dubbed it, "Tough on Black Artists or Asses' circuit. This circuit was all black, but it took her into large theaters in the South, East, and Midwest, whereas Ma seldom ventured out of the South except for recording sessions in Chicago.

Though Bessie is said to have urbanized the blues, she disliked sophisticated Negro audiences; she preferred the simple people who came only because they wanted to see her perform and never failed to let her know it.

Bessie Smith was described as "beautiful," "Junoesque," "regal," and "majestic." As one person put it, "she was beautiful even when she appeared in New York in 1923, tall and fat and scared to death." Her appearance obviously contributed to her charismatic hold on audiences. Carl Van Vechten, one of the few whites who saw her perform, tells of his conversion to Bessie Smith (and it was that) and his enthusiasm suggests a magical quality about Bessie.

> . . . her face was beautiful, with the rich, ripe beauty of Southern darkness, a deep bronze brown, like her bare arms. . . . she walked slowly to the footlights. Then, to the accompaniment of the wailing, muted brasses, the monotonous African beat of the drum, the dromedary glide of the pianist's fingers over the responsive keys, she began her strange rites in a voice full of shoutin' and moanin' and prayin' and sufferin', a wild, rough Ethiopian voice, harsh and volcanic, released between rouged lips and the whitest of teeth, the singer swaying slightly to the rhythm.
>
> "Yo' treated me wrong;
> I treated yo' right;
> I wo'k fo' yo' full day an' night.
>
> Yo' brag to women
> I was yo' fool,
> So den I got dose sobbin' h'ahted
> Blues."
>
> And now . . . the crowd burst into hysterical shrieks of sorrow and lamentation. Amens rent the air. Little nervous giggles, like the shivering of Venetian glass, shocked the nerves.
>
> "It's true I loves yo', but I won't take mistreatments any mo'."
>
> "Dat's right," a girl cried out from under our box.
>
> "All I wants is yo' pitcher in a
> frame;
> All I wants is yo' pitcher in a frame;
> When yo' gone I kin see yo' jes'
> duh same. . . ."[26]

Musicologists are generally ecstatic about Bessie Smith's artistry. "What, in a musician's terms," asks writer Gunther Schuller, "made Bessie Smith such a superior singer?"

> . . . it is a combination of elements: remarkable ear for and control of intonation, in all its subtlest functions; a perfectly centered, naturally produced voice (in her prime); an extreme sensitivity to word meaning and the sensory, almost physical, feeling of a word; and, related to this, superb diction and what singers call projection. She was certainly the first singer on jazz records to value diction, not for itself, but as a vehicle for conveying emotional states.
>
> . . . perhaps even more remarkable was her pitch control. She handled this with such ease and naturalness that one is apt to take it for granted. Bessie's fine microtonal shadings could color a pitch in relation to a particular word or vowel, . . . move into the center of a pitch with a short, beautifully executed scoop, or "fall" out of it with a little moaning slide; . . . she could hit a note square in the middle—these are all part of a personal, masterful technique of great subtlety, despite the frequently boisterous mood or language. I am not saying hat she knew these things in the learned "conservatory" sense, but simply that she knew how to do them at will, by whatever combination of instincts, musicality, and physical equipment she possessed.[27]

Bessie Smith's image survives in her musicianship, but also in the complexity of her personality. She was called rough and brawling, coarse in conversation, earthy in her humor, ugly in manner when she was drunk, addicted to gin, capable of great bursts of generosity and also of inflicting hurt on musicians and associates. Where, one wonders, amid all these descriptions is the real Bessie? Bessie's story has been compiled and preserved primarily by whites, but a few blacks remember experiences.

Ethel Waters tells the story of a TOBA booking that brought her into an Atlanta vaudeville theater on the same program with Bessie, who had evidently heard about Ethel's "low, sweet and new way of singing the blues." Bessie made it clear to the management that she would not tolerate another blues singer on the program, and after a heated argument, with Bessie shouting plenty of "Northen bitches," it was decided that Ethel should not sing. But neither Bessie nor the management had counted on the audience's desire to hear Ethel Waters' "new blues." The people out front set up a clamor, and Bessie finally agreed to let Ethel sing one song—"St. Louis Blues."

Of this unexpected confrontation Ethel Waters was to write: "I sensed this was the beginning of the uncrowning of her, the great and original Bessie Smith. I've never enjoyed seeing a champ go down, and Bessie was all champ. When I closed my engagement in that theater Miss Bessie called me to her. 'Come here, "long goody," ' she said. 'You ain't so bad. It's only that I never dreamed that anyone would be able to do this to me in my own territory and with my own people. And you know damn well that you can't sing worth a damn.' "[28]

In the Twenties Bessie dominated classic blues. After she recorded "Down Hearted Blues," written by another great blues singer, Alberta Hunter, her name rose like a missile and soon she was the biggest star in Negro vaudeville, with Columbia selling between 8 and 10 million records.

What led to her decline? Some say man trouble. She replaced Frank Walker, a white manager, with Jack Gee, a Philadelphia policeman she had married in 1923, and soon her financial and booking problems were in disarray. Jack was either untrained in these matters or systematically frustrated by whites who still controlled bookings. She began to depend on liquor more and more; there were public fights with friends, lovers, managers, musicians. As show business people say, she "hit the skids." Few places wanted to book her. She began to show up late, and gradually the number of engagements dropped off. Most critics agree that Bessie continued to record blues and non-blues songs like pop tunes with artistic success, though her stardom was declining and the sale of her records added up to financial failure.

Bessie may have had a streak of self-destruction, but by 1929 the collapse of the record business also played a part in her decline. Though she had enlarged her repertoire, black people looked upon her as strictly a blues singer and preferred other black female singers, like Ethel Waters, who were moving into the sophisticated supper clubs singing blues but also ballads.

In 1933 John Hammond persuaded Columbia Records to arrange a session for their Okeh race label, and Bessie was paid a flat \$50 for each side as compared to the \$1,000 advance against 5 percent royalties she had commanded in her heyday.

In the end she was reduced to working as a waitress in a gin mill dressed in a Mammy outfit and singing pornographic songs for tips. Even toward the end of her life, however, there were some good experiences, and efforts to "come back" as a top-billed performer seemed to be working for her.

According to *Esquire,* her impromptu performance in a jam session at New York's famous Door on Fifty-Second Street in 1936, one year before her death, was so overpowering that Mildred Bailey, the first white woman singer accepted in jazz, decided she would not follow her.[29]

Bessie had finally found a man with whom she was building a warm, constructive relationship. Contrary to reports that she was broke, by black standards she was financially secure, with a home in Philadelphia and a farm in New Jersey. She and Morgan, her new husband, had driven their Packard down South to join a touring tent show.

At least one person, Dave Oxley, a drummer in the band, remembers the last song she sang. "Bessie sang, 'Can't you see what love and romance have done to me? I'm not the same as I used to be, this is my last affair.' "

It was her last affair, professionally and romantically. After the show she and Morgan headed up Route 61 along the Mississippi River toward Memphis. They were headed toward an engagement with the Silas Green Tent Show. Somewhere near Clarksdale there was a car accident and Bessie Smith was killed.

Herein lies the seed of the legend of Bessie's death. Did she die because a white hospital would not give her medical attention? Was Edward Albee's play *The Death of Bessie Smith* essentially true?

Sally Grimes, in an *Esquire* article, attempted to get at the facts of Bessie's death and interviewed the orthopedic surgeon who happened to be traveling down the highway soon after the accident and stopped to give aid to the victims. He said that while he was attempting to lift Bessie, who was then 200 pounds, into the back seat of his car, another car traveling down the highway plowed into the back of his car. Reports vary about whether the ambulance was from Memphis or Clarksdale and whether she died in it or at the black G. T. Thomas Hospital (now no longer in existence) in Clarksdale.

No matter where Bessie Smith was taken, it is the surgeon's professional opinion that "Bessie Smith didn't have a chance. I have no way of knowing the course of that ambulance, but I'll still say this, it wouldn't have made any difference if she'd been hurt with her injuries on the front steps of the University Hospital in Memphis. In 1937 with no blood bank and a lot of new techniques that weren't available then, she didn't have a prayer to survive. And it's quite probable that even in this day and time, she wouldn't have made it."[30]

Sally Grimes' question is ironic: "Either a nigger or a great artist was killed in that car crash. Which one survived?"[31]

The survivor is Bessie Smith, great artist—the greatest blues singer in history, many say. Her records are now posthumously enjoying a wide circulation among black youth and blues buffs.

The real thrust of racism, you see, did not take place at the site of the accident, but at the moment Bessie's show ended that night, and she and the others, like black troupers before and after, had no place to sleep and were forced to wind their fatigued way down narrow, dusky Southern roads in the dead of night, searching for simple lodging. It is this racism that "wore out" many a star and about which Billie Holiday, Marian Anderson, and Lena Horne would have more to say later.

Mamie Smith and the Decline of the Blues Women

After the record business began to fall apart, most blues singers found themselves out of the limelight. Most died broke and forgotten. Among them was Mamie Smith (no relation to Bessie), the blues singer who did not really like to sing blues, but who nevertheless, according to Willie the Lion Smith, was the first Negro woman to record a blues record. Mamie's breakthrough into the recording business, won by the dogged determination of Perry Bradford, a black songwriter, opened up the "race records" business for others.

Mamie recorded "Crazy Blues," with the Lion at the piano leading the band. He says: "We got 25 dollars apiece for the two sides, and we had to wait two months to get our money. In those days it didn't matter how long it took you to get the sides down satisfactorily—the money was the same, regardless of the time, and no royalty deals."[32] " 'Crazy Blues' was released in 1920 by Okeh and in no time at all it was selling like hotcakes in Harlem. It put Mamie Smith on the map, but it also put a lot of other singers in demand."[33] Most of them lived well while they were on top. Derrick Stewart Baxter writes: "All the blues queens were larger than life, most of them carried the regal myth into their everyday lives. Their fans were their subjects, the musicians and their managers were their cabinet ministers, there to pander to their will, and surprisingly enough, they did just that! Thus, for part of the time they lived in a world of their own, a world of fantasy and daydream."[34]

It was a world which expanded; gin mills gave way to supper clubs, and before long there were to be black faces accenting the Great White Way and black talents helping to build legends in the golden years of both radio and TV.

Dinah Washington: The Transition Blues Queen

As always, there are persons like Dinah Washington who mark the trail for such transitions. Bessie Smith was the Empress, but Dinah wore well the crown of Queen of the Blues. She started as a gospel singer. Her blues singing marked a departure from the blues-bound turf which good black women singers occupied; they had been confined and isolated there because white promoters would not let them record ballads and booked them in black dives or "fringe clubs" that existed somewhere between the black and white communities. Discjockeys somehow heard Dinah's recording of a ballad, "Unforgettable," and began to play it along with songs recorded by white female ballad singers. Soon she was leading a line of black female singers, singing and recording blues *and* ballads, eventually gaining visibility on the Great White Way. Dinah Washington lived much of the "mistreated woman" tragic overtones of former blues singers, dying tragically at the age of 43. But she was to pass along to young singers that wonderful ability to mix gospel and blues and ballad singing that would one day be known as *soul.* That indeed is a legacy.

THE GREAT WHITE WAY

There is more to the word "white" in the Broadway scene than the symbolism of electric lights radiating from the marquee, or the flash of great names in neon signs.

The Great White Way and the Great White Father are synonymous in many ways. Whites control the entertainment world, from sheet music to talent. They control the critics' establishment. Angels who invest money in talent and entertainment are white. Consequently whites have traditionally decided who is good and what should be allowed to live. Until the advent of Motown in 1949 the gatekeepers of "The Way" were all white men. With rare exceptions, they made you or broke you.

Motown, the complex of show business operations including music publishing, talent, and the production of records, films, and television shows, was started by Berry Gordy in Detroit and predictably by 1972 it had become the number one black business in the nation.[35] And why not? Music and entertainment have always been a natural black resource in this nation, but until Motown, all of this was mined and exploited solely by whites.

Not until Ruth Bowen (Queens Booking Agency) became manager-agent for Dinah Washington, and later for superstars Aretha Franklin, Sammy Davis Jr., and Redd Foxx, did black talent connect with a black institution in a profitable and productive relationship.

W. C. Handy attempted to edge into the record business in the era of race records. Handy, considered the father of the blues, wrote and arranged much of the music of that time, but his company, the Black Swan Record Company, even with Ethel Waters as a recording star, could not compete with entertainment giants like Columbia, Victor, and MCA who made millions from black artists. Handy's music company lasted up to the time of his death, but it was not a financial success.

It took a Supreme Court decision to break the MCA monopoly of the entertainment field, freeing many black artists, including Lena Horne, who then were allowed to control and market their talent in their own way—but not before years of exploitation had passed.

No matter what black audiences preferred, sooner or later black singers were forced to please whites—white producers, white critics, white audiences. While whites owned the TOBA circuit, and other circuses and vaudeville theatres in which Ma Rainey and Bessie Smith starred, black audiences were the ticket buyers and what they liked and disliked was an important marketing factor. But even on those black circuits white agents were given first choice in booking their clients and black performers were forced to choose white agents to book them. There was just enough mismanagement of talent and money between singers and black manager-husbands to discourage many female singers from such an arrangement—the classic reminder for all of them being Bessie Smith—but many female singers did try to combine a business and romantic marriage. However history does not record one successful business marriage among all who tried. In most cases neither business nor marriage lasted.

Black husband-managers were not so much inadequate as inexperienced in show business management, and more than one black male manager found whites blocking him at every turn, rendering him powerless to make things work.

HARLEM AND THE WHITE TREK

Broadway is not the only "white way"; other ways included the control of race records, which at first circulated to black audiences. A few whites ventured into this market as listeners, and some became interested in seeing the black performer in person. Some white singers coveted the style of delivery as well, as in the case of "The Rocking Chair Lady," Mildred Bailey, who spent night after night in Harlem listening to Billie Holiday; and Sophie Tucker, "The Last of the Red Hot Mamas," who paid Ethel Waters to give her private lessons so she could imitate her technique. The whites, enamored of the persons who communicated this new music, began the trek to Harlem. First came the promoters, always eager to market a good thing; then came the white performers, listening, learning, imitating, enjoying. And finally came the thrill seekers, in search of new kicks and other exotic pastimes.

A popular "white way" became the after-hours joints in Harlem where whites sneaked in to observe and occasionally mix with black customers. They came in couples when they were slumming, but they came in singles when their jaded appetites lusted for more intimate relationships.

Edmond's, Leroy's, and other popular Harlem places were all owned by blacks "until 1920," according to Willie the Lion Smith, "when things changed and the hoodlums, who furnished the booze, came up and took over." All of the greatest musicians and entertainers worked these places at one time or another. Even when blacks made "the Great White Way," they frequented these Harlem spots.

Ethel Waters started whites coming to Edmond's Cellar in Harlem. Prior to working there she sang a blues repertoire, but she began to include popular ballads and "white society folks began to come to hear her." Both Ethel Waters and Willie the Lion Smith mentioned the slumming parties organized by Mississippi ("Sippie"), the one black horse-and-buggy driver in Central Park. He would gather a group of white VIP's and take them on a personally conducted tour of Harlem night spots, including Edmond's and Leroy's. Willie the Lion Smith said: "As word got around town that a lot of show business celebrities could be seen at Leroy's, we began to get some white-folks trade from downtown. Leroy didn't particularly like this because he thought the mixing of races tindery. There were three groups of ofays allowed in—personal friends of Leroy's, big names in the show world, and anyone brought by 'Sippie.' . . ."[36]

Since whites controlled show business, it is not surprising that black singers and entertainers were at least curious about their popularity with white audiences, even though some did not like these audiences very much. Ethel Waters, never a show business personality to be associated with black causes, wrote in her autobiography:

> White people generally bored me, and we didn't speak the same language. . . . They seemed to get little fun out of life and were desperately lonely. . . . I'd look around at those pale faces and weary eyes and I'd think, "They are only here to kill time." In spite of the countless advantages they enjoyed as the master race they looked . . . as though they hated life itself. When you worked in

> front of them you had to do the whole job. . . . But in Negro night clubs the customers worked with you. They had come to the spot to cut loose. . . . High spirits weren't forced on them. They came in with bounce and éclat, checking their troubles at the door. . . . As far as I could see, the white man was full of mental pains and psychic aches. . . . If he came to night clubs it was only to escape whatever the hell it was that ailed him. And I couldn't help wondering, if he was really like that, what good were all his fine homes and jobs, trips to Florida, silk hats, and his poses of superiority?[37]

Billie Holiday recognized a long list of celebrities who caught her act—Paul Muni, John Hammond, Benny Goodman, and of course Mildred Bailey.

> Every night the limousines would wheel uptown. The minks and ermines would climb over one another to be the first ones through the coalbins or over the garbage pails into the newest spot that was "the place."[38]

As impressive as these big names were, however, Billie thought the black audience at the Apollo Theater in Harlem (still today a testing ground for black audience response) the supreme test of her talent. "There's nothing like an audience at the Apollo. . . . They didn't ask what my style was, who I was, how I had evolved, where I'd come from, who influenced me or anything. They just broke the house up. And they kept right on doing it."[39]

Langston Hughes expressed the feelings of many blacks toward this white invasion of Harlem clubs: ". . . nor did the ordinary Negro like the growing influx of whites coming toward Harlem after sundown, flooding the little cabarets and bars where formerly only colored people laughed and sang. He resented whites staring at black customers, as well as the performers—like amusing animals in a zoo."[40]

Negroes did not share such attitudes with whites, said Hughes. "Negroes are practically never rude to white people. So thousands of whites came to Harlem night after night, thinking the Negroes loved to have them there. . . ."[41]

Gradually the black club managers and musicians began to cater to whites. "Gladys Bentley," said Langston, "sat and played a big piano all night long, literally all night, without stopping—singing songs like 'St. James Infirmary.' . . . sliding from one song to another, with a powerful and continuous underbeat of jungle rhythm . . . a perfect piece of African sculpture, animated by her own rhythm."[42] When whites began to flock there and the place became well known, "she acquired an accompanist, specially written material, and conscious vulgarity." Then she moved to a larger place, downtown (white clubs), and finally to California, carrying with her "the old magic of the woman and the night and the rhythm. . . ."[43]

Even the famous Harlem Savoy Ballroom, "The Home of Happy Feet" which popularized the Lindy Hop, the Susie Q, and Truckin', and kept the Charleston and the Black Bottom authentic, began to draw white audiences.

THE COTTON CLUB

But racial mixing was not really what whites wanted. The biggest insult to black people was the world-famous Cotton Club built right in the middle of Harlem, owned by Owney Madden, a white gangster who seldom went there. Bootleg whiskey and a control of Harlem cuisine was really what the Cotton Club was about. Yet it spawned some of the greatest black talent in history—an accident, not a purposeful intention.

It was here that whites came in droves. It was here that black talent exploitation and "Jim Crowism" walked side by side and made millions for whites. Here, also, black entertainers really grasped the meaning of "the Great White Way," what it took to make it there and at what cost. And perhaps the first "dues" paid was the black performer's self-respect. Cut off from black audiences, and thus alienated from the source of their talent, some eventually reclaimed a black following, but many were manufactured for white consumption, via the Cotton Club route, with little or no identity with their own people.

"I was never there," said Langston Hughes, "because the Cotton Club was a Jim Crow club for gangsters and monied whites. They were not cordial to Negro patronage, unless you were a celebrity like Bojangles. So Harlem Negroes did not like the Cotton Club and never appreciated its Jim Crow policy in the very heart of their dark community.[44]

According to Hughes, the celebrated W. C. Handy was refused admission, even though his music was used in the show. Whites resented his record company, and this was a part of his punishment.

Lena Horne remembers that black sporting and gambling men, members of the black underworld, were often given tables in the back, while the parents and relatives of the performers had to sit behind the stage, out of sight.[45]

Whites dominated everything in the Cotton Club even the "on stage" performance. Lew Leslie, who was associated with Florence Mills' success, was one of the Cotton Club's first musical producers. The scores were written by whites, including Dorothy Fields and Harold Arlen. Though Rosamund and James Weldon Johnson, Noble Sissle, Eubie Blake, Wil Marion Cook, and Bob Cole were recognized black composers, whites wrote the music, controlled the staging and direction of the black talent.

Both Cab Calloway and Duke Ellington began their phenomenal rise to fame at the Cotton Club. Harold Arlen wrote "Stormy Weather" for Ethel Waters, who insisted on scrapping the mechanical devices simulating bad weather and sang it from the heart: "Only those who are being burned know what fire is like. I sang 'Stormy Weather' from the depths of my private hell in which I was being crushed and suffocated." Miss Waters immortalized the song and was asked by Irving Berlin to take a starring role in *As Thousands Cheer.* In the Broadway show starring Marilyn Miller, she became the highest paid woman performer on Broadway.

Adelaide Hall and Ada Ward were stars in several Cotton Club shows. And in the chorus at one time or another were Leslie Uggams' mother and Bessie Buchanan, who later became the first black woman elected to the New York State Assembly.

Toward the end of the Cotton Club's history, a young teenager, dubbed "the little squirt from Brooklyn" by Cab Calloway, reluctantly dropped out of school, joined the chorus line, and went on to become a legend! Lena Horne was forced into show business by a stagestruck mother and stepfather who needed her earnings to survive.

The Cotton Club did not swell her head, since she really wanted to remain in school.

> Working conditions were terrible. There was only one ladies' room, and the people in the show were discouraged from using it—it was for the customers. There was practically no room backstage. We did three shows a night—8:30, 11:30, and 2 A.M.—seven nights a week, and we were paid $25 a week. On top of that we were frequently obliged to take the show downtown and play a week in one of the vaudeville houses, in addition to our regular schedule, and then too, we were expected to play smokers and conventions—anything some politician or local big shot asked the owner to do, with no extra pay. As I said, I assume the older girls were expected to entertain important people when the boss asked them to.[46]

She had pride in associating with great talent.

> . . . there is no question that they lived up to the somewhat patronizing line in one of the club's brochures, which promised "the cream of sepia talent, the greatest array of Creole stars ever assembled, supported by a chorus of bronze beauties. . . ."
>
> The Cotton Club shows . . . were wonderful. But for the employees, it was an exploitative system on several levels. The club got great talent very cheap, because there were so few places for great Negro performers to work. Duke Ellington . . . was . . . the greatest jazz composer ever, but the white audience was convinced that Paul Whiteman and Isham Jones were the last words in jazz. So for many years Duke had to sell his songs and arrangements to a white publisher for far less than he deserved. There were few places for Duke except Europe or some joint like the Cotton Club.
>
> . . . They were also very clever at exploiting Negro stereotypes, of catering to them in order to bring in the white people. That made it hard for people who didn't fit the stereotypes to get work there in the first place.[47]

Lena believed it ironic that such expensive and lavish entertainment actually went on in the middle of Harlem during the Depression years, a time of great suffering for blacks.

> One that I remember as particularly ironic was a thing about sailing to Europe, and the boys in the show carried out eight or ten deck chairs in which we reclined to sing the number. Considering who we were and where we were, it must have seemed pretty silly. I'm sure a lot of people came there just to get a laugh out of our pretensions.[48]

"The Depression," said Willie the Lion, "easy-to-obtain liquor and the end of the vogue for Negro shows on Broadway lessened Harlem's attraction to downtown celebrities. . . . The Cotton Club moved to Broadway and Forty-Eighth Street, only to fail after two years."[49]

Perhaps it could be said that during this time many whites were exposed to black entertainers, creating a much wider money-paying audience for their talent. Also, many black entertainers had an opportunity to star in lavish productions and develop versatile showmanship. White entertainers regularly visited black clubs and raided their talent and styles, but rare was the opportunity for black artists to see white performers at work so they neither had an opportunity to copy their material, nor were they too much guided by white tastes and preferences.

What did emerge for black female entertainers during the Cotton Club vogue was a "Lena Horne syndrome"—white preference for a black woman who was as much a carbon copy of a white female beauty as possible, with a few exotic quirks thrown in to make it tantalizingly different. Lena Horne became the ideal role model for black performers. Gone were the Bessie Smith "fat mama" images. And performers who didn't "look like Lena Horne" were pushed into the background unless pure talent and a wide acclamation by blacks stormed through and demanded that attention be paid to them.

BROADWAY

The greatest of the Great White Ways is perhaps Broadway. Promoters and songwriters who discovered outstanding black performers siphoned off the best and packaged and commercialized them for a white Broadway audience. Just as Ma Rainey and Bessie Smith wanted the fame of a huge record following, those who followed in later years craved a Broadway role. At first, it was possible for blacks to sit in the balconies of Broadway theatres, but when black entertainers left Harlem for Broadway, their black audiences diminished. Neither the prices nor the shows attracted large black audiences. Perhaps they also felt uncomforable in white surroundings. In any event, to gain success on Broadway, black performers had to be acceptable to whites.

The exception was *Shuffle Along*, the first all-black musical staged on a legitimate Broadway stage.[50]

There had, of course, been several musical shows produced, conceived, directed, and managed by Negroes since 1898. By 1910, when Bert Williams became the first Negro to have a specialty act in the Ziegfield Follies, he had already established himself among Negroes as a top entertainer. Bert Williams, in blackface, was the only black in the show, and he exited each night to a roar of applause. He died in 1922 at the age of 47, still going strong on the Great White Way. But he was unique.

Noble Sissle and Eubie Blake wrote the music for *Shuffle Along*, which featured several hit tunes including "Just Wild About Harry."

Conceived primarily for Negroes, produced on a shoestring, *Shuffle Along* just managed to open in New York in 1921. Blacks loved it, even though forced to see it from the balcony. Overnight it was a fantastic success. It played on Broadway for one year, and at least three companies played in different cities for two or more years.

The show was loaded with black female talent. Caterina Jarboro and Josephine Baker were in the chorus. Trixie Smith, the blues singer, sang "He May Be Your Man But He Comes to See Me Sometimes." Adelaide Hall was a star at one time. But it was Florence Mills (replacing Gertrude Saunders) who skyrocketed to fame.

Shuffle Along began the vogue for Negro musicals that followed for at least a decade. Though the succeeding black revues were staged and written by whites, three women—Florence Mills, Ethel Waters, and Josephine Baker—hit the Great White Way with such impact that they dominated it from New York to European capitals.

Florence Mills: The Little Blackbird

Florence Mills was an overnight star, moving on from *Shuffle Along* to unprecedented international fame. At age 32, five years after the show, and at the height of her fame, she was dead.

Entering show business as a child, first in a sister act, later appearing in vaudeville, she played in at least one Williams and Walker musical.

What made Florence Mills so great? She didn't sing the blues like Bessie Smith, or even Ethel Waters, for that matter. In fact, Ethel Waters rather offhandedly said of her: "Florence Mills was vivacious, a cutie, and a whirlwind when it came to selling a song and dance. But she had a small voice. They had been using a choir around her to get volume, and then Florence would come in and sing the punch line."[51] "She was all eyes," says Eubie Blake, "that's what grabbed you."[52]

Even today, years later, people who knew and admired her are unable to describe her in comparative terms. She evidently was one of a kind, the likes of which were never seen before or since in black entertainment. And what a pity! Maybe like Edith Piaf she was a theatrical artifact, a find for a time and period that completely departs from established norms of beauty and excellence.[53]

Her talents did not go unnoticed by Broadway managers and producers. *Variety* ran an item concerning her on July 31, 1909:

> Florence Mills, petite and pretty, is the personification of daintiness and refinement. She possesses not only beauty of face, but of figure as well and a large measure of that intangible, but effectively magnetic quality, chic.
>
> This little lady . . . has been brought prominently to the attention of theatrical managers by her admirable work of a quality and temperament unusual in the burlesque field.[54]

Among the many descriptions of Florence Mills, this one by a *New York World* critic reviewing *Blackbirds of 1926,* makes an attempt to capture her personality and talent, and manages somehow to convey a fantastic spirit.

> The gods should send down a watchmaker from heaven to discover what makes Florence Mills tick. The rest of us might be gayer if we knew. A droll, dainty creature, like a human-sized mosquito that draws laughter instead of blood, her skin is not dark, but rich and burnished, and more alive than whiteness, she goes flitting about, tilting our funnybones, or she is a mad, bewitching monkey, or a flippy-floppy, flirty blackbird. The last when she sings, heart-taking bubbles of sound thronging out of her throat as champagne from a bottle.
>
> Have you heard blackbirds sing? They make sudden molten notes, flinging them off like poets, and then wind up a dismal squawk. Florence Mills is like that, only from the molten notes she goes into jazz slides and minors that somehow make music. She becomes all mouth in a moment. She makes faces. Her hands become crazy pointers. Her body struts and stalks and makes golliwoggles. She flings herself into hilarious postures and all as spontaneously as a blackbird flitting his feathers while he whistles at the sun.[55]

She had been wooed away from *Shuffle Along* by Lew Leslie and continued to star in his shows until her death. Sissle and Blake remember: "She came to us and said she had this offer for a considerable amount of money from Leslie, but that she wanted to remain with us if we could match the money. Of course, we could not. We had been hearing about a girl who was playing in one of the *Shuffle Along* road shows. And when we saw her, Josephine Baker went into the show as a replacement for Florence."[56]

Eventually the show *Blackbirds of 1926* went to Paris and London, and Florence Mills was the toast of Europe, with a string of celebrities and royalty dancing at her feet. It is said that the Prince of Wales saw the show thirteen times.

Always she came home to Harlem, to her family and friends. She could be seen many nights listening to Willie the Lion, or visiting with Ethel Waters at Leroy's. She had married a dancer much earlier in her career and they were Harlem's model of a happily married show business couple. "One thing," said a club manager, "success never changed her . . . she always did her best. She was a hard worker; no gay parties, never spoiled, and she was good to her mother." She was a highly esteemed and accepted black artist.

On her last trip to Europe her health began to fail. She closed *Blackbirds* and went to Baden Baden and other European health centers, but was advised by physicians to return to America for an operation. Upon arrival she found her mother seriously ill and delayed the operation, perhaps too long. She died following an appendicitis operation, but surely because of other complications as well.

Florence Mills was buried in that grand style black folks adore, laid to rest in a $10,000 coffin, dressed in a silver lamé dress. Some 57,000 people viewed her bier, 5,000 crowded into the church for the service, and 50,000 people lined the Harlem streets to pay their last respects. Choirs, singers, and sermons had extolled her virtues and the flowers and telegrams from the great and near-great duly acknowledged her. In her last final moments, Florence Mills played to a packed audience and even this was a Great Show.

As the funeral cortege wound its way to Woodlawn Cemetary, a flock of birds circled overhead as a final tribute to the Little Blackbird.

The American press was as impressed with the funeral (probably the first black funeral many reporters had covered) as it was with the woman. Among the hundreds of press tributes, one from the *London Daily Telegraph* stands worthy of historic note:

> To speak of the art of Florence Mills is perhaps to use too pretentious a word. Perhaps, after all, it was her personality, and no more than that, which made the sudden news of her death so strangely, disturbingly painful. There is always something tragic in the extinction of youth, and still more when it is youth endowed with such electric vitality as hers; but "Queens have died young and fair" before today, and a Queen of Revue who delighted for a little while the hearts of English audiences might well have died and been forgotten amid the rush of everyday affairs. And yet there was something in Florence Mills which made her unforgettable . . . the queer little break in her voice and her soft lisping accent will haunt us as poignantly now that we know we shall never hear them again. . . .
>
> . . . It was not surprising, somehow, to learn that off the stage she was a grave, serious woman, who thought much of the status of colored people, and fought hard to establish them as men and women with the same claims on the world as the whites. All was implicit in her voice when she sang the sentimental rubbish which no one but she could have made worth a hearing. Somewhere one sensed the sad dignity of a race which the world had treated unjustly—a kind of sensibility, which made all our memories of

> nigger-minstrel buffoonery seem shabby and dull. This was Florence Mills' real message, which her delicious artistry kept hidden, or almost hidden, because at the moment it was irrelevant. She herself believed that hard work and achievement were worth all the protests in the world if the Negro was ever to come into his own. The memories of London playgoers, at all events, are not likely to disappoint the faith that she held.[57]

Ethel Waters

Billed as "Sweet Mama Stringbeans" on the TOBA vaudeville circuit, it was young Ethel Waters who began to steal some of Bessie Smith's limelight. Some claim that once Ethel Waters appeared with her sophisticated brand of blues singing, Bessie Smith's popularity began to decline.

Among educated blacks who found it difficult to appreciate Bessie's gutsy shouts and moans, this brown-skinned blues singer was a favorite. Yet, according to Zora Neale Hurston, she "was never comfortable with educated blacks."

With that unerring sense of empathy, Zora Neale Hurston predicted, "I have a terrible fear that the world will never know her." She was partially right. Those who feel that blacks who make it owe it to their black brothers and sisters to become involved in black causes and organizations will find little kinship with Ethel Waters.

This generation of young blacks saw her as a Billy Graham crusader. Her religiosity was understandable, but this evangelical zeal moved her toward a white middle American evangelist. Somehow Billy Graham's cause won her embrace while Martin Luther King, who combined religion and civil rights advocacy into a cause that few blacks could resist, never evoked her response. She used her money to send some black children through school, and to patronize a Catholic Church, but she so disliked both the feminist and black movements that she took the time on national television to disassociate herself from both, saying, "God will take care of those who do his will and work."

God's will and work blessed Ethel Waters with as much talent as any black woman has ever possessed, before or since. Ethel Waters was a star! She went as far as blacks were allowed to go in her time. Hers has been a versatile career as singer, dancer, and actress. She was one of the first black actresses to perform movie parts other than that of a domestic and starred in both radio and TV shows. She paid a lot of dues and got a lot of lumps along the way, and she made the Great White Way with impact and distinction.

She grew up without the love she needed from parents. "When it didn't come I cried inwardly; I also began to build up my defenses."[58] While working as a maid in a hotel she began to frequent various nightclubs, learning to shimmy and to sing for fun. A vaudeville couple heard her sing and persuaded her mother to sign the necessary papers so that she could join a traveling vaudeville show. She sang "St. Louis Woman," and both she and the song became hits. Before reaching Leroy's in New York, she spent many one-night stands in circus sideshows, black vaudeville, and even played in burnt cork as a Jane Crow character at one time.

As a major recording artist for Black Swan Records, she attracted a large listening audience, but it was a long time before she felt comfortable enough with white people to forsake the all black shows and work in white vaudeville. "I was scared to work for white people. I didn't know very much about them and what I knew I didn't like. The very idea of appearing on Broadway in a cast of ofays made me cringe in my boots."[59]

After starring in a Lew Leslie Broadway musical which ran well even during the Depression, she went on to the Cotton Club and finally to "an ofay show," *As Thousands Cheer,* often stealing the applause from Marilyn Miller. In this show she sang Irving Berlin's "Suppertime," a song about a woman preparing supper knowing her husband had been lynched, a classic even now.

Then, completely switching from musicals to drama, Miss Waters executed a stirring portrayal of Hagar in *Mamba's Daughters,* winning plaudits from every New York critic. From there came *Cabin in the Sky,* both the play and screen hit—but much bitterness was to follow.

Being rejected even for a chorus part in *Shuffle Along* was a slight that so incensed her that she was "determined to show the *Shuffle Along* men they had made a mistake in rejecting [her] services."[60] And of course there was always the jealousy she expressed about other female performers, from Florence Mills to Lena Horne.

She almost passed up the part of Berenice in Carson McCullers' *Member of the Wedding* because she did not like the characterization, But given creative license to portray Berenice as she saw her, Ethel Waters in 1950 delighted in concluding that a "fat, gray-haired lady" could still bring the house down. And this she did.

Hers was a great talent . . . such great promise. . . .

Perhaps she turned more directly to religion as a source of comfort because there was never really a base of acceptance anyplace and her initial rejection was by blacks. The fact that Ethel Waters, who wrote "I never belonged," and who came late to friendships with whites—eventually joined Billy Graham as a singing evangelist, is hard to accept. Black people know well the need for spiritual strength, but her apparent alienation and rejection of fellow blacks in favor of an essentially white crusade is sad. She was often bitter, despite her religiosity. Perhaps a closer connection with her own people might have been a healing balm. She died in 1977 as she had lived: a marginal misfit who found no home with whites or blacks.

Josephine Baker[61]

Now, meet the woman credited with creating the vogue for jazz in France. A militant in every respect, the opposite of Ethel Waters on race matters, Josephine Baker probably never could have survived in the America of her day.

She left St. Louis at age fifteen to dance in a Bessie Smith show, then joined the chorus of *Shuffle Along*, and for a while replaced Florence Mills. She was in the chorus of *The Plantation Review* when Ethel Waters starred there, and when Ethel turned down an offer to go to Paris (requesting too much money), Josephine Baker was asked instead and her life story became sensational. She owned a chateau, married an Italian count, and had "all Paris at her feet, permanently.

Within a year after her Paris arrival, she was a sensational star of the Folies Bergere, with her name in lights twenty feet high. Josephine Baker made it to the Great White Way via France, bringing millions of dollars into Parisian box offices.

She was an acknowledged world star when she returned to America in 1936 to play in the Ziegfield Follies. She was less warmly received by the press and American audiences, perhaps because, as one writer puts it, "The American audiences, before the days of Eartha Kitt, were not accustomed to seeing a Negro in Fath or Patou gowns singing French songs in French, or American songs with a French accent." Her cold reception sent her back to France and she did not come back to the United States for fifteen years.

Josephine Baker's recent biographer, Stephen Papich, verifies the stories about Josephine Baker's rich and famous lovers, including sheiks and the Crown Prince of Sweden. By Papich's accounts, she lived in the grandest manner imaginable, possibly creating a "role model" that suggests to young black performers that they too can be another Josephine Baker and receive some Prince Charming backstage who will shower them with sables, diamonds and wealth! She was the first black performer to set a style of opulence in such a grand manner.

Josephine Baker, however, was more than talent and glamour—she was a fighter for causes. An important figure in the French Resistance Movement, she received many distinguished medals, including the Legion of Honor and the Medaillion of the City of Paris.

She did not return to Broadway until 1951 and then broke all box office records at the Strand. This time she was warmly received by the press and audience. *Ebony* wrote of her 1951 American reception: "The legend named Josephine Baker has come home again to her native land to score an artistic triumph that show business historians will probably call the most remarkable of our times. The fabled Negro star . . . at the age of 44 achieved the one great success that ironically eluded her in the 26 years of her remarkable career: A smash hit in her own U.S.A."[62]

She made nationwide newspaper headlines, however, fighting discrimination. She was refused admission to the Stork Club, then a favorite social center for celebrities. She fought back, making this a cause célèbre. She declined to perform in Miami Beach, declaring: "I have been told that Negroes cannot go to nightclubs in Miami. I cannot work where my people cannot go. It is as simple as that." The Copa City Club in Miami, anxious to get her, changed its policy and other clubs followed soon after. In the short time that she spent in the United States in the Fifties, she established herself not only as a great entertainer, but as a fighting civil rights advocate.

There were unique facets to this woman's history; her heart was as grand as her talent; her dedication to humanity was a personal commitment she translated into a way of living. As Josephine Baker toured throughout the world, she gathered up a large family of orphaned children from every race and nationality. These youngsters lived in her rambling home outside Paris, learning the lesson of love and acceptance their foster mother thought of utmost importance. She was proud of her children, keeping them all with her even when times were hard toward the end of her career. In an interview on Japan's National Television Network in the summer of 1972, Josephine Baker made it clear that her method of breaking down hate and racism was by starting with the children, helping them see beyond the color of a person's skin, the kink in his hair, or the set of his eye.

When she was nearing sixty she appeared again in New York, "a champion show queen still." No superlatives were too excessive for describing the Josephine Baker that the American Great White Way had rejected. From the New York Library of the Performing Arts clipping files, the critics raved: "An eyeful and an earful . . . One of the century's most durable and inimitable stars. . . . The electricity of a superb artist sending waves of excitement across the footlights . . . that voice, that youth and that figure that have made a fool of time."[63]

She died in 1975 in Paris, an expatriate and with very little money.

Like Josephine Baker, several black singer/dancer/actresses sought to gain American acclaim via Europe. Two in particular achieved success: Eartha Kitt and Josephine Premice actually made the Great White Way, both doubling as nightclub singers as well as actresses.

Commediene Singers: A Vanishing Breed

One day in a Houston restaurant a man turned to his wife and said, "I think that's Lena Horne!" Confirming this with a look backward, the woman replied with obvious sarcasm, "So what, she ain't so hot, and besides she's not even as funny as Pearl Bailey."

Pearl Bailey is a funny lady—a singer who sang her way into the hearts of Americans through a combination of comedy and goodwill. "Here comes love, here comes joy, here comes—Miss Pearl Bailey!"[64] That's how she flashed onto our TV screen when she became one of a half dozen black entertainers ever to be given a national television show. Hers is a world that recognizes no wars, racial discord, or violence. Or, if she recognizes these problems, she has devised a philosophy which says, "All the things that seemed ugly have been washed away by the beauty I've found in living with humanity. . . ." She is the original child of the Age of Aquarius, the eternal optimist. And this, all of this, has catapulted her to the top of the entertainment field. Already a big attraction in nightclubs, with movie parts in *Carmen Jones* and *Porgy and Bess,* she broke all records in the Broadway musical *Helly Dolly.* Furthermore, President Ford appointed her to the U.N. delegation—an appointment not particularly heralded by the black community.

It is said that constant and abrasive irritation produces pearls, a kind of disease of the oyster. Pearl Bailey's life certainly had its share of "oyster disease." A broken home, bad marriages and illnesses, the usual show business knocks "before integration" and a few after integration, out of such stuff blues singers are made. It made of her a black cultural hybrid, a female comedienne.

There has been only one other black female comedienne, the late "Moms" Mabley. Moms' get-up, those sloppy dresses and shoes, floozie hats, toothless gums, black speech idiom, plus the black material she used, kept her popularity high among blacks.

Moms singing (if you called *that* singing) was only a small part of her art. She was a standup comedienne, the greatest!

Pearl Bailey, on the other hand, works in gorgeous gowns, waving her elegant hands around in hand talk, singing, throwing away rambling asides, dancing a few steps. She is probably the last of the black female comediennes; there are no young ones coming along.

Pearl Bailey is a cultural hybrid in many ways. First, she probably has a larger, more enthusiastic white following than black. Unlike "Moms," whose black audiences used to stand around the block of the Apollo to see her, Pearl has a small black following. She rarely if ever articulates any identification with blacks.

This nonblack identity, of course, poses no threat to her white audience. Like Ethel Waters, whom she greatly admired, she is seldom, if ever, on record as being concerned with black causes. She never suggests in anything she does that America is anything but "the land of the free and the home of the brave." President Nixon made her his Ambassador of Love, and asked her to advise him on the question: "How am I going to communicate with your people? I'm not too big with them." It is not clear what her advice was, but she might have responded: Neither am I!

The aching feet and the soul food inserts are funny, but beyond this, little about Pearl Bailey touches on the black experience. And the lesson we draw from this is that the Man recognizes talent when he sees it, but he chooses to give the breaks to those among us who make him laugh without making him uncomfortable, and who keep alive the myth that love, and love alone, especially when it's not anchored in black identity, will make the world right.

THEY MADE IT THEIR WAY

Beyond the Great White Way of Broadway, some of the most talented black singers were making their way as "girl singers" in small jazz bands and in the Big Bands of the Thirties.

Billie Holiday, Ella Fitzgerald, Sarah Vaughn, Carmen McCrae achieved the coveted designation of "musicians' singers," having won the highest accolades from this tough group.

Ella, Sarah, and Carmen are rarely seen on TV even in guest spots, though very mediocre white girl singers get constant exposure for a season or so and then disappear. These three represent, however, a small cadre of fantastic black singers who go on year after year steadily drawing fans to their concert and nightclub appearances. They survive and satisfy—to blacks they are superstars.

When these Malindys sing, it is pure musicianship, an experience in good jazz, or rhythm and blues, blending the blues of their ancestors with the sounds and musical expressions of this generation. And always their way.

"Lady" Day: Billie Holiday

It is not surprising that Frank Sinatra attributes his style of singing to Billie Holiday. "It was Billie Holiday," Sinatra said, "whom I first heard in Fifty-Second Street clubs in the early 1930's, and who was and still remains the greatest single musical influence on me . . . with a few exceptions, every major pop singer in the United States during her generation has been touched in some way by her genius."[65] And it is the essence of black irony that her style, her delivery, her very art was perceived by her as something that came naturally. "I don't think I'm singing. I feel like I am playing a horn. I try to improvise like Les Young, like Louis Armstrong, or anyone else I admire. What comes out is what I feel. I hate straight singing. I have to change a tune to my own way of doing it. If you find a tune that's got something to do with you, you don't have to evolve anything. You just feel it, and when you sing it, other people can feel something too."[66]

All about Billie Holiday—why she sang, what she sang—is central to the black human struggle and defines for all times her place in black history. When she sang, black folks (and some white people) felt something of her anguish and shared it. But importantly, we still feel it.

Billie's legend is a bucketful of woe in that historic well of black rage passed on from generation to generation. Tortured in spirit, Billie Holiday died unrelieved of unendurable pain—at once screaming to die, then again for drugs—while white-frocked M.D.'s hid behind inhumane laws governing the treatment of narcotics. Billie was arrested while dying and the police guard who hovered inside the sickroom itself was removed from her presence, by court order, only three hours before her demise.

Nikki Giovanni, in a TV interview in February 1971, asked Lena Horne: "You grew up professionaly with Billie Holiday and Dinah Washington and you survived and they didn't. Why?" Lena's answer was: "I didn't want them [whites] to destroy me. I was strengthened by my active disinvolvement—hidden—but it kept me surviving." Nothing like this worked for Billie.

Billie was a slum victim, prey to all the pathology of black poverty—parents who were too young, racial discrimination, and a persistent hunger for a nourishment of the body and heart. Put out to work too soon, the child within yielded to the social demands of womanhood. "I was a woman when I was sixteen. I was big for my age, with big breasts, big bones, a fat healthy broad, that's all. So I started working out then, before school and after, minding babies, running errands, and scrubbing those damn white steps all over Baltimore."[67]

Eventually (and who hasn't seen this script) the rape of the female child paved her passage from childhood to adolescence. Throw into this black female scenario the years spent in institutions and the base is laid for the blues. All that is needed now is the particular individual style of blues singing created by Billie Holiday. "I've been told," she wrote, "that nobody sings the word 'hunger' like I do. Or the word 'love.' And for good reason." She sang from sheer gut, having written many of the lyrics herself.

Billie Holiday wanted to be a dancer, and failing that, turned to singing. John Hammond arranged for her to record six songs, all for thirty dollars. Among them was a Holiday classic, "I Cover the Waterfront." Miles Davis said: "After the record started moving she tried to get more and later was able to make $75 for two sides."[68]

Billie wrote several social protest songs and regularly packed civil rights messages into songs despite the fact that she was almost always a nightclub singer. "Strange Fruit," which later inspired Lillian Smith's novel, told of a lynching and reminded her of her father's death. Despite its sadness, it was a favorite with fans and sometimes for the wrong reasons: "Over the years I've had a lot of weird experiences as a result of that song. It has a way of separating the straight people from the squares and cripples. One night in Los Angeles a bitch stood right up in the club where I was singing and said, 'Billie, why don't you sing that sexy song you're so famous for? You know, the one about the naked bodies swinging in the trees?' "[69]

Billie often faced discrimination and an odd sort of racism. While singing in Count Basie's band in Detroit she was forced to put on dark greasepaint because she was "too yellow" to sing with all the black men in the band and might be mistaken for white. Though she protested, the management was protected by the contract.

On the other hand, when she traveled with Artie Shaw's band, she often had to sit behind the band because she was too black to sing with a white band!

After the jazz craze left Harlem, music centered on 52nd Street in New York. Though the music up and down 52nd Street was a direct steal from black musicians, Swing Street was an all white scene. Eventually Billie made it, though she and Teddy Wilson were the only black entertainers there, and were subjected to considerable humiliation.

"There was no cotton to be picked between Leon and Eddie's and the East River, but man, it was a plantation any way you look at it. And we had to not only look at it, we lived in it. We were not allowed to mingle any kind of way. The minute we were finished with our intermission stint we had to scoot out back to the alley or go out and sit in the street."[70]

Once she sat at the table with Charlie Barnet, a white musician, and was immediately fired. But after a while the "plantation owners" were forced to include black musicians and customers, and many musicians began to work there. Billie Holiday was the headliner, however, who gave Swing Street that special glitter for most of her working years, and most of its life.

Now she is remembered as much for drug addiction as for her sad songs. The sad songs came first, based on hard times and bad lovers. Her first husband introduced her to heroin when the marriage began to fail. Soon she was making a thousand dollars a week but: "I had as much freedom as a field hand in Virginia a hundred years before.

"I spent the rest of the war on 52nd Street and a few other streets. I had the white gowns and the white shoes. And every night they'd bring me the white gardenias and the white junk."

Drugs finally sent her to the Federal Women's Reformatory at Alderson, West Virginia, for a year's sentence. She had to kick the habit "cold turkey" in Alderson, and came out clean, though she was on and off drugs during the rest of her life.

Actually Billie paid high dues for the year spent at Alderson. She couldn't work in New York clubs where liquor was sold because the police department did not issue a working permit to entertainers with police records.

Though Billie herself said, "There isn't a soul on this earth who can say for sure that their fight with dope is over until they're dead," she saw her habit as an illness and very much wanted to be treated that way. On the last two occasions she was framed and claimed that she was only in trouble with law officials whenever she tried to go straight. Her autobiography describes the corruption in drug traffic.

Billie's legend continues to grow, however—so much so that

Columbia has reissued all of her records in stereo. Diana Ross was nominated for an Academy Award for her portrayal of Billie in the movie *Lady Sings the Blues.* It was less a movie about the real Billie Holiday than it was a salute to a spirit, a legend of black womanhood.

Ella Fitzgerald[11]

While Billie Holiday was moaning her "petulant sex-edged moans," as one critic put it, another singer took a simple nursery rhyme, "A Tisket, a Tasket, I Lost My Yellow Basket," and in a swinging little girl way made the song and herself an overnight sensation.

The song, like Ella, is a kind of wholesome approach to life and living. She is the First Lady of Song and nobody around has tried to dethrone her. Bing Crosby, who was himself a legend, paid her the highest compliment: "Man, woman, or child, Ella is the greatest singer of them all."

Ella began her career on the stage of the Apollo as an amateur night contestant. She won, of course, and got a job singing in Chick Webb's band.

A vocal virtuoso, Ella is at ease in a wide range of musical eras and styles. A Motown "chart" hit, "scat singing" from the earliest jazz days, love ballads, bossa nova, rock-oriented music—name it and she sings it. Also known as a "musician's musician," band men say they tune up to her voice, so true is it.

Her life had none of the personal tragedy of Billie Holiday's. Her life style is simple and hard working. No slacker in civil rights, though given to shyness, she wrote a beautiful song after Martin Luther King's death entitled "It's Up to Me and You."

New York Times critic John Wilson once wrote: "Ella Fitzgerald, a big shy woman whose willowy, little girl voice . . . has none of the mystique of a Dietrich or a Garbo, nor the instinct for the spotlight of Tallulah. She is neither garrulous nor gregarious and, in general, is a poor source of news copy. She just sings."

Ella Fitzgerald sings!

LENA

There is only the need to write "Lena." No other descriptive title, no other adjective is needed. The name conveys the message, multi-media McLuhan style! When you see the name Lena, you know to add Horne.

Because Lena Horne is an institution, her life is instructive. Consider the long line of black female singers who skyrocketed to fame or were picked to succeed because some agent or some impresario thought they had something of Lena Horne in them.

She embodies strong authoritative principles which have survived. In the butcher shop of show business, the fact that she gets better, more interesting, more relevant, and more beautiful with age defines her as an institution. Like Cinderella *homo habilis,* she endures. Like Harriet Tubman, she leads with a passion for black freedom. Like Florence Mills, she defies the white impressario's labels. And like Billie Holiday, she has a lot to sing soulful about.

How did Lena Horne make it so big in show business? Was it her talent, brains, physical beauty—what?

She arrived on the stage as a chorus girl in the Cotton Club, dancing and singing music written by whites, for a white audience.[72] The glamor of the Cotton Club might have gone to the head of a stagestruck teenage girl, but Lena never wanted to be in show business. Unlike so many others, she had tasted some of the warmth and security of family life, even experiencing the fierce protection and indoctrination of a bourgeoisie first family of Brooklyn. She preferred to be in school and to lead a normal life. This is a preference she was never to lose.

Lena's story is a classic case of a stagestruck mother who could not make it in show business herself but plotted and schemed to have her daughter achieve what she could not. The plotting began with her mother's spiriting Lena away from her socially conscious grandparents who reared her during the earliest formative years, instilling in her an enduring respect for formal education and race solidarity. Her grandmother's belief in membership in black causes probably caused Lena to become supersensitive to the earliest demands from civil rights organizations that she project a "good racial image," and she was pulled between becoming a cause célèbre and a person with thoughts and ideas of her own. When in the Fifties she decided to really become involved in civil rights, she startled the Deltas and National Council of Negro Women by participating on the "gut" level of organizational life and displaying brilliant tactical and political strategies of organizational know-how. In a day when one expects stars to do "image-making" jobs in women's organizations, Lena Horne—very much her grandmother's child—is an active and involved black female superstar who works at the business of black liberation.

Removed from the stable, loving influence of her grandparents' home, Lena lived under the pressure of her mother's meager theatrical career. She never knew when her mother would show up and spirit her away. She was boarded with many different families and learned to build sturdy emotional barricades against hurts and disappointments. She learned the fine art of role-playing for survival. This cut her apart from her mother and later even her grandmother, with whom she was reunited for one last year before both grandparents died.

Lena was shuttled about from grandparents, to mother, to other relatives and a series of families who "took in children" for pay throughout her pre-Cotton Club days. When, in her early teens, she was pressured by her mother to audition for the Cotton Club, she had had the benefit of dancing and drama lessons. These were "musts" for all little middle-class Negro girls, but certainly not with a career in view. Internalizing her grandmother's attitudes, she grew up thinking show business sinful. Her mother eventually married a white man, whom Lena resented, and brought Lena to live with them during the Depression. Since neither her mother nor stepfather could get a job, and Lena was alienated from her grandparents and friends, she agreed to her mother's plan for an audition at the Cotton Club. Even when she got the job, it was just that—a job. She had no aspiration to become a star, and because she was under age, her mother chaperoned her so closely that she never really became a member of the "in" show business crowd. It was only after the producer pulled her out of the chorus and featured her with Avon Long (the original Sporting Life in *Porgy and Bess*) that her mother began to really see that Lena could, with her help, become a star.

In the grip now of her mother's dream, demoralized by her failure to fit in ever again with her old school crowd, really not caring one way or another, she moved on in show business.

After leaving the Cotton Club, she sang with Noble Sissle's Society Orchestra. "I couldn't sing jazz and I couldn't sing blues." Noble Sissle really wanted her to sing like Florence Mills (as did Lew Leslie later). What was beginning to emerge was the need for an identity. She was neither Florence Mills nor Josephine Baker. Who was she? She was neither Ella Fitzgerald nor Billie Holiday, both of whom were traveling with big bands. But again, black people rarely played a part in her identity formation, for the Sissle Society Band played mostly for white parties or a few black middle class affairs. She sang what they liked.

Show business has always been perceived by Lena as a substitute for something else she would rather have done. It is, however, something that, if done well, pleases people close to her and provides for their comfort and needs. That fact helped her to survive the rough and tumble life of being black in a white world of entertainment. Early in the game she began to see the Great White Way for what it was, and she carried no illusions about any aspect of it. One consistently agreed-upon adjective which describes Lena is "professional."

Lena ran away from show business into "the normal life of marriage" with a black college graduate. She ran back into show business when an agent called to entice her into a show at a time when her marriage was in financial straits.

In rehearsing for a new Blackbirds show, Lew Leslie tried to make her another Florence Mills. Once he began to accept the fact that Lena could not be forced into another performer's pattern, he worked to help her find her personal musical identity. As she began to realize that her marriage was not working and she was going to have to take care of her two children without a husband, she began to work harder and harder at her craft. She obviously excelled at it.

Then began a long list of firsts: first Negro to become a Hollywood star in a nondomestic role, first Negro to sing in fashionable supper clubs. She paid dues for it all. The movie department attempted to create a pancake makeup that would match her skin with her co-star, Rochester (Jack Benny's sidekick). This failed, but they discovered a formula that made white skin dark enough to "pass" as mulatto. This cut blacks out of certain roles. Lena herself lost the role of Julia in Showboat to Ava Gardner. Black actors were further enraged over her refusal to play maids' parts. Calling a mass meeting, they labeled her a "tool of the NAACP," fearing the elimination of the only movie roles available to blacks. With the exception of Hattie McDaniel, the greatest of the Mammys, Lena incurred the wrath of her fellow actors. She said she was not against domestic roles, but preferred to act other parts. She got a contract that excluded playing menial roles. "They did not make me into a maid," she said, "but they didn't make me anything else either. I became a butterfly pinned to a column singing away in Movieland."

When she went the supper club route she paid other dues. She hated being the first Negro "sex symbol." And less by choice than by accident, she found herself involved in a "peculiar kind of pioneering."[73] She had to be sexy to make it in white clubs.

Though Lena's "pinned to a column" movie posture was conveniently dubbed into the picture so that Southern theatres could cut it out, she gained an international reputation as a movie star in two black movies, *Cabin in the Sky* and *Stormy Weather.* In the latter movie her name began to replace Ethel Waters' as the interpreter of that song. This must have been painful to Miss Waters, who seemed to be threatened by Lena at every turn of her Hollywood career.

The song and the movies turned Miss Waters against Lena and dampened Lena's enthusiasm for singing "Stormy Weather." (Even today she doesn't really like singing it very much, though audiences clamor for it.) Miss Waters' rejection, plus the realization that some blacks in show business resented her "new" image, developed in her a cautious attitude toward other black female vocalists and their material. She wanted to steer clear of their territory, i.e., whatever they deemed to be special to their success. As she moved more and more into an incisive, almost merciless, analysis of her strengths and weaknesses, she pioneered on a unique path of personal development which led to superstardom.

That Lena Horne rose rapidly to international fame, smashing record after record, being the first Negro entertainer here and there, all of this is now history. Critics recognized her talent and everywhere there were accolades . . . "this particular kind of mesmerizing which Miss Horne practices is not merely accidental endowment by a capricious generous nature, although nature has been a spendthrift in her case. It has come about because she has learned her business, which is singing the songs she knows she can sing. At this particular business of hers, she is a master. Forget the beautiful face, the graceful hands, the fabulous clothes sense, the warmth of her eyes, the intimacy of the smile. Forget Lena Horne and just listen . . . and she will come right to you and lead you down the enchanting pathway to song."[74]

After those first frustrating years of singing before segregated audiences (and going back to the Negro neighborhoods to eat and sleep), Lena began to sign only those contracts that stipulated a nondiscriminatory audience policy. After the racial restrictions were removed, however, she still faced audiences that consisted of affluent whites and blacks, and far too few of the latter. Years later, after singing a simple spiritual, "This Little Light of Mine," at a Jackson, Mississippi, rally a week before Medgar Evers was assassinated, she turned to him in the midst of the most tremendous ovation and said, "There is no feeling like this, to be applauded and accepted by my own people."

Her friendship with Paul Robeson and others caused her to be blacklisted during the McCarthy days. But the need for a more intimate connection with her own people began during the run of the musical *Jamaica* in 1957 and 1958.

Jamaica was written for Harry Belafonte but Lena was anxious to get a Broadway role at that time. She liked the Arlen-Harburg score and agreed to take it, provided it was rewritten so that Savannah, the role she was to portray, could be a "really basic earthy human being." That never happened to anybody's satisfaction, but she took what she was given and made the musical a smash hit. Working in that show opened her eyes to the ideas and world of young black activists, some of whom danced and sang in her show. Her famous parties began to include new breeds and crossbreeds—young black activists, organizational leaders, African revolutionaries, and other intellectuals, all destined to play important roles in the black revolution.

She began to relax the protective shields, to engage in the intellectual ferment generated by these blacks and to accept a role that obviously these people (whom she thought at first would shun her, or use her) expected of her. She became Lena Horne, black sister in the movement who had ideas to share.

A kind of inertia and melancholy followed the closing of *Jamaica.* To fight her way out of this depression, she turned from simple "moon-June," "love-dove" songs and became more and more involved in organizational life, not as a symbol, but as a creative member. She "wanted to act now as I knew my grandmother would have acted. I wanted, at last, to be my own woman, to be sure of my own motives, my place in society, my rights and privileges, as she had been."[75]

Following the Sixties, Lena became even more meticulous about the lyrics she sang. During the civil rights movement she sang of the cold hate which killed the four children in a Birmingham church and of black demands for justice in a song called "Now"; the song was immediately banned from many radio stations as too militant and offensive. But her choice of songs was to change—not to militant cause songs, but to songs with lyrics that expressed her interests. Today there are love songs that she polishes off to perfection, even a few "moon-June" songs. But always there are social statements in enough songs to make the thinking listener ponder the injustices of this nation. There is still the glamor of a beautiful, elegant lady on the television screen, but in place of the sex symbol there is the beauty of a black woman fully in command of her senses, reaching out to sensitize her listeners and viewers to positive human relationships.

On Educational Television's *Sesame Street* she sang a touching song to a frog puppet, "It's Not Easy Being Green." While the song shows empathy for a frog, it can be translated to mean: it's not easy being black!

The Lena Horne Syndrome

Not only did Lena Horne make it in the world of show business, she opened the way for dozens of young black women to follow her path to fame. She became the one to copy; she set the mold for white acceptance of the black female singer. She herself said of her image: "I've lived through all the deadly 'firsts'—the years of the white impressarios looking for the white hope Lena Horne, and . . . some of the same impressarious looking for the black Lena Horne . . . I am so glad that no Negro girl has to accept any yardstick but her own ability now. I like to think that if any comparison is made to me and my career, she will not be embarrassed by me 'the person' even if the stereotype 'me' is distasteful."[76]

In a TV interview with Nikki Giovanni she acknowledged that white bosses tried to make her a chocolate Hedy Lamarr and that she was "picked at the time to be what *they* thought a black woman was like." This molded view had really nothing to do with the inner woman, but with her physical looks, sophisticated style, and elegant dresses. Of course, every black woman who gained fame after Lena was established has denied that she consciously attempted to imitate her, but most agree with Leslie Uggams, who said, "There is no Negro woman in the world not aware of her, but I'm not like her."[77]

A kind of Lena Horne syndrome emerged as a result of Lena's success. Any singer whose hair, physical features, and color were more nearly white than black, but who retained enough blackness to tantalize the spectator with "exoticness," would fall into this category. Add to this fashionable clothes and a life style of white oriented and dominated business and personal associations, and a Lena Horne Syndrome emerged. Those singers who could match these descriptions could be groomed to follow her into the supper clubs where the big money was. The difference was that Lena became more and more emotionally detached from her own syndrome, while others were often overcontrolled by it, and a few were even destroyed.

A tragic example of the "syndrome sisters" is Dorothy Dandridge, who died in 1965 at the age of 42. Her biographer, Earl Conrad, wrote that "certain friends unintentionally hastened her death by warning her that if she told her life history she would hold back the march of black womanhood."[78]

Black people have always been uncomfortable about interracial marriages, but in 1964 they were certainly in no mood to read about a black woman whose avowed ambition was "hellbent to marry a white man"[79] and to be accepted in the white world. Hence a book that described such a woman's life was destined to be disgraceful in the eyes of blacks. In 1970, five years after Miss Dandridge's death, when the book was finally published, the coauthor would have been kinder to this performer's historical image had he heeded the words of her friends and "let the dead past bury the dead."

The million dollars she made before age 35, the nomination for a best actress Academy Award, the stardom she achieved in singing and acting, all ended in financial and emotional bankruptcy.

By the time Dorothy Dandridge arrived in Hollywood, she knew what it meant to be poor, to be fatherless, and to survive in a ghetto. She had sung in a family group on the gospel circuit. Her first marriage to a black dancer produced a mentally retarded child and ended in divorce. Outside of this, the only black identity she mentions is a liking for soul food, "all the pig products—emotional food." When she became famous she boasted, "My looks were acceptable in the way Lena Horne's appearance was also acceptable to whites. . . . The audience could . . . 'integrate' with a colored woman who had Caucasian features. . . . I would make the most of this stage of acceptance, publicly and privately . . . it was to be a trademark of mine. . . ."[80]

There was much about Dorothy Dandridge that was talented and promising. She was an excellent actress seriously committed to the craft, who preferred acting to singing. She took the nightclub route to fame because the black singer's role was emerging as acceptable to white America.

She studied diligently and received favorable reviews for star roles in *Carmen Jones* and *Porgy and Bess,* though many black organizations were displeased with both films, believing them to be a perpetuation of stereotypes. Dorothy Dandridge's fame began to decline, the course hastened by the fact that there were few films for blacks to star in, by unwise counseling from those whites who cautioned her not to take certain roles, by her disappointment in love, and always by her anxiety about her mentally retarded child. She began to hit the skids.

Her death, debated by some as suicide, was the result of a bathtub fall, but precipitated by depression, pills and drinking.

Nancy Wilson was one of at least a dozen black singers cast in the Lena Horne image and making it big with the same carriage trade that was then discarding Dorothy Dandridge. Enough fancy nightclubs were opening up, the Las Vegas strip was getting longer and longer, and soon as many as three black singers could be working in the main rooms of the hotels. Others (not in the Lena Horne image) might also be working in the lounges.* Though she was considered "heir apparent to Ella Fitzgerald, following the great tradition of blues, torch and jazz," she looked enough like Lena Horne. Uniquely, among all the "syndrome sisters," Nancy Wilson's records sold in the millions, earning several Gold Records. She established herself in both the supper club and recording worlds.

Dorothy Dandridge's path had crossed that of another of the "syndrome sisters"—Diahann Carroll. She had played the role of Clara in *Porgy and Bess,* but actually did not sing "Summertime," the big number associated with the show and a kind of symbol for many black female singers. (The voice of Marilyn Horne, the white opera singer, was dubbed in for this.) This was no comedown for Diahann. She went on to phenomenal success as a singer in all the posh places of the world, and as an actress in such Broadway musicals as *House of Flowers* and *No Strings.* Everywhere she drew critical accolades, with praise for her voice, stage presence, and looks. And always, the comparison with Lena Horne.

In 1968 Diahann had the distinction of being the first black woman to star in a TV series. *Julia* was welcomed by some, and severely criticized by others. Curiously the greatest objection was lodged by a white critic. In Moynihan fashion, Robert Lewis Shayon criticized the use of the black female figure as the lead when the problems of Negro youth and Negro men urgently required attention. "What curious irony," he wrote, "that this well-meaning TV program would contribute to the castration theme in the history of the American Negro male."[81]

After the show had run two seasons, Miss Carroll said, "I'd like to make films just the way we are . . . films which show the black world as it is." She admitted that the show was a copout. According to an article by Shayon: "She does *Julia* for 'money and power . . . money is power . . . and power means freedom . . . to do what I want to do.' "[82] The irony is that she did not get enough money and power to do her own thing—whatever that might be.

The hope for a "syndrome sister" with money and power is that she does not become too alienated from the life of grassroots blacks, and that she does use her influence both to stimulate

*It was only after the advent of soul music that Aretha Franklin made it to the main room.

interest in shows that reflect the way things are in the black community, and to change negative images that block black progress.

By the time Leslie Uggams opened in *Hallelujah Baby,* she had had an even less typical black background. Her parents were respectable; her mother was a retired Cotton Club chorus girl with time to devote as a stage mother, and her father made an adequate living. She had been successful in show business since the age of six, when she was a precocious regular on Ethel Waters' *Beulah* show. During her childhood and adolescence, she won one TV breakthrough after another, from prize-winning on *Name That Tune* to stardom on the *Sing Along with Mitch* TV show.

When she shed the girlishness of Mitch's "fun and games" format, which bugged her, she broke into the supper club world where she could "sing all the sexy songs Mitch wouldn't let me do." There she came face to face with another image. Privileged or not, she was black and the path to success was the one trod by Lena.

Leslie faced comparison even more intensively when she was asked to play Georgiana in *Hallelujah Baby,* the musical Arthur Laurents wrote originally for Lena Horne. Lena had hoped the musical world would be a vehicle for further expression of her social commitment to the black revolution, something that would engage her evolving societal concerns. *Hallelujah Baby* was clearly not that relevant; in fact its story was too vague and the whole show was riddled with stereotypes. As much as she wanted to do a Broadway show, she was too committed to the black liberation movement to lend her name and talent to that one. Lena bowed out.

Enter Leslie. Some asked: "How can she possibly play a Negro? She's never been one." Suffice it to say, Leslie didn't take the role of Georgiana that seriously, and so she sang, danced, and cavorted in such an engaging and winning way that she deservedly won a Tony Award.

The "ghost of Lena Horne," according to Rex Reed, "still overshadows every moment of the show." Leslie was able to sing and dance as if the musical never was intended to engage the racial pride and fire that comes through in Lena's most inspired performances. Indeed Georgiana was the old image of Lena pinned like a butterfly to an MGM column. It was charming, but not for real. Leslie was an entertainer first, an excellent one, a musical comedy star, and she used those skills and that image to make Georgiana *her* unique role. She out-witchcrafted the ghost!

With her undisputed success in *Hallelujah Baby,* Leslie was signed in 1969 to replace the Smothers Brothers' weekly show. Her show received a mixed reception. Blacks particularly objected to the weekly skits featuring Leslie as a bossy black wife with a "no-good" husband. Again, she was great as long as she sang sophisticated and popular songs, but her black "situations" lacked emotional conviction. Perhaps that's part of the reason the show was cancelled midseason.

As time went along, glamor in the way of Lena Horne and plain good singing, plus changing views about black female beauty, brought singers like Diana Ross and Natalie Cole, daughter of Nat King Cole, into the places Lena had dominated.

Some, like Dionne Warwick, are at home in R & B (rhythm and blues, the soul music category) and popular ballads. Dionne's background as a gospel singer equals that of Aretha's and she is considered one of the best singers of Burt Bacharach's sophisticated tunes.

In 1971, when the Grammy was awarded to two singers, the winners in the rhythm and blues category stole the show. One of them was Dionne Warwick, whose rendition of "Let It Be" was as close to soul singing as anybody's. The other, of course, was Aretha Franklin, undisputed Queen of Soul! Soon the clamor to be Lena Horne would yield to soul—with Lena herself saying: "If I could only sing like Aretha!"

SOUL SINGERS

"Soul defined is soul necessarily misunderstood," says *New York Times* critic Clayton Riley, ". . . soul is Black, the ebb and flow of dark memory."[83] The late Godfrey Cambridge described it this way: "Soul is getting kicked in the ass. . . . It's being broke and down and out, and people telling you you're no good. It's the language of the subculture; but you can't learn it because no one can give you black lessons."[84]

Soul includes body movement and language, special sounds, food, and even funky smells. "It is stomping and shouting with gospel music. It is Mahalia Jackson singing gospel and the blues of Bessie Smith. It is Ray Charles throwing back his head and shouting 'Oh Yeah,' and transmitting to everybody an inner feeling of goodness. Then he comes on with "Don't it make you want to feel alright?" Soul comes to you in Harlem where you can see and feel an infinite variety of rhythms. "When I go downtown . . . everybody's walking the same, you dig? . . . when I walk on Eighth Avenue, man I see rhythms I don't see downtown, polyrhythms. One cat goes bop, bop-bop, and another one goin' bop de-bop, de-bop. These are beautiful people."[85]

Soul is most often associated with music, and singers with

names like The Temptations, The Supremes. But you see it in other forms. It's as much body movement as words and songs. It's Flip Wilson's Geraldine saying: "What you say!" Or, "What you see is what you get." It's Judith Jamison hoisting a white umbrella dancing Alvin Ailey's "Wade in the Water" in his superb soul ballet *Revelations.* And, surely, for black women it's Judy dancing Ailey's solo "Cry," which is dedicated "to all black women everywhere, especially our mothers." Soul emerges spontaneously in the most dignified places, such as the funeral of Whitney Young (former Executive Director of the National Urban League), when Leontyne Price sang, "When I've Done the Best I Can/and My Friends Don't Understand/ Then My Lord Will Carry Me Home," and some of us heard Congresswoman Shirley Chisholm intone, "Yes, Lord," just like those sisters in Big Bethel!

Soul is not about surviving; that's left to spirituals and blues—though there is something of both of these in soul. Rather, soul is about using one's wits to become a winner—to get what's to be gotten as one's just due. It is the self-assurance that propels you to do your own thing while others do theirs—different strokes for different folks! But above all it's telling it all "like it is," and reading the emotional signs from other blacks correctly. Right on! means that if nothing more. In another way, soul is both individual expression and communal togetherness. It's "I'm me!" but it also is, "Here we all are, in the same boat."

It's neither hot nor cold in emotional quality; it's regenerative energy that expresses an oppressed people's triumphs in "keeping on, keeping on."

Soul demands a freedom of expression which claims a right to love lustily, to value the commonplace, the "little moments," to laugh at the ludicrous, cry at the painful, and just *be*!

In a mechanized, computerized society it is spontaneously doing what comes naturally. In this impersonal society, Soul means emotional touching. Soul is the essential black message in America: "Accept us on our own terms, or forget it!"

"The relationship of the black listener to the music that he regards as 'his' always has been a very deep and personal one, quite often reflecting a great deal about his subordinate position in the society," says Phyl Garland. "In contrast to all the things the black man has not had in this country, he has always had 'his' music. This has been his special province, and any infringement upon it, either by whites seeking out black music as presented by black performers, or by white artists offering convincing duplications of black music, is likely to be resented."[86]

There are many excellent soul singers. Four, however, typify the style and range of soul musicianship: Nina Simone, Aretha Franklin, Roberta Flack, and Novella Nelson.

Nina Simone: High Priestess of Soul

In the old days (the Fifties) you didn't decide on a moment's notice that you'd catch Nina Simone's act at New York's Village Gate. You had to make proper preparation to enter a temple ceremony, presided over by Simone—the sorceress.

Nina Simone is labeled a soul singer, but according to Phyl Garland "there is in her choice of songs all the major streams that have gone into the making of modern music. Her music is heavily laced with the classical techniques she learned at Juilliard in New York and at the Curtis Institute of Music. There is the 'touch of Bachian counterpoint' intermingled with the improvisation of jazz and blues."[87] Her musicianship is based on a foundation of gospel music, since her mother was a minister and Nina traveled with her playing the piano in countless revival tents and storefront churches in North Carolina before she was out of her teens. As with Aretha, the road to soul expression for Nina Simone was paved in gospel music.

The title "High Priestess of Soul" did not come because of her audience scolding and early singing in supper clubs. Until the Sixties she appealed mostly to whites, black middle-class intellectuals, and club trotters. In 1962 Langston Hughes wrote:

> She is strange . . . she is far out and at the same time common . . she is a club member, a colored girl, an Afro-American, a homey from down home. . . . She is unique. You either like her or you don't. If you don't you won't. If you do—wheeeouuueu! You do.[88]

She had won a small following as a piano player in small clubs on the Eastern seaboard, supplementing her income as a respectable music teacher and studio accompanist in Philadelphia. And always she studied to become a concert pianist. In order to separate her nightclub work from this "serious" work, she changed her name from Eunice Waymon to Nina Simone. In Atlantic City a club owner insisted on a singer/pianist, and desperate for work, she sang, won a crowd of devotees, and was soon drawn completely into the popular music world.

After the 1959 record hit "Porgy," New York and its supper clubs became her base. She became a songstress for the elite, a small select crowd who regularly came "to be under her spell." In those days, as Maya Angelou says, she sat at the piano "looking like a curved G." She also wore all the trappings of posh place singers, complete with wigs and sequins. Unlike the singers in the Lena Horne syndrome, Nina Simone had none of the "look like a chocolate Hedy Lamarr qualities" sought by white impresarios, In all probability she might have played the fringes of the carriage trade pleasure houses, always attracting a select crowd of loyal Simone aficionados, but not destined to fulfill her real mission—to be the High Priestess of Soul.

Then came 1963—and Birmingham, and the bombing of the church and murder of the four little girls trapped in it. And after that Medgar Evers was assassinated in Mississippi. Nina Simone, already enraged over racial matters, emerged from underneath those cafe society trappings and wrote "Mississippi Goddam," a protest song which she sang with such rage and fury that it became clear to all: Nina Simone was a soul sister, a protest singer, an artist whose carefully educated and practiced musicianship was now turning into an arsenal of revolutionary music, designed, determined, and dedicated to freeing black folks from racial oppression.

> Alabama's got me so upset;
> Tennessee made me lose my rest;
> And everybody knows about Mississippi—Goddam!
>
> Yes! You lied to me all these years,
> You told me to wash and clean my ears
> And talk real fine, just like a lady
> And you'd stop calling me Sister Sadie
> Oh! This whole country is full of lies
> I don't trust you anymore
> You keep on saying "*Go slow*!"
>
> Why don't you see it, why don't you feel it
> You don't have to live next to me
> Just give me My Equality[89]

"Mississippi Goddam" was either banned from radio stations or broadcast by black disc jockeys whose stations made them delete the offensive words. Imagine "Mississippi beep beep!" With this song Nina Simone established herself as the leading black protest singer. She is, of course, a singer capable of pulling on all the listeners' emotions. But there are so many Simone originals that protest or speak directly to the black experience and with such intensity and fervor, that it is for these protest songs of black liberation that history will best remember her.

In remembrance of Lorraine Hansberry's untimely death she wrote the hauntingly lovely "To Be Young, Gifted and Black." In introducing it to an audience she said: "It is not addressed to white people. It does not put you down in any way. It simply ignores you. For my people need all the inspiration and love they can get." The song is a plea for black unification: "Don't divide us, unify us, Lord. Help us to get it together. . . . To be young, gifted and black, that's where it's at."

Aretha: Lady Soul

How did Aretha come to be the living embodiment of soul? It is clear that from the black community have come some fantastic singers, male and female. Aretha considers Dinah Washington "the greatest of them all." How is it then that a young woman, essentially shy, almost withdrawn, "daughter of a preacher man," came to be "a standard bearer for the Black Movement of the 1960's."[90] Until 1970 no really strong black protest statement was associated with Aretha. In fact, she is alleged to have said: "It's not cool to be Negro or Jewish . . . or anything else . . . you don't have to be Negro to have soul. . . ."

Aretha Franklin is the youngest black ever to appear on the cover of *Time* magazine. All three were singers; the other two, Marian Anderson and Leontyne Price, are classical singers. The *Time* article made it clear that Aretha's vocal technique—as fabulous as it is when ranging over a full four octaves, and delivered direct and natural—is not alone the reason for her title Lady Soul. "What really accounts for her impact goes beyond technique: it is her fierce, gritty conviction. She flexes her rich, cutting voice like a whip; she lashes her listeners—in her words "to the bone, for deepness."[91]

Phyl Garland wrote: "To hear her is not to be entertained; it is to undergo a baptism of emotion that leaves one weak and yet fulfilled, as in the aftermath of good sex. This is the soulful side of Aretha Franklin that springs from a sheer sensuality, baked down in the brimstone expressiveness of her Baptist upbringing. But there is more to it than that: a fine sense of musicianship that leads her to place her rhythmic accents in all the right places; a fundamental knowledge of the blues as a pianist as well as a singer; a dramatic instinct on which to build her shrieked and wailed climaxes."[92]

Aretha's Grammy-Award-winning recording of "Respect" was far from a call to militancy and a statement of racial injustices and neither are 99 percent of her songs. "Aretha is about a black woman loving a black man," said a friend. Her songs, many written by Aretha and her sister Carolyn, tell, shout, and moan about getting a man, keeping him, and facing the loss of him. In Otis Redding's "Respect," she sings:

What you want baby I got it
What you need you know I got it
All I'm asking is for a little respect
When you get home.

I'm about to give you all my money
All I'm asking in return honey
Is to give me my propers when you get there
When you get home.[93]

Now that may not qualify as a Negro national anthem, as it was called by *Ebony* magazine, but it does touch solidly on a lot of black women's concerns and troubles.

Unlike the blues, which often have a self-pitying "I'm so down and out" feeling, Aretha's "soul" singing celebrates the ecstasy of trying to cope with life, the hope that it will all get right someday and the fun of having had "it" while it was there. It carries a feeling of self-pride: "Baby, baby, baby, I'm the sweetest thing you ever had." A man is made to feel important: "I've got a man named Dr. Feelgood. That man takes care of all my aches and pains."

Ruth Bowen, her agent, says: "Aretha is one of those rarities that are born every generation or so. She is a natural and everything she sings, she feels. She will not sing a song unless it has a meaning."[94]

Without dwelling too much on the lyrics, there is a "'New Negro anthem" expressed in the spirit of Aretha. She once said, "I'm 26 going on 65." She seems to bear witness to a lot of black realities that enjoin us all: a broken home, a strong religious background, dashed hopes . . . discrimination.

"After her mamma died," said Mahalia Jackson, "the whole family wanted for love." Aretha grew up without financial concern; her father is still one of the most popular evangelistic black ministers on the circuit, commanding $4,000 an appearance. But the Detroit slums were just around the corner from Aretha's home, and the life style of the Franklins was geared more to the poor constituents in the church than the amount of money father banked.

Traveling with her father's gospel caravan, criss-crossing the country, Aretha witnessed how segregation and discrimination took their toll on tired and sleepy talented folk who couldn't find food and lodging. When she started in the pop field she had a miserable four years "singing to the floor most of the time." Only after Atlantic Records backed her with Southern musicians (the Memphis sound) did she develop the soul groove that catapulted her to greatness.

Often plagued by personal problems, she once told Mahalia, "I'm going to make a gospel record and tell Jesus I cannot bear these burdens alone." She finally did, and "Amazing Grace" sold millions of albums and became a classic. In 1968 her fans were saddened to learn that Aretha had reached the breaking point, canceling her Las Vegas engagement at Caesar's Palace after only one performance. Though obviously hoarse and weary, she was still Lady Soul for that one show. By midnight the word was out—something's wrong with Aretha. "I was all fouled up," she said later.

The feeling in the black community surrounding that year's leave of absence bordered on hysteria. "When is Retha coming back? Suppose she doesn't come back?"

Aretha has rarely sensed her real impact on people, or her symbolic value to the black revolution or to black people. She shuns the public, prefers a quiet family life. People tend to forget that, symbol or not, it's tough being a female in the entertainment field.

The fact that she is so important brings a warning and a large measure of compassion from Nikki Giovanni in her "Poem for Aretha," which says in part:

> . . . it's a shame
> the way we are killing her/
> we eat up artists like there's going to be a famine
>   at the end . . .
> of those three minutes/when there are in fact an
>   abundance
> of talents just waiting/let's put some
> of the giants away for a while and deal with them like
>   they have a life to lead
>
> aretha doesn't have to relive billie holiday's life/
>   doesn't have
> to relieve dinah washington's death/but who will
> stop the pattern?[95]

Aretha came back stronger after her leave of absence, with a decided social consciousness. In December 1970 she offered to pay bail for revolutionary Angela Davis, "whether it's $100,000 or $250,000."

> "Angela Davis must go free," Miss Franklin declared. "Black people will be free. I've been locked up for disturbing the peace in Detroit, and I know you've got to disturb the peace when you can't get no peace.
>
> "Jail is hell to be in. I'm going to set Angela free if there is any justice in our courts, not because I believe in communism but because she's a black woman who wants freedom for all black people.
>
> "I've got the money; I've got it from black people . . . they've made me financially able to have it, and I want to use it in ways that will help our people.[96]

The greatest help to us from this Malindy might well be the elevation of our spirits and the nourishment of our souls.

Flack Power

Roberta Flack seemed to be a 1970 "soul phenomenon." She knocked all the black vocalists aside and won the "Best Female Singer" award from *Billboard.* She did a standing-room-only performance at the New York Philharmonic Hall, having won the total approval of the Apollo Theater's crowd the week before. She was "The New Musical Messenger."[97]

It looks very much like Roberta Flack appeared overnight. She taught music at a Junior High School in Washington, D.C. Like Nina Simone she studied hard to become a concert pianist. An all-around excellent music major at Howard University, she was well along towards a Masters Degree when the death of her father made it necessary for her to discontinue her studies and take a job. One of the many "extra" music jobs she had was accompanying opera singers at Mr. Henry's, a restaurant in Georgetown. When things were quiet there, she played blues and popular songs for the waiters. Everything else she did musically was, as told to Phyl Garland, "deep into classical music." Yet, this playing for the enjoyment of waiters delighted the owner of the restaurant, who persuaded Roberta to play for Sunday brunches at Mr. Henry's.

By word of mouth Roberta's fame spread and the owner of "Mr. Henry" soon built a special room with church pews, paneling, and stained glass windows, naming it "Roberta's." With this much encouragement and success, she decided to become a full-time popular singer. Over the next few years a cult of followers grew, spreading the word around the country, and soon she was the first Washington "hometown" performer to win recognition at home before becoming acclaimed outside Washington, something that delights Washingtonians no end.

Les McCann, a musician and one of Roberta's first mentors said, "Roberta can take you all the way inside and clean your soul—out!"

Roberta said at one time that she was not a soul singer—much to the dismay of a growing black audience. She chooses her songs with care; the lyrics and sounds make her a love balladeer of great distinction, but many of her songs deal with social problems. She introduces "Angelitos Negros" with "Painters, why do you always paint white virgins? Paint beautiful black angels."

There is in Roberta's repertoire the songs of protest, earthly love reminders like "The First Time Ever I Saw Your Face," and black religious selections like "I Told Jesus." She's got her "soul bag together."

Roberta Flack stands today at the crossroads of an exciting musical career: she can go the Mancini, Bacharach, Lennon route, join the glamorous, misunderstood sisters of the Lena Horne syndrome (which her idol, Lena Horne, still likes to reject), or continue to cultivate even more exciting and creative soul musical expressions in her own way. Jeffrey W. Kimmel's poem does seem true of her:

> She is a woman of mirrors.
> Mirrors are superficial, usually distorted
> and they reverse you.
> Left is right and what appears to be right
> may be wrong.
> So you see, Roberta doesn't sing at all.
> Her songs are not songs, they are prayerful tales
> Her songs are not just sung, they
> are moanful wails.[98]

Novella Nelson: Look in My Face

When Novella Nelson strolled from her dressing room (combination kitchen, office, storage room) through the artsy craftsy Village Vanguard crowd, bound on the same path that took Harry Belafonte and Pearl Bailey from this historic landmark to fame, one was immediately reminded of Leontyne Price's panther qualities. Everybody knows panthers don't attack, they serve notice that "just in case it's needed" they have the ultimate lethal power!

Aretha makes her triumphal entrances with a huge musical aggregation and you are readied for big sounds; Nina Simone and

Roberta Flack warm up to audiences through those pianos which sometimes seem to absorb their bodies. Novella just stands there alone, like some Ashanti Queen Mother, and commands! Ethos and charisma she has in great abundance. But what Novella Nelson has at once and forever is *presence.*

Not once does she request silence or anything else from her audience. Unlike Simone in her early days of performer-audience battles, Novella has an elegant sense of self and mission that heels the audience to her feet.

She turns first to the musicians with whom she works: "After all," she says, "we make love together, project social statements and create other moods together. I am not up there by myself—ever! We work as a group." When she has her group dynamics together, she turns to the audience, the spotlight frames her face, there is a faint smile of acknowledging her audience, and she begins to sing:

Do you want to see this land?
Then listen to what I say
Do you want to see this land
Look! Look in my face!

I'm a cotton field in the burning sun
I'm the lash of the whip when the day is done
I'm a mother taking her son from the ends of a rope
I'm the pain my mama put down while she was breaking that corn
Cause the boss man made her work til the hour I was born[99]

All about black womanhood is in this song and you are looking at one of the most incredible black women making music today. To "look, look in her face" is to think Black! Black! Black! It is a face with the strength of the Dahomey Amazons molded into the high cheekbones, the flaring nostrils, the full lips, but all put together as if chiseled for posterity. It is also a face with the softness of an African mother at a name-giving ceremony for her firstborn.

These are the hands that fixed the food with a smile
For in my mamma's lap she rocked the boss's chile
A ghost from my past guides me from day to day
And to know I'm going right keeps me on my way
Do you want to see this land?
Look! Look! In my face![100]

Throughout the evening the strength and softness of Novella's face and singing play a gentle game with each other, fighting for equal time. When she sings "Strange Fruit" (Billie Holiday's classic), strength has won and you are transfixed by the incredible amount of grief black women have endured and survived. But when she sings "Do what you gotta do, but come back to see me when you can," the eyes begin to smoulder and then comes the softness and tenderness of a woman understanding what a black man has to do to survive, but loving him anyway, anyhow and anytime. Oh, she can play and scat and bop, sing rock and gospel, and she is easily at home poking fun at "Dixie" in a satirical song about the magnolia smells of the dear ole racist smelling Southland.

There are many facets to this "face you look at." The warmth and sensuousness of black femininity, the strength and constancy are so mixed in Novella Nelson that she could easily become a black Edith Piaf or a reincarnation of Billie Holiday, Bessie Smith, and Florence Mills, all embodied in one person. Critics are unanimous in their praise of her talents, and one, Kevin Kelly of the *Boston Globe,* even said: "Novella Nelson well may be the most talented undiscovered singing actress in the theatre."[101] She could easily become as big a superstar on "soulville" as anyone.

But it will take a mature America to grant her commercial stardom, for she sings about cold water flats and freedom and wars and being black and a woman—and about human values. This is noncommercial fare and it sells well with a select crowd, but such audiences don't make superstars. And also there is the uncompromising Miss Nelson, who once was asked not to sing, "Johnny, I Never Knew You," a bitter war protest song about a soldier returned to his lover as a paraplegic. "It came down to being too strong a statement for television, but how could I change that? I have to sing that kind of material. That's my commitment to my given place in my given time. I'm not just able to get up and start with an up-tune. That isn't me, that's not what I'm all about or how I estimate the world around me. So I didn't do the show. It was as simple as that."[102]

She is unusually successful, even so, probably because she doesn't fit into a safe category. *New York* magazine calls her "a definitive blues singer," which is only one of her styles. It's been said, "she's a protest singer"; but there is all that lovin' she sings about—and what about the fun things? As one critic said: "Miss Nelson is such a different kind of vocalist that audiences are compelled to re-evaluate their preconceptions of what a night-club singer could be."[103]

Novella is yet another phenomenon on the soul scene. She says about herself: "I am an actor who sings, not a singer who acts." This accounts, perhaps, for the great presence she brings to the stage. It is there in the way she moves her body, the accents here and there on phrases, the facial expressions, the timing, the cadence. She clearly sees herself in just that order—actress, singer! Her dramatic roles proved her skills as a tragedienne as well as comedienne.

She started singing only a few years ago because "I can project my feelings better through song." "As an actress," she said, "I spoke playwright words, words I sometimes did or did not agree with. As a singer I choose what I will sing and it is a very personal thing . . . I choose material that has meaning to me."[104] She had an excellent opportunity to practice her singing and build a repertoire while serving as Pearl Bailey's understudy in *Hello Dolly.* She sang the role about 60 times during the run, but on most other nights—since an understudy has to be accessible on a moment's notice in case the star is suddenly incapacitated—she waited out the time at Hilly's, singing for fun and to please the crowd. She made a successful debut at the Village Vanguard, and was on her way. The supporting role of Missy in *Purlie*, the musical based on Ossie Davis's play, *Purlie Victorious,* brought her to Broadway for six months, where she just about stole the show from stars Melba Moore and Cleavon Little.

> What is lacking in *Purlie* is the quality brought to the stage by one of the supporting actresses, Novella Nelson. As Purlie's sister-in-law, Miss Nelson communicates the spirit of soul and of a hard life, wisely and barely survived. She is the only performer in *Purlie* with a three dimensional past.[105]

This soul singer is a strong black woman whose exposure came mostly from "Soul," the black TV show, and other black television programs, as well as supper clubs like Reno Sweeney's. Friends have advised her to compromise, get rid of "Johnny, I Never Knew You" and sing songs people recognize. This counsel must be difficult to ignore, for Novella knows the feel of success, the applause of Broadway, the first-night flowers. Perhaps there will be compromises along the way—one has to have bread.

But somehow the word spreads about soul singers such as Novella. Standing there at Reno Sweeney's, resplendent in African dress, closing an hour of intense musical involvement where the tears somehow show through, there is the last song. There is never an encore!

> I wish I could tell what it
> means to be free . . .

Perhaps the words set the context of soul singing best of all—

freedom to be and do what you feel you must as a black woman in America today. That Novella Nelson claims and lives to do. For that, she has to be a very special soul sister.

When dealing with soul singing, it's always impossible to eliminate personal preference completely and to analyze every performer's background and style. Gladys Knight (and, of course, the Pips) is surely one whose contribution to the art and industry of Soul deserves more than the physical limitations on the size of this volume would ever allow.

The important thing to bear in mind is that as black women grow and flourish as artists, there will always be newer voices raised, newer interpretations of the age-old themes of coping with sadness, overcoming despair, and reaching new heights of love and joy. We have paid some dues as Malindys, but we have made our mark as singers.

THE CLASSICAL MALINDYS

The obvious differences between singing in one of the plush main rooms in Las Vegas and singing on the stage of the Metropolitan Opera House may obscure some of the similarities. The training differs, language requirements certainly differ, as does the material, but there is a connecting thread of human emotions which ties the two forms together. Communication is the key, and when Leontyne Price as Aida sings "O Patria Mia," the words may be in Italian and understood by only a few, but it's also a woman singing of loss and sadness and alienation and that's the heart of the blues. So where do the paths split? What leads a young black girl into a life of formal music lessons and years and years of training?

Spirituals, blues, and gospel singing were seldom the preferred musical careers for those sisters whose talents were discovered by choir directors and schoolteachers. The music of the black experience may have motivated the musical interest of the young girls, but their mentors heard a different music. Opera and the great concert stages of the world where Wagner and Bach were sung were most often the ultimate goals of musical achievement. Singing "serious music" is what they strived to instill in their pupils. And while this or that Malindy's voice lifted the rafters singing, "Swing Low Sweet Chariot," some teacher or choir director was usually thinking, "Maybe this one will make it to Carnegie Hall, yes, or even to the Metropolitan Opera!

For years, however, those who pursued serious music down the long arduous road of formal music education and concertizing were to experience a special kind of racism, very different from that experienced by the blues singers. Few were to make it before the Fifties.

The serious music power structure is controlled by rich and educated white American aristocrats and intellectuals. In America, music has generally been stratified into good and bad, high brow and low brow. Even when records were first cut by blacks, their defined category was "race records." Blues singers achieved their limited success not because whites helped and welcomed them, but because their singing sprang from the musical heritage of their own people. Whites could not at first steal the beat, the sound, and the musical material without allowing a few black singers some projection and visibility.

The young girls who departed from gospel singing and spirituals and began to sing Italian and German songs were on very strange turf. There were gaps in experience and upbringing to traverse. Not only were they singing in a segregated land where whites and blacks were totally separated, and white tastes and ways were foreign to them, but most of them were poor and the stylized formal singing demeanor was as strange to their black audiences as were the foreign words and sounds. Black captive audiences listened to the foreign sounds only because they believed in the young artists. They patiently suffered through classical programs knowing they would be rewarded with a few spirituals at the end. That so many unschooled poor black church congregations tolerated their odd performances is a testimony to their determination to do whatever is necessary for a young artist's development.

Of course, as time went on the artists also helped expand the musical tastes of their congregations. Marian Anderson, for example, did not understand the music and lyrics of the classical songs she heard as a child while listening to guest artists in her church, but she liked what she heard and was motivated to become trained to sing such music.

For generations these young singers went virtually unnoticed by whites, gaining appreciation only among the few college and middle-class audiences. When Marian Anderson, Mattiwilda Dobbs, Leontyne Price, and Grace Bumbry first started, their sororities could be counted on to present them in recitals throughout the country. And of course the black colleges scraped together enough money to present these artists in recitals for student populations. But the black audiences for classical music had to be cultivated, and this could be done only by black artists who moved them, not by teachers telling them what was "good" music.

Certainly, the growing popularity of blues singers was a source of jealousy for many classical singers. *The Chicago Defender* (September 14, 1929) ran an article entitled "Prima Donnas Grumble Over Blues Singers."

> Time was when folks who carried the name of "blues singers" were classed decidedly below the standard of prima donna. But with the sweeping popularity of jazz mania the standing may be the same, but the shekels and contracts go to those who are bluest . . . [the prima donnas] deplore the fact that the years of training and self denial to perfect their art are now going to naught with the cashing in of every little former chorus girl or even less who can shout a jazz tune.[106]

The seeming effortless achievement of the blues singers has always been overstated, for their rise to fame was also compounded on hard knocks and exploitation. Nevertheless, the anguish of the classical music singers was well founded, as was their plea for just recognition of years of arduous training.

Whereas Bessie Smith and other blues singers played the tent circuit and dives of the country in order to gain entry into the big theaters, black classical singers as well as whites traditionally spent their apprenticeships in Europe, gaining recognition there before winning even minor acclaim at home.

At least four women gained limited recognition before Marian Anderson's spectacular breakthrough into the world of classical music. As early as 1850, Elizabeth Greenfield, born a slave in Natchez, Mississippi, in 1809, won some success as an opera singer in Europe. A Quaker woman took the slave to freedom in Philadelphia when she was only one year old, and educated her for a musical career. Her voice, one critic remarked, "ranged from 27 notes, from a sonorous baritone to a few notes above even Jenny Lind's highest." Though she gave a command performance before Queen Victoria before leaving England, she never achieved fame in America.[107]

Sissiretta Jones once sang at the White House and was later signed for roles in *Aida* and *L'Africaine* at the Metropolitan in 1892. She did not get a contract to sing at the Met and her singing drew only small audiences until Bob Cole built a musical show, *The Black Patti Troubadours,* around her. Though she was never to gain recognition on the concert stage, hers was an unusual spot in show business. She appeared in only one act, usually the last, singing only operatic numbers, even though the rest of the show was in the musical comedy tradition, complete with the cakewalk. Black Patti was a huge success.[108]

In 1933 a "tall, voluptuous soprano" named Caterina Jarboro, who had been in the chorus of *Shuffle Along,* sang the role of Aida in the New York Hippodrome. Jarboro created such enthusiasm that she persuaded her husband to send her to Europe, where she stayed several years, taking vocal lessons, coaching for leading roles, studying languages, and trying to get roles in European opera houses. Somehow she managed to sing "Aida" in Milan. The Italian public liked Jarboro, and many of the provincial opera houses engaged her for both *Aida* and *L'Africaine.*

She returned to America and became a "first" Negro, appearing with Alfredo Salmaggi's American Opera Company. She triumphed here, but her success was short-lived. There was nowhere else for black Jarboro to go in white operatic America, and she soon retired.

Before Jarboro there had been Madame Lillian Evanti, believed to have been the first Negro woman to sing the coloratura roles in *Rigoletto* and *La Traviata* in European opera houses. When she left Washington to study and sing in Europe, there were few black singers in this field, and she helped to open the doors of European musical circles for them.

Many fine singers continued studying and some, particularly Dorothy Maynard, won critical acclaim and gained some financial success. It was not until Marian Anderson came along, however, that any of this music and its artists captivated the enthusiasm of the black masses. Only the small "cultured" black middle class and liberal white music lovers patronized their concerts. Rejected by whites for the most part, and strange to their own people, these singers were faced with too few ticket buyers to make a full-time living. That any of them made it is perhaps among the most phenomenal stories in black history.

Marian Anderson: "The Big Wheel Runs by Faith"[109]

On Sunday, April 18, 1965, Sol Hurok presented Marian Anderson in a farewell tour which culminated four decades of Miss Anderson's reign as the world's greatest contralto.

There was a special elegance that evening, even in the program notes, all befitting the Lady from Philadelphia whose life has been an inspiration and whose musical stature has surely brought more musical pride and beauty to black people than perhaps anyone in our history.

Much of Marian Anderson's young adult life was similar to that of other young black singers. There was an encouraging choirmaster and church members who believed in her. Young Marian not only sang contralto, but also tenor, bass, and soprano in the church choir. She credits the range of her voice, sometimes described by critics as "two voices," to all the experience of filling in for absent soloists and "singing any note in any register."[110]

Also, consistent with a black tradition which long believed that guest artists appearing in a town should also hear and judge local talent, young Marian was billed on most visiting artists' programs as "assisting artist."

Like most American singers, white or black, Marian Anderson studied voice with various teachers and eventually studied and performed in Europe. But, for Marian Anderson, singing to the critical acclaim of European critics was a significant historic breakthrough. For countless black people throughout the nation—especially the children—the news of Marian Anderson's European triumph was like Joe Louis's winning the world heavyweight boxing title. In classrooms and churches, teachers and preachers proclaimed, "Children! one of us has made it!" Grasping newspaper clippings, black teachers read that Toscanini had proclaimed Marian Anderson's voice "one heard once in a hundred years," and that Jean Sibelius had exclaimed, "The roof of my house is too low for your voice."

Overnight, music appreciation was eagerly pursued. Masses of blacks wanted to know all about the music Marian Anderson sang, and in their impoverished homes and churches they struggled to grasp the relationship between young Marian Anderson's European acclaim and what lay ahead for her in establishing American fame. Around the country, prayers for Marian Anderson's success became a part of regular church services.

Marian Anderson, according to American tradition, had "pulled herself up by her bootstraps" and was a black female Horatio Alger, the kind of individual achievement symbol around whom legends are born. Everything about her background—except her blackness—would have made the kind of Cinderella story destined to win her proper entry into American history.

It is difficult to communicate what Marian Anderson meant to blacks in those days. A black hope? A race model? A credit to the race? Yes, all of this.

How desperately have we blacks identified with those among us who make it against the odds of racism! White Americans understand overcoming all obstacles of the human condition except this one. Consider the grinding put-down of poverty and segregation and discrimination—all of which Miss Anderson knew well by the time she reached the first step of her escalating career.

Overcoming the psychological consequences of words and deeds that label one stupid, dumb, lazy, or the niceties of racism which on another level come clothed in sentences like, "Negroes naturally have good voices," must have posed difficulties. Add the sentence, "He or she is an exceptional Negro," which blacks decode to mean that whites don't expect significant numbers of us to achieve excellence, and there is the stress of being the token one, the lone one. Marian Anderson's acclaim has to be understood against all of this psychology.

Marian Anderson was born poor in Philadelphia. Her father died early and her mother, like so many others, worked as a domestic. At fifteen, she took her first formal music lesson, paid for by her church congregation. A white principal became interested in her and paid for an audition, but not before Miss Anderson had been told by one conservatory, "We don't take colored."

Nurtured in the warm appreciation of her family and church, she studied, supplementing her small income with domestic work. She won important singing prizes and finally, in 1930, departed for Germany to perfect *Lieder* (German art songs of the nineteenth century by Schubert, Brahms, Wolf, and others), the backbone of a concert singer's repertoire and eventually the cornerstone of her art.

When Marian Anderson returned to the United States she was a European success. On December 30, 1935, her Town Hall debut established her as an American success. Howard Taubman, *New York Times* music critic, was one of many oustanding critics who covered the concert.

> Let it be said at the outset: Marian Anderson has returned to her native land one of the great singers of our time. The Negro contralto who has been abroad for four years established herself in her concert at the Town Hall last night as the possessor of an excellent voice and art. Her singing enchanted an audience that included singers. There was no doubt of it, she was mistress of all she surveyed.[111]

Appraisals were generally favorable, sometimes describing her as "the coloured contralto," "the Negro contralto," or simply "the Negress."

Recognizing the racism of America, but choosing not to deal with this, Howard Taubman concluded his article with this challenge:

> . . . in the last four years, Europe has acclaimed this tall, handsome

> girl. It is time for her own country to honor her; for she bears gifts that are not to be feared.[112]

Though Europe celebrated her genius, a good many Americans thought her first and foremost, a black second-class citizen. She was refused hotel accommodations throughout the South and had to stay with friends and sorority sisters when singing there. Atlantic City offered her the key to the city, but no first-class hotel would give her a bed. In New York she could not live in first-class hotels. She would sing before the "crème de la crème" of New York society and trek back uptown to sleep in the Harlem YWCA. (Later the Algonquin offered her accommodations.) Her contracts contained a clause against segregation in audiences. The Jacksonville chapter of her sorority, Alpha Kappa Alpha, refunded ticket money to 250 white persons after authorities told them that races couldn't be mixed in the audience. Some few whites slipped in anyway.

Among all the racial insults and indignities she endured, one reached the status of an international disgrace: the DAR's refusal to let her sing at Constitution Hall in the nation's capital. Mrs. Henry M. Robert, the president, gave two reasons for her denial:

> The hall was engaged for the afternoon of the date when a night appearance was asked and rules forbid rival musical attractions at the Hall on the same day.
>
> A rule was adopted more than seven years ago "because of unpleasant experiences in attempting to go contrary to conditions and customs existing in the District of Columbia." [Mrs. Robert] did not outline the rule, but apparently referred to one restricting use of the building by Negro artists.[113]

Eleanor Roosevelt promptly resigned from the DAR and floods of protest letters reached the White House and the news media. The DAR refused to back down; the white school system refused the use of its white high school facilities on similar grounds, and the verdict was clear to black people everywhere: no matter how high a black person's accomplishments take her, when the chips are down, all blacks are treated like niggers! Some are just niggers with talent!

This must have been in the minds of the millions of black people who listened that Easter Sunday morning in 1939 when the Marian Anderson Lincoln Memorial Concert was broadcast over radio. Secretary of the Interior, Harold Ickes, made the steps and mall of the monument available for a free concert after the DAR's rejection and 75,000 people attended. The following June she sang for the King and Queen of England in the White House.

Undaunted and arrogant, the DAR offered to allow Miss Anderson to sing in Constitution Hall during World War II to raise funds for a war cause. Again she agreed to sing provided the hall was not segregated. The DAR refused on the grounds that they could not depart from local custom. Miss Anderson sang, however, believing the war cause greater than the cause of desegregation. This incident as well as other responses of hers to racism have not escaped criticism from time to time. Many blacks have wanted her to be more outspoken. But she always proclaimed "music is my way" and simply did not see herself as "a fearless fighter."[114]

Deeply religious, possessed of a humility expressed in a speaking pattern which substitutes the editorial "we" for "me" or "I," she certainly has identified with black causes and has paid her dues in ways known and appreciated by all.

The fact is that during the years of her fame America would hardly have allowed a militant, angry Marian Anderson to survive. Would whites have supported her had she been outspoken about the treatment of blacks, even herself? Is anybody naive enough to really think that white Americans could separate genius from an unpopular political or social commitment?

Sooner or later the Metropolitan Opera had to recognize the existence of Negro talent, and when that door was finally opened in 1955, it was fitting that Marian Anderson be the first to enter. The Met might have chosen any number of other Negro singers; by that time there were many fine young singers inspired by Miss Anderson who were clamoring for musical recognition. But the "first" to sing at the Met would command a dramatic moment, and a dramatic choice was demanded.

It was, however, little more than a gesture. First of all, Miss Anderson had had little operatic experience, with the presence of other people and scenery and props such as one finds on the awesome Metropolitan stage. Furthermore, her voice, while no less beautiful under proper circumstances, was no longer the size for that kind of auditorium and she had to force to be heard. Third, Ulrica in *Un Ballo in Maschera* is black, so the breakthrough gave the audience a safe role to accept as a first. Nevertheless, Miss Anderson took it on with her accustomed grace and a precedent was set.

Ten years later, on April 18, 1965, Marian Anderson sang her farewell concert at Carnegie Hall, but her career had already taken on the dimensions of an elder statesman. Each year the Marian Anderson fellowships, established by her, make it possible for young talent to receive training. Some of these winners are now singing at the Metropolitan Opera. In 1958 President Eisenhower appointed her to the United States delegation to the United Nations. This Grande Dame of Music has won nearly every distinguished civilian award and tribute accorded great artists and humanitarians, and serves on the boards of some of the most powerful "cultural establishments." A black people and an entire country could say "Amen" again and again to Alan Rich's lovely tribute: "Marian Anderson is a whole series of symbols for our age and the ages to come. The fact that her musical qualities are so rich and noble merely adds a touch of the miraculous. . . ."

Brava! Leonessa! (Divine! Leontyne)[115]

> *First voice*: Brava, Leonessa!
>
> *Second voice*: She is more like a panther than a lioness.*

When Leontyne Price reached the stage of the Metropolitan Opera, black people at last had someone with whom they could enthusiastically identify and claim as a soul sister. Everything about Leontyne was destined to "turn them on"—not the college crowd alone, but the countless brothers and sisters in the ghettos, in the schoolrooms, on the blocks. Never mind that she wasn't the second, after Marian Anderson. That distinction goes to Mattiwilda Dobbs, who appeared in 1956 at the Metropolitan Opera in the principal role of Gilda in *Rigoletto.* Though Mattiwilda was then an outstanding soprano, she chose to return to Sweden and take up permanent residence with her Swedish husband. Removed from blacks geographically, Mattiwilda was also a member of the distinguished black Dobbs family, whose six brilliant and beautiful daughters had all accomplished great achievements. She would have had to consciously cultivate the love of the poor black masses, for little of her repertoire or life style was comfortable to them.

Blacks have long held the insidious phrase "a credit to your race" as a label whites reserved for blacks they like and reward. The black masses often question: "How much self-respect will this 'credit to the race' buy for black people? When the chips are down where will that sister stand? What has she ever done for us?" So black acceptance of black artists is a separate matter. Either in one's style or one's involvement in black causes, some sharing of the artists' feeling for the pain and suffering of black humanity—something has to get across to black people. Increasingly and certainly, by the time Leontyne reached the Met, black people were

---

*La Scala, 1960

expressing more and more a desire to identify artists with black causes. *They,* not white critics and opinion makers, were beginning to confirm and affirm the new idols of black history.

Leontyne emerged as such an idol—confirmed and affirmed by her people as great.

Take the matter of Leontyne Price's hometown, Laurel, Mississippi. Even if her father had been a doctor and not a humble sawmill laborer, and her mother a housewife and not a midwife, just the sound of that place in the state of Mississippi creates an immediate bond of black identity. She must have paid dues! Even after Leontyne overcame racism, the local newspaper editor said: "This gal is a good example to other Negras. She wasn't hurt by attending a Negra school." He made her discrimination a condition for success. When Leontyne cooks chitlings (which she does very well) you know this is no acquired effete fad; this is experienced cooking perfected when soul food was simply eating to keep alive. For any black person, a woman at that, to make it out of Laurel, Mississippi, and become a diva, a world prima donna, the world's greatest Aida and all the other great things associated with Leontyne, means she was extraordinarily gifted, bright, and determined. Add to this her impoverished (even for whites) segregated hometown, the marginal poverty of her parents, and their dependence on the leading white family, the Chisholms, and it becomes apparent that one also has to have a little bit of gall—chutzpah, as the Jews say! All this is bound to create among black people a common kinship.

For Leontyne Price, the climb to the Metropolitan Opera was routed through a typical black experience. She played the piano and sang in the church choir and at all the black community occasions in Laurel. She was an expressive funeral singer; she once whipped a group of mourners into such a frenzy at a funeral that the funeral director had to tell her to stop singing. Even then she had star quality, for she vowed, "That's the last funeral I'll ever do."

Like many little black girls she was often taken to the Chisholm's big house by her aunt, who had worked as a domestic in the family for over forty years. One must credit Mrs. Chisholm, a kind of modern-day Fannie Kemble of Laurel, for responding to Leontyne's obvious desire to learn the music she observed being taught to the two Chisholm children. Credit also Leontyne's parents' expectation that she and her brother would amount to something, and Wilberforce University (now Central State) for giving her a scholarship.

At college she sang in the choir and was considered a student leader. Sorority hazing was difficult in those days. One day while she was walking across the campus, a Delta Sigma Theta soror stopped her and ordered her to sing. There in full hearing of the entire noontime campus, she sang "Because" with such beauty and force that all within the sound of her voice stopped in their tracks and applauded.

Leontyne soon realized that New York and Juilliard had to become her base if she was to realize a musical career. Paul Robeson, after hearing her sing, appeared at a benefit in her honor where $1,000 was raised. Mrs. Chisholm offered to pay Leontyne's living expenses in New York, and with a scholarship from Juilliard she was able to study there for the next four years.

During those four years she was signed by Virgil Thomson to sing Saint Cecelia in a revival of *Four Saints in Three Acts.* Ira Gershwin auditioned her for *Porgy and Bess* and she sang the role of Bess on Broadway, then on national tour and throughout Europe.

A kind of romance with a happy ending culminated in her marriage to William Warfield, the distinguished tenor who played opposite her as Porgy. In this marriage she assuaged the fears often expressed by blacks that Negro artists always marry white men when they reach the top.

Meanwhile, as Leontyne said, "everything I put my hand on musically turned into gold." She filled in for ailing sopranos in Europe and San Francisco. "My career," she says, "was launched on the appendectomies of Italian sopranos."

She made her opera debut in 1957 at the San Francisco Opera. Herbert Von Karajan invited her in 1958 to make her European debut with the Vienna State Opera in *Aida.* In 1960 she walked into La Scala as Aida, without one stage rehearsal. "After all," she said, "the Nile can only be upstage." She had sworn never to enter La Scala except as a prima donna, and she did just that. One Italian critic wrote: "Our great Verdi would have found her the ideal Aida."

The dream of her lifetime came true on January 27, 1961. "Since I first began to train as a singer my special goal and ambition has been to sing at the Metropolitan Opera in New York." She sang Leonora in *Il Trovatore,* and her unremitting hard work in concert halls, opera houses, recording studios, and practice and coaching sessions was rewarded by audience enthusiasm and unanimous critical acclaim. She had taken her place as one of the reigning prima donnas of opera.

At first some people thought that Leontyne's color would keep her from many parts. A La Scala official, however, put such thoughts to rest in considering her for other roles. "The public will have to get used to it. If she sings Butterfly and anybody objects, we'll say she's a sun-tanned Butterfly." For this role, however, Leontyne does whiten her skin, giving this reason: "Why should I go struggling out on the stage looking anything but Japanese? A geisha puts rice powder on her face." Why not Leontyne? Otherwise she doesn't believe in "putting white stuff on me."

The Chisholm family's financial investment in Leontyne's career has been repaid a million times. If there is immortality in the Chisholm name it comes from their title, "Patrons of the Great Prima Donna, Leontyne Price," and not from their identity as one among other white Mississippi families.

Leontyne's life style has spawned memorable stories that somehow give a down-to-earth, human quality to her life. There is one about her threatening suicide over a Haitian fellow who spurned her love. It is alleged that she came to her senses when told to put on her shoes first before jumping into the Hudson. Or, more recently, the night of Martin Luther King's assassination Leontyne invited some of her white aristocratic friends to dinner. They were greeted by Leontyne wearing a new Afro hairstyle moving about the house in an angry fashion (Panther fashion?). After reading them all out about American racism and declaring her intention to become more involved in the black revolution, she ordered them out of her house and made arrangements to attend the funeral in Atlanta.

A look at Leontyne's total life experience, her earthy presence, her commitment to black causes, the daring ventures into musical firsts—opening the Metropolitan Opera House at Lincoln Center, yes, even riding a horse onto the stage in *The Girl of the Golden West* as a black woman and not as a "blonde American type," makes for popularity among blacks. She is the symbol of the first black woman who became a Prima Donna Absoluta.

While Leontyne was claiming the major spotlight at the Met, there were many other singers gaining fame in Europe, only waiting for the proper moment to appear on the stage of the Metropolitan Opera. Gloria Davy actually made it to the Big House before Leontyne, but preferred to return to Europe where the roles offered her were more suitable to her taste. Felicia Weathers also went to Europe after a brief stint with the Metropolitan.

Margaret Tynes tried the *Porgy and Bess* route, with strong inducements to follow "the pretty black girl" Lena Horne route and take the supper club path to success. She opted for opera in

Italy and Canada, and attained popularity in the Balkan countries. Except for standby roles, she will not come to the Metropolitan stage unless the right roles are offered her, a condition more and more black singers now make.

By the middle of the twentieth century almost every major opera house in the world had Negro singers on their rosters: Olive Morehead in Oslo, Charlotte Holloman, Ella Lee, and Annebell Bernard in Saarbrücken; and with the Berlin Opera, Gloria Davy, Vera Little, and Meryl McDaniel. At the New York Opera House, Camilla Williams, Adele Addison, and Margaret Tynes sang various leading roles.

Actually with Leontyne's debut and wide range of starring roles at the Metropolitan, there was no special glory for black women to gain entry into the Metropolitan Opera. The firsts were already established in history. The later comers could afford to live the less intense and more informal life of European stars. There seemed to be no rush, in fact a reluctance to arrive at the Met. In Europe they could escape the problem of being black and avoid participation in the fight for black liberation which surely would have placed demands on them. By experiencing an artistic life in Europe and South America they often escaped notice by American blacks, so much so that by 1971 many people were surprised to discover that at least four black prima donnas were established in starring roles at the Metropolitan Opera.

They had come there by different routes, but were indeed present, disproportionately represented some might even say. There were seasons when two of them starred on the stage in the same opera. Grace Bumbry, Shirley Verrett, Martina Arroyo, and Leontyne Price were there; Peri Grist was coming later. More Malindys had triumphed! They were neither Great Black Hopes nor "whitewardly mobile blacks"—just great singers!

CHAPTER 8
NOTES

[1]Paul Laurence Dunbar, "When Malindy Sings," from *The Complete Poems of Paul Laurence Dunbar* (New York: Dodd, Mead & Company, 1968), pp. 131–134. Reprinted by permission of Dodd, Mead & Company, Inc.

[2]Judith Gleason, *Agotime, Her Legend* (New York: Grossman Publishers, 1970), pp. 113–114.

[3]*Ibid.,* p. 137.

[4]*Ibid.,* p. 138.

[5]Frances Anne Kemble, *Journal of a Residence on a Georgian Plantation in 1838–1839* (New York: Harper & Brothers, 1863), p. 129.

[6]LeRoi Jones from *Blues People* (New York: William Morrow and Company, 1963), pp. 25–26. Copyright 1963 by LeRoi Jones.

[7]*Ibid.*, p. 28.

[8]*Ibid.*, p. 42.

[9]*Ibid.*, p. 42.

[10]Mahalia Jackson, with Evan McLeod Wylie, from *Movin' On Up* (New York: Hawthorne Books, Inc., 1966), p. 72. Reprinted by permission of Hawthorne Books, Inc. Copyright 1966 by Mahalia Jackson and Evan McLeod Wylie.

[11]*Ibid.*, pp. 30–33.

[12]*Ibid.*, p. 63.

[13]*Ibid.*, p. 59.

[14]*Ibid.*, p. 66.

[15]Paul Oliver, *The Story of the Blues* (Philadelphia, New York, London: Chilton Book Company, 1969), p. 6.

[16]LeRoi Jones, *Blues People*, p. 81.

[17]Paul Oliver, *The Meaning of the Blues*. Reprinted from *Blues Fell this Morning: The Meaning of the Blues*, copyright 1960 by Paul Oliver, by permission of the publisher Horizon Press, N. Y.

[18]Erik Erikson, *Identity: Youth and Crisis* (New York: William Norton and Company, 1968), Chapter 7.

[19]From *Music on My Mind: Memoirs of an American Pianist* by Willie the Lion Smith with George Hoefer. Copyright © 1964 by Willie Smith and George Hoefer.

[20]One of the most famous of these black minstrel stars was James Bland, graduate of Howard University. According to journalist Phyl Garland, unbeknown to whites, Bland wrote many of the "ole Southern songs," such as "In the Evening by the Moonlight" and "Carry Me Back to Ole Virginny." Bland eventually performed in Europe, where he did not have to wear burnt cork in order to gain acceptance.

[21]See Oliver, *The Story of the Blues*, especially page 13, and Langston Hughes and Milton Meltzer, *Black Magic* (Englewood Cliffs, N.J.: Prentice-Hall, Inc., 1970), pp. 16–32.

[22]*Ibid.*

[23]Copyright © 1970 by Derrick Stewart Baxter from the book *Ma Rainey and the Classic Blues Singers*. Reprinted with permission of Stein and Day Publishers, New York; also Oliver, *The Story of the Blues*, and Hughes and Meltzer, *Black Magic*.

[24]Stewart Baxter, *Ma Rainey*, p. 42.

[25]See Oliver, *The Story of the Blues*, and Hughes and Meltzer, *Black Magic*.

[26]Carl Van Vechten, "Negro Blues Singers," *Vanity Fair*, March 1926, p. 67.

[27]Gunther Schuller, *Early Jazz: Its Roots and Musical Development* (New York: Oxford University Press, 1968), p. 229. Copyright © 1968 by Oxford University Press, Inc. Reprinted by permission.

[28]From *His Eye Is on the Sparrow* by Ethel Waters, Copyright 1950, 1951 by Ethel Waters and Charles Samuels. Reprinted by permission of Doubleday & Company, Inc., p. 92.

[29]Sally Grimes, "The True Death of Bessie Smith," *Esquire*, June 1969, pp. 112–113.

[30]*Ibid.*, pp. 112–113.

[31]*Ibid.*, p. 112.

[32]Willie the Lion Smith, *Music on My Mind*, p. 105.

[33]*Ibid.*, p. 105.

[34] Baxter, *Ma Rainey*, p. 53.

[35]"The Top Ten," *Black Enterprise*, 3, no. 2 (June 1973), 37.

[36]Willie the Lion Smith, *Music on My Mind*, p. 96.

[37]Waters, *His Eye Is on the Sparrow*,, p. 194.

[38]Billie Holiday, *Lady Sings the Blues* (New York: Lancer Books, Inc., 1969), p. 34.

[39]*Ibid.*, p. 95.

[40]Langston Hughes, *The Big Sea* (New York: Hill and Wang, 1940). Reprinted with the permission of Farrar, Straus & Giroux, Inc. Copyright 1940 by Langston Hughes.

[41]*Ibid.*

[42]*Ibid.*, pp. 225–226.

[43]*Ibid.*, p. 226.

[44]*Ibid.*, pp. 224–225.

[45]From *Lena* by Lena Horne. Copyright © 1965 by Lena Horne and Richard Schickel. Reprinted by permission of Doubleday & Company, Inc.,

[46]*Ibid.*, p. 57.

[47]*Ibid.*

[48]*Ibid.*

[49]Willie the Lion Smith, *Music on My Mind*, p. 139.

[50]See Hughes and Meltzer, *Black Magic*, p. 71.

[51]Waters, *His Eye Is on the Sparrow*, p. 183.

[52]Interview with Eubie Blake, New York, April 7, 1970.

[53]Perhaps a lasting tribute and recognition of Florence Mills' artistry is best experienced in the dance *The Mooche*, choreographed by Alvin Ailey, which features four black women artists, Bessie Smith (danced by Judith Jamison), Marie Bryant (danced by Serita Allen), Mahalia Jackson (danced by Enid Britten), and Florence Mills beautifully portrayed in Estelle Spurlock's dancing.

[54]See Florence Mills file at the New York Library of the Performing Arts, Lincoln Center, New York City. Also Joe Nash's collection on the Florence Mills Story, Library on Black Dances, 475 Riverside Drive, 7th floor, New York.

[55]*Ibid.*

[56]Interview with Eubie Blake and Noble Sissle, New York, April 7, 1970.

[57]London Daily Telegraph, November 2, 1927.

[58]Waters, *His Eye Is on the Sparrow*, p. 64.

[59]*Ibid.*, p. 148.

[60]*Ibid.*, pp. 138, 139.

[61]See Josephine Baker clipping file, New York Library of the Performing Arts, and Joe Nash's collection, Library on Black Dances. See also Stephen Popich, *Remembering Josephine* (Indianapolis: Bobbs-Merrill, 1976).

[62]Clipping file, New York Library of the Performing Arts.

[63]*Ibid.*

[64]See Pearl Bailey, *The Raw Pearl* (New York: Harcourt Brace Jovanovich, Inc., 1968), and *Talking to Myself* (New York: Harcourt Brace Jovanovich, Inc., 1971).

[65]Arnold Shaw, *The World of Soul* (New York: Cowles Book Company, Inc., 1970), pp. 52–53.

[66]*Ibid.*, p. 53.

[67]Holiday, *Lady Sings the Blues*, p. 9.

[68]Nat Hentoff, "An Afternoon with Miles Davis," *Jazz Panorama*, ed. Martin Williams (New York: The Crowell-Collier Press, 1962), p. 162.

[69]Holiday, *Lady Sings the Blues,* p. 83.

[70]*Ibid.,* p. 95.

[71]See Ella Fitzgerald clipping file, New York Library of the Performing Arts.

[72]Horne, *Lena.*

[73]*Ibid.*

[74]John Chapman, New York *Daily News* in Lena Horne clipping file, New York Library of the Performing Arts.

[75]Horne, *Lena,* p. 206.

[76]*Ibid.,* p. 221.

[77]The *New York Times,* Arts and Leisure Section, Sunday, May 7, 1967, p. 1.

[78]Dorothy Dandridge, and Earl Conrad, *Everything and Nothing* (New York, Toronto, London: Abelard-Schuman, 1970), p. vii.

[79]*Ibid.,* p. 192.

[80]*Ibid.,* p. 84.

[81]Judy Stone, "Black Is the Color of Diahann's 'Julia,'" quoting Robert Lewis Shayon, *The New York Times,* Arts and Leisure Section, Sunday, August 18, 1968, p. D17.

[82]Robert Lewis Shayon, "TV-Radio," *Saturday Review,* April 18, 1970, p. 46.

[83]Clayton Riley, "That New Black Magic," *The New York Times,* Sunday, May 17, 1970, p. D15.

[84]Godfrey Cambridge, in an article "No Music Like That Music," *Time* Magazine, June 28, 1968, p. 66.

[85]*Ibid.,* p. 66.

[86]Phyl Garland, *The Sound of Soul* (Chicago: Henry Regnery Company, 1969), p. 31.

[87]*Ibid.,* p. 170.

[88]Langston Hughes, *New York Post,* June 10, 1962.

[89]Lyrics excerpted from "Mississippi Goddam" by Nina Simone, © 1964 Sam Fox Publishing Co., used by permission.

[90]*Current Biography,* December 1968.

[91]"Lady Soul: Singing It Like It Is," *Time* Magazine, June 28, 1968, pp. 62–64. Reprinted by permission from *Time,* The Weekly Newsmagazine; Copyright © Time Inc.

[92]Garland, *The Sound of Soul,* p. 191.

[93]"Respect," Otis Redding, *Atlantic Records.* Copyright © 1965 East Memphis Music/Time Co., Inc. All rights administered by East Memphis Music.

[94]Interview with Ruth Bowen, Las Vegas, April 1968.

[95]Nikki Giovanni, "Poem for Aretha," from *A Broadside Treasury,* ed. Gwendolyn Brooks. Copyright © 1971 by Broadside Press.

[96]*Indianapolis Reader,* December 12, 1970.

[97]Phyl Garland, *Ebony,* January 1971, p. 54.

[98]Jeffrey Kimmel, "She Is a Woman of Mirrors" (Liner Notes), Roberta Flack, *Chapter Two,* Atlantic Records.

[99]"Do You Want to See This Land?" by John W. Anderson, also known as Kasandra.

[100]*Ibid.*

[101]Kevin Kelly, *The Boston Globe,* January 12, 1970.

[102]Novella Nelson clipping file, New York Library of the Performing Arts.

[103]Hollis West, *Washington Post.*

[104]Novella Nelson clipping file, New York Library of the Performing Arts.

[105]D. Mayerson, *Villager.*

[106]"Prima Donnas Grumble Over Blues Singers," *The Chicago Defender,* September 14, 1929.

[107]Hughes and Meltzer, *Black Magic,* pp. 26–28.

[108]*Ibid.,* p. 48.

[109]Marian Anderson, *My Lord, What a Morning* (New York: The Viking Press, 1956).

[110]*Ibid.,* p. 24.

[111]Review in *The New York Times* by Howard Taubman, December 30, 1935. (Marian Anderson clipping file, New York Library of the Performing Arts.)

[112]*Ibid.*

[113]*Ibid.* (see *The New York Times,* April 19, 1939).

[114]Anderson, *My Lord,* p. 188.

[115]See *Time* Magazine cover story on Leontyne Price, March 10, 1961, pp. 58–69; Irving Kolodin, "Leontyne Price: I Live Opera, But. . . ." in *Saturday Review,* September 1972; *Current Biography,* May 1961; Emily Coleman, "Girl of the Golden Voice," *The New York Times* Magazine Section, October 15, 1961, p. 37.

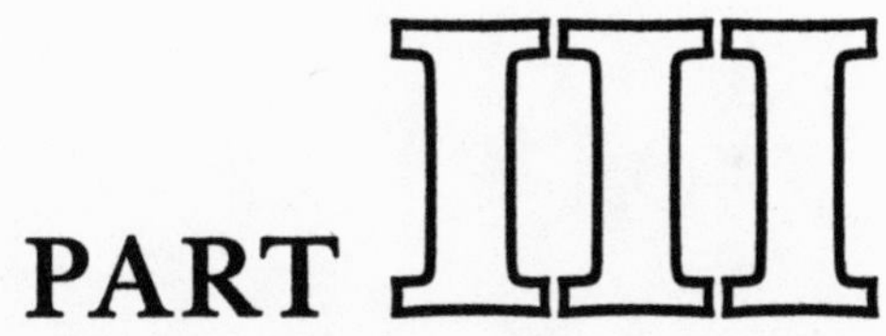

PART III

PRESENT AND FUTURE

We black women have been called many things. . . .
Foxes, matriarchs, Saphhires, and recently . . . Queens!
I would say that black women have been a combination
of all them words . . .
'cause if we examine our past history, at one time or another,
we've had to be like them words be saying.
But today, there are some words we can discard,
There be some we must discard,
For our own survival, for our own sanity,
For the contribution we must make to our emerging Black nation
And, we must move as the only Queens of this universe
To sustain, keep our sanity, in this insane . . . messed up . . .
Diet conscious, pill taking, masochistic
Miss Ann oriented society
Got to be dealt with.
'cause that's us. Y'all hear me? US! Black Women!
The only *Queens of this universe*
Even though we be stepping unqueenly sometimes
Like . . . It ain't easy being a Queen in this unrighteous world
Full of . . .
Miss Anns and Mister Anns
But we steady trying!

SONIA SANCHEZ[1]

9

"It Ain't Easy Being a Queen in This Unrighteous World Full of Miss Anns. . . ."

Leaving aside for now the unrighteousness of this world, it *is* full of white women. There are 93 million Miss Anns compared to 89 million Mister Charlies.[2] These women never died in wars (though too many have cheered them); they live longer than their men (though aging is so frightening to them that they strenuously combat it with millions of dollars spent on cosmetics, dieting, and exercising). And, given their share of psychological problems, white women are still the healthiest group in America. "Miss Ann" is a huge collective presence in America, an institution with values and traditions which add up to the American Woman—the ideal homemaker, mother, lover and citizen.

If white woman is the ideal, what are we black women? Neither white women nor black men have ever fairly defined black women, nor are they able to do so. We must do that ourselves, being careful to recognize our two identities as blacks and as women. Whether the talk is of black revolution or of women's liberation, where do we fit in . . . how do we move?

In the Sixties we dealt with a basic question: What is the black woman's role in the black revolution? How can we develop positive relationships with black men and work together toward black liberation? In the Seventies we began to face another urgent question: What is our responsibility, if any, toward the women's liberation movement? Particularly, can we ever hope to form a successful alliance with "Miss Ann"? Certainly, black women are not joining the movement in large numbers; some even call it "the white woman's liberation venture." And, while it may be claimed that continuing black problems have first priority with black women, this only partially accounts for the reticence, hostility, indifference, and questions in the minds of black women as they wonder and ponder calling white women "sisters."

Some claim that historical alliances of the past make us natural kinfolk. Some women's liberation leaders were surprised during the early years of the women's movement that black women did not become blood sisters and eagerly embrace the goals of the women's movement. While credit must go to many white women, especially the New England Schoolmarms, the abolitionists, and others who were active in anti-slavery movements, there is little historic basis for automatic trust between black and white women. Unlike the common kinship born of a historic American oppression shared by all blacks regardless of sex, black and white women are not natural allies. Old and new enmities, painful jealousies, and plain old indifference to the white woman's so-called plight weaves throughout black women's psyches, causing us collectively to either turn off, hold off, or steer a different course; thus we invest little organized group energy in the women's cause.

Got to be dealt with!

ON THE POSITIVE AND NEGATIVE SIDES OF HISTORY

The white women who went south during Reconstruction, the New England Schoolmarms, were the first real white help many blacks realized. But there were also women of the South with a sense of conscience that are also worthy of note. Their good works began during slavery when a remarkable group of women began to speak out.

Fanny Kemble, Mary Chesnut, Lucy Carter, Mary Blackford, and the sisters Angelina and Sarah Grimké[3] all achieved personal identity in the slave culture of the antebellum South, taking what for the time were radical steps against repressive laws and customs. These women saw the damaging effects of slavery and recognized its broad scope, its corruption of the white society which seemed to benefit from it. Because they all felt the frustrations of their own status as women, believing themselves to be as disenfranchised as any slave, they worked to unify the human rights courses of both blacks and whites. Each of these women began to search out ways to affect change. Mary Blackford was indignant over the failure of the church to protest the abuse of slaves. Fanny Kemble was unable to persuade her husband to improve conditions on the plantation and equally unable to obey his orders to stop interfering; her marriage was to end in divorce as a result. Sarah and Angelina Grimké traveled to the freer culture of the North and discovered that without the vote, there was only one right that women could exercise as citizens, the right of petition; but they marshalled their forces and made the best use of the tools available to them.

Although they did not always behave exactly as was prescribed for young gentlewomen of the 1880's, these women all lived with spirit as well as with purpose. Mary Chesnut, Mary Blackford, and Angelina Grimké Weld were all married to men who respected their intelligence and independence of mind. The only "spinster" in the group was Sarah Grimké, who seems to have remained single by an act of will rather than lack of opportunity. As a group, these women put the lie to another myth which even today tends to equate liberated women with those who are "anti-men." Far from it, these women included their husbands in their meetings, welcoming their support.

No list of white women who were sympathetic to the cause of black freedom would be complete without mention of Harriet Beecher Stowe, author of *Uncle Tom's Cabin,* and Julia Ward Howe, who wrote "The Battle Hymn of the Republic."

Elizabeth Stanton, Lucretia Mott, and Susan B. Anthony were Northerners whose lives intertwine throughout anti-slavery history and, of course, theirs is the designation in history as leading, if not founding mothers, of the suffrage movement. Mrs. Mott and Mrs. Stanton were Quaker women reared in the nonviolent traditions of that faith, but both stood firm against mobs, refusing to be frightened even by threats of tar and feathers. Indeed, all these women were able to walk with dignity through torrents of rotten eggs and cayenne pepper, with no show of timidity.

Although Harriet Tubman was a conductor of the underground railroad, and blacks were continuously involved in this work, many of the stationkeepers along the way were white women, some single and others forming a team with their husbands. In fact, white women were largely responsible for its operation. Today's women's movement leaders might well remember that the success of these early female activists generally seemed to flourish more readily when they used their energies outside the political system and when they were involved in other humanistic endeavors, in this case the abolition of slavery.

So timeless were Lucretia Mott's ideas that her words seem to speak out to modern opponents of the Equal Rights Amendment (ERA)—the "Total Woman" movement; the Pussy Cat League, a group of women so enamoured of their place high on the pedestal that they've dedicated themselves to maintaining the status quo, campaigning to keep all women in the Dark Ages; as well as the men who parade through midtown Manhattan bearing signs proclaiming, "We Want Wives Who Obey." Mrs. Mott reasoned that by men and women treating each other as equals, the principle of equality is enhanced for both sexes, providing protection for each sex against errors, hard feelings, and outright exploitation and tyranny on the part of the other sex. Deprivation of responsibility went along with deprivation of rights. Since irresponsibility enabled women to avoid many unpleasant duties, it was easy to become satisfied with an inferior position, in much the same way as some slaves become accustomed to their chains. More than any other leader, Mrs. Mott kept the relationship between emancipation of slaves and women's rights in perspective, and placed both movements on the sound footing of self-respect and social concern rather than petty self-seeking.

Susan B. Anthony and Elizabeth Stanton were jointly responsible for establishing the group which was to be known as the Women's Loyal League; after the Civil War the League revived the call for both Negroes' and women's rights. They helped bring the vote to black men. This League spread farther across the country than had any other group formerly dedicated to either cause alone. But the women were in for a rude disappointment. After all their work, they found sentiments of men in the Republican Party and in New England so strong against allowing women to get the vote that the word of the Fourteenth and Fifteenth Amendments, which they had fought to change from "male" to "persons" ultimately guaranteed suffrage to Negro men, but ignored both black and white women.

Actually white women abolitionists had encountered sexism among some male members of the anti-slavery movement all along. In 1838 the Massachusetts Anti-Slavery Society admitted women to full membership with the right to hold office and vote on all issues, but not without intense protestations led by Nathaniel Culver and others. Later that year, at the London Convention on Anti-Slavery, Culver—assisted by a black man from the West Indies, curiously—championed the adoption of rules which eventually excluded women from the deliberations, charging them as "constitutionally unfit for public and business meetings." Thus, Lucretia Mott, Elizabeth Stanton, and others whose fight against slavery in America was beyond "any call of duty" and equal to that of any man's found themselves escorted to seats behind a barrier. Though William Lloyd Garrison and other male abolitionists objected to such action, Culver and others were triumphant in the execution of their idea that woman's place was in the home. For Lucretia Mott and Elizabeth Stanton, this exclusion from the Anti-Slavery Conference in 1840 was the first step that led in 1848 to the first convention of the Women's Rights Society held in Seneca Falls, New York. As a matter of fact, one wonders if the women's suffrage movement would have been started at all had women instantly been fully accepted in the anti-slavery movement.

After half their battle had been lost, Mrs. Stanton acknowledged that women had learned an important lesson—that it is impossible for even the best of men to understand women's feelings or the humiliation of their position, and so gradually women awoke to their duty to themselves. Perhaps it was just as well none of them knew that more than fifty years' work lay ahead before suffrage could be granted to women, followed by still another fifty years' struggle to gain equal protection of women under the law.

Susan B. Anthony continued the fight, later serving as president of the Women's Suffrage Association, performing ruthless acts when she felt justified, but none more puzzling to blacks than her seeming insensitivity to their plight. In 1899 a black convention delegate introduced a resolution before the Suffrage Association in Grand Rapids, calling upon the railroads to provide more comfortable accommodations for black women, stopping the practice of requiring them to ride in smoking cars. Miss Anthony stepped down from the chair and advised the members to bear in mind that their organization was dedicated to women's suffrage, and that they must settle race questions elsewhere. The convention stood with their president and voted down the resolution.*

This kind of action not only is hard to accept but is a grim reminder of current concern: Will white women leaders again abandon black causes in favor of their own cause? Surely, history will and does repeat itself in pitting women against minorities. If ever there was a woman who had clearly been cheated by history, it was Susan B. Anthony. As president of the Women's Loyal League, she had crossed the country, pleading the case of anti-slavery and women's rights. She had seen loyal friends desert the women's suffrage issue. Though the Women's Rights Society formed in order to give visibility to the women's amendment, and the Anti-Slavery Society had almost identical membership, when she and other women moved to merge the two and pursue dual goals of full citizenship right for Negroes and women, Wendell Phillips led the Anti-Slavery Society constituency in voting against merger and joint efforts. Phillips feared for the fate of Negroes if the claims of women were pressed upon a reluctant Congress.

Elizabeth Stanton was persuaded of his tactical realism in giving priority to the rights of freedmen. Susan B. Anthony kept saying that one-half of the Negroes were women. She recalled that at the Seneca convention Sojourner Truth had called for all women, black and white, to be enfranchised along with the freedmen. It was then and there that Susan Anthony declared flatly that she would rather cut off her right hand than ask for Negro suffrage without women's suffrage.

As the Women's Rights petitions continued to pour into Congress, there were other deserters. Horace Greeley, publisher of the anti-slavery *New York Tribune,* at the New York Constitutional Convention of 1867 actually denounced his own wife's position on women's suffrage.

Frederick Douglass advised the women to yield to a higher claim of black men and postpone women's suffrage indefinitely. His parting words with his old friend Susan B. Anthony were the most bitter of all, and perhaps today an instructive warning to black women. Frederick Douglass said: "I do not see how anyone can pretend that there is the same urgency in giving the ballot to women as to the Negro. With us, the matter is a question of life and death, at least, in fifteen states in the Union."[4] This was one-upped by Miss Anthony's nasty remark: "If you will give the whole loaf of

*See minutes of 1899 Suffrage Association in Sophie Smith Collection, at Smith College, Southampton, Massachusetts.

suffrage to the entire people, give it to the most intelligent first.... If intelligence, justice and morality are to have precedence in the Government, let the question of women be brought up first and that of the Negro last."[5] Racism had reared its ugly head and its spokeswoman had clay feet!

In some respect, Miss Anthony can be likened to many white women's liberation leaders who worked so diligently in the student nonviolent movement but left in anger at the onset of the Black Power thrust. Susan B. Anthony knew that the Southern states must vote on suffrage and that the majority of black women lived in the South. She concluded that the loss of Southern white women to the suffrage cause would be enormously expensive for her, and so she chose to ignore black women.

Whatever the level of logic, that development, perhaps more than any other, marked the separation of the women's rights and black movements. This meant an end to a single women's movement broad enough and dedicated enough to fuse all human rights issues including the plight of black women into an instrument for social change. Black women, finding no common cause, have simply ignored white women's groups, recognizing them as largely unheeding of their needs.

Following the dissolution of the Women's Suffrage Association came the League of Women Voters, an organization which was clearly noncontroversial, steering a course directly down the middle of the road, coldly and objectively dedicated solely to political education. As important a function as this was and still is, few black women cared to join, nor are many attracted to it today.

Still with an eye on the history of black and white women working together, it would be impossible not to consider yet another course taken by the Young Women's Christian Association, which did win the respect and dedication of black women.

THE YWCA

The National Board of the YWCA of the USA was formed in 1906, bringing together two national coordinating councils for local associations having varying constituencies and program emphases: girls, working women, college students; residence, health and recreation, family service, counseling, and adult education. Bringing together this varying collection of local associations and developing a clear, specific program was in itself a major feat of organization.

In 1936 a Standard Study was mounted, with some rather discouraging findings. Although the membership was fairly representative of women in the community, shortcomings were found in representation of Negroes, Orientals, industrial employees, and foreign-born women. Board members were predominantly middle aged, married, Protestant, and white. The study recommended positive measures for developing a YWCA membership that was a cross-section of the community, and for building a Board representative of the membership.

However, there were branches where prevailing segregation laws and/or customs made it difficult to get full participation from the Negro membership in the general association program. Resistance to the pressure of segregation became a real test of the strength of the YWCA, in maintaining its work, in bringing all the membership together across racial, national, religious, and economic lines, against the financial pressure brought to bear in community after community.

At the 1940 convention, the national student groups within the YWCA proposed that the matter of participation be carried a step further, ultimately eliminating all segregation and discrimination.

In order to insure adequate service to Negro women and girls, representation on the committees from the Negro membership was recommended—personnel, finance, program planning—and in the professional staff. It was proposed that staff positions be filled by Negro professional, clerical, and maintenance people immediately, where vacancies occurred, and that all salary and wage differentials between Negro and white staff members doing the same work be wiped out. When all had been said, the recommendations for interracial practice in community YWCA's were adopted; the convention unanimously adopted the "Interracial Charter of the YWCA's of the USA."

Thus the YWCA became the first predominantly white women's organization to take the women's movement past another milestone. The rights of women were fused with the rights of Negroes as well as other religious and racial minorities.

Other women's groups were to follow, including the Girl Scouts. Here in these two groups black women were to focus much energy and dedication. Not that they were to find racism eliminated, although the YWCA is now committed to "the elimination of racism, by any means necessary," but they can relate to specific projects and issues that black and white women can work on together, realizing the mutual benefits to both groups.

In recent years both national organizations have moved beyond "token" integration of their boards and staffs. By 1975, the YWCA had appointed Sara Alice Wright, a black woman, as

Executive Director and the 3.5 million Girl Scout movement had elected Dr. Gloria Scott, also black, as its first National President.

FROM HISTORY—IS THERE COMMON COURSE?

Many critics have stated that with the passage of the Nineteenth Amendment the women's movement collapsed.[6] White women had, indeed, promised a lot: a more humane society, freedom from overt violence, a social system based on justice for all people—they promised much. But nothing really changed. "Women voted much as men did, except on a handful of issues concerning personal morality . . . politicians had to be more careful of their drinking and wenching, but otherwise the enfranchisement of women meant little to them."[7]

It is also evident that the women's vote has done nothing to change the status quo for blacks. None of the empathy and justice women were supposed to bring into the political arena were visible to our eyes.

MISS ANN'S CAUSES

Throughout the Thirties, Forties, and Fifties, Miss Ann's causes, so inspiringly begun by the Grimké sisters, Lucretia Mott, and Elizabeth Stanton, were perhaps slightly more humanistic than male ones, but not serious enough to make much difference in the lives of black women.

By the time Simone de Beauvoir and Betty Friedan wrote their provocative books in the Sixties, restating and underscoring the plight of women, even claiming that they were worse off than ever, a host of studies and so-called scientific theories had ensconced women on a procrustean bed from which few dared or even desired to rise. "Man's world, woman's place remain," Elizabeth Janeway wrote, "and our society continues to ascribe different psychological attributes to each sex, and to assign different duties and ways of living to men and women, because it is assumed that they have different capabilities, moral and social and intellectual as well as physical. . . ."[8] This was written in 1971, when Women's Liberation, the new feminist thrust, was shocking a country that had already gone through changes and revolutionary revelations amidst the black revolution.

But here they were, the women again, and like some great historical repeat performance, they were following immediately on the heels (if not in lock step) of the black liberation movement of the Sixties.

Herein lies the crux of the matter—the timing of the two movements and the claim by some that they are similar. What should black women do now, being both black and female?

We certainly share some of the problems of white women, working for less wages than our white male counterparts. The need for decent wages and equal pay is most crucial to black women since, as already pointed out, so many black women rear children alone or contribute heavily to family solvency.

But what assurance do we have that Miss Ann will want to share whatever other advantages she gains with us? Does she really want us to have the kind of power we want for ourselves? Perhaps we should take a good look at just who is represented in the women's liberation movement, and how "powerless" white women really are?

Statistics tell us that a major portion of this nation's wealth is controlled by white women. Are these women seeking liberation? There are female Rockefellers (other than Sister Abbey), Mellons, Whitneys, and others, some of whom are identified with humane causes; but who among the liberation leaders—Gloria Steinem, Betty Friedan, and Co.—has dared to confront the monied ladies' group for support?

It is difficult for us to sympathize with those seeking more power for white women when the financial power in their midst has rarely and too superficially been used to right injustices and to deal with the liberation of the poor, the disenfranchised, and the racially different.

Some women's liberation leaders claim female powerlessness to the extent that some of them see themselves as "niggers" and continuously insist on making comparisons between the black experience in America and the historic treatment of women. Toni Morrison says it is a "ladies' liberation" movement, but having ignored the rich ladies, the movement is just now in the middle-class recruitment phase. Looking back over long history, one can see a "niggerization" of women, but of a different order. Black women can't be expected to work in both movements as if they are the same. Miss Middle-Class Ann is simply not as powerless as she claims, and nowhere as powerless as blacks. This is perhaps best demonstrated in the numbers of organized women's groups who advocate that "they like the status quo," and the fact that consciousness raising is essential to prove to some women that they are an oppressed group. *All* blacks know they are oppressed, even though they may differ on tactics to relieve the burden.

Proportionately few blacks feel as indifferent as white women generally do about the way they are treated in America. This alone alienates some black women from the women's cause.

Take the women of the "silent majority." They become very noisy when their children are bussed into interracial neighborhoods. In fact, who can forget the faces of the white Little Rock mothers? Most of the faces on the TV screen screaming against bussing are white women. Boston! Elsewhere! If, in fact, white women are weaving a humanistic thread throughout America's institutions, such as the schools, where they have some chance of exerting power, this humanism would be reflected in their demand that integration be geared toward a humanistic training of children who live in a multi-racial neighborhood. The reverse is all too sadly what black women see.

White women don't have a history of "paying dues" for their right to vote. They have never been turned away from the polls, beaten, or lynched for casting a vote. Certainly not anything like the historic case with blacks. Where are the white Fannie Lou Hamers and Uneida Blackwells, whose blood was shed because they dared to vote? And this question must again be raised: on school and other social welfare issues, do blacks or women tilt the nation toward a more just society? How can black women trust the masses of white women to be different from white men on social issues? Why, many ask, empower further this mass of insensitive souls?

Furthermore, this silent majority woman cops out on some sensitive issues. She is the first to cry "rape," yet keeps alive the fantasy of sexual prowess among black men. In her dependency on white men's ideas she perpetuates the fear of crime on the streets, which all too often comes to her mind in the shape of a black male.

Historically, many Miss Anns have participated in black causes, as well as peace movements, proportionately more than white men. Soon, however, they hasten to appropriate the techniques and tactics of a black cause for their own purposes, seeking to link together the struggle of both blacks and white women. All too often this alienates black men and turns off too many black women who could benefit from both if issues were more clearly delineated. All too often the rhetoric of white women engaged in the "woman cause" appears to make the cause of blacks mild by comparison. This is probably why black men generally consider the women's movement distracting. Since most black people believe that there is no oppression like black oppression, too few women liberation leaders have bothered to make clear the difference.

It is not that black women don't want equal rights. It is more the case that we are "hanging loose" from total immersion in any other liberation movement unless and until the "new" liberators prove the depth of concern for the liberation of all people—black, poor, "other," as well as women. In a real sense, "Physician, heal thyself."

AND ALWAYS: MISS ANN'S "IMAGE"

There has always been a psychological toll of "self-hatred" associated with the put-downs of black female strength and beauty when wrongly compared with the "ideal Miss Ann image."

White women are the standard-bearers for that which white men have deemed desirable in women. While many white women leaders would like to change this concept of women, it is slow to go.

How this projection of what standards of beauty and life style contributes to self-hatred among black women is illustrated in *The Bluest Eye* by Toni Morrison in Pauline's obsession:

> The onliest time I be happy seem like was when I was in the picture show. Every time I got, I went . . . the screen would light up, and I'd move right on in them pictures. White men taking such good care of they women, and they all dressed up in big clean houses with bathtubs right in the same room with the toilet. Them pictures gave me a lot of pleasure, but it made coming home hard, and looking at Cholly hard. . . .[9]

Pauline, depressed, escaped to the movie fantasy world, seeking a substitute for reality. She was introduced to a standard of beauty that neither she, her husband, nor her children, would ever approximate and the conflict affected her relationship with every person in her life.

> Along with the idea of romantic love, she [Pauline] was introduced to another—physical beauty. Probably the most destructive ideals in the history of human thought. Both originated in envy, thrived in insecurity, and ended in disillusion. In equating physical beauty with virtue, she stripped her mind, bound it, and collected self-contempt by the heap. She forgot lust and simple caring-for. She regarded love as possessive mating, and romance as the goal of the spirit. It would be for her a well-spring from which she would draw the most destructive emotions, deceiving the lover and seeking to imprison the beloved, curtailing freedom in every way.[10]

On the other hand, the extent to which this "image" has corrupted the black man's concept of feminity and caused him to make unfair comparisons between the women of his family and white female beauty standards enrages black women and causes many of us to resent white women, especially those who talk liberation for all women by day and sleep with black men by night. It would be nice to be open-minded about this, but black women generally want access to only one group of men—black men! Even if black women wanted to marry white men, they would have little access to white male power brokers, because white men are penalized socially for marrying black women, and their traditional drive for power often causes them to repress any natural inclination toward a permanent relationship with a black woman. Yet the white woman now has and wants access to both white and black men. About this we smolder, we resent, we anger, and some among us—the under-thirty black women especially—rage.

In fact, one can never be sure whether so many of the under-thirty black women hate the women's liberation movement for other reasons, or because they are really angry at white women who in ever-increasing numbers become romantically involved with black men. Never mind whose fault it is, or whether "who sleeps with whom" is a private matter and has nothing to do with liberation—the feelings are negative with almost every black woman. It is a fair conjecture at this point to claim that the women's liberation movement is lacking black female support for many complex reasons, one of the most difficult ones being the black woman's resentment of interracial romancing.

Just what has Mr. Charlie designed as his "ideal woman"?

A close look at how white men design this ideal reveals a "Miss Ann" who is almost rootless, allowing herself to be blown in any direction, just as the white males of Madison Avenue decree. Beyond the realm of fashion, she has traditionally allowed herself to be caught in the net of personality demands Mr. Charlie throws over her to keep up his own image. The movie *The Stepford Wives* is not too removed from this image.

The "ideal" white woman is expected to monitor the children's education, yet limits are placed on what she can really do. She has little collective voice in reforming the school system; she most often deals with its problems piecemeal and mostly through direct interviews with teachers about her child's progress. Women seldom elect other women to school boards, preferring to let men control the one institution they should have found compatible with their interests and claimed a right to lead. If the white woman is so reluctant to organize to place women on boards of education where the fate of her children rests, how can she be counted on to elect blacks? Again, white women make little use of the power *they already have.*

Forward, outgoing, and aggressive are definitely not traits traditionally associated with white women. Even now, the key words for Mister Charlie's approbation are passivity and submissiveness, with complimentary and nurturing running a close second. As a just reward for exemplifying all these characteristics (for she works hard at it and deserves it), Miss Ann can expect a hearth and home designed for happiness. Such is her ultimate goal and reward; but even if she is found in the business world, the hospital, on the stage, or in the halls of academia, it is considered a real coup to game one's brains through America's achievement maze, projecting the outward appearances of Miss Ann, the housewife, while acting out an occupational role. Even if she makes it, she must keep within the bounds of femininity, whatever that is.

While much of the black female's rejection of women's liberation is political and dispassionate, a lot of hesitation is based on black female empathy. Black women have always been "hip" to white women and know them for their pretensions and weaknesses, as well as their potential strengths. This knowledge of white women is born of centuries of washing their laundry, cleaning their homes, and taking care of their children. As Lorraine Hansberry put it, "Our lives have been intertwined with white women—in the kitchen, in the schoolroom, in the marketplace, and in the volunteer board room. We probably know Miss Ann better than Mister Charlie does, and surely far better than our black brothers do—because sex has little to do with knowledge of total life styles—positive or negative. The roles we have played in society give black women a special vantage point of observation."[11] Few black women deny this claim.

FROM THEIR OBSERVATION POSTS . . .

Black women had long realized that Miss Ann's image was false, unrealistic, and costly. They first recognized this when the "Pedestal treatment" for white women was enshrined in American culture. Mostly they observed it as domestics. They knew this defined "woman's place" was confusing to whites and stunted their emotional growth. Pedestal placement exaggerated white women's weaknesses, causing whites to fall back on the strength of black women. Lillian Smith wrote that white men respected the strength of black women, though in doing so they defined them as something inferior to their own women. The strength of black women, both emotional and otherwise, was also demonstrated by many who became mother surrogates to white children whose mothers found hard to manage or didn't think it ladylike to care for their daily needs.

The influence of black women on the children of white households was an indelible mark of their power. Many of them wet-nursed white children when their own mothers were dry or unable to produce proper nourishment. They cared for the children when sick, rocked them through the night, treated them with the strange ancient remedies and teas which characterized the witchery of black communities, often against doctors' orders, scolded the naughty children, played with and listened to them.

Lillian Hellman, the distinguished playwright and civil libertarian, noted her black nursemaid Sophonia's influence on her painful childhood, and recalls running away from home to find solace in her presence long after Sophonia had quit. Later, when Miss Hellman became a famous writer, Helen, another domestic, became a substitute for Sophonia. She even loved her fatness: "In this period of nobody grows old or fatter, your mummy looks like your girl, there may be a need in many of us for the large strong woman who takes us back to what most of us wanted and few of us ever had."[12]

Lillian Smith believed that the personality soil of the white psyches was well fertilized with the black domestic's nursing and her bosom much too comforting to forget. Generations of whites, according to Lillian Smith, were in conflict over the natural love they felt for the black nurse who was never too busy to comfort them, and the biological white mother, who was often too busy to give them "the time and concerns . . . hungered for." They were forced by custom to reject the one they clung to, for the clinging-vine mother on a pedestal. The "Oedipus Complex" seemed by comparison "almost a simple adjustment."[13]

While white women were malingering on the pedestal, black women were developing domestic management skills, becoming toughened and realistic in human relationships, and while later some would consider this education a hardening one, basic to all of it was a deepening of their nurturing qualities.

All groups stood to suffer from crowning Miss Ann sacred and placing her on a pedestal: white men, white women, black men, and many middle-class copycat black women.

White women were not allowed to think of their bodies as sensuous, though their body image was strengthened by the assurance that their white skin color was a heavenly blessing. Yet, since their children, and sometimes their men, preferred black women as love objects—no matter if they were Mammies, concubines, or whores—white women surely must have come to believe that all a woman could expect from the lofty position of the exalted heights of a pedestal was a frosty chill. Long before women's liberation leaders struck a blow against sexual repression and demanded full freedom to explore their sexuality more extensively, black women had recognized how sexually repressed the pedestal treatment had made *everybody*! Thus, black women seldom screamed about "sexual liberation" as a priority, but shouted "equality for blacks," knowing that this would free people to claim and reclaim a natural sexuality.

White men paid dues for male chauvinism. Many were turned on to the freedom they felt in expressed affection for domestics who never turned away from soiled diapers or funky smells, or looked in shock at nakedness or other natural functions. White men generalized from this to a similar acceptance of their "sowing of wild seeds" among black women. They turned to black women for sexual activity, a white women's resentment that has been long chronicled.

Black men also developed negative attitudes as they viewed the exploitation of their women. These will be dealt with later in this book. Suffice it to say, the view from where they stood was myopic, for they devalued black women and continued the enshrinement of Miss Ann, long after white men began to dethrone white women, and surely long after black women knew them for what they were—human!

And, of course, the bourgeoisie black woman all too often galloped after the chastity belts discarded by white women and donned them, hoping that sexual repression and denial of spontaneous sensuousness would give them also a respectable place in God's mixed-up world. If not blue eyes, like Pecola desired in *The Bluest Eye,* then *respectability*—like Pauline?

What has emerged from this history, then, is a need for new definitions that black women can recognize as meaningful and not superficial to themselves. If there is to be a sexual revolution born of women's liberation, it must acknowledge tenderness and compassion, for the rough and tumble of brutal sex has long been the black woman's stalker and hers is, as Aretha sings, a need for a man to "Try a little tenderness." If there is to be talk of birth control, black women's mothering qualities which helped us to survive must be valued; few would negotiate freedom from motherhood. If there is to be a collective women's claim that "I am strong, I am invincible, I am woman," Helen Reddy style, then the prototype is the black woman. Invincible strength does not come because it is legislated, though this helps; it develops out of the crucible of life's struggles. The real question is: Are white women too spoiled to "hang in" through the battles that will inevitably get rougher, as they press on for a share of the white male's power holdings?

Unlike Miss Ann's grandmothers, who found some allies among black women, this generation of women's liberation leaders are faced with a new challenge: how to woo and win the support of black women, who if won over, could probably persuade black men to join common cause. Then, as blacks and women moved together to reach affirmative action goals, there might develop an unbeatable alliance!

THE BEAUTY MARK

A new black female image is growing nonetheless and we are becoming aware of ourselves, our true selves. Part of the black woman's liberation is freedom from those white standards of beauty and being which for years have set goals we couldn't hope to meet. We are moving away from that false mark of beauty, showing ourselves to be originals, no longer content to be carbon copies of Miss Ann.

In the Seventies we have TV commercials for cosmetics designed for black complexions, not for preparations to create the illusion of slightly less than perfect white beauty. Only when we are confirmed in the actuality of our own special beauty, can we project that image with assurance and pride.

A recent news feature reported that in the early days of presenting black models, the only ones who could make it were those women with the palest tan tones and the most Caucasian features; now pale is out and black is in. There is no longer a prize for winners in the Miss Ann Look-Alike contest.

In the affirmation of the beauty of blackness there is certainly no attempt to follow the white woman's ascent to the pedestal. That lofty position is reserved for those content with a life of submissiveness and noninvolvement we don't want. There is a positive sexuality exuded by a strong, sure-minded woman, one who values herself and her own unique qualities. Not only do we reject the pedestal for ourselves, we want no part in helping Miss Ann stay up there, for without generations of sturdy black women to do her scrubbing, her polishing, her dirty work, her hands could not have stayed so lily-white.

One thing is sure, black women have begun their own mental

liberation and this allows us to acknowledge some progress accomplished with the help of white women.

President John Kennedy called together the women's organizations of America and asked them to help pass the 1964 Civil Rights Act. They succeeded in mobilizing wide support for the eventual passage of the bill. Sargent Shriver attempted to gain the same dramatic response for the salvation of the Poverty Program. The women succeeded in rescuing some parts of the program, but they were not powerful enough to forestall the national dismantling of this program, often done in insidious, sneaky ways. Not enough (hardly any) women were in local power positions to save the poverty program, for there in the state and municipal houses of law, the "maximum feasible participation of the poor"—black poor—had threatened the city fathers' power base and they were bound and determined to kill the poverty program. This proved that women lacked power at the local level, but were somewhat formidable in their national associations. It is precisely this need—to organize with white women's organizations on *specific issues,* local, state, and national, so that a more just and humane society eventuates—that attracts black women to joint efforts with white women.

Yet the nagging question remains: How can black women cast their lot with the white women's liberation movement when the power of white women is still so unpredictable, and there are so many factions within it vying for prominence?

WOMEN'S LIBERATION: THE UNFINISHED BUSINESS OF WOMEN'S RIGHTS

Norman Cousins, a long-time advocate of liberal causes, is one of many white male opinion makers who became disappointed in the women's liberation movement. "Liberation," he says, "is one of the most exalted words in history. It has produced towering ideas and efforts. It has been the inspiration for some of the world's finest and most enduring literature. It has been the greatest single force behind human progress."[14]

Mr. Cousins had watched a television show featuring a number of women prominently identified with women's liberation. He had not observed this program with an open mind, but, despite the nobleness of his expectations, he had preconceived ideas concerning what *he* wanted from the movement. "We were eager to learn," he said, "about the prospects for mobilizing women to abolish war, reduce violence, and impart a quality of tenderness to the management of human society."[15] He was upset and disappointed because, in his judgment, little was said about those topics, but "the conversation made it appear that the most important thing about liberation was freedom to masturbate and talk about it in public."[16] He concluded that the televised women leaders did not know what liberation was all about and "it quickly became evident on the program that the freedom of women was being subordinated to the freedom to bore."[17] And since "liberation can overcome anything except boredom,"[18] he was bored. Exit (was he ever there?) a potential friend for women's liberation.

Norman Cousins is one of many white men, joined by most black women and almost all black men, plus vast pockets of white women, who have defined for themselves what the women's liberation movement should be about, and what elements of it they will and will not support.

Actually, the movement's objectives are very complex. When black women are asked their opinions of women's liberation, they seldom respond to the diversity of goals among its advocates. Yet every black would quarrel with the lumping of Muslim, Black Panther, CORE, Urban League, and NAACP ideologies in the same category. One had only to be present at the historic Black Political Caucus in Gary, Indiana, in 1972 to understand varied black points of view—from bussing for the purpose of integration to separatism. So too would a gathering of current feminists range from women who want to abolish conventional sex roles, to those wanting to give up sex entirely, to those who stress equal pay for equal work and day care centers for working mothers, to those who refuse to bear children at all. Their strategies range from radical rhetoric—for it must be said in their favor that they are an articulate lot—to the introspective T-Group oriented consciousness-raising rap sessions that quietly engage a host of women who simply need to explore how it feels to be a woman and how to identify for themselves Betty Friedan's "problem that has no name." They have burned bras and picketed Mory's,despite the fact that Kingman Brewster bravely withstood the pressure of many millionaire Yalies to coeducate "Old Blue."

Like blacks, they fight stereotypes, tokenism, and unjust laws. Their tactics have been about as varied as the sit-ins, freedom riding, picketing, and legal actions which marked the black revolution. They make a lot of noise; theirs is a growing scholarship borne of the patient research done by lawyers and scholars, planning and programming. When white women say, "the movement," it is just that! It is a conglomerate of organized women's groups and a grapevine of unorganized sympathizers.

There is definitely a war to be waged and in the best rules of battle, we must take care to know our enemy. And so, it would be well for all women to bear in mind that the people who are most imprisoned by the caste system, who are least willing to take the initiative in the cause of human rights, who stand in the greatest peril of losing power, are white men. The people who are most involved in the crisis of personal identity, in the perils of insecurity and uncertainty in a crumbling caste system, are black men. Women have no stake in the caste system, and they are in the best position to transcend its barriers, finding other alternatives for patterns of human relations.

And finally, this strong note from black sister Mary Ann Weathers: "If we are going to bring about a better world, where best to begin than with ourselves? We must rid ourselves of our own hangups, before we can begin to talk about the rest of the world, and we mean the world, and nothing short of just that. (Let's not kid ourselves.) We will be in a position soon of having to hook up with the rest of the oppressed peoples of the world who are involved in liberation just as we are, and we had better be ready to act."[19]

IT AIN'T EASY . . .

No, indeed, "it ain't easy being a Queen with all these unqueenly Miss Anns," or the ideals they are supposed to represent. Becoming and being a queen—a black queen—requires strength, endurance, the resourcefulness to survive without much help from any of America's institutions, including a continuous monogamous marriage and an intact family. Being a queen (or a strong woman) means involvement in a constructive, cooperative relationship with black men in building strong black institutions and communities. A black queen is neither superior nor inferior, she just does what she has to do.

The struggle to be queenly—strong and self-reliant—has been a relentless and thankless metamorphosis; but all of the historical circumstances, our African heritage and our American slavery and oppression, have produced a special kind of woman, a woman different from the Miss Anns in their statistics or as they are projected in *Harper's Bazaar* and on the TV screen. Forged from this historical struggle comes—say it loud and clear—a beautiful Black Amazon! In short, the black woman emerged strong and proud from her history and only finds today that she is in style, at least with the women's liberation leaders who maintain there are more role models of the so-called liberated woman among black women than are to be found within their own ranks. They are struggling for assertion and self-reliance in decision-making, among other things. The black woman, by force of historical circumstances, has demonstrated an abundance of such qualities.

These qualities, so often identified with black women, now emerging as good, even queenly, have never fit the Miss Ann image and this fact has contributed toward black self-hatred of our womanhood. And we've got to have time to sort it all out for ourselves before jumping wholeheartedly into the women's liberation movement.

But in the meantime: "We steady trying."[20]

CHAPTER 9 NOTES

[1]Sonia Sanchez, "Queens of the Universe," from *A Blues Book for Blue Black Magical Women* (Detroit: Broadside Press, 1974), Part I, pp. 11–12.

[2]Table 5: Population by Age and Sex: 1973, in *The Social and Economic Status of the Black Population in the United States, 1973,* U.S. Bureau of the Census, Current Population Reports, Special Studies, Series P-23, No. 48 (in thousands).

	Black	*White*
Men	11,337	89,424
Women	12,464	93,625

[3]See Eleanor Flexner, *Century of Struggle: The Women's Rights Movement in the United States* (New York: Atheneum Press, 1968); and *The History of Woman Suffrage,* published in six volumes. Volumes I to III were edited by Elizabeth Cady Stanton, Susan Anthony, and Mathilda Joslyn Gage. The first two volumes were published in Rochester, N.Y., in 1881; the third in 1886. Volume IV, edited by Susan B. Anthony and Ida Husted Harper, was published in Rochester in 1902. Volumes V and VI were edited by Ida Husted Harper and published in New York in 1922.

[4]See Minutes of the New York American Equal Rights Constitutional Convention of 1867 (Sophia Son: the Collection, Smith College, Northampton, Mass.).

[5]*Ibid.*

[6]See William O'Neill, ed., *The Woman Movement: Feminism in the Unied States and England* (Chicago: Quadrangle Books, 1969); and Elizabeth Janeway, from *Man's World, Woman's Place: A Study in Social Mythology* (New York: William Morrow and Company, Inc., 1971). Reprinted by permission of William Morrow and Co., Inc. Copyright © 1971 by Elizabeth Janeway.

[7]O'Neill, *The Woman Movement,* pp. 92–93.

[8]Janeway, *Man's World,* p. 9.

[9]Toni Morrison, *The Bluest Eye* (New York: Pocket Books, Division of Simon & Schuster, Inc., 1972, 1974), p. 97. Originally published by Holt, Rinehart and Winston, New York, Chicago, and San Francisco, 1971, p. 95. Copyright © 1970 by Toni Morrison. Reprinted by permission of Holt, Rinehart and Winston, Publishers.

[10]*Ibid.,* p. 97.

[1]Lorraine Hansberry. By permission from Robert Nemiroff, Executor, Hansberry estate.

[12]Lillian Hellman, *An Unfinished Woman* (New York: Bantam Books, 1970; published by arrangement with Little, Brown & Company, 1969), p. 206.

[13]Lillian Smith, *Killers of the Dream* (New York: A Doubleday Anchor Book, 1963 (originally published by W. W. Norton & Co., Inc., 1949), pp. 97–120 in Anchor edition.

[14]Norman Cousins, "The Uses of Liberation," *Saturday Review,* July 24, 1971, p. 33.

[15]*Ibid.*

[16]*Ibid.*

[17]*Ibid.*

[18]*Ibid.*

[19]*Mary Ann Weathers,* "An Argument for Black Women's Liberation as a Revolutionary Force," in *Voices from Women's Liberation,* ed. Leslie B. Tanner (New York: Signet Books, The New American Library, 1971), pp. 303–307.

[20]See *Who Is My Sister,* a corporation for Public Broadcasting videotape produced by Michigan State, 1975.

Some man did a woman wrong.
Now she wants to rip us off.
Her hate is exposed like an itch.
She' sick, she's sad, what a bitch.
Maybe one day she will meet
A real fine man who'll treat her sweet
She will not be a bitch no more
She will not be a witch no more.
She will not make a bitch's brew.

CHRIS ACEMADESE HALL[1]

Bitch's Brew

Bitch! You black Bitch! Of course, most women have been called bitch one time or another, but there is that special intonation, that nonverbal meaning that accompanies the epithet "bitch" when it is hurled at a black woman by a black man.

Black bitch images stalk us from the pages of fiction, from radio, television, and stage plays. In the Amos and Andy years, Sapphire was the quintessence of a bossy, fussy matriarch. Flip Wilson's Geraldine combines sassiness, toughness, and "all for my man Killer" qualities, packaged in a Pucci dress. (And blonde wig?) More recently, from the Broadway play *River Niger* "superbitch" emerges as a positive expression of the respect and affection one man associates with his wife's strength and inventiveness in facing family tragedies and life problems. Are "we black women," as Sister Sanchez says, "all these words be saying"? Or do black men mostly associate negative qualities with the term, Black Bitch?

"Black consciousness" and "Black is beautiful" have supposedly moved from rhetorical posturing to functional realities in the life style of black people. By now "black unity" and "black solidarity" are supposedly internalized in the minds and actions of blacks so that very practical results of working together can readily be seen in community programs and black institutions. "Say it loud! I'm black and I'm proud!" sang James Brown. "It's nation-building time," proclaim brothers Imamu Baraka and Jesse Jackson.

And yet, black men and women, who must work in a partnership in nation building, all too often aren't constructing together. We aren't making music together. The notes are all too jarring, too sour, perhaps, too phony. In a sense, black women and men may well be farther apart today than ever before.

On the economic and social level, black men are advancing, certainly too slowly, but at a faster rate and pace than black women with comparable skills and education. Now that affirmative action programs have been instituted in most major institutions of America requiring employers to deliberately recruit and advance minorities and women, it's become commonplace to say that black women profit the most, since they are "twofers" (two for one): To hire and advance a black woman is counted twice in a company's statistical reporting. Yet, the facts simply don't add up to significant economic breakthroughs for black women. We are definitely lagging behind white women and black men.

Often the strongest complainers about the perceived hiring preference for black women are black men. It seems as if too many of them believe that black women should not be given a chance in the world of work if there is the slightest possibility that a black male might be threatened.

This attitude, above all else, will bring more and more black women to see that there is a stake to be had in working more actively in the women's liberation movement, for the economic need to work is deeply ingrained in black women's psyches, and most would rather work at something they like and progress up the achievement ladder while doing it!

Some brothers have a way of saying: "Black women cannot afford to get sidetracked by white women in their domestic quarrels with white men. We must stick together as black people." As we've already seen, there is ample reason for us to distrust any alliance with whites, and during the early stages of women's liberation, black women did abstain from direct involvement with the women's movement, openly restating time and time again that the black movement needed their energies. The cause of black people was their primary cause.

We are thoroughly aware that white men control the jobs, the breaks, the values of society, and are largely responsible for the powerlessness of black men as well as women. There is, however, the continuing reality that black women face in their daily lives: We are the most powerless group in America. And often we carry this burden, feeling that everybody forgets it.

The plight of women rearing children as "heads of households'" continues to be a major social problem, as much in evidence today as it was when "I Have a Dream" resounded throughout the Lincoln Mall in 1963 and Martin Luther King struck hope in our hearts. Black women on welfare, black women unemployed and underemployed, pose just as serious a problem today as they did when Stokely yelled, "Black Power."

Sadly we have had to face in the Seventies what we dared not think about in the Sixties: There is serious, destructive black male chauvinism flourishing in the midst of white racist, sexist America. Often black women are too ashamed to confront it directly, because most of us take seriously the need to keep a united front. For many black women, too, there is always an ambivalence about our right to jobs, promotions, and a share in decision-making when it comes to competing with black men. Many of us have internalized the myth of the "Moynihan mystique" and feel black men should get more opportunities than women do. But it is no secret that black women talk among themselves about the injustices they suffer at the hands of their own black brothers. Moreover, during the summer of 1972 a major black women's organization had enough cases to bring up affirmative action appeals on behalf of well-trained black women seeking employment in two of the largest black organizations in the nation. At the last minute they decided that it was not sisterly to complain.

On college and university campuses affirmative action was beginning to mean hiring and promoting white women and black men. And, when black men were asked to speak on behalf of black women, few seemed to care. Black female professors on black campuses continue to be the most underutilized minority group in America. In another instance, the only black man on a prestigious selections board cut the ground from under a black female candidate whom the rest of his white colleagues preferred, persuading them to choose two black males rather than one male/one female, on the theory that the honor would be more beneficial to a black male. And the whites gave in believing that, after all, he was black; he should know!

Divisiveness threatens to drive a wedge between us. It is foolish to say that black men don't control some jobs and wield some influence in America, or to ignore that there are some black women in powerful positions. But when you list them, a disproportionately few number of black women really control jobs or policy. It is not enough to say that black men don't have their share of American opportunity. We all know that. But it will not help in the negotiation process for black men and women to fight for the few jobs available, with women shouting "black male chauvinism," and men hurling back charges of "castration." It is unfortunate that too many black men forget the statistics of reality which show that black women need to work in order to (1) feed family and/or relatives, and (2) supplement family income. Once that is established, psychological energy is greatly dissipated when black men "keep us down in the marketplace." More and more black women are singing with brother Jerry Butler, "Don't rip me off."

Chafing at black male chauvinism makes for much stress among black women. But this problem pales into insignificance when compared with interpersonal problems growing out of the lack of enough marriageable black men in the black community and the disproportionate number of black men who seek companionship and sex with white women.[2]

There are few choices and fewer alternatives. The two life styles that practically guarantee a mate, the Muslim religion and Imamu Baraka's commune, also demand rigid compliance to rules that practically put a woman in purdah. Few women will pay this price. The major bone of contention, further limiting options, is "the white woman thing."

It's a painful scene. Black men running after white women. White women throwing themselves at the feet of black men. Black men and white women, walking hand in hand across the nation's campuses, down the urban boulevards, locked in lovers' clasps. In nightclubs, in restaurants. "They're everywhere," said one sister. "There are some restaurants I refuse to patronize 'cause I'm sure to see some of *them* in there," said another.

Black men marrying white women, by the dozens, the thousands—maybe one day the millions? Black men negotiating for blacks—including the 52 percent of us who are women—at the White House and in other places of power, but who appear to be hung up on white women, prefer them, flaunt them at every opportunity as *their* women. Black men with clenched fists yelling "Right on," putting their arms around white women "right on." For many black women there appears to be a significant message here: Black men are not liberated from white women. A minority group can tolerate some exceptions from the rule, some interracial marriages and alliances. But a lot of black women fear that the exceptions have become the rule. They write about their feelings in *Essence*; they are duly noted in *Jet* and *Ebony*. Once they merely whispered about the black male put-down. But more and more of them are outspoken, and on a few campuses black co-eds refuse to participate in black student movement activities led by brothers with "white fever," as they call it. Increasingly it becomes clear that what one campus sister calls "the eventual sexual obsolescence of black women" might wreak havoc in any group solidarity. For unless the black women's sexual and companionship needs are reasonably met, there will be no black togetherness, no black unity, no black movement, and definitely, *no black nation.*

THEORIES OF BLACK MALE/WHITE FEMALE ATTRACTION

Several theories have evolved over the years to account for the preoccupation of black men with white women, and their failure to see their women—their own sisters and mothers, daughters and wives—as preferable. Why do some prefer the females of the oppressor group?

1. The Conspicuous Consumption Theory

Calvin Hernton and others mention the influence of the mass media in exaggerating the desirability of white women.[3] It is surely a fact that the white woman is an overcommercialized product. Her face, hair, body, teeth, hands, feet, smile, and body odor are constantly discussed and advertised. Everything but Miss Ann's brains has become salable, plastered on billboards, TV screens, and magazines for all to desire. She purrs on cars. She brazenly begs: Fly me to Miami! Mind you, not "fly with me to Miami," but "fly *me*!" It doesn't take much imagination to guess what is implied. Miss Ann is constantly portrayed as a sex object, a fact that the women's liberation movement groups abhor and are now campaigning to change. Here and there a black woman pops up in an ad (mostly the mothering types), but the overwhelming sex symbol is the white woman. She is traditionally a part of the Big Sell and as American as apple pie and baseball. But wait a moment! Few white women look like those models paraded before our TV screens. A recent Playboy Bunny of the Year exposed the mythology of feminine perfection, even by modeling standards, when she admitted on television that the bunnies are posed at favorable angles with a play of trick lighting which gives the illusion of perfection.

This kind of commercialization is detrimental not only to black women, who cannot identify with such beauty symbols, and black men who are seduced by the Big Sell, but to white women as well. Long before NOW pronounced its objections, psychiatrists, including Karen Horney, had warned against false beauty, "tyrannical shoulds" imposed on women by society. A woman should weigh so much, be so and so in the bust, so and so in the waist, and so and so in the hips. Using case studies to document her point, Horney warned that large numbers of women were starving themselves and spending untold hours in beauty treatments in an effort to live up to the "idealized self" which one should be. Since a positive body image is essential to the development of a healthy personality, the continual reign of the "tyrannical shoulds" has to be seen as detrimental.[4]

For the sake of mental health, then, both black and white women should fight to eliminate the barrage of unreachable and unrealistic images being commercialized for public consumption. We should fight for the same range of human models that has been appropriated by white men. The variety of white male models paraded before us in attractive ways is almost inexhaustible. From Carroll O'Connor (Archie Bunker), Telly Savalas (Kojak), and Joe Garagiola, for many years featured on *The Today Show,* we learn that one can be fat and bald and still be lovable to the American public. From Dick Van Dyke we see that a man can be a stumblebum and still be considered lovable. Of course, there are the Paul Newmans and other pretty boys, also the tough Marlon Brandos and Karl Maldens. There is the bad boy Dean Martin, but also wholesome Johnny Carson. White men are portrayed in a variety of roles—all aimed at *including* most types as desirable. It is bad for everybody when so many people are excluded from the field of attraction and self-worth.

So persuasive is the pull of conspicuous consumption that many settle for anything that reminds them of the real thing. ". . . images form a society's mythology and govern its actions, thoughts and attitudes. . . . The passive viewer lets the TV image subvert his own . . . and the viewer is removed from the possibility of alternatives."[5]

It is said that men buy a certain car because it reminds them of the girl in the advertisement whom they can't buy. So it is that too many black men are often caught in a similar trap. They may buy a car, but the image of a white woman still whets their appetite, and they settle for very ordinary looking white women. They might stand out in a black group because of color contrast, but many are "plain Janes" with nothing unusual about them. Few marry white women who look like TV models. One of Frantz Fanon's sources in his chapter on black men and white women suggests that "choosing white partners often means marrying persons of a class and culture inferior to their own, whom they would not have chosen as spouses in their own race."[6] This kind of settling for less in a majority group than you might attract in your own group often provokes black women to cutting remarks like: "What does he see in her, that stringy-haired paleface?" Or "Is that *all* he could drag up?"

One suspects, however, that even if black men married international beauties with much education, money, and position, black women would still be angry. As indeed they are even when a black man marries an occasional movie star.

2. The Forbidden Fruit Theory

It has been said that man, the constant explorer, will always seek to scale Mt. Everest simply because it is there. It is a challenge. That which seems beyond one's reach somehow is supposed to motivate a person to try, to risk all in order to reach the unreachable. As the song from *Man of La Mancha* says: "To dream the impossible dream." How much of this is arrogance born of Western values which socialize little boys to feel that they can and should conquer everything and anything in order to be masculine, and how much is innate in the human condition, has been adequately debated elsewhere.[7]

Without a doubt, the conquering spirit is associated with manhood. Since Western white men are the role models for all men, for those black men who envy and emulate them it makes sense that some would see the white woman as Mt. Everest. She, in her remoteness, on her unreachable pedestal, has to be scaled. Never mind that Mt. Everest is there due to an act of nature, and the "white woman on a pedestal" was a manmade notion contrived by white men, for such black men she simply has to be had! For some, not to conquer her, to possess her, is to have a piece of one's manhood missing.

Until recently society threatened the black man with death when he even "looked at a white woman." She then became the ultimate prize, for to win her was black man's most dangerous feat. Black men became ensnarled in the white man's madness, and the sons and grandsons of slaves who knew fear better than lust, began to ponder, "What if. . . ." And that "What if . . ." ended with "What if the white woman really is the most desirable sex partner? If the white man is so superior, and he protects his women so, then she must be superior. If I am to prove myself equal to that white man, then I must also have access to his possession—his woman."

Though times have changed and white men are less concerned with "who sleeps with their daughters," seeming to be more concerned with barricading economic and power positions against black men, too many brothers still live as if white women are "forbidden fruit." Actually, there is growing evidence that white men could care less. Substitute "white" for "upper class" and Norman Mailer's analysis has a ring of truth: he suggests that the upper classes are obsessed with sex but actually are asexual. "They use up too much sex in their manipulation of power. In fact, they exchange sex for power."[8] White men want economic power!

Though a few white women have been killed by their own relatives for consorting with black men, the custom today is simply to banish them from the family or ostracize them. But, as Mailer suggests, we can pretty much count on white men turning more and more toward their drive for social and economic power. As women win first the sexual revolution and become freer in expressing their sexuality, they will then move to change other institutions and white men will become busier and busier saving their institutions instead of their daughters and sisters.

In fact, some white men capitalize on what they perceive to be the black man's sexual preference. The "Rent-a-Bird" (pay your money and get a female companion for the night) agency flourishes in Florida. "When I asked Mr. Brudd what kind of Bird he would send to a black male customer, he replied, 'We send a white girl every time unless a black girl is specified.' "[9]

3. The Orgiastic Transformation from Black to White

The "quest for white flesh" by some black men can be explained as an effort to forget their color and its negative consequences. Fanon speaks of "a coal-black Negro in a Paris bed with a 'maddening' blonde . . . shouting, 'Hurrah for Schoeler' " (Himmler Schoeler, an abolitionist, helped free the brother legally. But, that is not enough. This man must recapture and validate his freedom in the arms of a white woman.)[10]

Fanon gives several examples of the "deracialization" process in which marrying a white woman becomes a wiping-out. One is cleansed of blackness, of the consequences of color prejudice. Union with white flesh becomes a purifying act. Observing the arrival of blacks from the Caribbean, Fanon noticed that "their dominant concern was to go to bed with a white woman. As soon as their ships docked in Le Havre, they were off to the houses. Once this ritual of initiation into 'authentic' manhood had been fulfilled, they took the train to Paris."[11]

4. The Violent Revenge

Of all the theories concerning black male attraction toward white women, the most dehumanizing is the sexual conquest of white women as an act of violence. Psychological humiliation, physical abuse, and in many cases, rape, appear to motivate some. The writer Chester Himes, though once married to a black woman, flatly admits his own preference for white women, yet acknowledges that in the final analysis, a black man's response to a white woman with whom he lives is violence.[12] After receiving a royalty advance from one of his novels, Himes found that his most intense desire was to have sex with a white woman. He found, according to his autobiography, a willing companion, a woman with some power leverage in the foundations which funded black causes, artists, and scholars. A tempestuous sex life with this woman included violence and alcoholic binges.[13] Sometimes long and permanent liaisons are based on a totally violent framework, such as Chester Himes writes about.

Malcolm X was one of many black men who spoke of the white woman as a needed possession in establishing oneself with "the boys." ". . . in any black ghetto in America, to have a white woman who wasn't a whore was—for the average black at least—a status symbol of the first order."[14]

Malcolm's Boston socialite girl, Sophia, paid for his clothes, followed him to Harlem, and gave him the prestige among Harlem men that he needed: ". . . all you had to do in those days was put a white girl anywhere close to the average black man, and he would respond."[15] Malcolm involved Sophia in criminal acts for which she was later convicted. He went to prison on a ten-year sentence and found Allah. She went to the Woman's Reformatory for one year and faded into obscurity.

Hernton admits that when an oppressed group begins to throw off the shackles of oppression, they desire the oppressors' women. The act of acquiring is, moreover, a violent acquisition. Frantz Fanon, perhaps the most influential writer for young revolutionary blacks, makes no apologies for violence as a cleansing force in overcoming the degradation of the oppressor. "Violence is seen as comparable to a royal pardon. The colonized man finds his freedom in and through violence."[16] So inevitably "the look that the native turns on the settler's town is a look of lust, a look of envy; it expresses his dreams of possession: to sit at the settler's table, to sleep in the settler's bed, with the wife if possible. The colonized (oppressed) man is an envious man."[17]

When *Soul on Ice* appeared, many blacks hailed its brutal truth and identified with it, especially some black men. Eldridge Cleaver's writings were definitely a radicalizing element in the eyes of many black youth during the Sixties. He thought it a matter of principle "to have an antagonistic, ruthless attitude toward white women." "I became a rapist . . . it delighted me that I was defiling his[white man's] woman."[18]

Black women might have believed such violent acts merely a part of the rites of manhood in the early days of the black revolution—something that black women simply had to endure. Some believe it is so today.

But as the years have gone on, too many acts of "achieving manhood" have become full realities, and more and more permanent liaisons between black men and white women have become the trend. The blood of rape, like that on Lady Macbeth's hands, cannot be washed away. The deeds have become the man. And if the defiling of Miss Ann was to be seen by black women as a revolutionary act at one time, then vast numbers of black women today are simply unconvinced of its worth.

What comes to mind when reading Cleaver's works is that he presents a classic example of one who uses the mechanism of projection to soften his own feelings. At one time in his life he preferred white women himself, but his bitterest words are placed in the mouth of a prison character in his book *The Accused*: "I love white women and hate black women."[19] Cleaver overstepped the bounds of reason, however, when he concluded that black women must feel the same way about white men. He might have been rationalizing his own attitudes toward white women, which might have been frightening to him and might also have aroused guilt for the black man's rejection of black women. To soften this guilt, he evidently had to feel that "black women prefer white men."

Opinions of some individuals like Chester Himes aside, evidence seems to point to the fact that black men often move toward white women because, among other things, they resent the role their mothers and grandmothers have traditionally played in socializing them to stay away from white women, in order to avoid lynching. There is the theme that black mothers did kill the aggressiveness boys need in order to be masculine in this society—simply to help their sons survive! An aggressive black male is the most feared human on earth; he always has been and doubtlessly always will be. Talking back and up to white people was too often punished by whites. But the greatest taboo of all was the simplest sign of aggression toward white women. Until recently black men not only were lynched for being caught with white women, but in places like Selma, Alabama, they were punished for talking to them in private and public places, except in very specific situations. Naturally, the mothers and grandmothers of young black boys made sure that their children understood the mores and folkways of the South so that they could survive. "The black mother . . . must produce and shape and mold a unique type of man. She must intuitively cut off, blunt his masculinity, assertiveness and aggression, lest these put the boy's life in jeopardy."[20] "As a result, black men develop considerable hostility toward black women as the inhibiting instruments of an oppressive system. The woman has more power, more accessibility in the system, and therefore she is more feared, while at the same time envied."[21]

Of course, this pattern of socialization is fast changing. The rhetoric of the black movement embraces such terms as "rearing young warriors" and "we shall have our manhood." One has only to listen to the mothers of George Jackson, Freeta Drumgo and other political prisoners in the jails throughout the country to realize that a "new" kind of mother is emerging, one who feels it is necessary for black boys to be reared with this aggressiveness intact.

But for many black men, especially those reared in the South who came of age in the Sixties, there smolders the resentment against their mothers, who, indeed, instilled in them a fear of open communication between them and white people.

"The taboo of the white woman," writes Calvin Hernton, "eats into [the black man's] psyche, erodes away significant portions of boyhood sexual development, alters the total concept of masculinity, and creates in the Negro male a hidden ambivalence toward all women, black as well as white."[22]

The price black women paid in their protective role as "socializing agents" was that of contributing to the "forbidden fruit" syndrome.

5. The "Same Bag" Theory

Of all the explanations put forward concerning the black man/white woman phenomenon, the most complicated and perhaps most infuriating one is the "fellow sufferer" theory.

Its genesis, according to Hernton, is in Marxist theory. Black men and white women occupy the middle position as shown in the diagram below,[23] a "squeeze position." This close proximity on the economic ladder pushes black men and white women together, aided by pressures from the bottom—black women.

Highest Status Group	White Men	Ruling Class
Middle Status Group	White Women Negro Men	Semioppressed Class
Lowest Status Group	Negro Women	Oppressed Class

Hernton rejects this theory, which cites marriage as the vehicle to accomplish the move upward, due to "mechanical reasons." He suggests that Negro women and white men have more of a common class interest than white women and black men. Since Hernton does not explain what this means, we can only assume that he bases this on the "Moynihan myth" of relatively more economic advantages accruing to black women than to black men. Also, he like so many others, may confuse the long-ago slave-time bartering of a black woman's body for economic advantages with her sharing affection, love, and commitment with a white man of her own free will. Even spatially, as seen on the Hernton diagram, the distance between white men and black women is far too great to be scaled any time soon. The median earnings (dollars) in the civilian labor force of workers 14 years and over in 1974 was:[24]

White men	$12,434
Black men	$ 8,705
White women	$ 7,021
Black women	$ 6,371

Black men and white women are still in the middle, the "squeeze position," with black men earning slightly more money than white women. Black men occupy the second rung; thus, a pronounced sexual cleavage cuts the diagram right in half. Black men can move up to ally themselves with white men when it is convenient and also move downward to embrace white women when this seems suitable. The black woman is so low on the totem pole that her position almost necessitates her alignment with white women in order to gain power leverage for dealing with both male groups. But realistically, how much power can an economic "have not" group (black men) and a marginal social "have" group (white women), both with no political clout, generate in an effective alliance without the participation of black women?

Alliances other than sexual ones between black men and white women have seldom resulted in more economic or social power for black men. When a white woman marries a black, the usual pattern is for her to take on his status rather than for him to assume hers. Affirmative action programs designed to recruit and promote women and blacks (plus other minorities) have tended to: (1) bring black men and white women into open competition for economic advancement, and (2) push the black woman into an "in-between" group, fearing to incur the wrath of either group. Federal compliance officers count black women twice in hiring columns, as black and as women, but we are all aware that this enrages both black men and white women, and that we are alone a sisterhood of black women who have to fend for themselves in the labor market.

While the white woman becomes associated with the black man's status, white men (outside of show business) are often so ambitious and desiring of high status, that they seldom if ever risk an interracial marriage. Can you see General Motors electing Chairman of the Board a white man married to a black woman? On the other hand, the black woman is so powerless that she is forced to accept, on a superficial level at least, any white woman the black man brings into black affairs, even accepting these men as spokesmen in leadership positions in black organizations.

With movies like *Shaft* and some of the current writings, the old stereotype of black men as sexual objects continues. Sex objects are quite different from men who are good lovers. Were the latter the case, black women might be proud to have their brothers so recognized. But amid all the talk of manhood, there comes the theme of sexual exploitation—an affront to a man's basic integrity. Sadly, some black men seek out such treatment.

Any relationship based on a sadistic-masochistic "rip-off," as suggested by Cleaver, Himes, Cobbs and Grier, and others who have examined the relationships between black men and white women, affects black women. The dehumanization of any black man's tenderest instincts, so difficult to cultivate in a people who have so many reasons to hate, leaves a man crippled for life. Likewise does he cripple the women in his own racial group.

No doubt some white women move toward black men because of other reasons. Both John Killins and Calvin Hernton believe that some seek out black men because they are interested in further emancipation of black people, and because they are altruistic. Doubtless some liaisons are based on such good intentions and goodwill. Few black women, however, accept many of these interracial liaisons on such noble and lofty terms. They tend to say:

(1) If the white woman wants to be helpful in the black movement, let her make some personal sacrifices, like hands off black men, so she can deal *directly* with white male racism and sexism.

(2) If the white woman really wants to be involved in the black liberation movement, she will increasingly be unable to do so as a black man's woman, because black women will not accept her on that basis. In fact, few will let such black men lead, let alone accept help from their women.

BLACK WOMAN/WHITE MAN

Black men declare: "We shall have our manhood. We shall have it, or the earth will be leveled by our efforts to get it."[25] They declare this in many ways: through aggressive moves to change the structure and institutions of society so that black people are the beneficiaries of shared power and not the victims of powerlessness; through individual efforts to gain entry into the system. But as has been pointed out, some black men appear to be gathering historical injustices, like unpaid, long overdue bills, and presenting them to white women for payment as a means of validating their manhood.

This is in direct contrast to black women's attitudes. Black women want their womanhood validated in personal relationships with black men as well as through involvement in the total struggle for black liberation. For many of us, growing closer to black men is inextricably intertwined with revolutionary struggle. To see black men hold their heads high, risk, seize, negotiate in the cause of black power, brought an overwhelming sense of pride and identification to the hearts of black women during the Sixties. To see brothers speak up for us—black women—brought ease to the weariness black women wear like an outer skin.

Nikki Giovanni's poem expressed the feelings of all but the most insensitive black woman:

i wanna say just gotta say something
bout those beautiful beautiful beautiful outasight
black men
with they afros
walking down the street
is the same ol danger
but a brand new pleasure

sitting on stoops, in bars, going to offices
running numbers, watching for their whores
preaching in churches, driving their hogs
walking their dogs, winking at me
in their fire red, lime green, burnt orange
royal blue tight tight pants that hug
what i like to hug

jerry butler, wilson pickett, the impressions
temptations, mighty mighty sly
don't have to do anything but walk
on stage
and i scream and stamp and shout

see new breed men in breed alls
dashiki suits with shirts that match
the lining that compliments the ties
that smile at the sandals
where dirty toes peek at me
and i scream and stamp and shout
for more beautiful beautiful beautiful
black men with outasight afros[26]

Nowhere, in poems, in novels, in songs, have black women idealized or rationalized personal relationships with white men in positive ways. Having had little tenderness in their relationships with white men, they seldom see a place for them in their personal lives.

The exception to this rule are those black women involved in the performing arts—show business—women whose life styles are quite different from that of the rest of their sisters and whose husbands are often tied into their careers. Even so, Lena Horne came recently to the conclusion that interracial marriages are divisive, and she would not marry a white man again. The implication is that an oppressed group is short-changed when a wife is trying to play down her own involvement in race problems, somehow softening her racial identity in order for the marriage to run smoothly. She is not free to really get into the fray of social change, for there is always the fear that she is casting her husband in the villian's role as a member of the oppressing group.

While black men have been more articulate in claiming a desire on black women's parts to be sexually involved with white men, white women seldom record similar views. Lillian Smith pointed out different observations in the South, saying that Negro women, whether upper class or not, have

> . . . a burning blasting scorn of white men . . . , making it a fairly dangerous thing for a white male to approach one of them.[27]

And while some white men may well take ego trips, believing that as they availed themselves of the women of a powerless group they were well loved in return, others saw black women as sexual receptacles, even teachers:

> When I was about fifteen the Negro came into my life with a wallop directly connected with the sex drive . . . the colored girl was the greatest underground sex symbol for the U.S. white man, the recipient of his trembling mixture of guilt, leer, and male-sadistic desire. Feeling inferior due to what I thought was my physical unattractiveness . . . I took refuge in heartless masturbation . . .

> and the Negro chick . . . became my glory-hole for imagined sex bouts. . . . Thus it was that the Negro girl became . . . someone who loved (in my imagination) to f--k. . . .[28]

Since the advent of Germaine Greer and Kate Millett, it does not take much arguing to assign the writer and his "Portnoy's Complaint" to the realm of Male Fantasy. Greer writes, "Adventure-sex is a matter of pyrotechnics, explosives, wild animals, deep-sea diving, rough riding. The ideal sex partner gives a promise of a good tussle. . . ."[29] The "Great Bitch" white woman, she continues, "is a worthy opponent for the omnipotent hero to exercise his powers upon and through."[30] If Miss Ann is the target of the Mailer, Miller, Lawrence "penis-as-weapon" battle as conceptualized by Kate Millett,[31] then it stands to reason that the black woman becomes a natural victim of white man's vilest depravity. Out of such sickness comes the fantasy that the Great Black Bitch is the best source for sexual catechism. Having "sown wild oats" with black women, the Great White Father is now ready for the Great White Bitch.

All too often, black men have recognized and capitalized on this horror psychology. In the Cleveland black ghetto, "the black men did not object to their women being whores of a kind, or at least vessels for the white man's lust. When the hunkies bought the black woman for sexual purpose they were called 'Johns.' The black men simply preyed for their livelihood, robbing the hunkies . . . and lived on the money their women made as whores."[32]

Not only Himes, but Cleaver, Fanon, Hernton, and others who make strong cases for black men choosing white women, attempt similar arguments to prove that black women also prefer white men. Few begin their arguments with the obvious: the white man as a sex partner has never been forbidden fruit—just marriage to him. This alone suggests a more intimate knowledge of white men and possibly accumulated wisdom in outmaneuvering him.

Fanon's theory is that black women seek white men to compensate for a perceived weakness—being black.[33] In bearing children by white lovers, they seek to "bleach the world." In this theory Fanon justifies black men's pursuit of white women because their relationships often lead to marriage. White men, being conquerors, according to this theory, have no romantic feelings for black women: ". . . they only take, they never marry them." One has only to read current literature, including James Michener's *The Drifters,*[34] to see that white women are just as capable of adventure-sex with black men sought out as studs.

Perhaps the most scathing analysis of black woman/white man relationships comes from Eldridge Cleaver, who pronounced: ". . . Jesus Christ the pure is the black woman's psychic bridegroom."[35] He put these words in his fellow prisoner's mouth:

> I always believed that marrying a white man, to a black woman, is like adding the final star to her crown. . . . Whitey is their dream boy. When they kiss you it ain't really you they're kissing. They close their eyes and picture their white dream boy. Listen to the grapevine . . . Jesus Christ the pure is the black woman's psychic bridegroom. You will learn before you die that during coition and at the moment of her orgasm, the black woman, in the first throes of her spasm, shouts out the name of Jesus. "Oh Jesus, I'm coming!" she shouts to him.[36]

Cleaver theorizes that history and social forces have ordered black and white males and females into the following categories: The Omnipotent Administrators (white men), who reject their bodies in favor of superior minds; the Ultrafeminine (white women), who are a weak but well-groomed, pampered "pin-up" lot with no brains; the Amazons (black women), strong, sub-feminine domestic workers; and the Supermasculine Menial (black men), who possess great bodies but no minds.[37]

According to Cleaver's theory,[38] the white man loses his virility to the black man (body) and the black woman relinquishes her femininity to white women. The white man compensates with the fruits of superior mental energy. While Cleaver suggests that the white woman desires the brute force of the black man, and the black man compensates for his unused mind with sexual prowess, the black woman wants to mate only with the white man. But, there is no reciprocal desire, for the white man chooses to mate with nobody! This would suggest that the black woman really has no psychic bridegroom. She might not respect the supermasculine menial because he lacks economic power and might be drawn toward the white man who is powerful, either because he uses his power to command her or because she seduces him to gain something. Does she have to surrender her psyche in order to gain some small measure of power? Does the white man really become her psychic bridegroom?

Black women have often been in positions, like Vy in *Happy Ending* to "pull the wool over white people's eyes." Maybe Cleaver is closer to the truth when he says: "The Amazon is lost between two worlds."[39] Substitute caught for lost and the black woman may well be caught between trying to neutralize the pull of the "squeeze position" between black men and white women while at the same time using her mind and, when necessary, her body to gain some advantages from the white man.

Because she is strong and self-reliant, as Cleaver admits, she really has no psychic bridegroom. She still awaits her bridegroom—the black man.

One suspects a fear lurking in all these theories and it may be the most potent "what if . . ." of all. What if white men really "dig" black women, and the two groups join forces to further oppress black men? This might well be in the minds of many who theorize about black women's desires while basing their observations on not one single article, book, or theory advanced by a black woman!

Others, but particularly Cleaver, insist that the love between black women and white men is one-sided, white men being too impotent to love, and black women too unlovable. Cleaver (again using another prisoner's voice) projects hatred of black men into the black woman's psyche:

> Anyway, every black women secretly hates black men. Secretly, they all love white men—some of them will tell you so to your face, the others will tell you by their deeds and actions. Haven't you ever noticed that just as soon as a black woman becomes successful she marries a white man!
>
> I'm going by what I know. I know one black bitch who always said that there ain't nothing a black man can do for her except leave her alone or bring her a message from, or carry a message to, a white man.[40]

Once having assured us that there is deep hatred of black men, he makes it possible to write off black women as enemies of the black man. She must be mistrusted, shunned. More than the white woman, she is his enemy. And as we all know, enemies soon go to war. Thus, the call to battle:

> There is a war going on between the black man and the black woman, which makes her the silent ally, indirectly but effectively, of the white man. The black woman is an uncommenting ally and she may not even realize it—but the white man sure does. that's why, all down through history, he has propped her up economically above you and me, to strengthen her hand against us.[41]

How could the daughters of Sojourner Truth and Harriet Tubman become, collectively, the enemies of black men? What could it possibly profit us to choose the Omnipotent Administrator? If the black woman sees the Supermasculine Menial as half a man, as Cleaver suggests, she does not necessarily turn to the Omnipotent Administrator because he is a complete man. She turns to him, as Cleaver's own words suggest, because "Strength gauges its own potency through a confrontation with other strength."[42] She measures herself against the white man's strength and puts her finger on his weakness. She uses his weakness, his sexual confusion, to gain advantages from white men. Most of the payments exacted—the trade of her body for sex, her bosom for solace, her energy for cleaning and keeping his house—have traditionally helped her family survive.

Did she surrender her femininity? If as Cleaver suggests, she is "alienated from the feminine component of her nature,"[43] one could only ask whether the "pampered power puff" image ascribed to white women by Cleaver, and rejected today by white feminists is really a constructive definition of femininity. So, what's to surrender?

Furthermore, how could Cleaver write so strongly about the deceptiveness of Mister Charlie, go on to make a case for a strong Amazon black woman, and not be forced, logically, to conclude that this strength makes her aware of Mr. Charlie's deceptiveness? How could she be strong, yet dumb enough to prefer the treatment she has traditionally received from white men? Once she gauges her strength against the Omnipotent Administrator, she could scarcely have any romantic notions about *him*!

What Cleaver probably misreads is the likelihood that black women share a belief that what black men say about preferring white women is probably true. They also believe that liaisons become unproductive alliances which will keep black men from confronting the real issue of power—economic and political potency.

Says Cleaver of black women in general, she ". . . seems to be full of steel, granite-hard and resisting, not soft and submissive like a white woman."[44]

It is difficult to build relationships with men who see strength as a quality which is so rigid that they are unable to find peace of mind in its presence. Black women know it's impossible to cuddle up to a piece of steel. And granite is no place to nestle! Many a black man has frankly declared that life is too trying for him to come home and face a tough woman, one who is so enmeshed in fighting the world herself that she has little time to assuage his wounds.

The answer seems to lie in mutual sharing of affection and work, both in and outside the home. Black couples should have provided the models for the new liberated men and women, for we have a longer history of both spouses working. It is now impossible for black women to be recycled to superfems. The drive to do, not be, and to survive is deeply rooted in us, and we are not likely to become totally dependent on men. And now, considering the women's liberation movement, black women will find their independency is likely to be strengthened.

Let it be noted that there are no good excuses for those women who have become domineering, demanding and unbearable. There is much truth in some black men's accusations against some of us. Yet these characteristics are not pathological nor incapable of modification. Usually, women develop them in response to heavy responsibilities that they feel are not shared with others.

Like all women, black women respond to tenderness and concern. They already know how to work hard. As more play and freedom come into their lives, the problems associated with "who is boss" will become insignificant. The answer really lies in equalitarian relationships, with each sharing, as Jessie Jackson points out.

> Man's and woman's traditional roles and functions may have to change. They should be based upon aptitude and intelligence, as I said, not about any prescribed route.
>
> . . . I think all of us must get to the point where we recognize that men and women should have oneness of respect but not sameness of roles, that there are some creative, complimentary differences between men and women. Those natural and complimentary differences are such that they give one something the other does not have and vice versa. This leaves neither with any justification for suppressing the other's mind, which is the most precious thing that a human being has.
>
> . . . There apparently has been a higher consciousness among black women than black men of the need to free ourselves from the white man. But then, that can be traced back. We became a maternalistic society not because of self-assertion by black women so much as because of the suppression of black men by whites. Black women developed a relatively stronger position based upon circumstances created by white men, not by black men. Therefore, black men should not get hung up on the maternalistic society we have come from but should deal more with the fact that we have survived, under indescribable conditions. The black woman's body was in fact the buffer between the barbarism of the white man and the helplessness of the black man. One should appreciate that and instead of pulling the black woman down pull the black man up, so that both can be buffers between the white man's barbarism and our chidlren.[45]

DIVISIVE ISSUES: BLACK MEN/BLACK WOMEN

To get to this consciousness level, however, some divisive issues must be examined, faced, and exorcised. The first, of course, is the nature of violence in relationships; the second, "the respectability syndrome" and last, "man: provider or partner?"

Violence

Fanon taught earlier that in one phase of revolutionary activity, "the niggers fight each other." Turning on each other, bruising the fragile relationship of lover-lover, husband-wife, parent-daughter, we have all too often brought the word violence ourselves into our history. How very sad! And how very true! But it goes beyond this.

Violence which reaches the lowest extreme is incest. This behavior is an unavoidable piece of the puzzle with which we must deal in order to understand the complex relationships between black men and black women. Without delving into the actual psychological reasons, we have enough evidence from some of those who have been victimized by forms of incest and physical beatings to know that often the man's motives combine unexpected elements of love, pity, and hopelessness. The thought frequently is not to harm the women involved, but rather to lash out against the frustration of a system which seems to have trapped them and made true victims of both the woman and man.

Dealing with this subject is difficult on all counts since there is revulsion at such outrage and at the same time, a need for understanding the forces that cause it.

Some violence perhaps grows out of a warped conception of what is best to control women.

> I asked the Accused, ". . . have you ever hit a black woman?"
> The Accused replies: "Black women take kindness for weakness. . . ."[46]

Some grows out of jealousy and misguided values. Bromfield, in *The Third Life of Grange Copeland,* had taken pride in Mem's speech pattern, but soon began to ridicule it. He embarrassed her in company, and when the men teased him about his schoolteacher wife, envying his ability to hold her, he gave as his formula: "I beats her ass. Only way to treat a nigger woman."[47]

Mem and Bromfield were truly in love. It was that pure and simple. Bromfield, angry all his life at a father who had abandoned him, was doomed to a life of everlasting tenant farming. Mem had barely emerged from "the culture of poverty," having pulled herself into a teaching career against all kinds of odds. She recognized in Bromfield all the loving qualities she needed in a man, and worked to purchase a small house, bore their children with delight, and loved him unashamedly and without the nagging for material possessions so often associated with black teachers. Still, he beat her instead of the system. In the end he killed her.

Louise Merriweather, Maya Angelou, and Toni Morrison speak of rape in their novels, and Maya Angelou, in an interview in *The New York Times,* vowed "to tell it because rape and incest are rife in the black community."[48]

The Respectability Syndrome

Another divisive factor between black men and women is the traditional view middle-class black women have held toward sexuality. Most middle-class girls have been closely supervised by mothers who were determined to overcome the myth of "the black woman as whore." The fear of pregnancy was early instilled in the minds of these girls. Pregnancy for black girls doomed them to poverty and a low social status. Chastity was always the key to catching men and upward mobility, so great care was taken in rearing girls to be respectable.

The respectability credo was a rigid one:

. . . To avoid downward slippage into the lower class one must be chaste. One cannot act like low-class women who are seen as "loose."

. . . Virginity and a college education are the best dowry to take a husband.

. . . If after you land a husband he chooses to leave you, sexual abstinence and education are still good insurance for the future.

Morality is more than the sum total of kisses and sex. There is the morality of justice, freedom, and fair play. This atmosphere of "black female upliftment" created a fantasy world that lured too many sisters into a phony society where fur coats and big houses and "keeping up with the Joneses" became the paramount dream. Culture and refinement stemmed not from a careful sorting of ideas, values, and experiences, but a slavish dedication to a white life style which they viewed from afar. There emerged a "copy-catism" of white people and a rejection of their own blackness and sexuality, a trade off of social status for sexuality.

The sexual revolution freed white girls to engage more openly in sexual relationships without demanding a life commitment from men. Some brothers feel that black girls are still the victims of Toni Morrison's "Mobile Respectability."

> These particular brown girls from Mobile and Aiken are not like some of their sisters. . . . They go to land-grant colleges, normal schools, and learn to do the white man's work with refinement; home economics to prepare his food. . . . Here they learn the rest of the lesson begun in those soft houses with porch swings and pots of bleeding heart; how to behave. The careful development of thrift, patience, high morals, and good manners. In short how to get rid of the funkiness of passion, the funkiness of nature, the funkiness of the wide range of human emotions. . . . Wherever it erupts, this Funk, they wipe it away; where it crusts, they dissolve it; wherever it drips . . . they find it and fight it until it dies. They fight this battle all the way to the grave. The laugh that is a little too loud; the enunciation that is a little too round; the gesture a little too generous. They hold their behind in for fear of a sway too free . . . and they worry, worry, worry about the edges of their hair.
>
> They never seem to have boyfriends, but they always marry. Certain men watch them . . . and know that if such a girl is in his house he will sleep on sheets boiled white . . . and pressed flat with a heavy iron. . . .
>
> What they do not know is that this plain brown girl will build her nest stick by stick, make it her own inviolable world, and stand guard over its every plant, weed, and doily, even against him. . . . A sidelong look will be enough to tell him to smoke on the bank porch. But then men do not know these things. Nor do they know that she will give of her body sparingly and partially. He must enter her surreptitiously, lifting the hem of her nightgown only to her navel.[49]

A healthy spontaneous sexuality combined with spiritual sharing, certainly not "Mobile Respectability," remains the best basis for relationships.

Man: Provider or Partner?

Most black women today are perfectly willing, even eager, to share the provider role, but have strong needs for a redefinition of manhood to include emotional provider as being essential to that role.

Man the Protector has taken too many white men into some of history's bloodiest wars. The role of protector has all too often meant taking up a gun to shoot someone who trespasses on one's property. Well, the idea of one's wife as property is obnoxious.

Furthermore, self-protection has become a necessity for everybody in this violent society, with women learning karate in order to protect themselves. It is too late for black men to dispense anger over their historical "powerlessness" to protect their women from rape and mistreatment by white men.

Bobby Seale, chairman of the Black Panther Party says: "The way we see it, the sister is also a revolutionary, and she has to be able to defend herself, just like we do . . . even to shoot. . . . Because the pigs in the system don't care that she's a sister; they brutalize her just the same.[50]

Of course, no woman wants to feel that her menfolk won't stick up for her, fight for her, in words and deeds. But this is more than "picking up a gun," this is a demand for emotional protection. This means a shoulder to cry on, a word said at a moment, a reaching out in the white world toward a sister, and looking the white man in his eye and daring to say: "Look, this black woman is *my* woman, my sister, and I'm standing by her."

The American family is in the throes of change. The term "head of the family" is as passé as a Model-T Ford. In the past this term meant that all final decisions were made by the man. It often meant that the man's needs were placed ahead of those of his wife. Today many couples reject this family model, though some still think black men need to be authoritarian.

Psychologist Charles Thomas in a *Psychology Today* article wrote: ". . . as a black man I feel that my family, my wife and children, must sacrifice everything for me. . . . My family realizes that if I don't make it, they won't make it either. . . . My family appreciates the fact that I have gained a taste of the thing called Freedom, the freedom to be what the feminists call being and becoming. Unless [my family] supports me, frustration will contaminate them."[51]

Black women are saying the opposite. They want to share freedom together. They want new relationships, not carbon copies. Lillian Benbow, Director of Housing, Michigan Commission of Human Rights, writes:

> I am hearing more and more about another disturbing thing which is surfacing—*black men acting like white men* in regards to the strivings of black women . . . what is especially painful is the callous disregard by many of the brothers in key positions who totally ignore the plight of black women. Black sisters are quietly discussing this situation, but it is now time to say to our black brothers openly that we will not take any more kindly to a *third* oppressor than we do to the original two (white male and female)!
>
> I have said on many occasions to white feminists that the black woman's fight is not with her fellow victims, the black male. That is

> still my position; because realistically his collective lot is ultimately no different from the black woman's. He can never be free, rich nor "middle class" independent of the black female, as long as he is black. When white women protest their unhappiness about the subservient social and economic roles they have been forced to assume by the white male, they are objecting to the total control which white males enjoy in the society. White males on the other hand contend, and not without some justification, that white women have been placed on a pedestal, and protected, *by them*; she has shared in the wealth, the good life that he controls; and that it is totally unreasonable and to an extent *un*feminine for her to aspire and agitate for equal status and power; for equal personhood.
>
> Black men, on the other hand, have never controlled *anything* in this country; they have never as a class been able to protect the black woman or to control the condition of her destiny, since even in ownership they do not *control* those forces through which life conditions are determined. Therefore, when black men begin to occupy some *spaces* of management and engage in the same sexist practices as does the white male, he cloaks himself in the false notion that he too can enjoy the fruits of sexism (against *black* women) as does the white male, while on his way to full liberation. History should teach our brothers that if in fact sexism was the white male's biggest hang-up (and he can join him in freedom via that route) then our black brothers would have been riding with the white brothers in the front of that bus, and the black and white sisters would have been in the back!
>
> Those without freedom cannot afford the illusion of it.[52]

Fannie Lou Hamer, the late stalwart Mississippi activist, said:

> You know, I see so many hangups in the North that I don't see in the South. In the South men don't expect their wives to be seen and not heard and not doing anything. We've always been used to standing by our husband's side and doing whatever is necessary to help the family survive. I think it's ridiculous to say that a woman's place is in the house, not doing anything but staying at home. Women have a duty to look after their babies, but now, what do you think would happen to us if my husband was making $15 a week if I didn't try to get out there and make the other$15 so that two times $15 would be $30 so them kids could eat, you know. I think it's ridiculous. It doesn't make me any less. I respect that man. And he knows it and he doesn't have any hangups about that.[53]

The history of relationships between black men and women has not been all negative. Black women writers through the ages have set down particular visions of positive relationships and models of mutual sharing which will endure for all times. We should look to those writers for "images" and actions. There are Teacake and Janie, Vy, and Ennis Brown, and other relationships that work.

BLACK FEMALE SEXUALITY

There seem to have developed through the years conflicting views of black female sexuality which may have some basis in fact. How is it that Toni Morrison's "Mobile, Alabama, women" evoke "uh huh's" from many black female achievers who readily admit that to become respectable in the eyes of others, sexual abstinence, regardless of personal feelings or social circumstances, was one of the rules they believed they should follow?

The socialization of black girls begins early and, as sociologist Robert Staples suggests, the training of a black middle-class girl "is puritanical."[54] And few would disagree with psychologist Kenneth Clark that when sex is tied to status and aspirations, "normal sexual behavior might well be inhibited."[55] If sexual abstinence is tied to achieving respectability and if the middle-class or socially mobile girl demands that each relationship be forever and not an expression of self-actualization "time contained with its own intrinsic worth and value,"[56] it follows that many black women eventually have to deal with a repressive sexuality. Consider this against other beliefs that black women are "potentially, if not already, the most sexual animal on this planet,"[57] actually heirs of a natural sensuousness that flows down through history from the African past, surviving slavery and subsequent repressions, hurled out from ourselves in artistic expressive ways, particularly through our music. All these conflicts add up to a potentially dangerous human condition which black women face today!

Perhaps this sexual dilemma is generational. Certainly the sexual liberation gains of the Sixties must have influenced the behavior of "under thirty" black women, granting them freedom to explore without being overly concerned about "respectability."

To some extent, of course, the current generation is less hung up about sex. But there is evidence, such as that revealed in a *Psychology Today* article, "Black Is Lonely," which reinforced what black coeds on campus tell us: "While nearly all blacks on white campuses often feel isolated and confined, it is the black woman who feels it most heavily."[58] In this study, black women overwhelmingly stated the belief that "Black students should date only black students," and at the same time they acknowledged and resented the white women who "jump fence"—invade black territory for mates.

Black women felt undesirable and ignored by black men, and they expressed distaste for white men.[59]

Many writers agree with Inez Smith Reid's summation of the feelings black women expressed in her study, reported in *Together Black Women,* "... black women everywhere are angered by any display of affection between black males and white females."[60] She further stated that the black female population most affected by this racial liaison is the college set.

The college women in the "Black Is Lonely" study also spoke despairingly of the "double standard" black men espouse which justified black men and white women liaisons but insists that black women should be reserved only for them.[61]

All of these factors, plus perhaps a lingering attitude of exclusivity when dating black fellows, a vestige of older black women's attitudes, suggests that problems in black female sexuality still abide.

By the time *Essence* magazine, very much "The Magazine for Today's Black Woman," appeared in February 1977 with an entire issue devoted to *All About Love, Giving, Forgiving, Growing, Sharing, Building toward a New Understanding,*[62] black women were already sorting out their feelings within today's social and cultural context. For self-actualization which includes responsible giving and receiving of love and which expresses a healthy sexuality is not a selfish, hedonistic goal; it is a confrontation and necessary resolution of needs that make for the greatest contribution of self to good works.

While some blacks might disagree with the solution Ntozake Shange comes to in her Broadway hit play *For Colored Girls Who Have Considered Suicide/When the Rainbow Is Enuf*, watching black women in the audience express "Right on," as they wince, laugh, and cry, is a good enough, even important, reason to count it seriously. The drama deals with the tragic and bitter "half-notes shattered" love/hate dimensions of black male/female relationships in a way that causes some to say the play is anti black men, even anti men, especially since the ending concludes that we black women have to find the rainbow within ourselves and even among ourselves. It is at the very least a statement of the unending search for respect, identity, and love among black women. In an interview with Jacqueline Trescott of the *Washington Post,* Miss Shange says: "I wrote these poems, this maliciousness and sorrow. I meant for them to have a devastating effect. I felt women have to explore these experiences with one another. . . ."[63]

Exploring the issues together is one of the solutions Toni

Cade Bambara suggests as she discusses workshops being held around the country with black women exploring the problems of man/woman relationships and trying "to analyze the way out of chaos and back to sane dialogue."[64] She also wants to create "new norms, ethics, and values which would lead to new kinds of contractive agreements . . . that reflect a better understanding of actual circumstances rather than of alien or opposed norms."[65]

FUTURE STRATEGIES—ALTERNATIVE LIFE STYLES—NEW NORMS

And what might these new norms, strategies, and life styles be?

Any concern about black male-female relationships is academic if the goal is a permanent monogamous marriage for every black woman.

The facts speak for themselves. After age fourteen, black females outnumber males at every age level. Even if every black male chooses to marry a black woman and makes no interracial crossovers, the black woman has a less advantaged marriage position than the white female.

Differences in the black and white sex ratios, 15 years of age, 1970[66]

Age Group	*Black*	*White*	*Difference*
15–24 years	93.0	98.8	5.8
25–34 "	84.2	97.8	13.6
35–44 "	82.8	96.2	13.4
45–54 "	86.3	93.8	7.5
55–64 "	85.1	90.2	5.1
65* "	76.4	71.9	−4.5

What then are the alternatives if fewer monogamous marriages can be foreseen?

The first alternative to the branding of children born "out of wedlock" is to validate the single head of household family style as legitimate.

Each census report, however, reveals an increasing percentage of black female-headed households. The numbers rose from 27.9 percent in 1970 to 31.8 percent in 1972, while white women continue year after year to head 9.4 percent of white families.[67] The black female-headed household has for too long been a "shush shush" shameful fact of life among black folks. It must be brought out of the closet where racial skeletons are kept and set forth as a fact of life, free from moralistic judgments.

Practically, this means that more and more black women will choose to have children when they have faced the likelihood that they may not have husbands. Nikki Giovanni made such a decision, one of many young successful blacks who refused to "wait until the right man came along," but decided she wanted a child. In an interview with *Ebony* magazine, she stated: "I had a baby because I wanted to have a baby and I could afford to. I don't say that any other black woman should do this if they can't afford it."[68] Nikki Giovanni has become a role model for many young black women, but this idea takes courage. Understanding and support from the respectable middle-class woman would greatly alleviate feelings of rejection some of these young women experience.

In an earlier study of black college women, the majority had entered into marriages with men who were considered to be in a lower social status than they. The impression was gathered that many of them entered into such marriages as last resorts and felt not only cheated but embarrassed by their husbands at every turn. The suggestion put forth in 1954 is more urgently relevant today "somehow we must de-emphasize the notion that a college graduate is superior to a non-college graduate . . . some women would affect better marriages with non-college educated men than with college men."[69] Today, as black men and women work together on the goals of black liberation, artificial barriers such as class and education soon become irrelevant and the skills and resources offered by each individual are seen as necessary to be shared. It is certain that black women cannot afford to be "hung up" on a man's degrees or his social status.

There is also the alternative to another standard rule of courtship and marriage all too often rigidly adhered to. It was said that a woman *must* marry someone older or her same age. Oh yes, one can give five years or so! Experts have derided this sexual taboo since a woman's sexuality lasts as long or longer than a man's. Yet the taboo continues. Black women cannot afford this! Increasingly more of them are developing relationships with brothers considerably younger than they are. Often, younger brothers are eager to develop a close relationship with a black woman, but are afraid of a younger sister's dependency. Or, they may not be able to finance heavy dating. Furthermore, they may not be ready for a lifetime commitment to a young woman who may be too eager to marry. Some of these brothers are not threatened by an older woman's job and don't feel competitive. They are often open to the new vistas older women can provide them. In such liaisons both parties gain.

While Staples suggests that black women tend to move more

readily into some form of polygamy than into lesbianism, certainly these two alternatives must be considered. Being too "butch" is so often associated with the word "matriarchy" that some black women bring more fear and taboos concerning homosexuality into their sexual explorations than white women. Others, who feel that polygamy is a "trick bag," as Inez Smith Reid found,[70] might be blocked by the need to "possess" someone. Some believe that a form of polygamy would again encourage black men to shrink from responsibilities toward "the provider role" and be too emotionally burdensome to black women.

Polygamy (and perhaps there is need for another word) requires, among other emotional strengths, financial sharing among independent individuals* All that requires a kind of liberation and openness which is difficult for black women, as has been stated before.

It is admittedly difficult to choose any alternative to a monogamous marriage in America. Even though that life style is in trouble among whites, the whole capitalistic system is geared toward its perpetuation. But black people have always had to improvise and settle for life patterns that bring them security and pleasure in different ways. What has been set forth here are models of different life styles that many black women may have to consider if they do not choose the life of total sexual abstinence—a rather lonely choice for any woman, but perhaps worse for us, given the burden of racism.

What is essential is a continuing role for black women as equal partners with black men. What must be clear is the fact that too many black women will still have to rear children alone and need adequate money from jobs. No social policy should be tolerated any longer that gives preferential treatment to black men. And surely the argument that more mouths will be fed in doing so is fallacious. America is simply not geared to double every black man's salary so his wife can stay home. Before that day, both salaries are needed to make the life black men and women seem to want. Once that decision is made, a partnership is already contracted. Black women have worked too long in the labor market to leave their jobs while large numbers of white women move out of the home and into the world of work. As much as black brothers glorify the "stay at home phenomenon," it will be increasingly

---

*Polygamy in this sense is a non-legal acceptance of a man having obligations and allegiances to more than one wife.

difficult to sell it since even the media will soon point women away from Ajax and Mr. Clean.

This means that the old days of letting brothers decide the goals of the black revolution and assign black women honorary or service roles is over. It faded in the years since the Meredith march when sisters came face to face with black male chauvinism and felt their interests ignored. It faded when the statistics related to interracial courtships rose and too many sisters began the lonely, unwelcome task of living outside a monogamous marriage. Today they feel that they have to protect their lives and their earning capacities. The fading of this custom began really when Harriet Tubman blazed a trail of resistance against repression during slavery and Angela Davis picked it up in a jail cell and said: *We* must free our brothers who are in jail!

Black women want to be involved. They demand to be involved. Black women want to be partners, allies, sisters!

Before there is partnering and sharing with someone, however, there is the becoming of oneself. And the search and discovery of authentic selfhood on the part of black women has begun.

One would agree with Inez Smith Reid that if one looked for concrete definitions of black women one would not find them. She says, "together" black women "are beautiful black sisters who cannot be pigeon-holed neatly into sterile categories."[71] Yet there is one theme that emerges suggesting a positive emotionalism that black women insist be present in their sexuality. In the *Essence* magazine issue on love, it was stated that "In this country there is a disdain for emotionalism, but we black people have never been afraid of our emotions."[72] Black women participated in the positive exploration of sexuality brought into focus in the Seventies, but they weren't about to cease asking questions about beauty in sex and commitments in relationships. Wherever and whenever they have been asked to speak out, as in the *Essence* issue, they insisted on discretion. In most causes they abhored group sex, thinking it exploitative, and they demanded understanding and romance from a partner. This reinforced Staples' finding that "although black women enjoy the physical aspects of sex, it is still linked with an emotional need of belongingness and human relatedness."[73]

Certainly Grier and Cobbs are right in advising that "liking oneself and seeing oneself as eminently lovable and worthy," indeed, some narcissism, is necessary for a healthy female sexuality.[74] Grier and Cobbs believed that some black women in their thirties abandoned their sexuality and moved into obesity and self-hatred because society devalued their looks, skin, color, and hair. Today one looks about and sees young black sisters who have changed the white-oriented standards of beauty and brought about the psychological redemptiveness for which Grier and Cobbs hoped. Today black women have become, are beautiful. We are beautiful and strong. And we can "Get Down" as well, with the feelings expressed by Marcia Ann Gillespie, editor of *Essence*:

> It's time to confess it all—I have an addiction. No I'm not strung out on drugs or deep in the bottle—I'm hooked on love. . . . .
>
> And in the course of my addiction I've become more understanding. Learned to love me more. Become more selective when opening up to my love and another. Been in love less frequently but far more intensely. Grown demanding of mutual respect and liking and communication. Must be friends and allow love to grow. Not looking for perfection but understanding. Knowing I can live without the love of another—if I love myself. But choosing to share and willing to take chances and risks that are all a part of the joy of giving and receiving love.
>
> I haven't kicked my habit, just refined it. Never intend to give up on love. Need it, want it, am a better person because of it. Love "ain't nothing but a feeling," and there ain't nothing more powerful than feelins, and we ain't nothing without feelins.*[75]

CHAPTER 10 NOTES

[1]Miles Davis, *Bitches Brew*, Columbia Records, GP 26, by permission of Emdec Music Co. Lyrics by Chris Acemadese Hall, written to a Miles Davis composition, recorded by Eddie Jefferson on an album entitled "Things Are Getting Better.

[2]See "The Social and Economic Status of the Black Population in the United States, 1973." Series P 23 #48 p. 78, Table 56, "Race of Husband and Wife: 1960–1970, and Decade of Marriage, 1970." Source: U.S. Department of Commerce Social and Economic Statistics Administrators, Bureau of the Census.

[3]Calvin C. Hernton, *Sex and Racism in America* (New York: Grove Press, Inc., 1965), p. 4.

[4]See Karen Horney, *Neurosis and Human Growth—The Struggle Toward Self-Realization* (New York: W. W. Norton & Co., 1950), Chapter 3; and Karen Horney, *Feminine Psychology* (New York: W. W. Norton & Co., 1967).

[5]Judith Adler Hennessee and Ivan Nicholson, "NOW Says: TV Commercials Insult Women," *The New York Times* Magazine, May 28, 1972, p. 12.

[6]Frantz Fanon, *Black Skin White Masks,* trans. Charles Lam Markmann (New York: Grove Press, Inc., 1967), p. 72.

[7]See Lionel Tiger, *Men in Groups* (New York: Random House, 1969).

[8]Norman Mailer, *The Presidential Papers* (New York: Bantam Books, 1964), p. 137.

[9]Judy Klemesrud, "If a Rental Gent Makes Passes, Take Two and Go Right to Politics," *The New York Times,* June 4, 1972, Sec. 10, p. 17.

[10]Fanon, *Black Skin White Masks,* p. 63.

[11]*Ibid.,* p. 72.

[12]Chester Himes, *The Quality of Hurt: An Autobiography of Chester Himes* (New York: Doubleday and Company, Inc., 1972), I, 137.

[13]*Ibid.,* p. 136.

[14]Malcolm X, with the assistance of Alex Haley, *The Autobiography of Malcolm X* (New York: Grove Press, Inc., 1964), pp. 66–67.

[15]*Ibid.,* p. 93.

[16]Frantz Fanon, *The Wretched of the Earth* (New York: Grove Press, 1965), p. 67.

[17]*Ibid.,* p. 32.

[18]Eldridge Cleaver, from *Soul on Ice* (New York: Mc-Graw Hill Book Company, 1968), pp. 13–14. Copyright © 1968 by Eldridge Cleaver. Used with permission of McGraw-Hill Book Company.

[19]*Ibid.,* p. 159.

[20]William H. Grier and M. Cobbs Price, condensed from *Black Rage* (New York: Basic Books, Inc., 1968), p. 62. Copyright 1968 by William H. Grier and Price M. Cobbs.

[21]*Ibid.,* p. 63.

[22]Hernton, *Sex and Racism,* p. 58.

[23]*Ibid.,* p. 32.

[24]The U.S. Bureau of the Census Correct Population Reports Series P-60, 101 *Money Income in 1974 of Families and Other Persons in the United States.*

[25]Cleaver, *Soul on Ice,* p. 61.

[26]Nikki Giovanni, "Beautiful Black Men," *Black Judgement* (Detroit: Broadside Press). Copyright © 1968 by Nikki Giovanni.

[27]Lillian Smith, *Killers of the Dream* (New York: Doubleday Anchor, 1963).

[28]Seymour Krim, "Ask for a White Cadillac," in *Beyond the Angry Black,* ed. John A. Williams (New York: Cooper Square Publishers, 1966), pp. 128–129.

[29]Germaine Greer, *The Female Eunuch* (New York: McGraw-Hill Book Company, 1970, 1971), p. 189.

[30]*Ibid.,* p. 186.

[31]Kate Millett, *Sexual Politics* (New York: Doubleday and Co., Inc., 1970).

[32]Himes, *The Quality of Hurt,* p. 19.

[33]Fanon, *Black Skin White Masks.*

[34]James Michener, *The Drifters* (New York: Random House, 1971).

[35]Cleaver, *Soul on Ice,* p. 169.

[36]*Ibid.,* p. 169.

[37]*Ibid.*

[38]*Ibid.*

[39]*Ibid.,* p. 188.

[40]*Ibid.,* pp. 158–159.

[41]*Ibid.,* p. 162.

[42]*Ibid.,* p. 183.

[43]*Ibid.,* p. 188.

[44]*Ibid.,* p. 159.

[45]Excerpted from "Conversation: Jesse Jackson/Marcia Ann Gillespie," in *Essence,* Essence Communications, Inc., July 1971.

[46]Cleaver, *Soul on Ice,* p. 158.

[47]Alice Walker, *The Third Life of Grange Copeland* (New York: Harcourt, Brace and Jovanovich, 1970), p. 56.

[48]Maya Angelou, in an interview in the *New York Times,* March 24, 1972, p. 28.

[49]Toni Morrison, *The Bluest Eye* (New York: Holt, Rinehart and Winston, Inc., 1970), pp. 68–69, in Pocket Book Edition.

[50]Bobby Seale from *Seize the Time* (New York: Random House, Inc., 1970), p. 398. Copyright © 1968, 1969, 1970 by Bobby Seale. Reprinted by permission of Random House, Inc.

[51]Charles Thomas, *Psychology Today* Magazine, September 1970, p. 51. Reprinted by permission of *Psychology Today* Magazine. Copyright© 1970 Ziff-Davis Publishing Company, New York.

[52]Lillian Benbow, "A Message from the National President," Delta Newsletter, May 1974, (Delta Sigma Theta).

[53]*Essence,* October 1971, pp. 53–57. Excerpted from "Fannie Lou Hamer Speaks Out." Copyright Essence Communications, Inc., October 1971.

[54]Robert Staples, "The Sexuality of Black Women," *Sexual Behavior,* June 1972, pp. 4–15.

[55]Kenneth Clark, *Dark Ghetto* (New York: Harper and Row), pp. 71–72.

[56]*Ibid.,* pp. 71–72.

[57]Hernton, *Sex and Racism,* p. 136.

[58]Charles V. Willie and Joan D. Levy, "Black Is Lonely," *Psychology Today,* March 1972, pp. 50–52, 76.

[59]*Ibid.,* pp. 76–80.

[60]Inez Smith Reid, *Together Black Women* (New York: Emerson Hall Publishing Company, 1972).

[61]Willie and Levy, *Black Is Lonely,* p. 26.

[62]*Essence* Magazine, February 1977.

[63]Jacqueline Trescott, *Ntozake Shange: Searching for Respect and Identity,* in the *Washington Post,* June 29, 1976, p. B1.

[64]Tony Cade Bambara in "The Sexuality of Black Women," by Robert Staples, *Sexual Behavior,* June 1972, p. 12.

[65]*Ibid.*

[66]Source of data: U.S. Department of Commerce, Bureau of the Census, 1970, census of Population, Advance Report, "General Population Characteristics, United States." PC V2-1 U.S. Department of Commerce, Washington, D.C., February 1971.

[67]"Census Essays Black Families," *The New York Times,* July 21, 1972.

[68]Nikki Giovanni, "I'm Black, Female and Polite," *Ebony* Magazine, February 1972, pp. 48–56.

[69]Jeanne L. Noble, *The Negro Woman College Graduate,* Bureau of Publications, Teachers College, Columbia University, 1956.

[70]Inez Smith Reid, op. cit., pp. 112–121.

[71]*Ibid.,* p. 379.

[72]Marica Ann Gillespie, "Getting Down," in *Essence* Magazine, February 1977, p. 46.

[73]Staples, "Sexuality of Black Women," p. 11.

[74]Grier and Cobbs, *Black Rage,* p. 39.

[75]*Essence,* February 1977, p. 46.

INDEX